INSIDE THE Art Studio

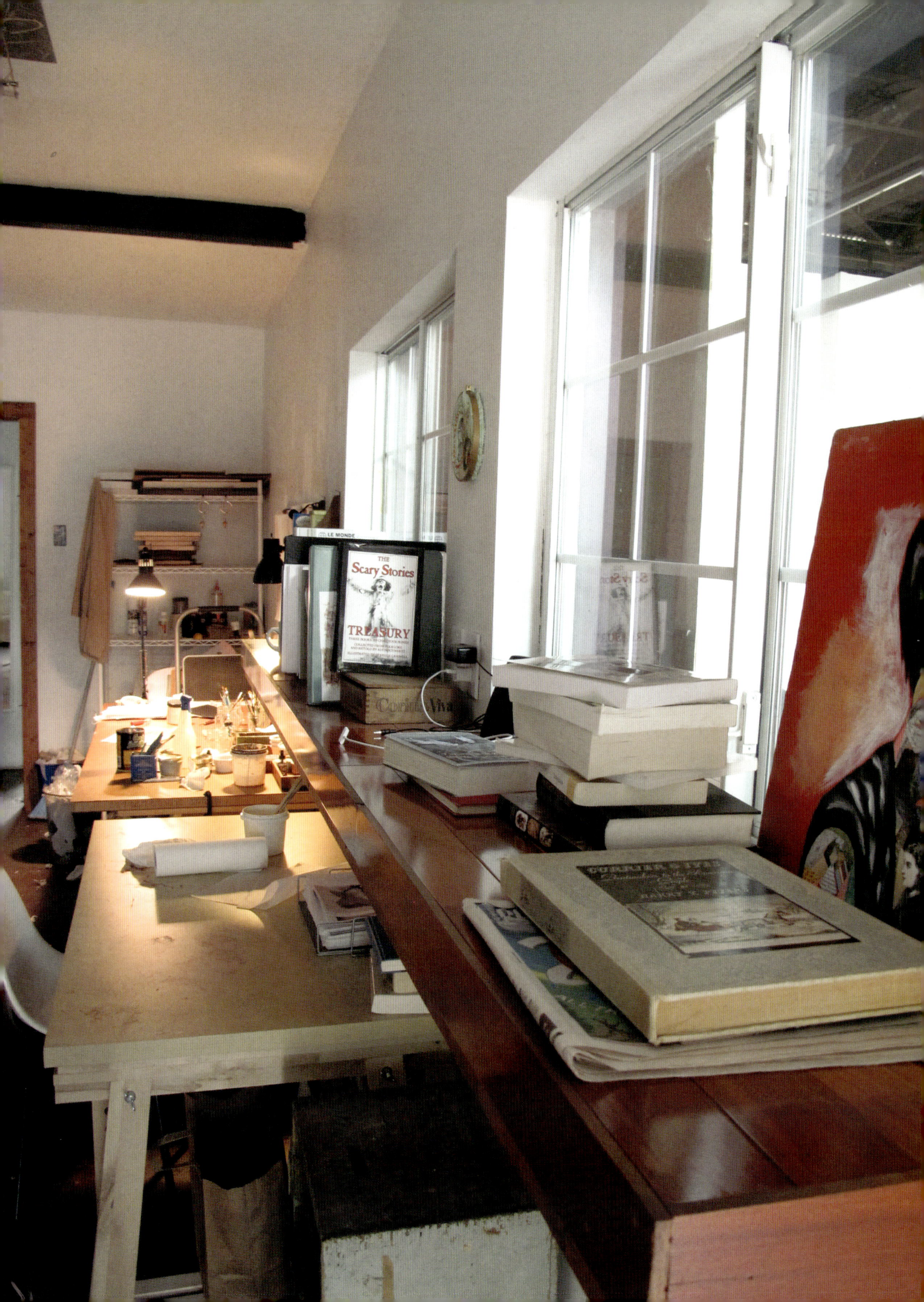
THE
Scary Stories
TREASURY
LE MONDE

INSIDE THE Art Studio

A GUIDED TOUR OF 37 ARTISTS' CREATIVE SPACES

Edited by Mary Burzlaff Bostic
and the editors of **AMERICAN ARTIST** magazine

NORTH LIGHT BOOKS
CINCINNATI, OHIO
www.artistsnetwork.com

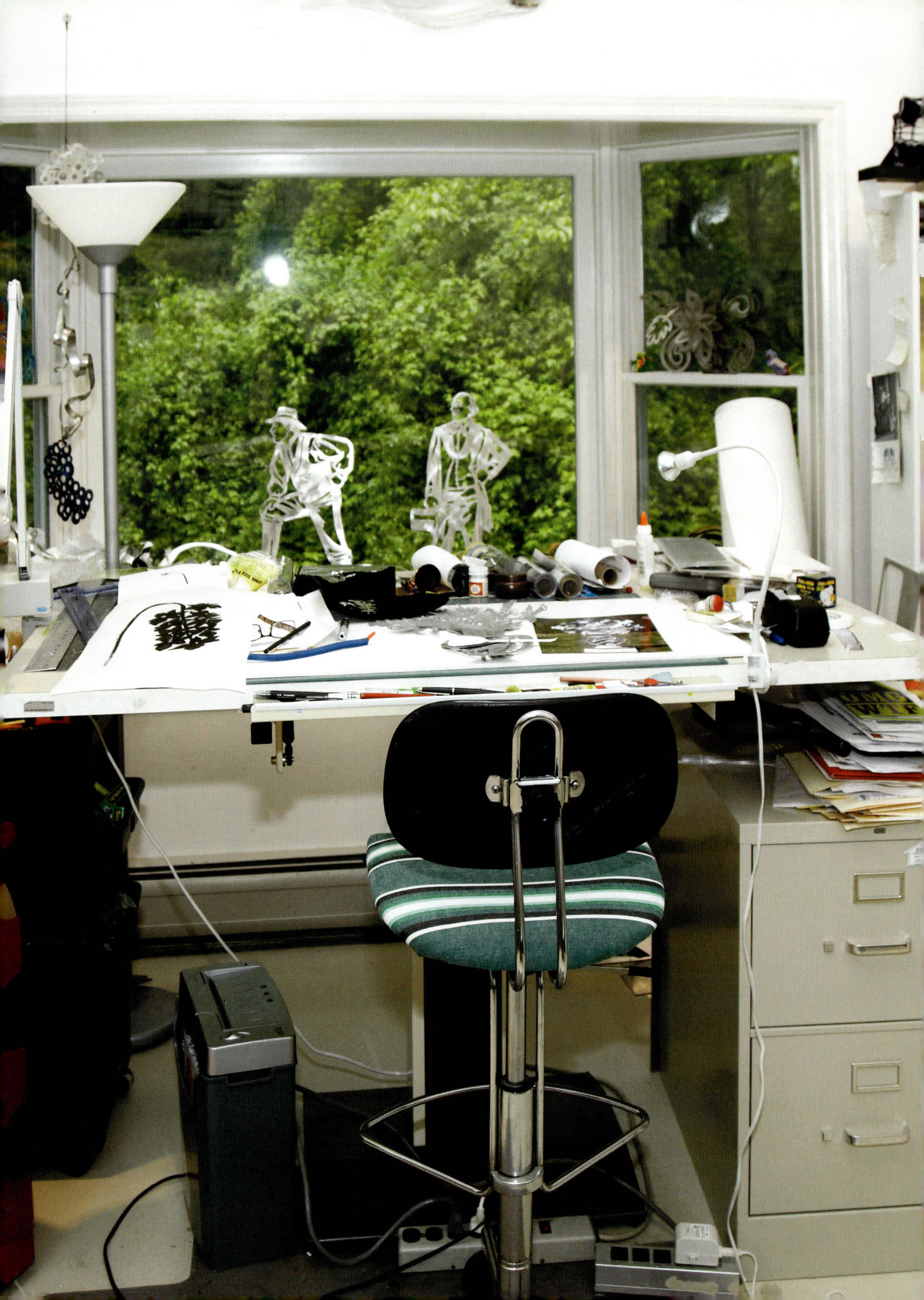

Contents

Introduction

Call me curious or just plain nosy, but I love touring artists' studios. Messy or tidy, large or small, old or new, converted or built to specification, the places where creative ideas are born and executed are fascinating. How does the magic happen? Can you see the influence of the space or location on the artist's work? I'm willing to bet that you like looking at other artists' studios just as much as I do, so I'm excited to share this exclusive look at thirty-seven artists' work spaces.

Culled from *American Artist*'s popular *Studios* series, *Inside the Art Studio* takes you inside the private studios of successful artists around the country and shows how these artists adapted existing spaces, added storage units, made the environments safer, designed work space to accommodate students or collectors, maximized a limited budget, or fulfilled their dreams. The featured artists' unconditional commitment to their studios, their artwork, and their lives and loved ones can serve as guideposts. Their experiences suggest numerous paths open to any artist wishing to further develop his or her creative life, both in and out of the studio.

Be inspired and enjoy!

Mary Burzlaff Bostic

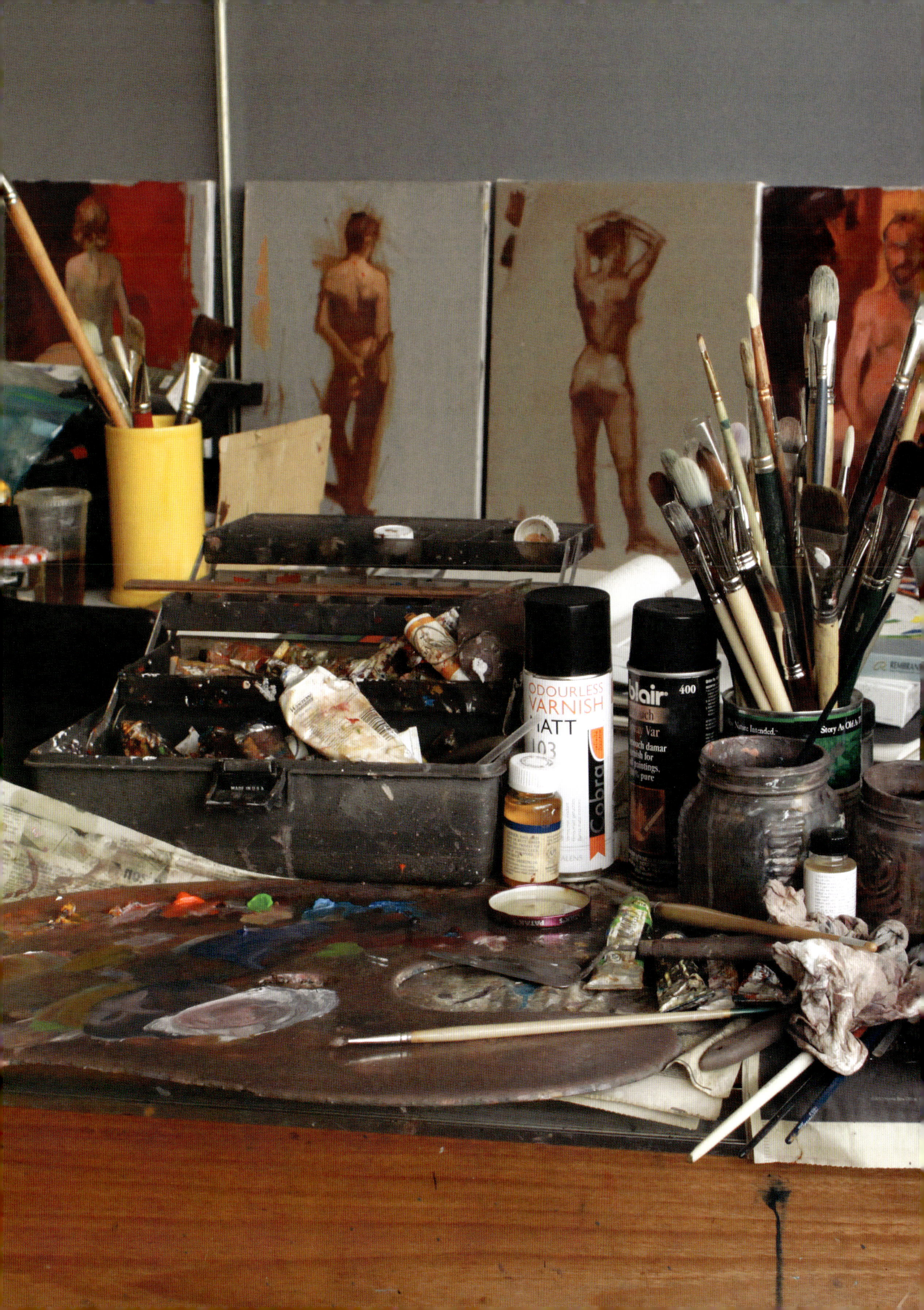
ODOURLESS
VARNISH
Cobra
blair

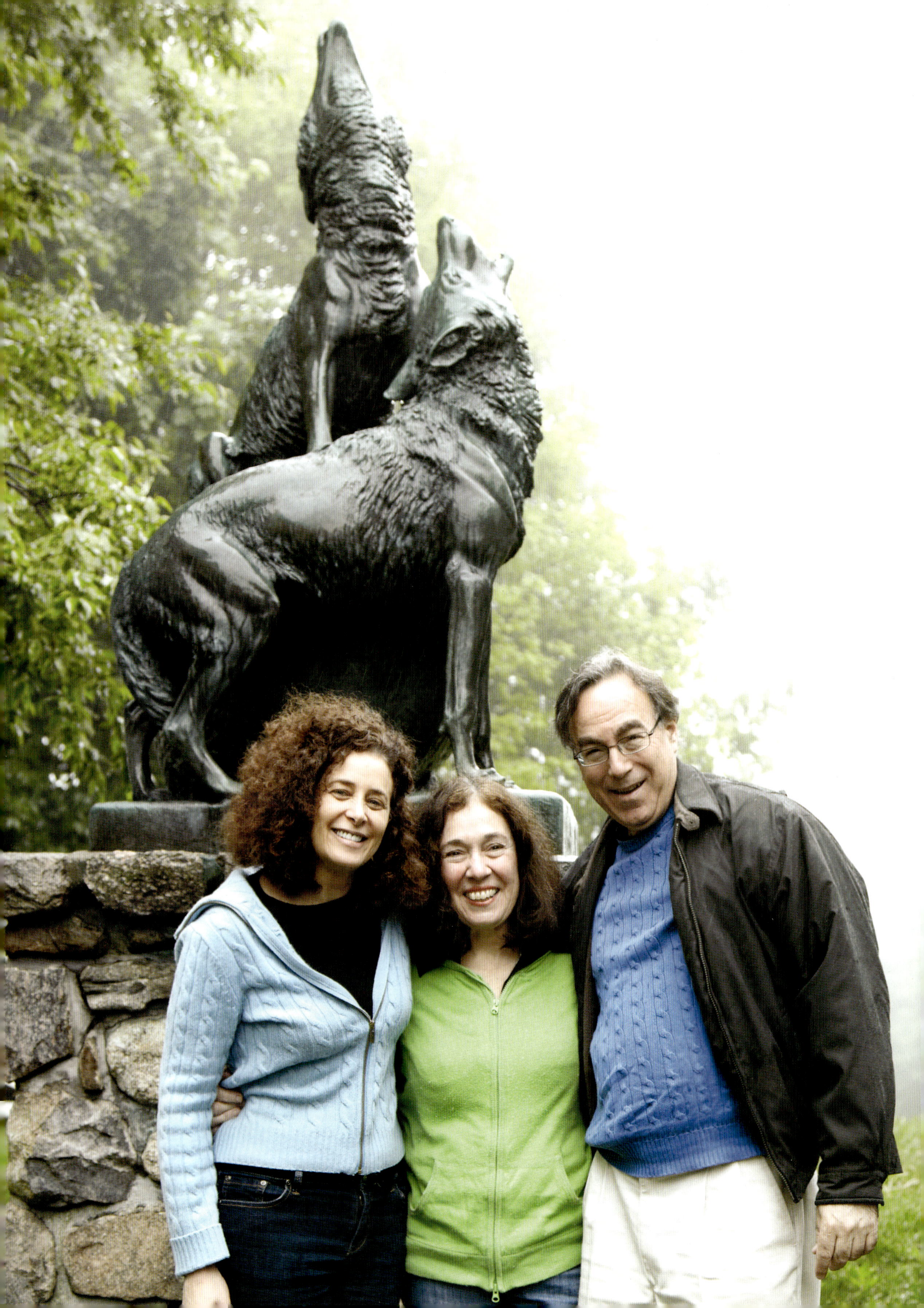

CHAPTER ONE

Pride of Place

"Fortunately art is a community effort—a small but select community living in a spiritualized world endeavoring to interpret the wars and the solitudes of the flesh."

—Allen Ginsberg

← Babette Bloch, Kathy Anderson, and Marc Mellon near their studios in Redding, Connecticut.

Beacon of Opportunity

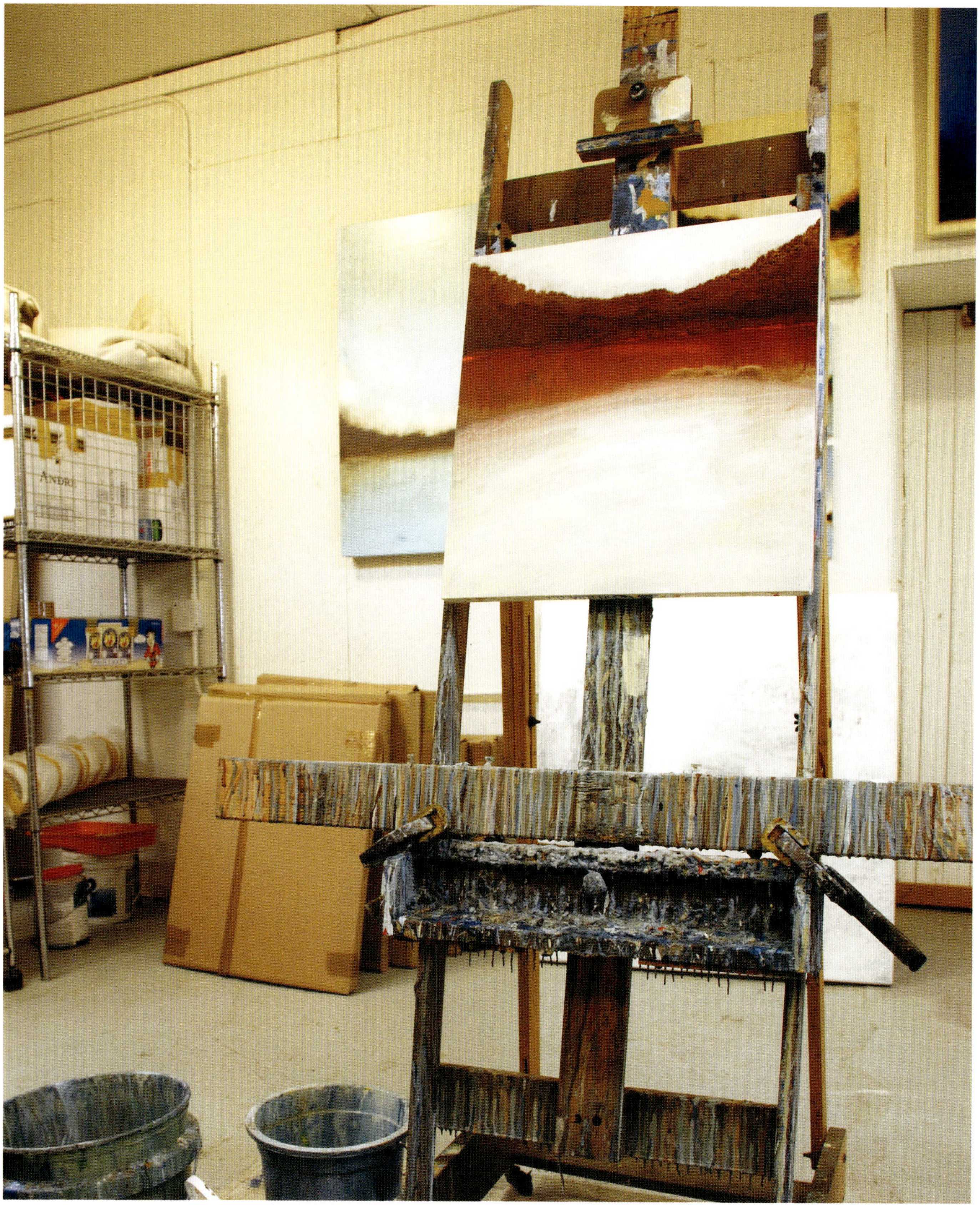

Richard Bruce has used the same Winsor & Newton easel for years, taking it with him through West Virginia, New York City, and now Peekskill, New York.

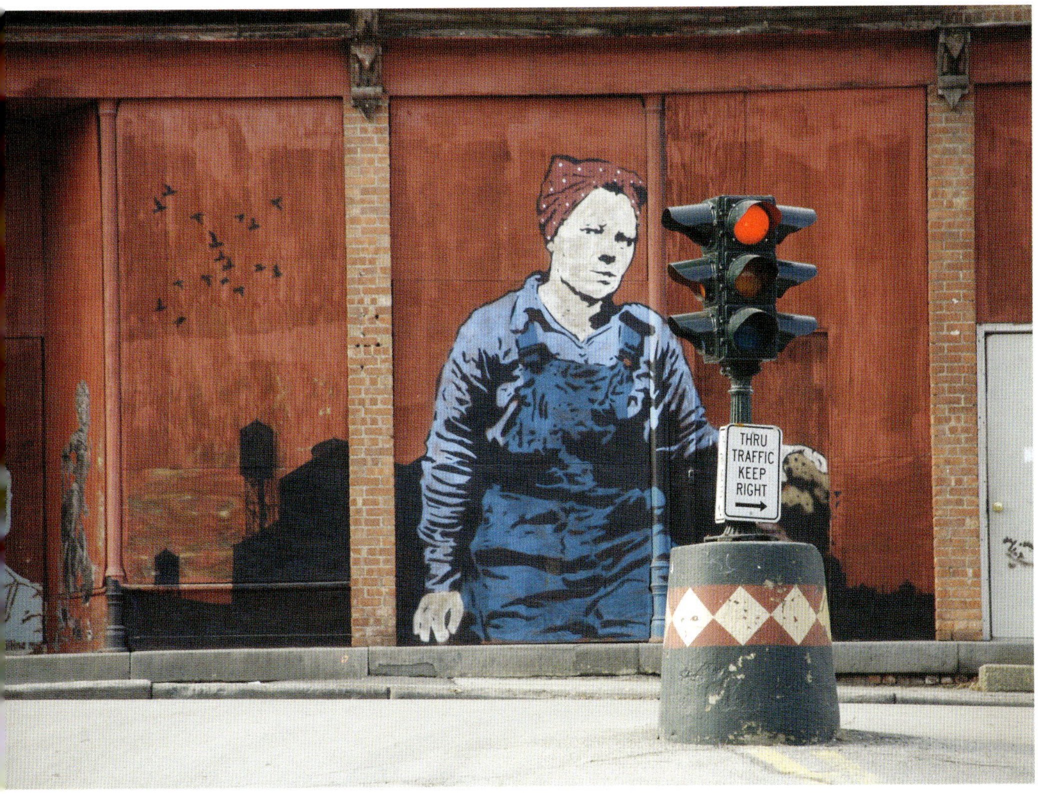

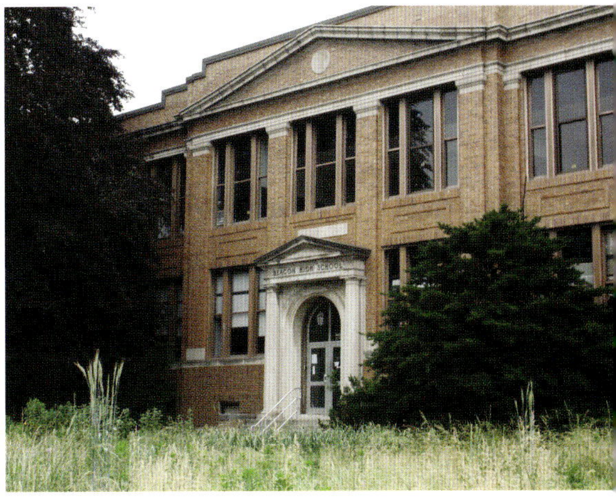

↑ Serving as the high school for Beacon, New York, residents since 1913, artists have utilized the classrooms as studio space since the school closed in 2002.

← Artwork and figurative graffiti enliven old factories and boarded storefronts along Main Street in Beacon, New York.

Before the Dia Art Foundation opened its museum in 2003, Beacon, New York, was a blue-collar city living in the shadow of its former boomtown days. Like so many Hudson Valley communities, empty warehouses and abandoned factories punctuated the string of boarded-up shops along Main Street. Over the last decade, the empty houses and vacant factories transformed into studios, galleries, cafés, and remodeled homes for upstart families as artists from New York City and beyond followed Dia to Beacon, bringing a surge of enlivened talent with them. The city was reborn, and the former high school—built in 1913 and serving the district until 2002—became a haven for artists looking for inexpensive studio space. Classrooms once lined with desks were now stocked with easels, canvases, and paints. Lofty rows of windows provided an abundance of natural light. And, perhaps most important, the hallways were again full of life and a sense of community.

Unfortunately, just three years after its rebirth, the school's mortgage defaulted. The district graciously allowed resident artists to maintain their studios while the building sat on the market, but as January 2011 ushered in a new year and a new owner, artists began bracing themselves for the unknown. "Grand designs for refurbished studios and gallery spaces were announced, but nothing seemed to come from it," says Rick Price, a Beacon resident and artist who currently maintains one of the last occupied studios in the former high school. "The rent went up and people got scared. Almost everyone bolted." Price has tentative plans to join Mill Street Loft, a multi-arts community educational center opening on the banks of the Hudson River, just a short walk from the train station. Although Price is excited about the new opportunity, getting over the loss of the high school hasn't been easy.

"It's definitely a transition period," he says. "It will be great to be in a place where I can interact with the community, but I feel we had something really special here in the high school—or at least the potential for something special." Frustrated by the realization that he would have to leave his studio, he took the advice of fellow Beacon artist Winston Roeth, who suggested that he use this "as an opportunity to change your life for the better." Price is trying to do just that, but the move will not be easy. His cozy studio is in one of the school's small conference rooms, but it is chock-full of artwork, supplies, and creature comforts, including audiobooks, CDs, and inspirational prints that line the walls. Two easels anchor his studio, and Price surrounds himself with a forest of Robert Simmons Signet Bristles (flat, filbert, and bright) and Blick Masterstroke Bristle (filberts), with a handful of Isabey and Raphaël brushes mixed in. He swears by Nova Color Artists' Acrylic Paint and uses a large rectangle of transparent acrylic glass for his palette, which rests atop a wooden podium forever smeared with the remnants of former mixes and hues.

The small size of his studio belies the scale of the artist's work. Price is an acclaimed muralist, and a great deal of his paintings are done outside the studio. Two local murals—the River Beacons Mural and the Howland Library Mural—are beautiful, colorful testaments to how much Price values the Beacon community, and how much the community values its artists. Artists have been welcomed with open arms, and as many of them scramble to locate new studio space, they are finding a variety of choices available to them. "Many artists are turning outbuildings and spare rooms in their homes into

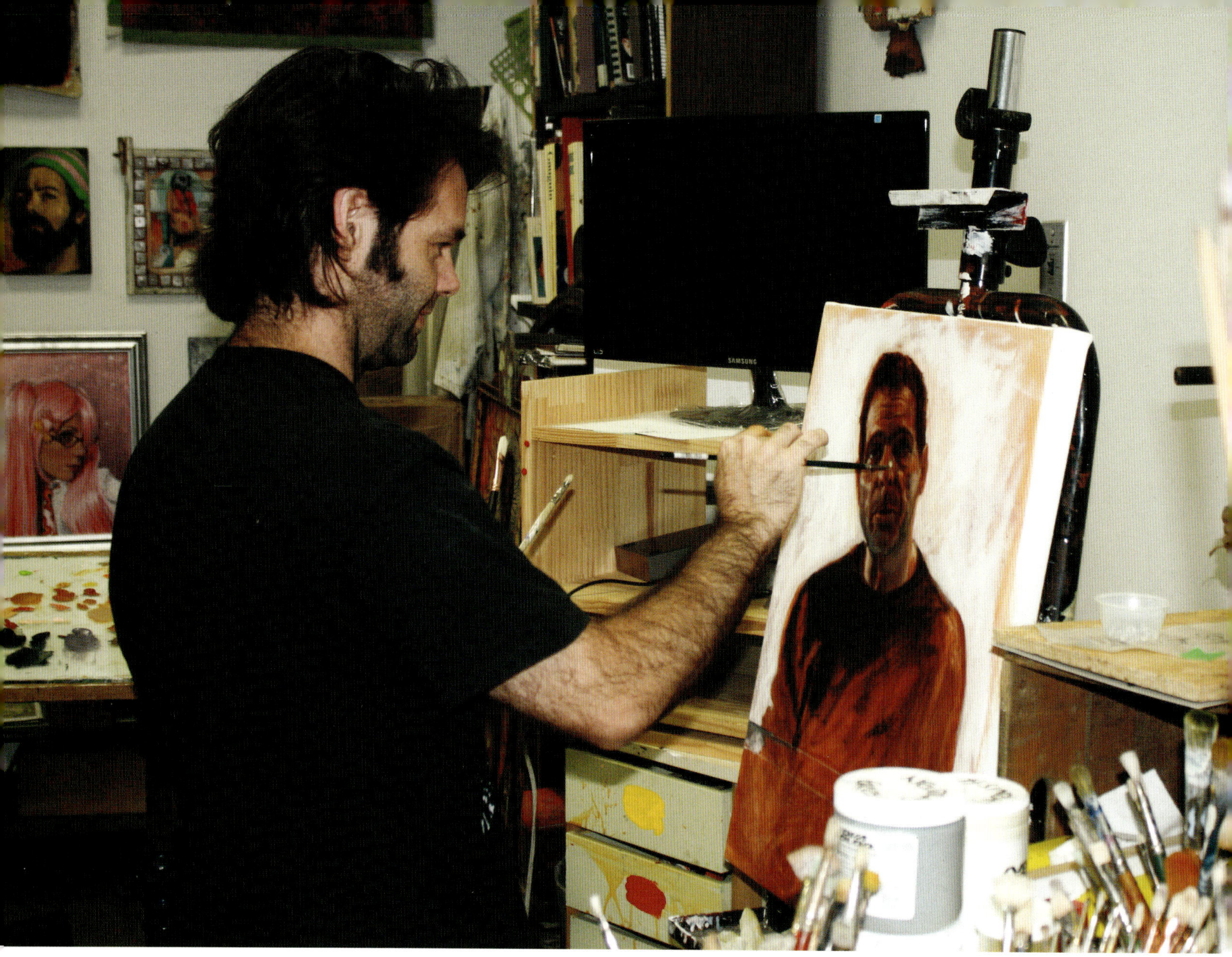

↑ Rick Price with his work in progress, *Howard.*

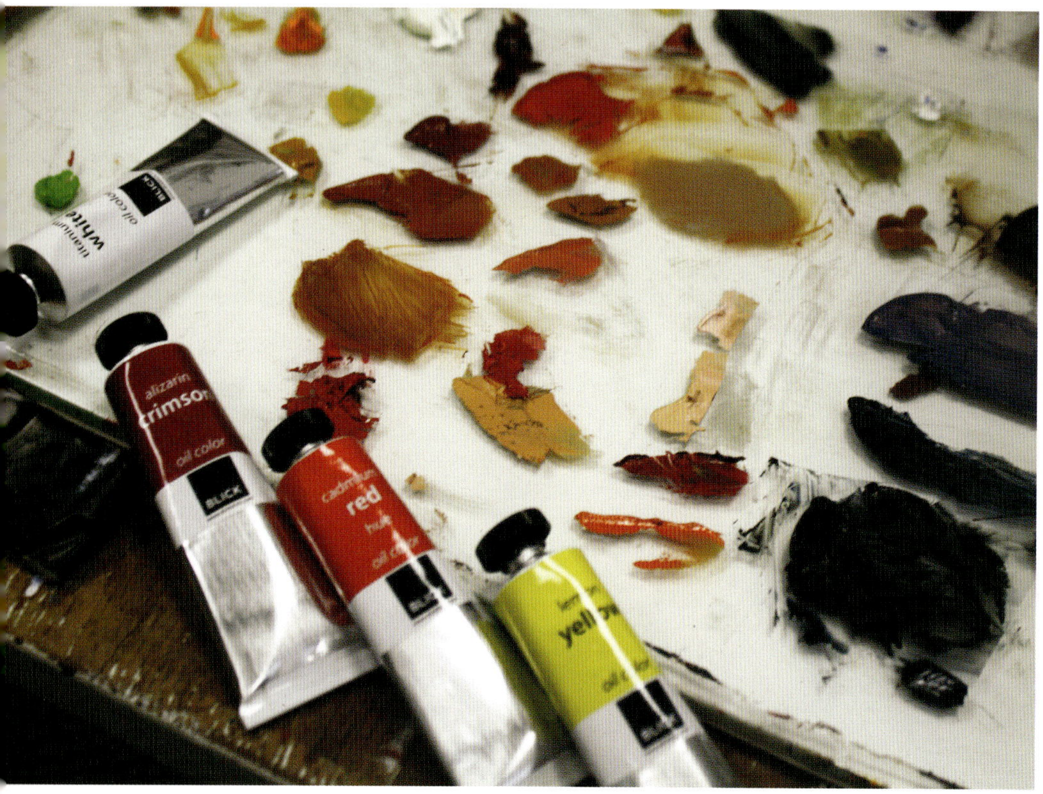

Price uses a large piece of Plexiglas for a palette, creating a playground of color experimentation.

studios," Price says. "Some have found those studios too close to home for their comfort and have discussed swapping spaces with each other."

Painter Richard Bruce took a different tact. When new owners moved into the high school, he not only left the studio, but he also left Beacon, choosing to relocate to Peekskill, New York, a thirty-minute drive south along the Hudson River. Housed in a small cluster of industrial buildings and loading docks just blocks from downtown Peekskill, Bruce's studio is a work in progress that, in some ways, exceeds his room in the old high school. "I don't have the big windows anymore, but that's OK," he says with a laugh as he shows off his new windowless work space. "The view was too distracting, and I've never found

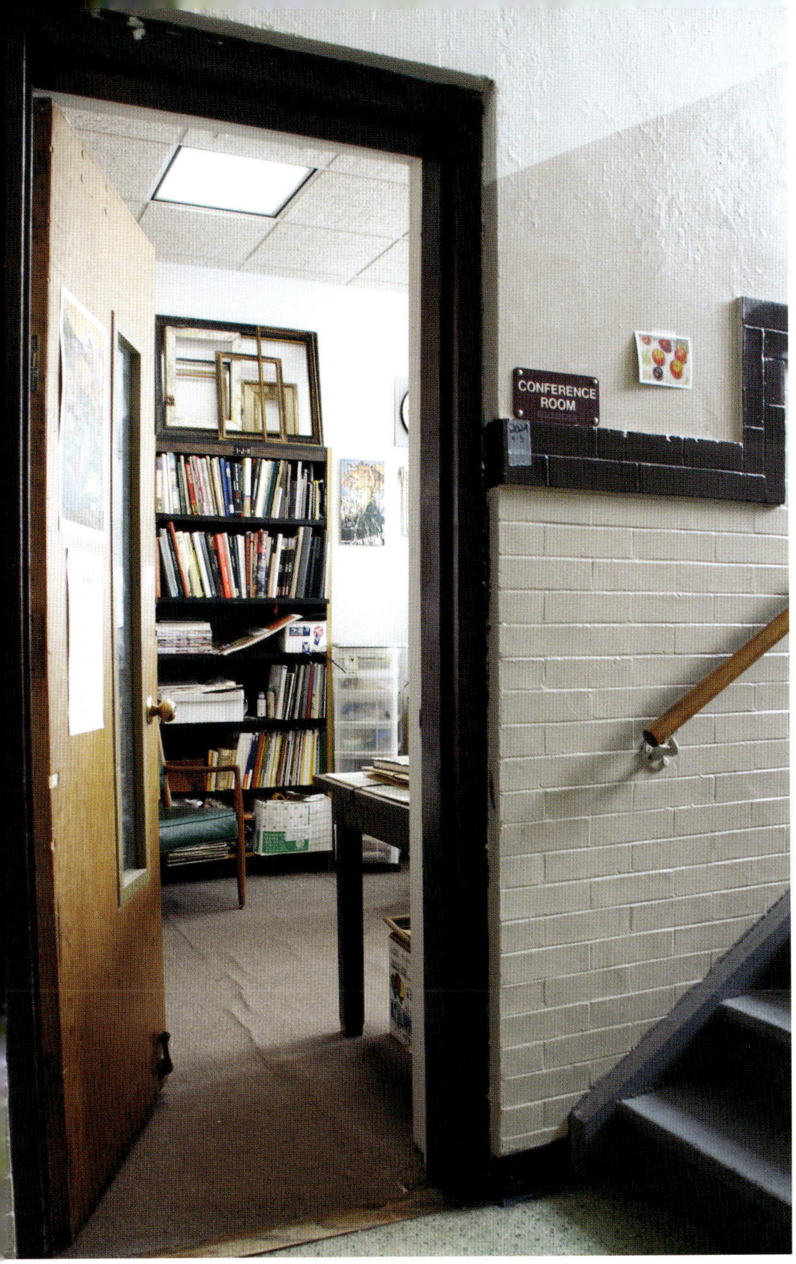

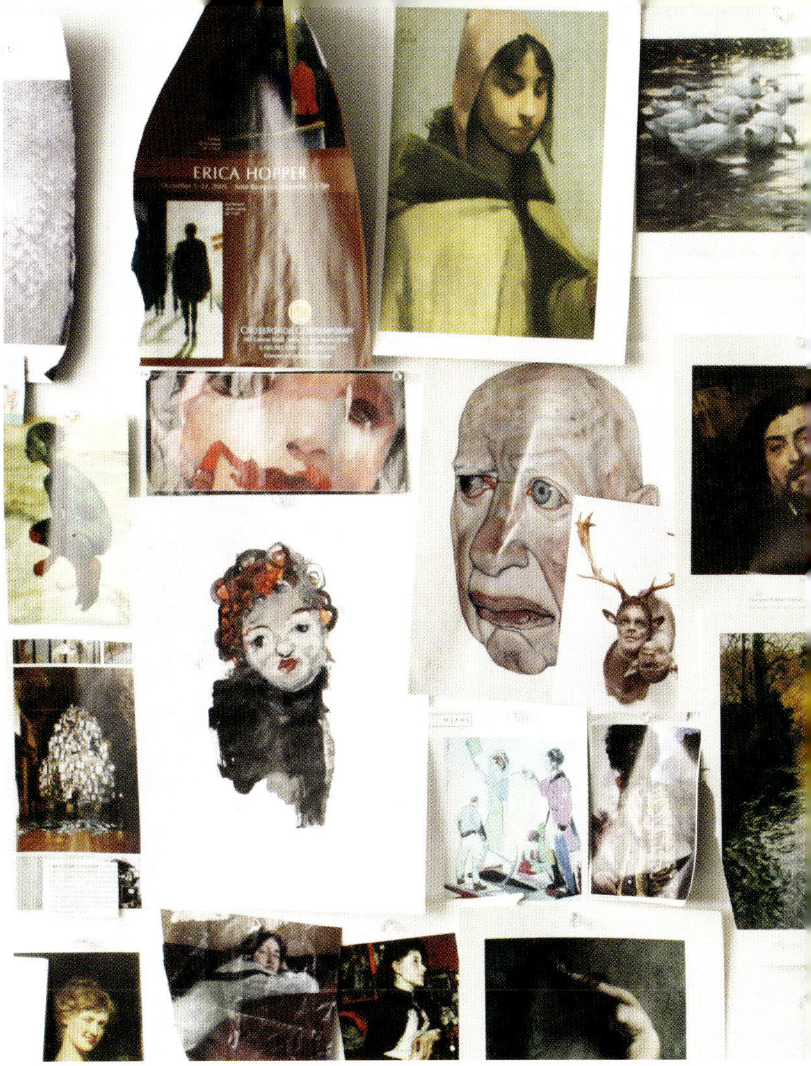

↑ Price fills his walls with inspirational images and an eclectic mix of his own artwork.

← Price's cozy-yet-bright studio space in Beacon's former high school was once a conference room.

that I needed a lot of natural light for my work." The artist explains that setting up a new studio is "a very personal thing," and most artists do so with a keen awareness of what their individual working process requires. "For example," he says, "I prefer painting on an easel, but I also like having wall space to hang works in progress, so I need to have that available. It's very important to have my work around me so that I am immersed in it and can get a real sense of what I am doing."

Bruce works with acrylic and varnish on wood to create his signature "horizonscapes"—ethereal depictions of the point where the land meets the sky. "It's a very spiritual, powerful place for me," Bruce says. "I grew up in rural West Virginia, and I did a lot of hiking and kayaking, and those experiences stayed with me. My work is based on my relationship with nature, but they aren't really landscapes. Landscapes don't interest me very much." Living outside of the city also affords Bruce the ability to kayak in the Hudson and hike through the Catskill Mountains whenever the mood strikes him, refilling his well of inspirational experiences with nature.

Although Peekskill's art community is smaller than that of Beacon, Bruce finds it more convenient to work there because it is closer to the city and, thus, easier to go to galleries and events in Manhattan. "It's still a challenge getting people to come up here, though," he says. "But I'm OK with that. Being a little more solitary can be a good thing." Bruce says his newfound seclusion helps to keep him on track and focused on his work.

Charlotte Schulz is another local artist in a transitional state. She found a small studio in Newburgh, New York, located across the Hudson River from Beacon, but she doesn't plan to stay. Even though a bridge and a ferry connect the two cities, Newburgh has seen little of the revitalization that Beacon experienced. With far more derelict buildings and empty spaces available, artists like Schulz have taken advantage of the cheaper rent and wider selection of spaces available, even if it is only a temporary measure. Her small yet bright room is part of a two-story, brick warehouse that carpenters, sculptors, and even a bookbinder now call home.

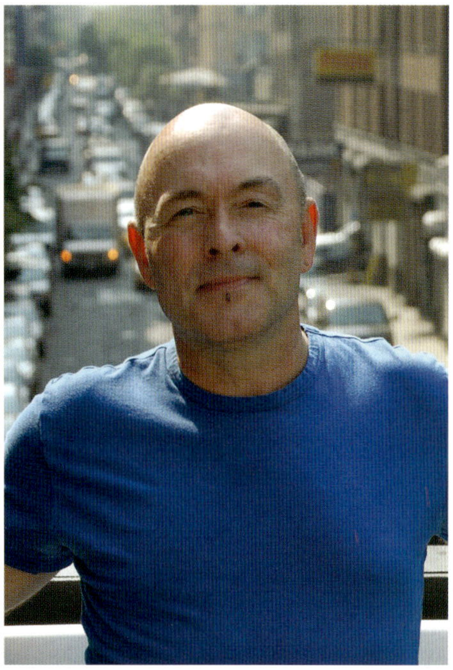

↑ Artist Richard Bruce.

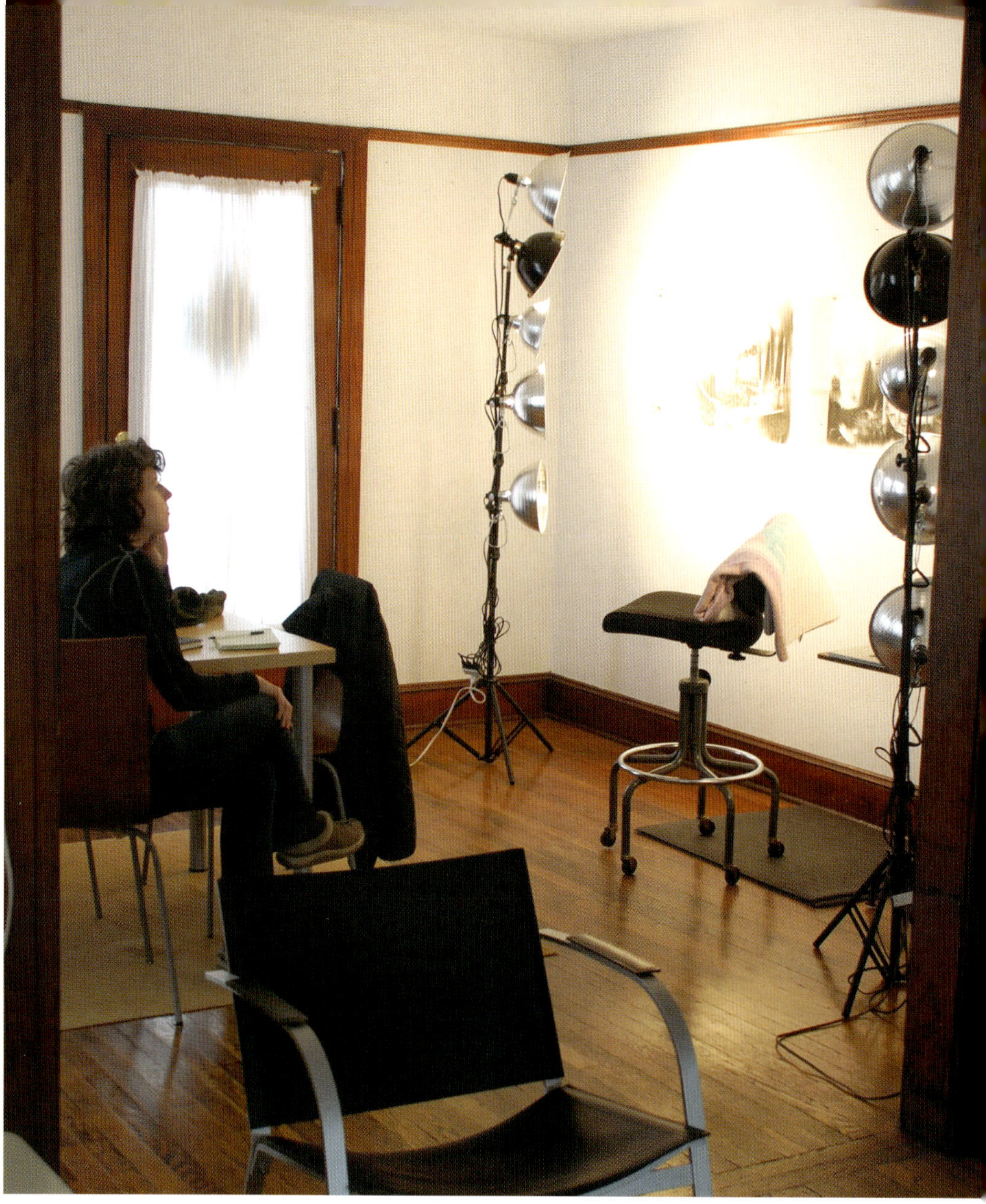

→ Charlotte Schulz in her home studio in Beacon, prior to moving across the river to Newburgh. Notice the power lamp stands she uses to eliminate shadows on her work in progress.

Schulz works with charcoal and paper, crafting fantastical vistas that have a cinematic feel, multiple perspectives, and an almost three-dimensional quality. While her art may look outlandish and eclectic, the compositions are always grounded in concrete, realistic images. The artist keeps her laptop nearby so that she can search for images that move her, and she also frequents the New York Public Library in Manhattan, checking out many of their old photographs to build upon her ideas. Paper is very important to her, and she often bends, folds, and wrinkles her sheets of Strathmore two-ply and Fabriano Artistico paper to add a visual texture to her work. Schulz tapes her drawings to the wall and stands or sits on a stool while she creates, preferring to move herself instead of the piece. Two columns of lights stand on either side of her so that no shadows block her view. The artist works the Alphacolor compressed charcoal into the paper and then teases out shapes and details with a variety of erasers. It is a long, delicate process, but as Schulz says, "One of the good things about living and working in this area is that you don't need to make as much money to maintain a quality studio space, so you can relax a little more and focus. You can enjoy the process."

Even more established artist/instructors such as Paul McCormack find truth in this bit of wisdom. McCormack moved to the area fifteen years ago with his wife because property was very affordable—and it still is, especially compared to areas closer to New York City. As his family grew, he moved his work outside of his home and now rents an impressive studio just down the road. "I love my studio," McCormack enthuses. "North-facing windows, 16-foot-high (5m) ceilings, 750 square feet (70 square meters)—what's not to love? It is, however, the first time in my entire life that my studio is outside of my living space. Although the commute is only 8 miles (13km), I don't think I've ever adjusted. If I want to work after dinner or into the early morning hours, it seldom happens. I miss rolling out of bed and walking into the studio with my first cup of coffee and planning out my day." Even so, McCormack makes the new situation work, and his experience as a top portraitist has given him ample knowledge about what makes a studio great.

"Good light has always been important to me," he explains. "In addition to the north-facing windows, I have fluorescent fixtures with color-corrected bulbs. I work mainly by the light of the

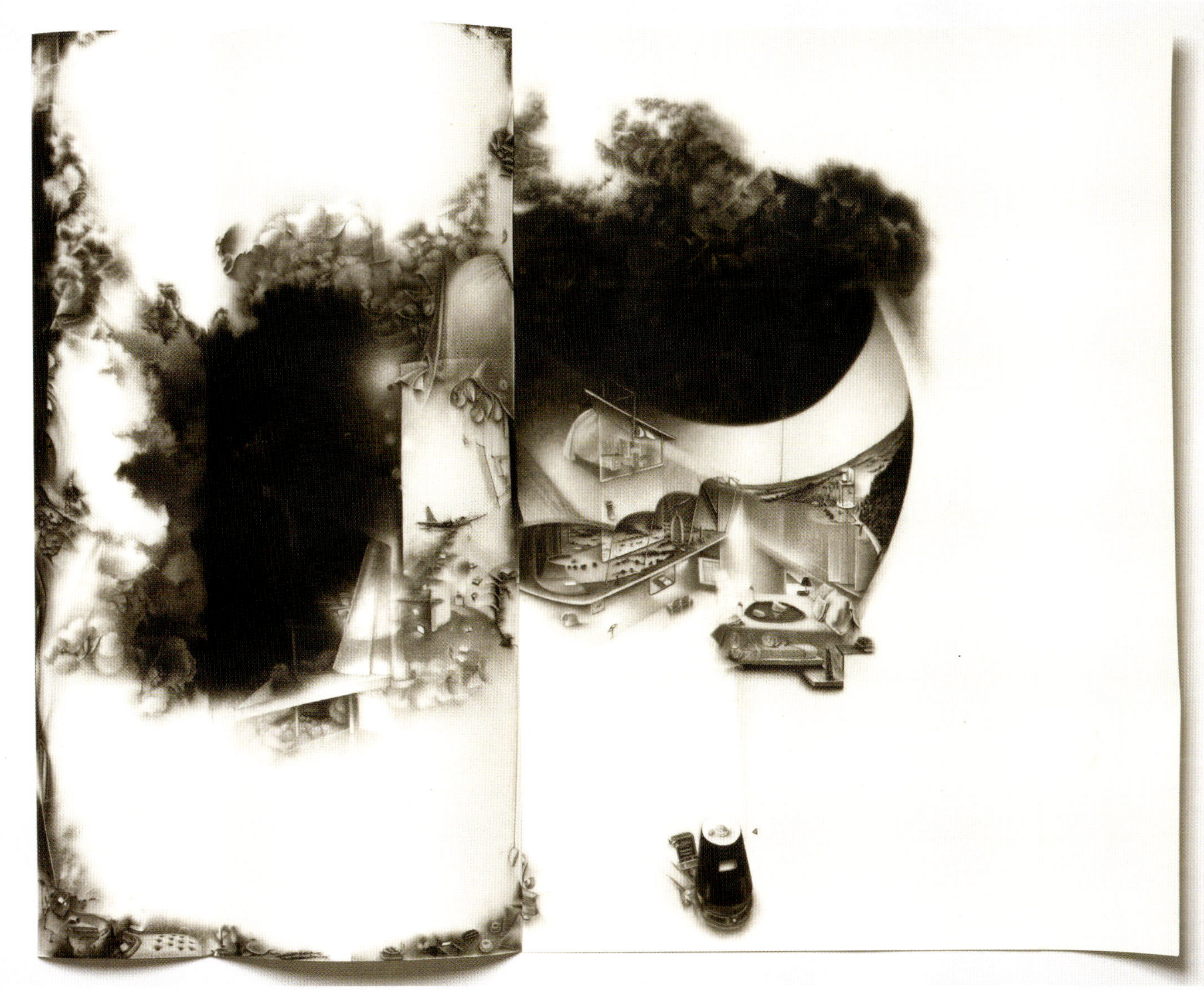

↑ **The uneven intensities of duration: tea and biscuits are set upon our object of destruction for those acting within the center without our knowledge**
by Charlotte Schulz, 2008, charcoal on paper, 38" x 45" (97cm x 114cm).

windows and use four of the fixtures as a light fill on dark days. The remaining fixtures light the rest of the studio when I hold classes and workshops." The artist's work space is ample, but he makes good use of every corner, sometimes as storage space. "Although they can take up quite a bit of room, I find that my flat files are indispensable for proper storage of paper and finished works," he says. "I also keep many props in the studio for models and for still-life setups. I have a large assortment of fabrics for backgrounds, hats, scarves, kimonos, as well as a few antique chairs." And for those just starting out, McCormack suggests you "avoid a basement studio at all costs.

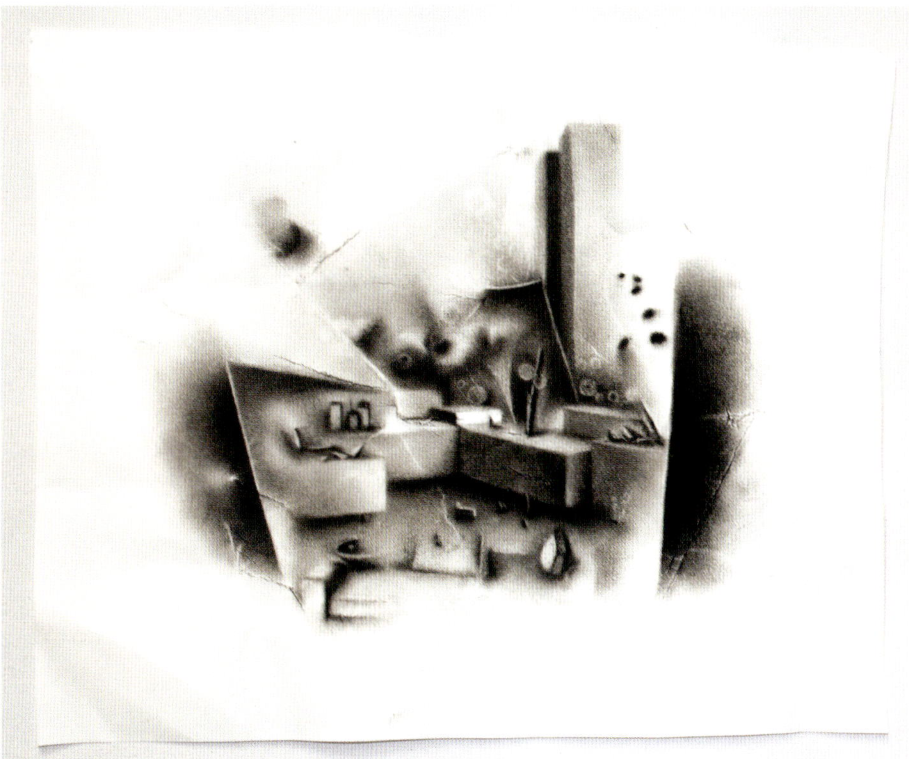

The impossibility of keeping borders: saturated with small events, the interior unfolds upon the screen
by Charlotte Schulz, 2011, charcoal on paper, 12" x 14" (30cm x 36cm).

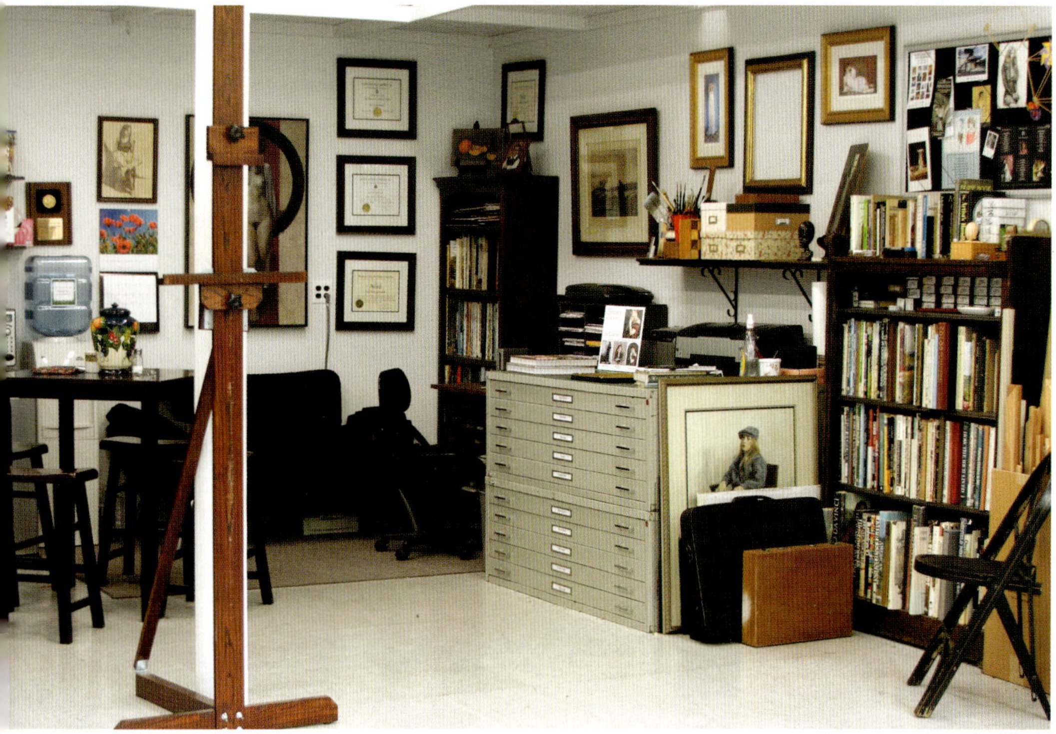

↑ Paul McCormack keeps an organized studio, due in no small part to his affinity for flat files.

→ The north end of McCormack's studio. The high ceilings and wide windows flood his space with natural north light.

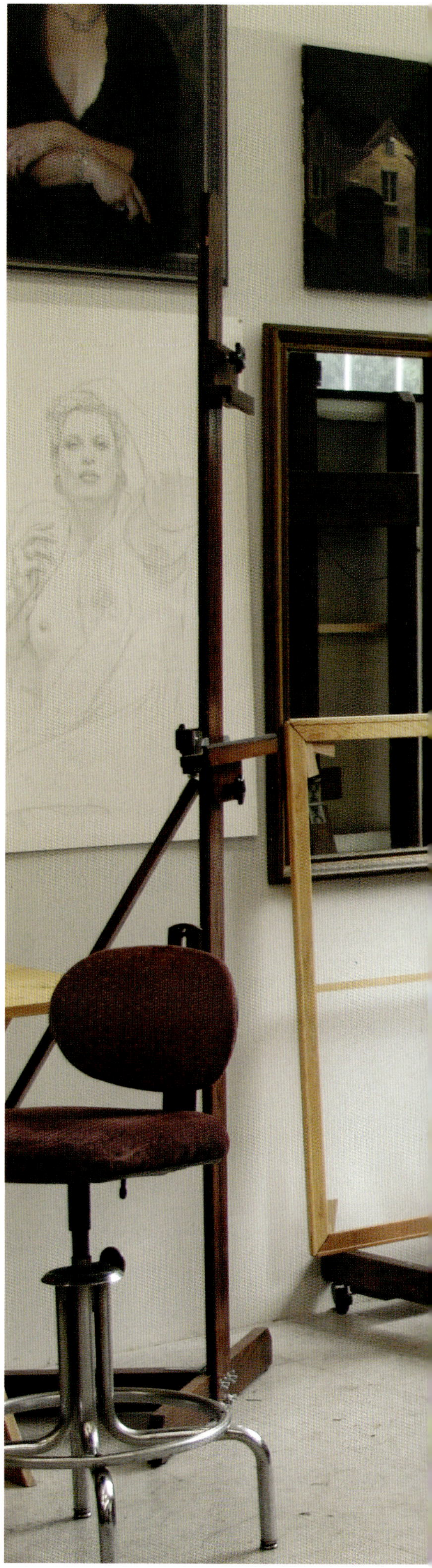

I know many artists and students that have set up their first studios in a basement and have later regretted the decision. There's something about a room with small or no windows at all and concrete that make a studio very uninviting. North light is nice, but it is definitely not necessary. Even a small spare bedroom can suffice when properly lit."

For artists starting out, the Hudson Valley has always been replete with unused factories and affordable homes with extra rooms perfect for what McCormack prescribes, but as time passes, these studio spaces may become harder to find. The Dia Art Foundation attracted the first waves of artists, but like moths to a flame, moneyed investors have followed, for good or ill. Much like the former high school in Beacon, large vacant buildings perfect for working studios are being bought with ambitious ideas of luxury suites and commercial spaces. It remains to be seen how many of these high-priced investments will benefit the working artisans and townspeople living along the Hudson River, but one thing is certain: Change is constant. It brought good things to the city of Beacon before, and the artists in the region remain hopeful.

For more on Rick Price, visit his website at www.rickprice.net.

For more on Charlotte Schulz, visit her website at www.charlotteschulz.com.

For more on Richard Bruce, visit his website at www.richardgbruce.com.

For more on Paul McCormack, visit his website at www.mccormackstudios.com.

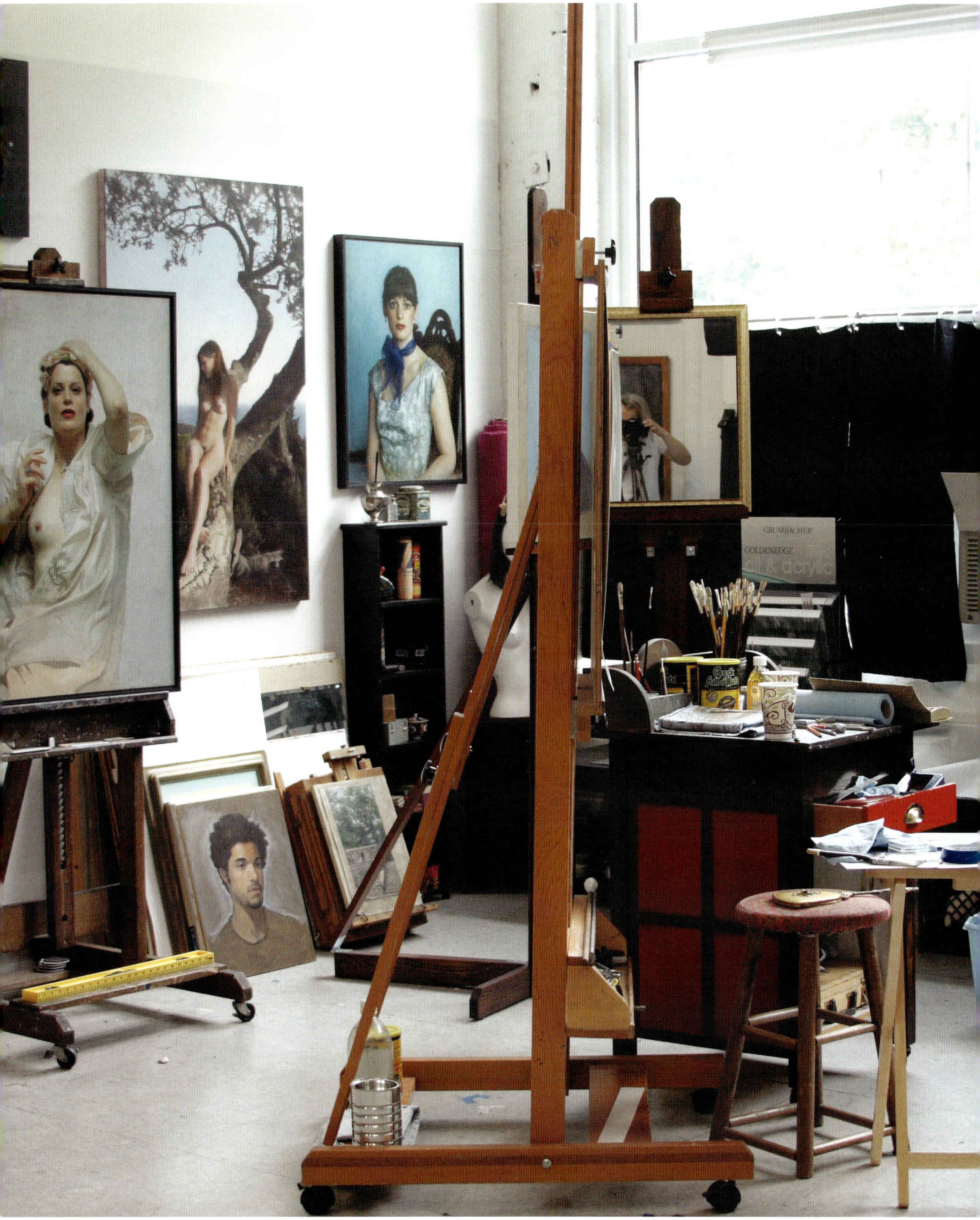

It Takes a Community to Make Art

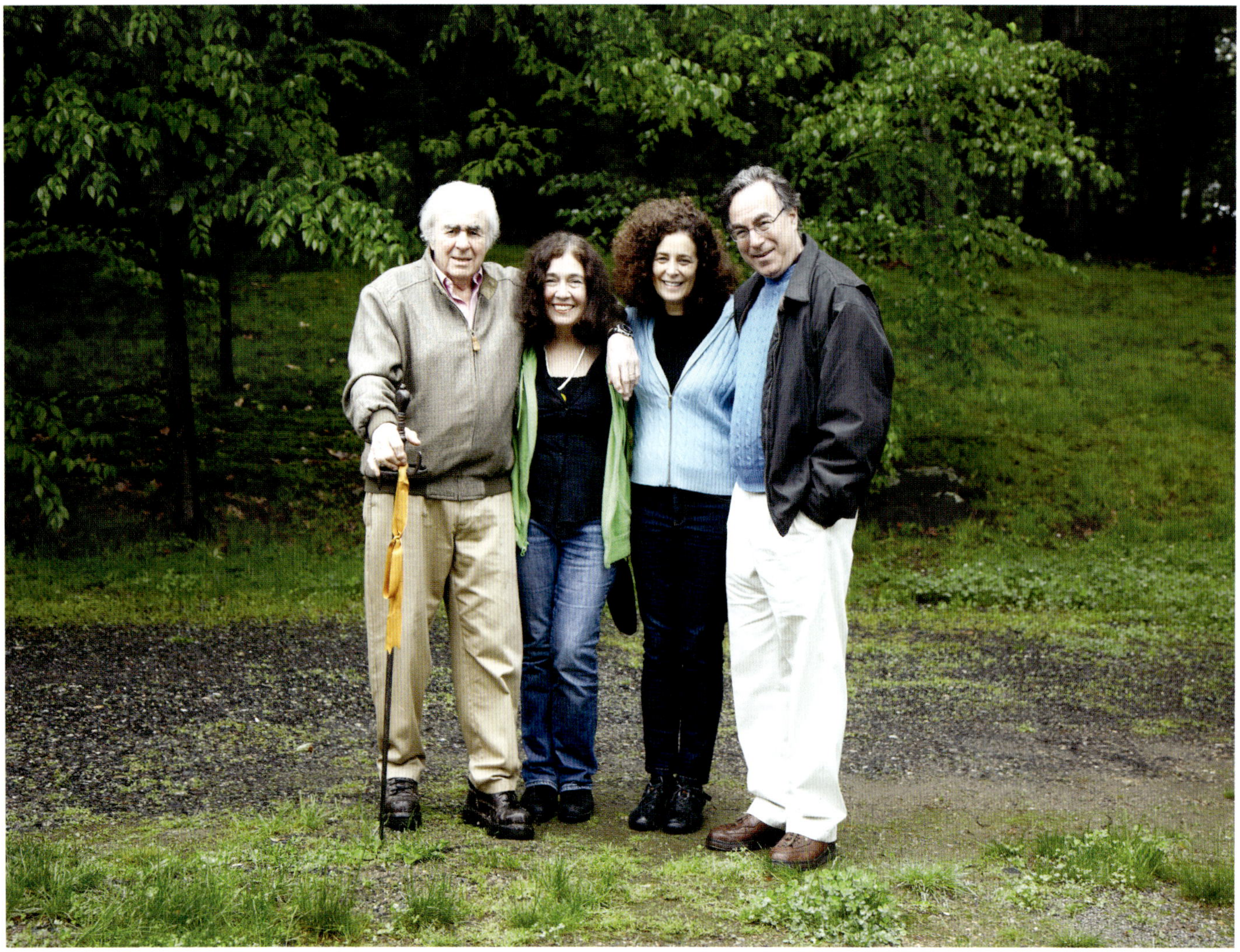

Left to right: Everett Raymond Kinstler, Kathy Anderson, Babette Bloch, and Marc Mellon.

Many factors influence where an artist decides to set up his or her home and studio. At the outset of a professional career, economic factors are of primary concern. Young artists also need easy access to exhibition venues, potential patrons, and ancillary employment. Such fledgling artists often gravitate toward major cities and towns, where they can pursue career advancement and take advantage of a wide range of affordable housing options and studio facilities. Historically, this trend has led to the formation of artistic communities, a boon both to the individual artist and to the general culture. These communities, which support a rich infrastructure including studio facilities, schools, and public meeting places, provide a fertile concentration for the creative exchange of ideas and the sharing of finite resources.

Alternatively, some artists are drawn to the natural landscape and prefer communities located a comfortable distance from urban centers. These artists tend to be more established in their careers and have developed the solid relationships with galleries, collectors, and students that provide a steady source of income.

Through my colleagues Wendy Walworth-Schrijver (page 58), a member of the National Arts Club (NAC), and Tim Newton, the chairman of the Salmagundi Club—both private cultural organizations in New York City that advance the visual and performing arts—I have become acquainted with a coterie of successful, midcareer artists

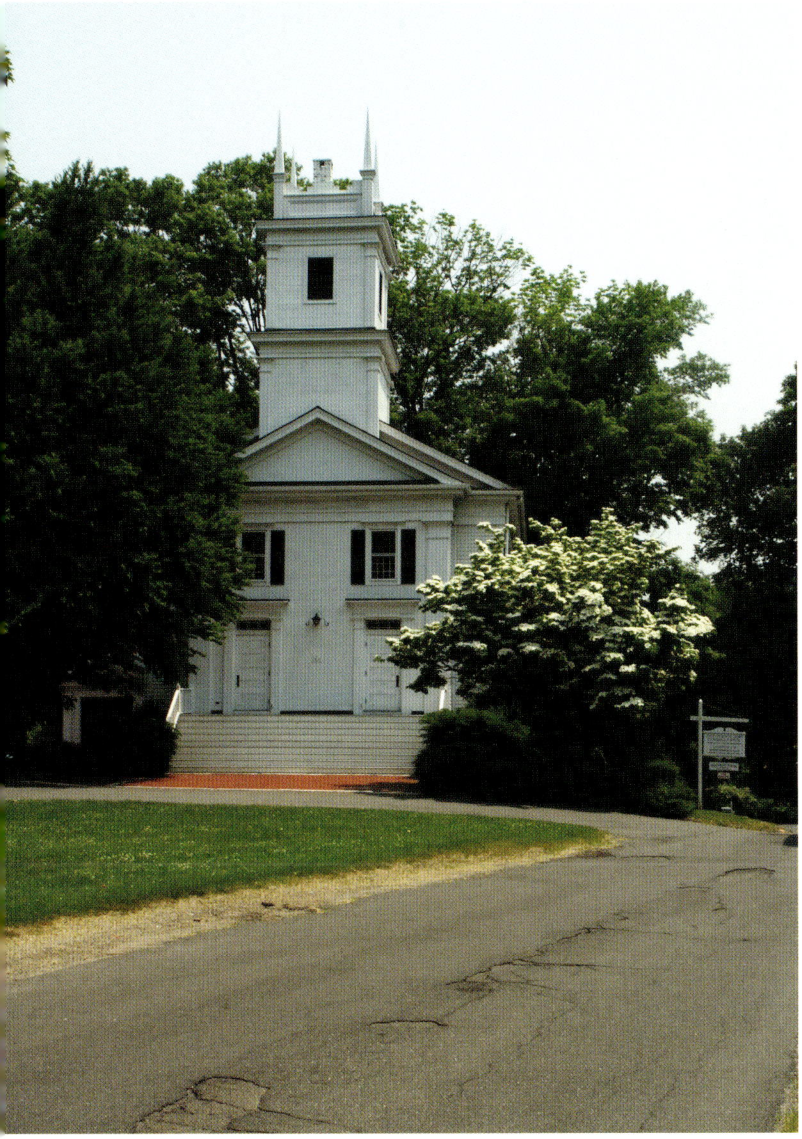

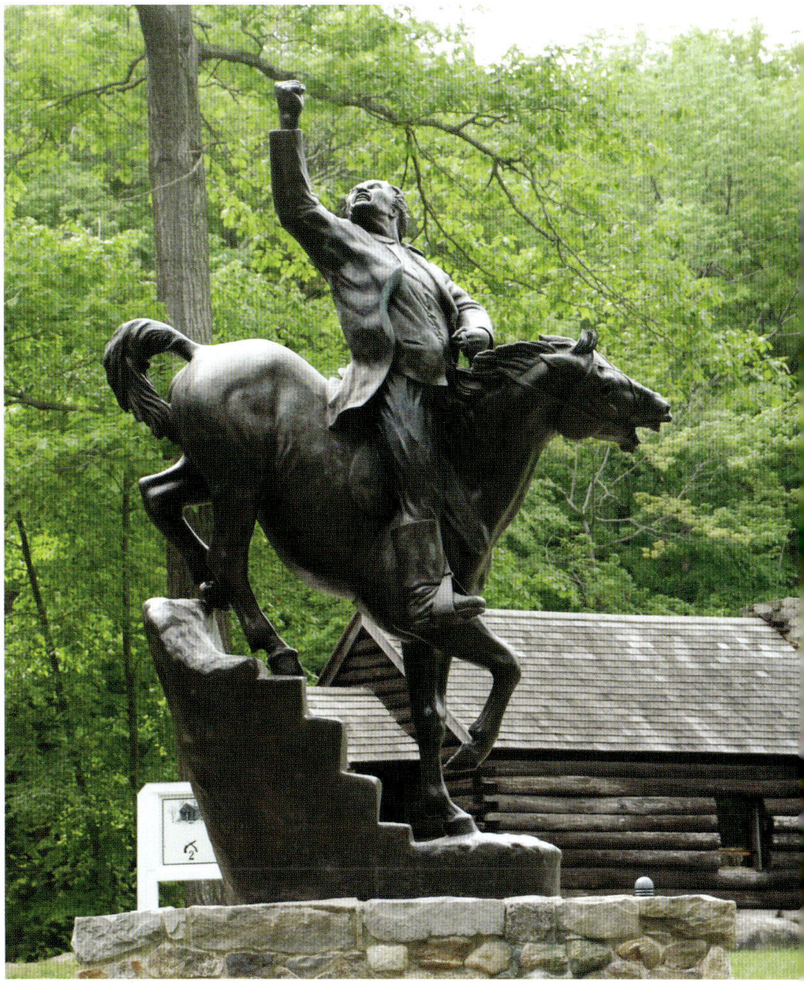

↑ Statue of General Israel Putnam by Anna Hyatt Huntington at Putnam Memorial State Park in Redding, Connecticut.

← The town hall in Redding, Connecticut.

who moved to the bucolic environs of western Connecticut and nearby parts of New York state, where they live in homes that also serve as their studios.

The next five articles explore the lives of these artists vis-à-vis their studio practices and their ties to one another. Throughout the process of writing and researching this article, it became clear to me that an art studio is much more than a physical plant conducive to the production of art. It is the nexus of an artist's life.

Building a Professional Studio Practice

Making art is largely a solitary practice, which can lead to challenging periods of discouragement. Upon leaving college and its myriad opportunities for interaction with peers and support from faculty and staff, many artists are unprepared for the isolation, monotony, and rigorous demands of studio work. This may explain the high attrition rates in fine-art practice that are reported by college and university alumni offices—by some estimates, more than half of art majors stop producing work within three years after graduating.

Meaningful social contacts seem to stem this attrition and play a significant role in the lives of successful artists. My observations suggest that successful artists—by which I mean artists who are relatively content and productive—have close friends and ties to family and community. Like many other successful professionals, they are members of collegiate organizations that help support and advance their respective careers. They also tend to volunteer their services to charitable and municipal collectives that seek to advance the common good, and they also teach and mentor younger artists.

It takes a serious commitment to decide to be an artist and to shape one's life accordingly. Staking a claim in a community implies the same level of risk and commitment. Yet the rewards offered—invaluable professional support and life-enhancing relationships—prove to be the magical ingredients that make for a contented and productive studio engagement.

Kathy Anderson
A Studio From Scratch

Kathy Anderson bubbles with a magnetic enthusiasm that can light up a crowded room. A prolific painter of nature scenes and floral still lifes, Anderson works in a fresh, alla prima style perfectly suited to capturing nature's beautiful, fleeting effects.

In 1979, Anderson moved to Redding, Connecticut, from Queens, in New York City, and loves what she calls Redding's "rural beauty." Unlike the overdeveloped suburbs that radiate out from city centers, the town has retained its country-hamlet charm. "Even going over to the post office is a thrill!" Anderson cheerily adds. "I recently participated in a wonderful plein air show on our local educational farm, founded by the late actress Carmen Matthews, and I am on a committee that mounts beautiful group art shows by Redding artists and photographers in our town hall. I also have many close artist friends here who I'm with all the time."

Anderson has always worked in her home. "I wouldn't change this," she notes. "I'd wind up never being anywhere, just driving around wondering where I was going." In 1993, Anderson added a sunroom to her home and uses this space to paint the floral still lifes and landscapes that have become her signature subjects. In 2010, as the market for her work increased and production space became an issue, Anderson decided it was time to build a professional studio. Her son Ben—a gifted craftsman who owns a construction business specializing in sustainable, environmentally friendly design—took on the task of building the studio addition to the Anderson home. With all the hallmarks of a New England barn raising, the building of Anderson's new studio was a joint family and community undertaking. The Andersons and members of their community did all the

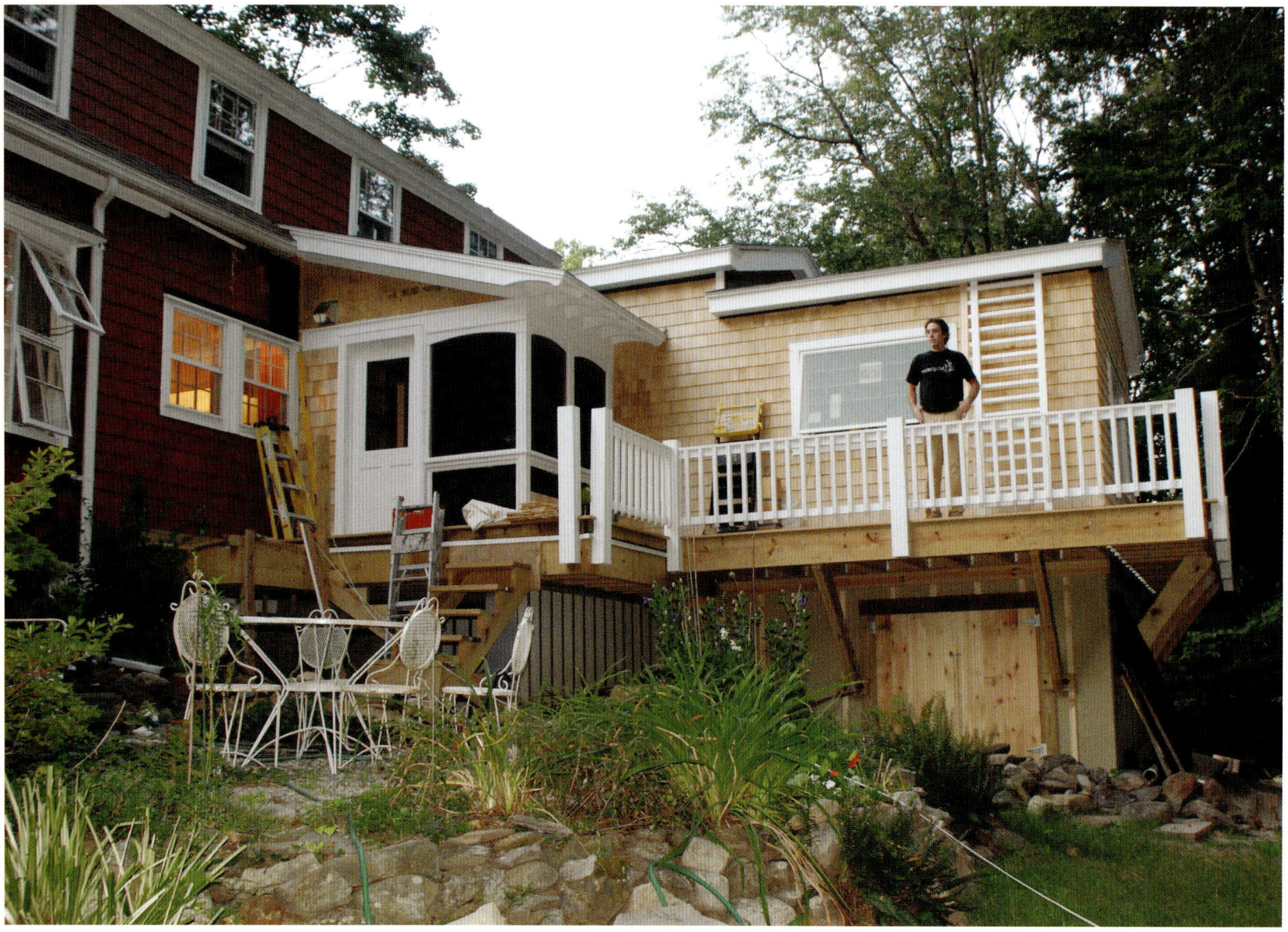

Anderson's completed studio addition, with a side entrance and kitchen nook.

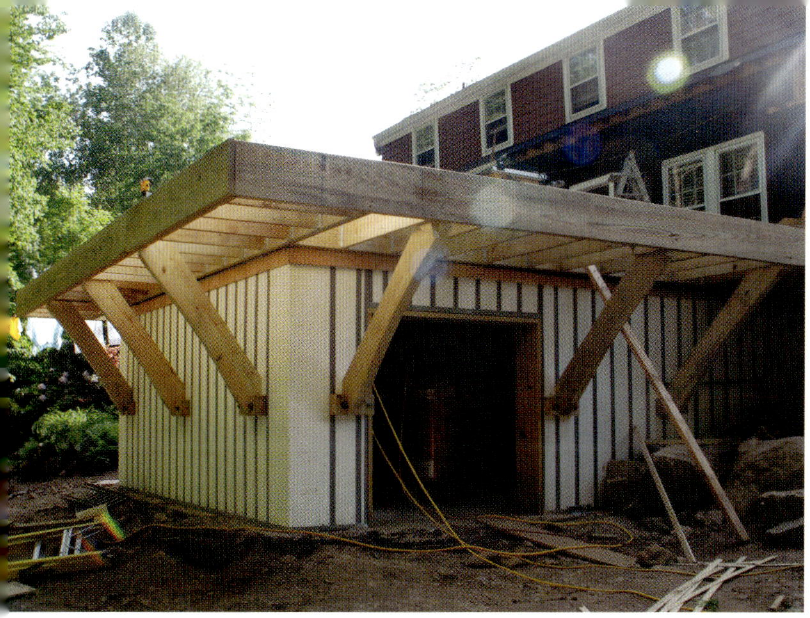

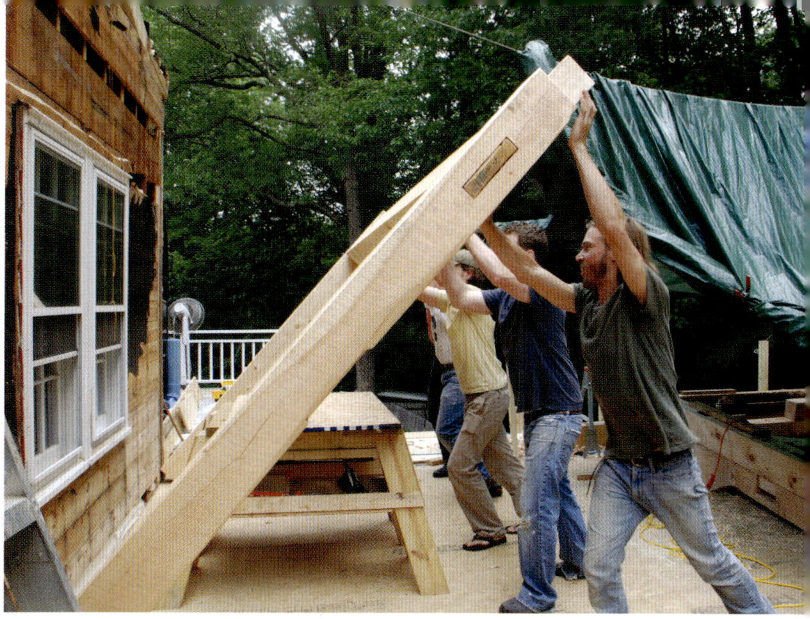

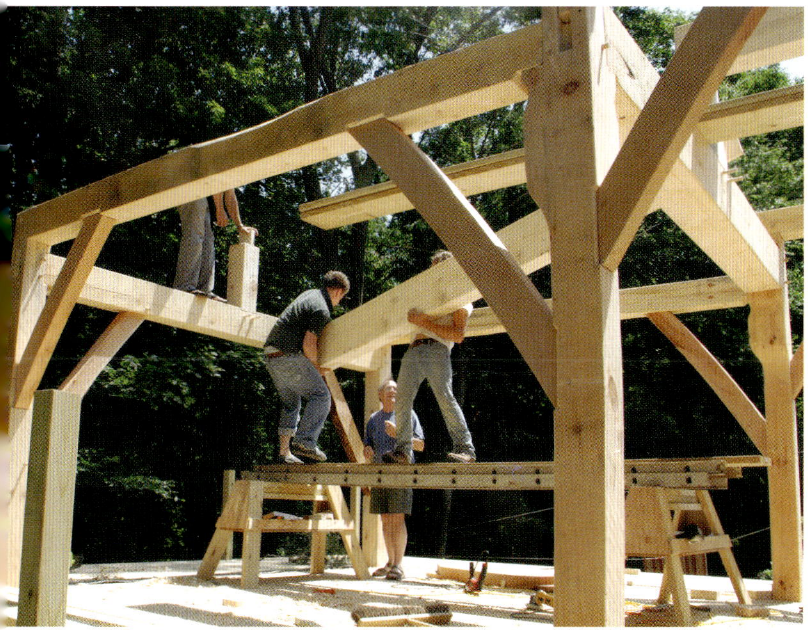

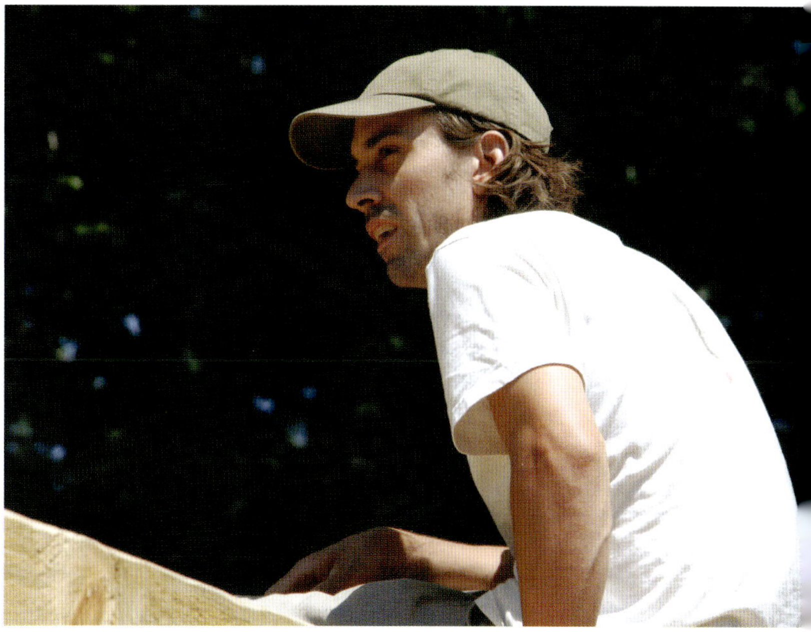

Above left: Floor beams attached to the foundation. *Above right:* Raising the hand-hewn timber walls. *Left:* Setting the roof timbers for Anderson's addition. *Right:* Ben Anderson, the artist's son, is a skilled wood craftsman and designer of sustainable homes.

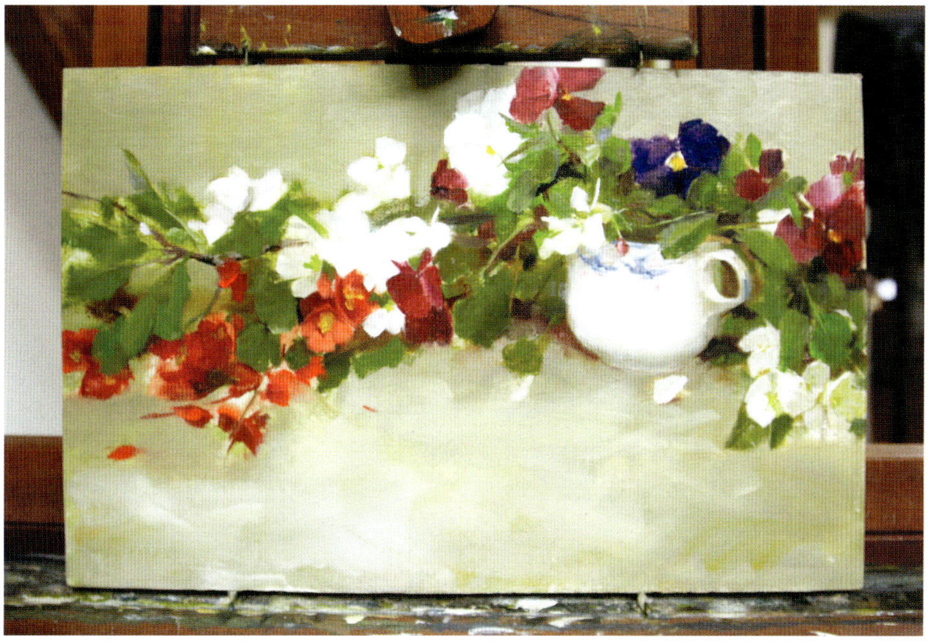

A still life in progress.

work, from clearing the land and pouring the concrete foundation to hewing and joining the traditional beam-and-post construction with wood dowels.

The new 15'-x-24' (5m-x-7m) timber-frame addition to Anderson's studio blends seamlessly with her country home. Its peaked ceiling, exposed beams, and multitude of windows lends the space an outdoorsy feel—more like a covered porch than an enclosed room. "It is heaven," Anderson joyfully notes. "I've basically tripled my space. I'm surrounded by windows with garden and woodland views. It is incredibly inspiring to be in there, and I wouldn't change a thing!

"My son did a wonderful job of interpreting my requirements and working within the constraints of the site and our budget," she continues. "We were somewhat limited by the orientation

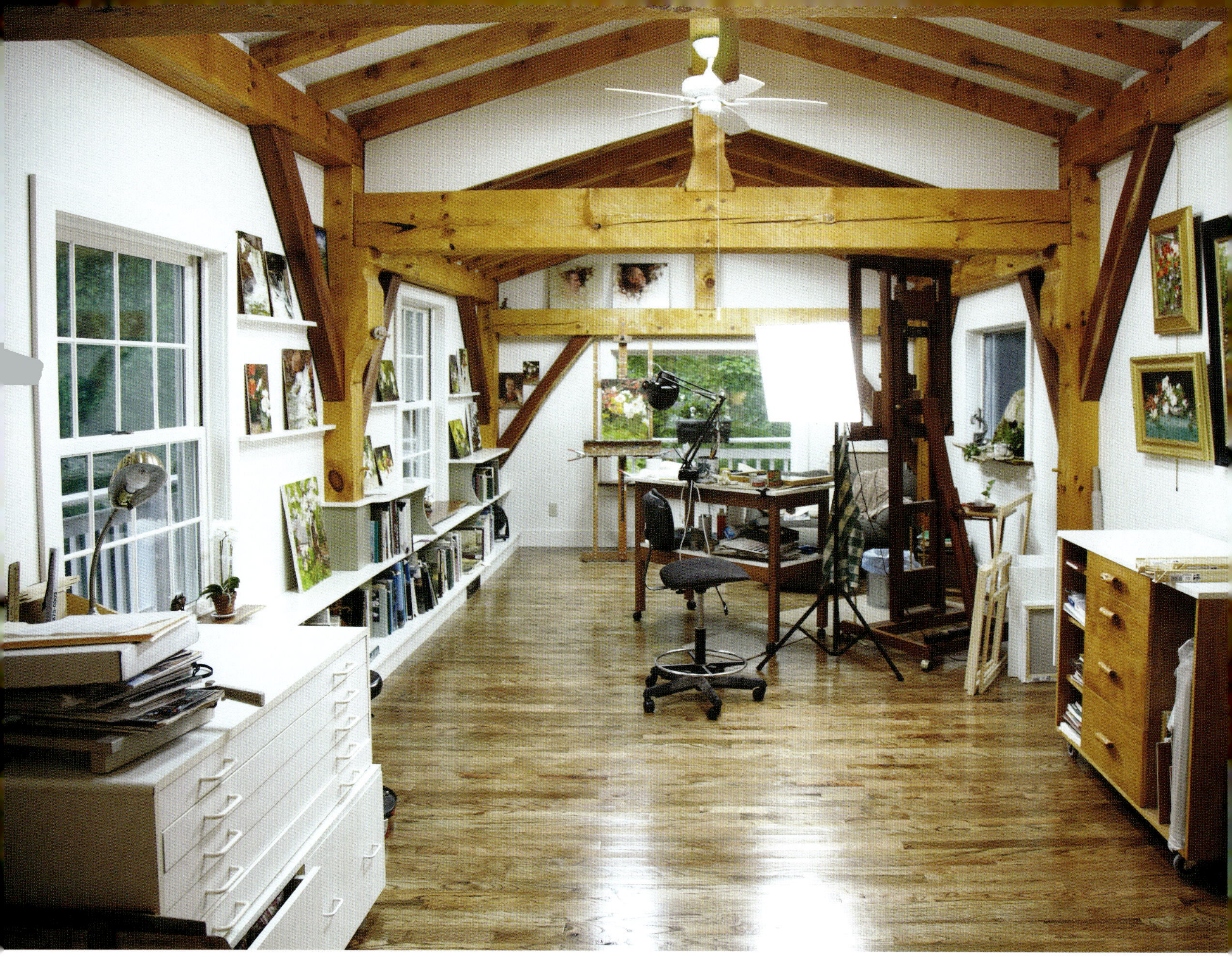

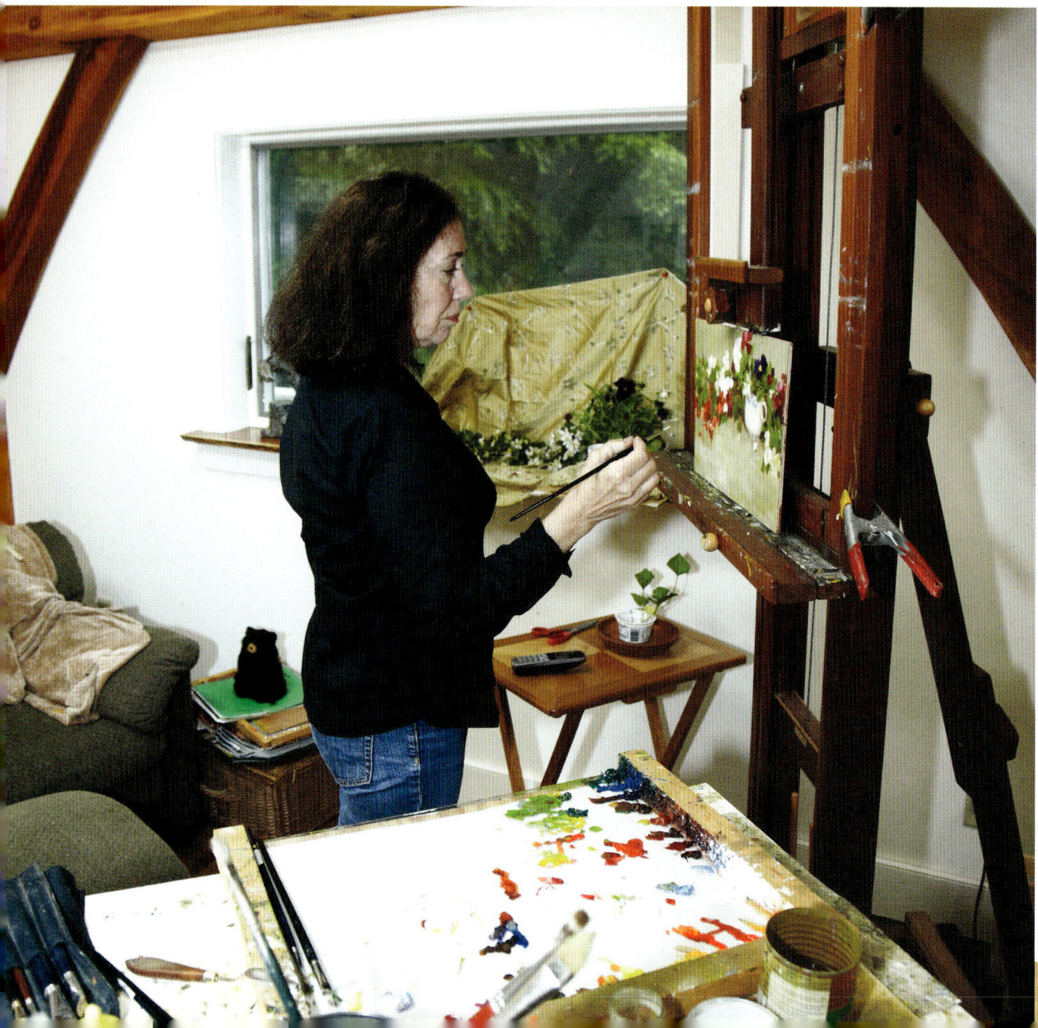

↑ Anderson's new studio addition features traditional pine construction.

← Anderson painting a still life.

STUDIO TIPS

When setting up an art studio, Anderson recommends careful thought and planning about storage issues. She also recommends checking light requirements and trying to make the best use of both natural and artificial light. Most important, Anderson notes that an artist needs to "make a space that you're so happy to be in—one that you never want to leave."

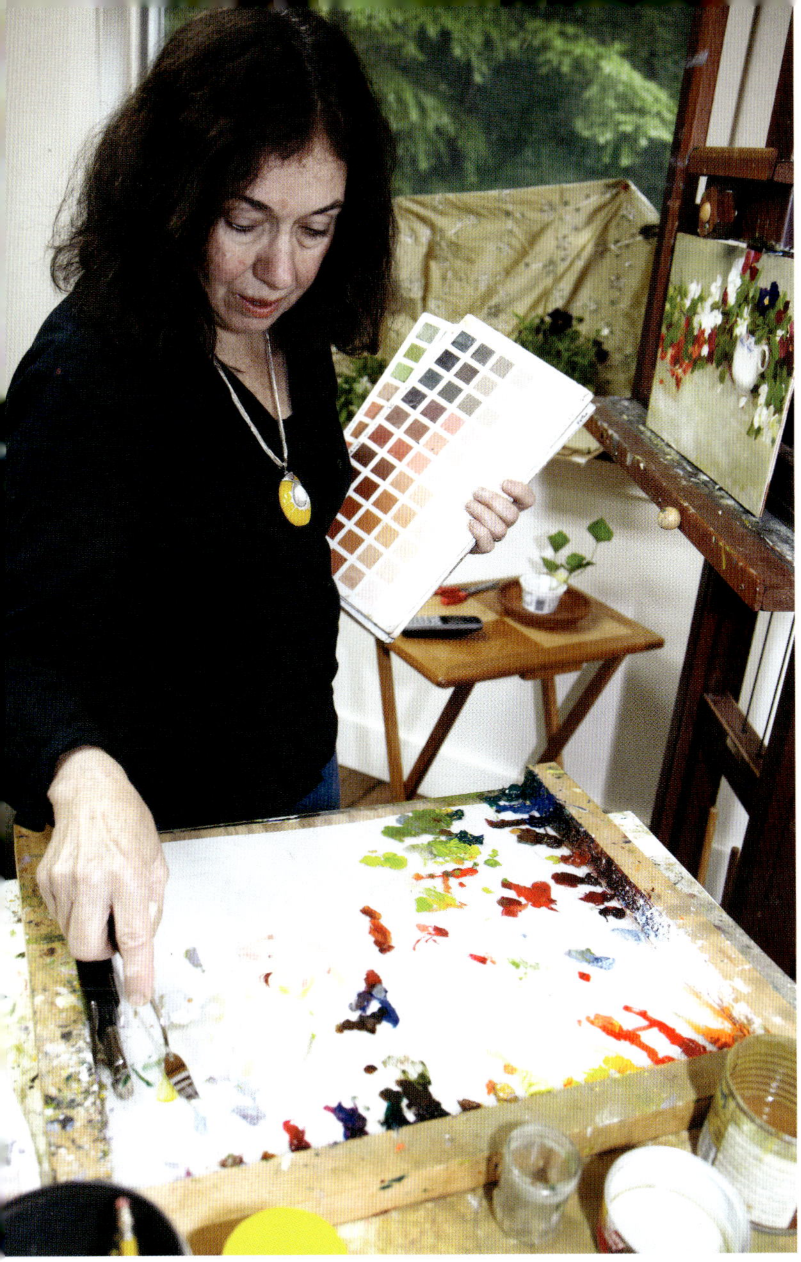

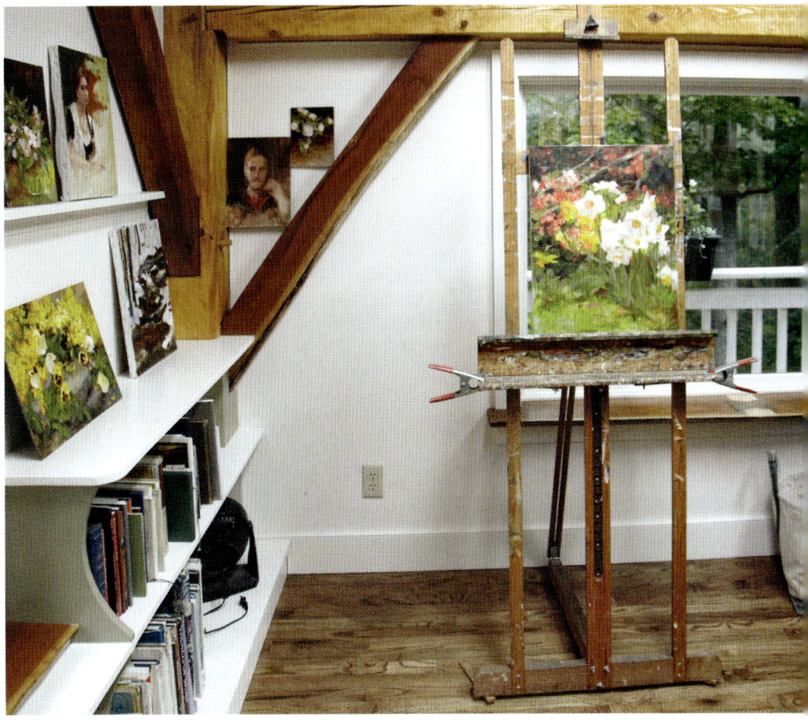

↑ The studio offers wall shelves for drying and displaying paintings and ample storage for books, supplies, and studio furnishings.

← Anderson mixes the complementary colors blue and orange to achieve the soft green-grays found in nature. She refers to the paint charts she completed in a workshop to help guide her paint mixtures.

of the house and the topography of the site. I don't have north light, but I have really good natural light and an excellent artificial lighting system. Everett Raymond Kinstler (page 36) was able to provide assistance on the lighting design; he's a good friend and is always available to offer support, a critical eye, and much-needed humor. I can also move around the studio as I need to, as all my work surfaces are on casters. I have hanging molding and good brass gallery rods, which give me lots of variety for rearranging my framed pictures. I also have lots of small shelves for panel works in progress, plenty of storage for paintings and art supplies, and lots of bookshelves."

Anderson is an easel painter and generally works on an intimate scale using braced birch boards over which double-primed linen is stretched. These sturdy supports are well suited to Anderson's painting process that often includes on-site work. She adds, "I will occasionally work from a photograph, generally when I've returned from a site and plan to finish the piece in my studio. The photograph helps me recall the details of the site that I wasn't able to record during the initial painting session."

When not on plein air excursions or completing those works begun on-site, Anderson paints from spare still-life setups that privilege a restrained, oriental-like design sensibility. During our visit to her studio, Anderson was working from one of these elegantly spare setups. A budding forsythia branch lay delicately over a drape of contrasting colored fabric; life and time was revealed by a light scatter of shedding petals. "Flower setups are always changing," Anderson notes. "The trick is to replenish the setup with fresh flowers, or it all starts to look a bit wilted."

Judging from the dozens of works that were drying in the racks that lined the walls—mostly panel paintings awaiting final touches and framing—one is bound to agree that Anderson is indeed inspired in her new studio. Luckily for Anderson, her artwork is a family affair. Her husband, John, handles her business affairs. A consummate craftsman, he also builds by hand the exquisite buffed enamel and gilded frames that adorn her paintings.

For more on Kathy Anderson, visit her website at www.kathyanderson studio.com.

James Prosek

Painting Nature Beside a Pond

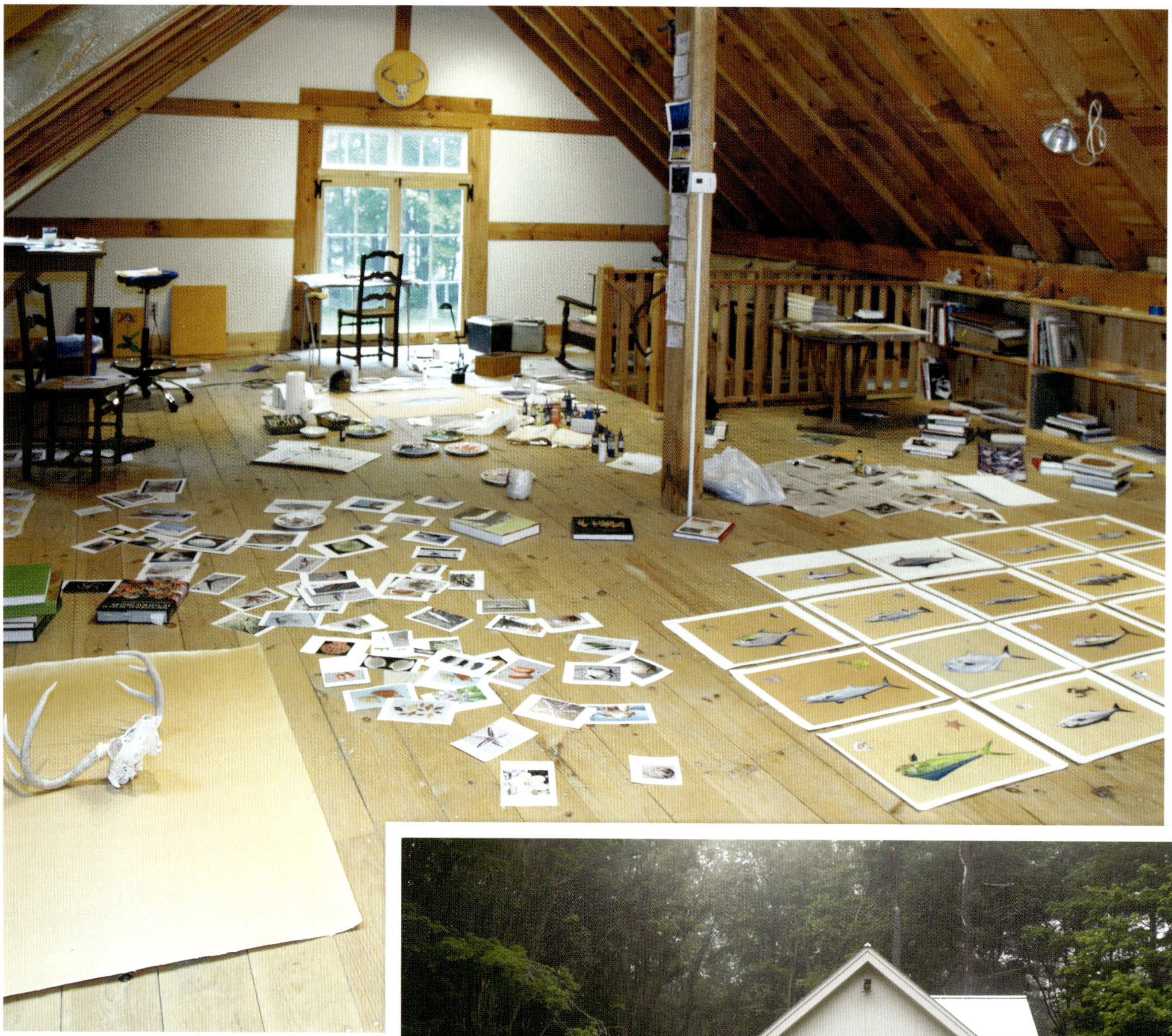

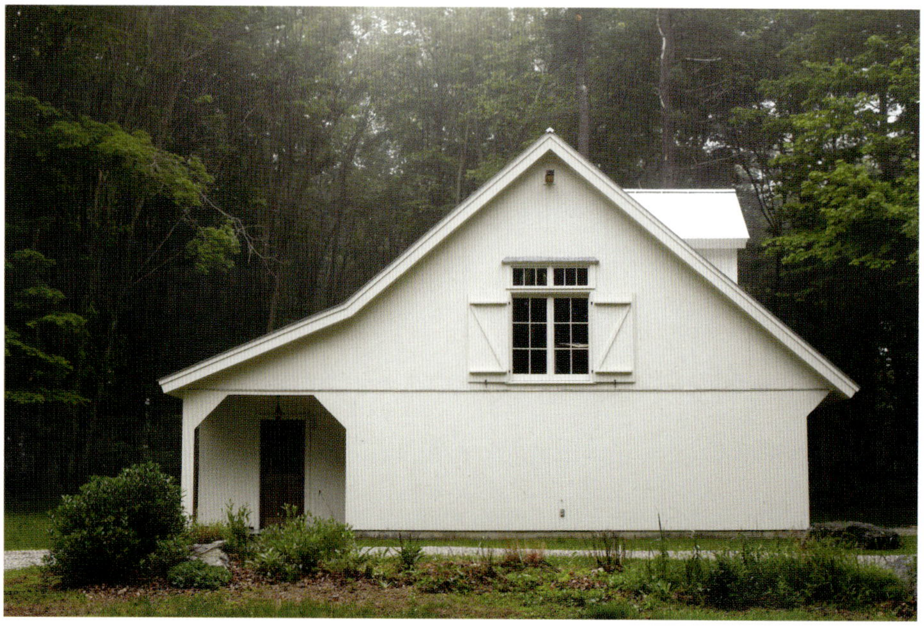

↑ Prosek's garret-like work space showing works in progress, drawing and water-media art supplies, and reference materials.

→ The exterior of Prosek's new studio.

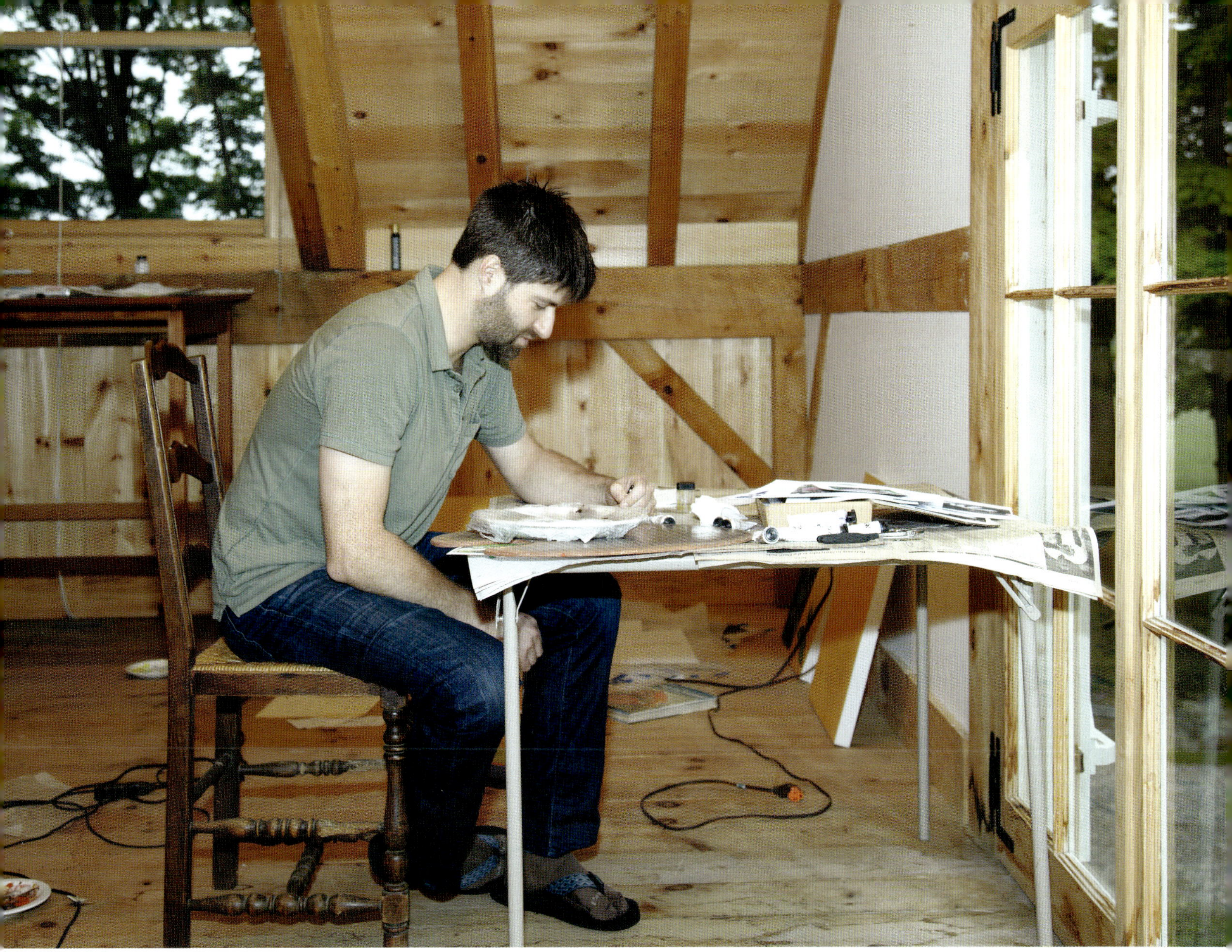

Prosek at his drawing table.

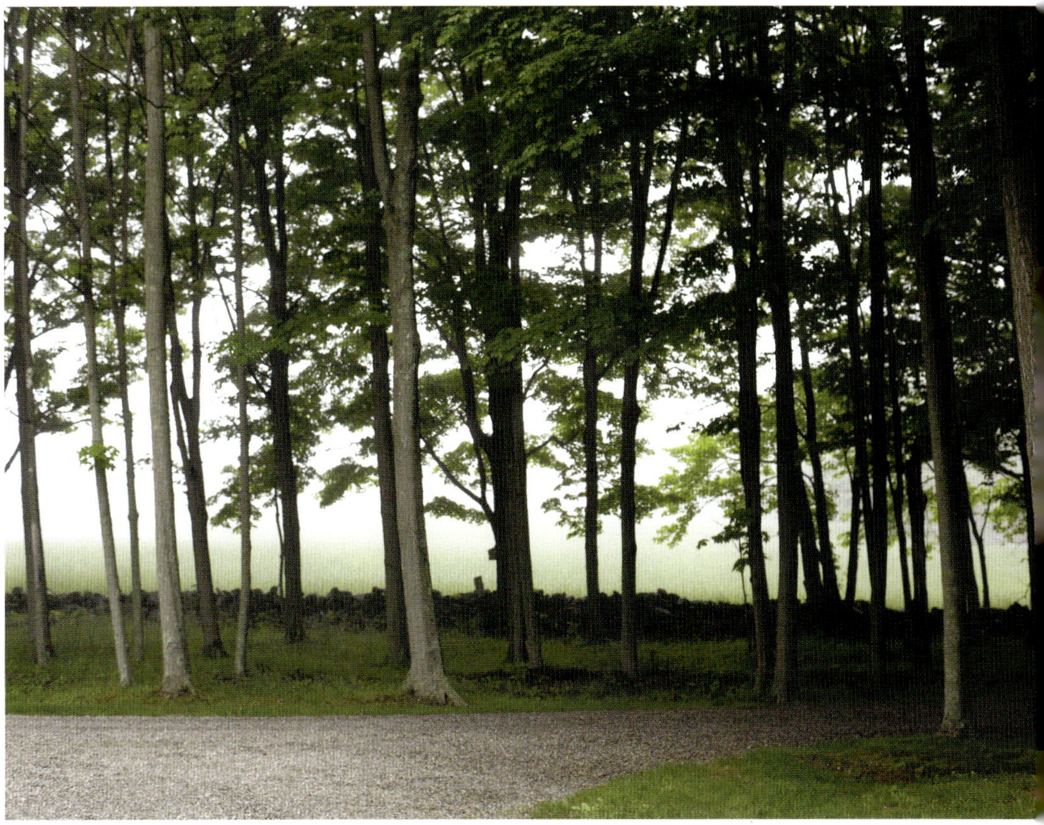

The pasture view outside Prosek's window.

James Prosek's home and studio is located in Easton, Connecticut, a short drive from the Andersons. His property abuts a large freshwater pond and the expansive pastures of a working farm—an ideal setting for an artist whose large-scale mixed-media drawings are a naturalist's exploration of flora and fauna.

Prosek is a Connecticut native and was raised in Easton. He studied at Yale University, in New Haven, where he initially enrolled in the architecture school. He eventually became an English literature major, and while still in college, he published an illustrated book titled *Trout: An Illustrated History* (Alfred A. Knopf, New York, New York), which catalogued more than seventy trout native to North America in bril-

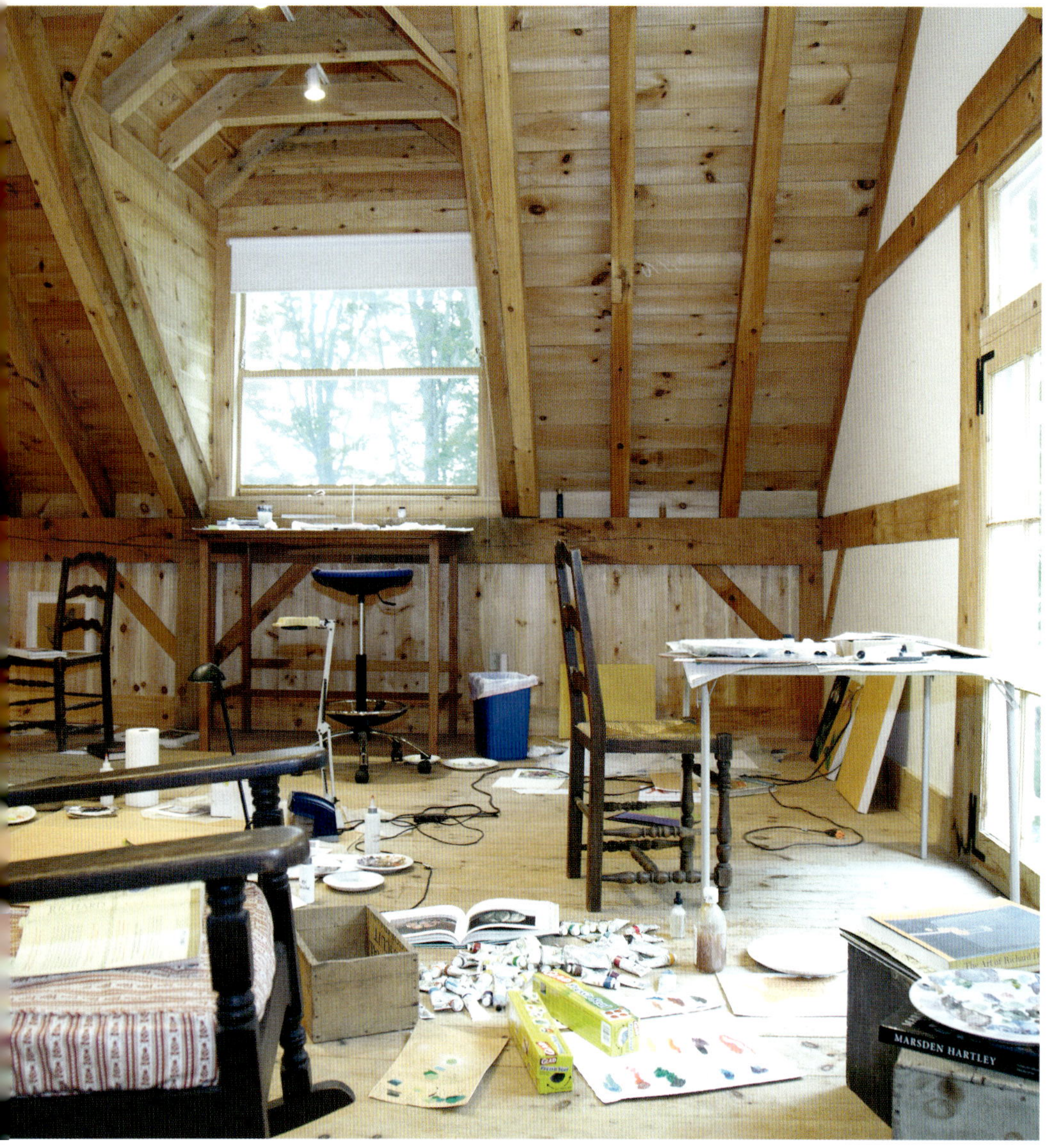

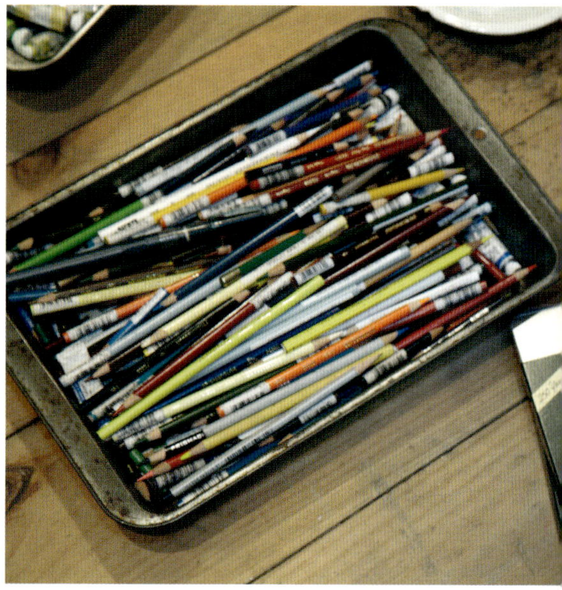

This page and opposite bottom: Prosek's studio is sparsely furnished, with bookshelves for reference books, colored pencils, and photographs.

Opposite top: **Sailfish With Spiny Lobster and Triton Shell** by James Prosek. Private collection.

liant watercolor paintings. A prolific author and visual artist, Prosek has since published nine more illustrated books, which have largely continued his exploration of the colors and forms of birds and fish—and on a more conceptual level, of the relationship of humans to nature. His paintings, many of them large watermedia works on paper, have been widely exhibited and collected.

Prosek's first studio was a historical rescue: a renovated one-room schoolhouse dating from 1850 attached to his home. Though certainly quaint, the school proved inadequate in terms of space, and two years ago Prosek renovated a larger building on his property—a post-and-beam barn—to use as his studio. Ben Anderson, who designed and built his mother's studio (page 20), did carpentry work on the building and dormers for Prosek's new work space.

Prosek's renovation, which involved removing collar ties and replacing them with a large beam and a post in the middle of the room, opened up a 750-square-foot (70-square-meter) space in the building's former attic. Left largely raw and unfurnished, the space exudes a palatable charm—a cross between a romantic artist's garret and a young boy's secret hideout.

Prosek's Spartan furnishings are limited to a small drawing desk nestled under a dormer and a scattering of wooden chairs. Abundant art books are stacked in piles on the studio floor; watercolor sketches, drawings, and hastily written notes accompany the volumes.

Prosek's watercolor and gouache drawings, which he completes on large sheets of tea-stained paper, lay about the floor in various stages of production. Nearby groupings of paint jars, assorted brushes, drawing implements, and reference photographs evince Prosek's methods; he generally works seated on the floor, late into the night.

A dedicated naturalist and adventurer, Prosek has traveled to distant parts of the world to document rare species of fish and birds for his drawings and writings. His humble studio, equipped with the barest necessities, mimics the hardy means and conditions of his outdoor adventures. Perhaps it's the quiet austerity of this setting, reminiscent of the peace Thoreau found at Walden Pond, that helps Prosek recall and retell his firsthand experiences with nature's elusive creatures with such compelling immediacy.

For more information on James Prosek, visit his website at www.jamesprosek.com.

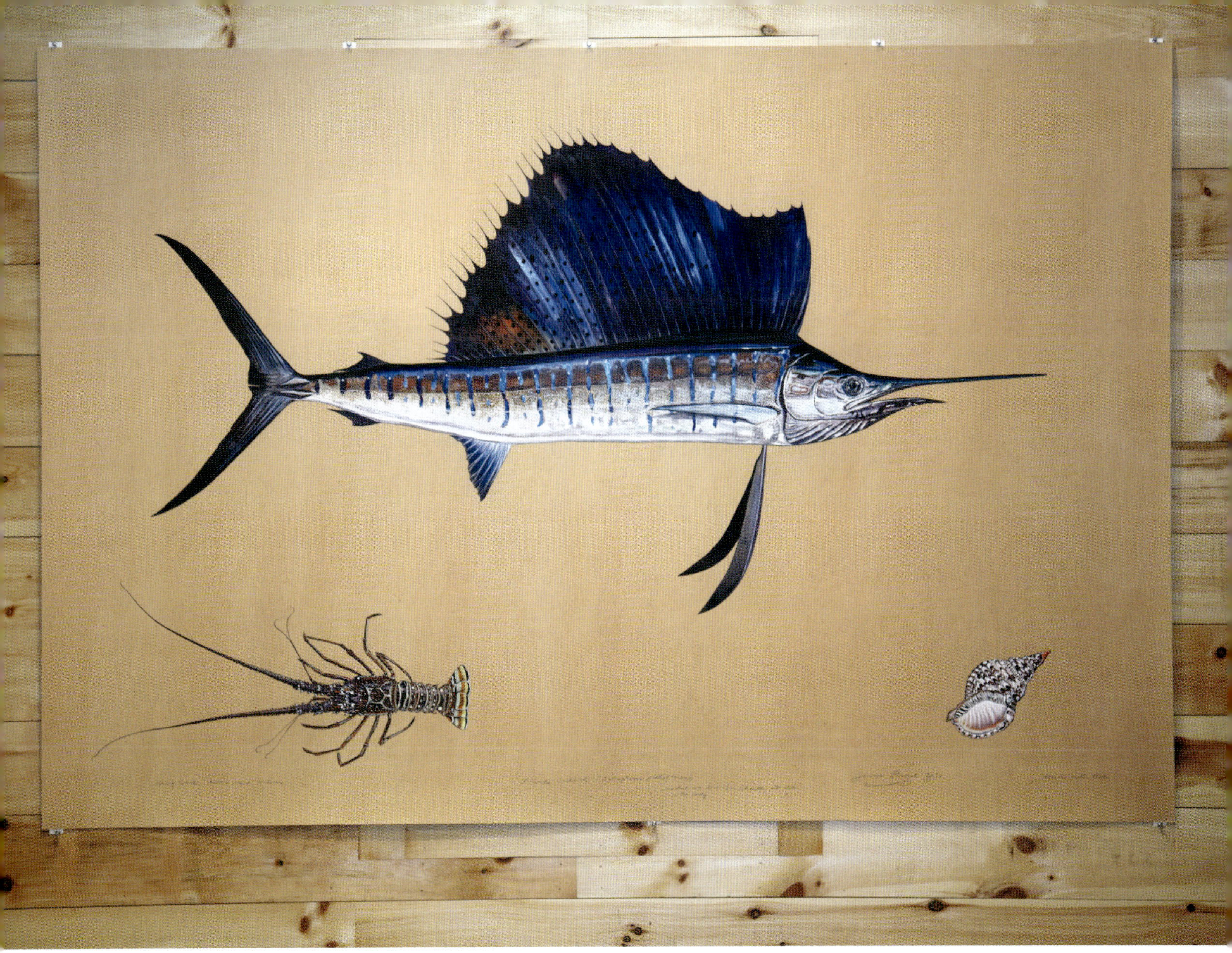

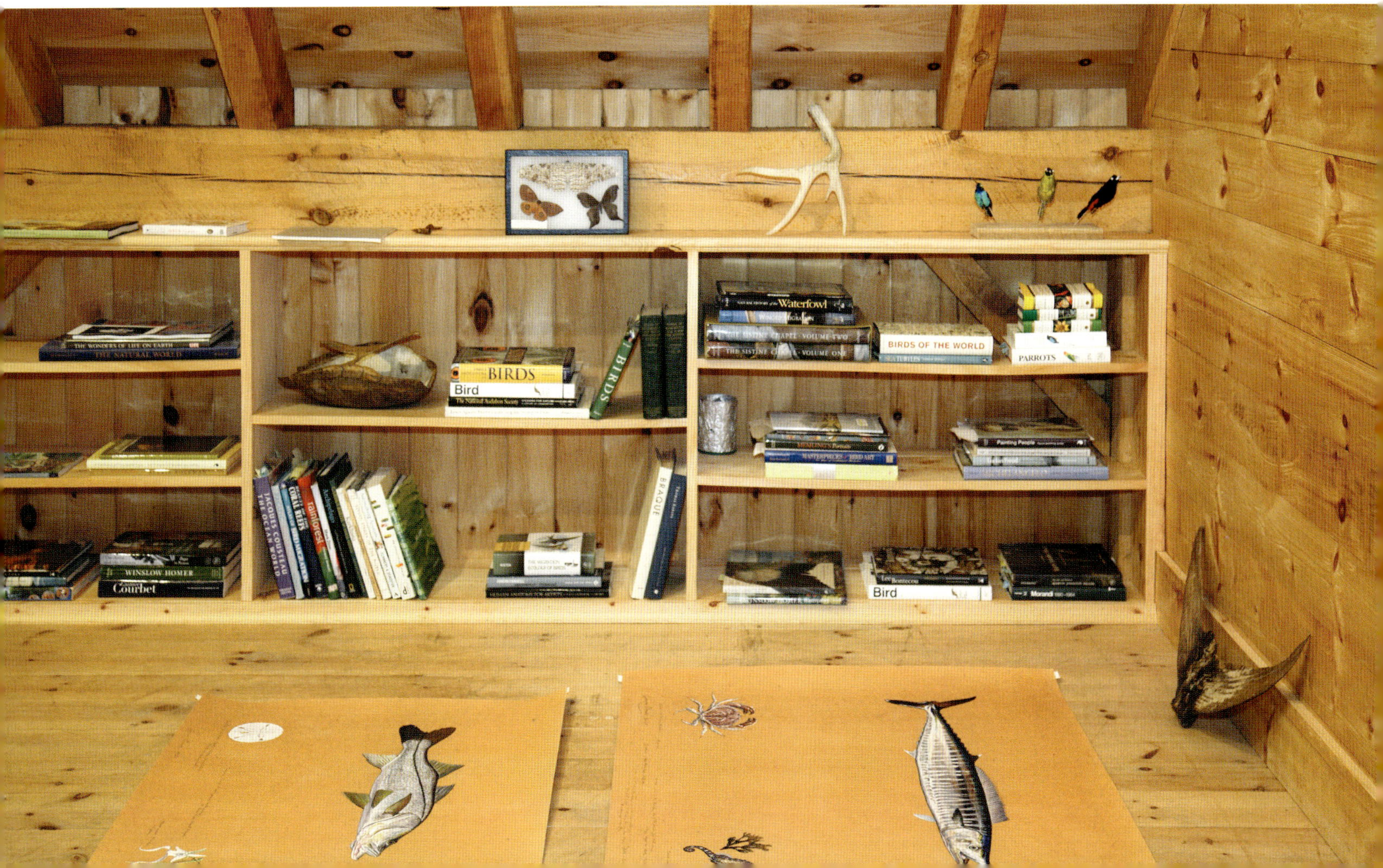
THE WONDERS OF LIFE ON EARTH
THE NATURAL WORLD
BIRDS
Bird
BIRDS
Waterfowl
BIRDS OF THE WORLD
PARROTS
WINSLOW HOMER
Courbet
Bird

Babette Bloch and Marc Mellon

Sculpting an Artist Marriage

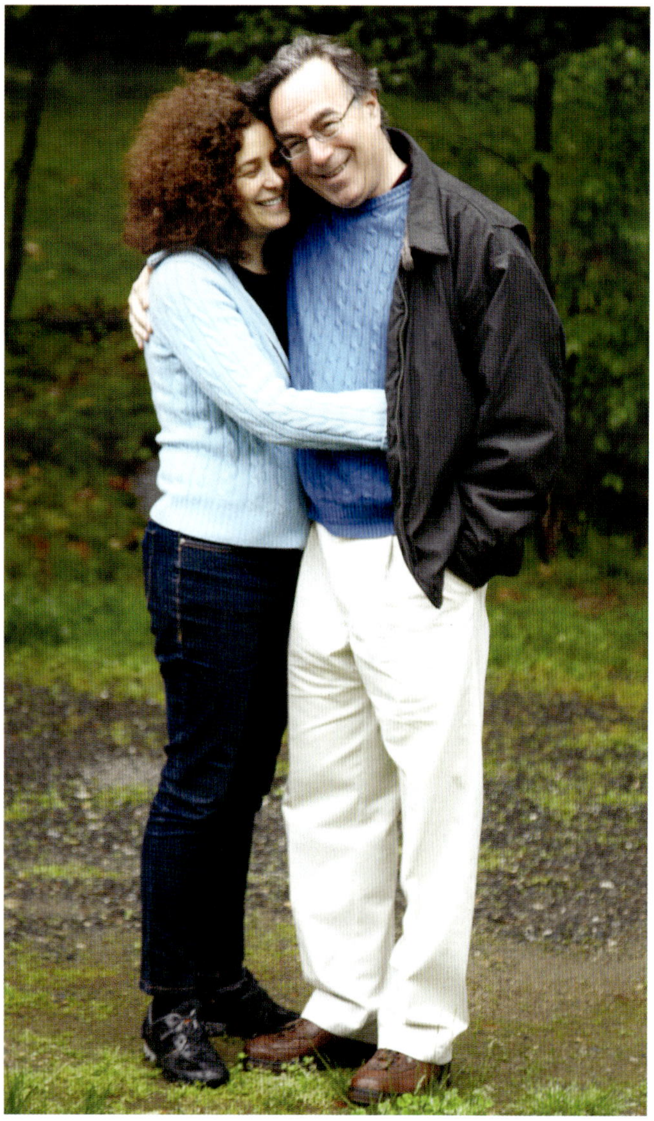

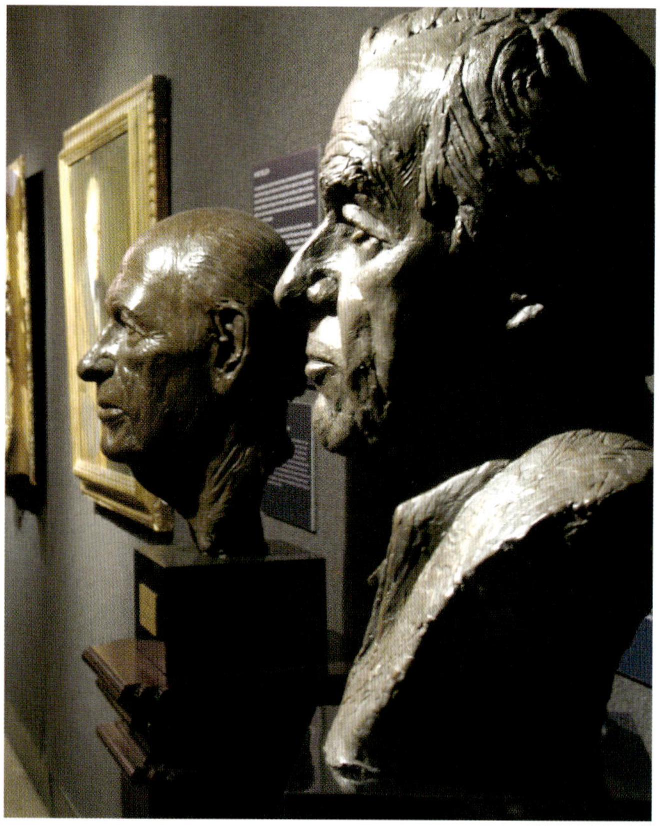

↑ Portrait busts by Mellon of Will Barnet and Everett Raymond Kinstler at the National Arts Club, in New York City. *Opposite top:* The north-facing view in Mellon's studio, with multiple model stands and various works in clay, plaster, and bronze.

← Babette Bloch and Marc Mellon.

Babette Bloch and Marc Mellon are sculptors who have been married for twenty-three years. Bloch hails from New Jersey; Mellon from Brooklyn. They met at a sculpture foundry on Long Island, lived in New York City during the early years of their marriage, and in 1989 they bought a house in Redding where they raised their two daughters. Like their friends the Andersons, they are members of the National Arts Club (NAC) and Salmagundi Club. Bloch and Mellon retain a small studio at the NAC—which used to be Mellon's bachelor apartment—for the convenience of Mellon's sitters and as a base for the arts programming Bloch has done for the NAC during the last twenty years.

Bloch and Mellon both have dedicated studio spaces in their Redding home. When they first acquired the house, Mellon used the family room as a studio, and Bloch set up her studio in the master bedroom. "At some point I tried to install a big crank easel so that I could work on bas-reliefs, and I found that it was too tall to stand in my studio," Mellon says. "I grabbed a broomstick and starting poking around and realized that I had a lot of space above the existing ceiling. We hired a contractor who removed the dropped ceiling, reinforced the roof, and put in a couple of skylights. It was a simple collaboration between me and a good old country builder."

When Bloch was pregnant with their second child, the couple decided to build an addition on the east side of the house, and they collaborated with the same builder to create Bloch's studio. Mellon continued working in the family

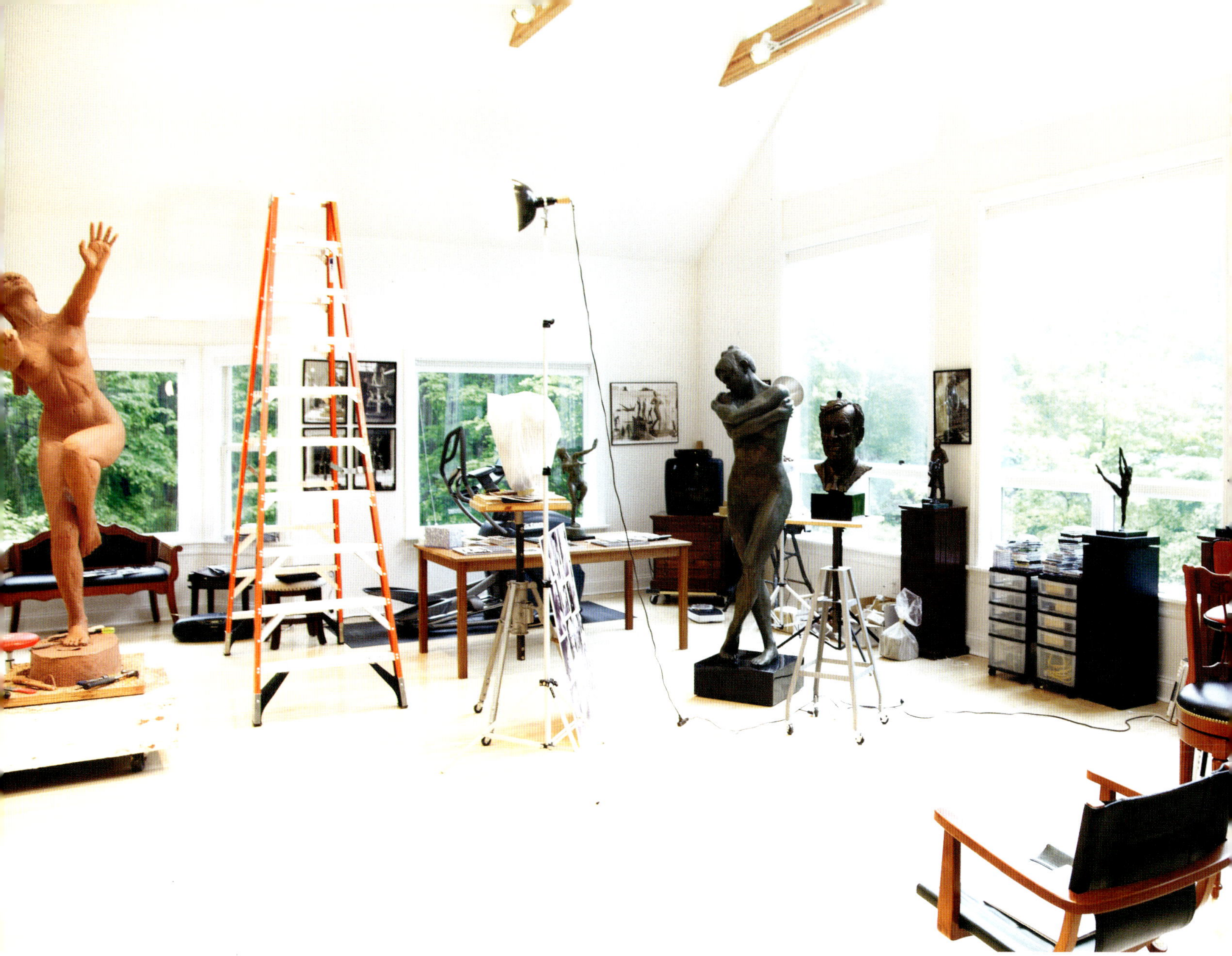

room for many years, but eventually he also wanted more space, and five years ago the couple built another addition. The build-out added a new studio for Mellon and also a lower-level garage large enough for two cars plus additional space for Bloch to paint or add surface texture to her works. Each artist's space has its own garage door and serves as a staging area for packing and shipping large works.

The couple hired an architect for this project, and the additional studio space has had a tremendous impact on Mellon's practice. "The bigger studio really allows me to think more expansively," he says. "In the old space, I'd walk in and would 'hear' numerous works in progress calling me. There was so much that needed to be worked on, and everything was so close to everything else that

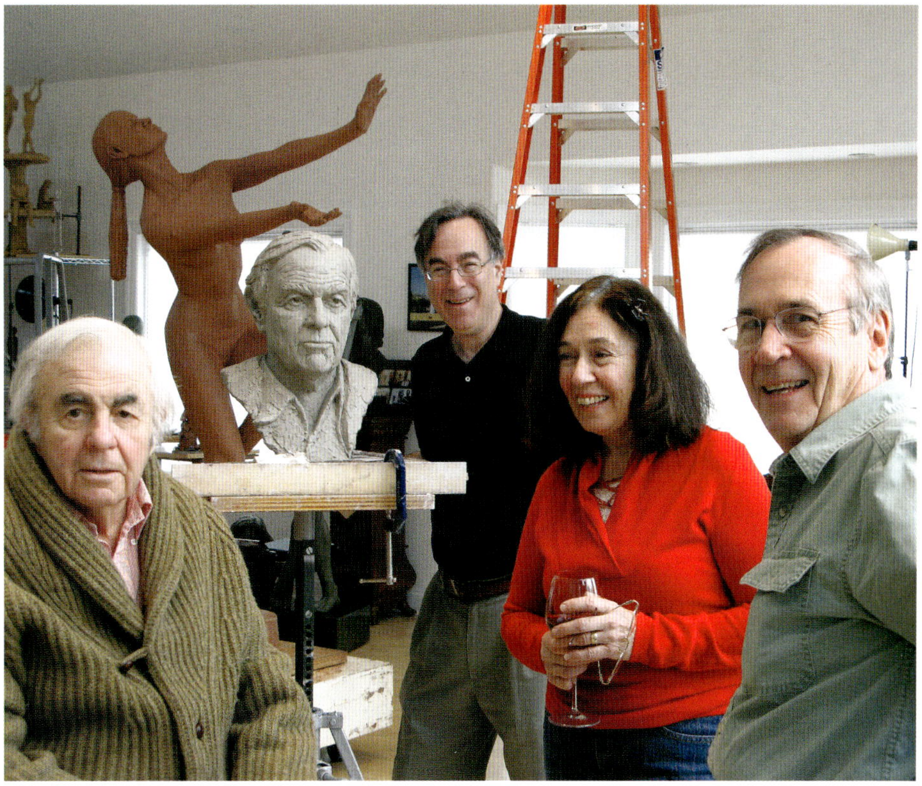

From left: Everett Raymond Kinstler, Marc Mellon, and Kathy and John Anderson, with a clay bust of Kinstler.

I would often walk right out. The big space allows me to work on numerous projects at the same time."

His new studio allows Mellon to exert much control over the light. "In addition to north light, I have 14-foot-high (4m) beams, and each side of each beam has a line of lights controlled by its own switch," he says. "I can selectively and simply amplify my lighting, including providing good directional light in the dead of night. The floor is a modified sprung floor, really a dancer's floor, and I installed 8-foot-high (2m) mirrors—again a dancer amenity. I love that my dancer models are comfortable and love the space as much as I do. The windows' shades are adjustable from the top or bottom, so I can add more or less directional light while screening the lower windows for privacy."

Mellon is the classicist of this artist pair. His figurative work references traditional sculpture processes and materials and demonstrates an impressive production output, including relief panels, medallions, full-figure pieces, and portrait busts that are first modeled in clay and then cast in plaster or bronze. The high level at which he practices his craft and his ability to capture a likeness have garnered him steady commissions. The time-honored processes that Mellon employs—beginning with exploratory clay studies and ending with the final surface chasing of his bronzes—are labor-intensive and highly technical procedures. Mellon is able to retain an aesthetic vision throughout this process, a tremendous artistic achievement.

In Mellon's cathedral-like space, there is abundant evidence of this classical production. Plaster portrait busts with patinas mimicking bronze casting tones line the walls. Graceful clay figures, in all shapes and sizes, teeter atop waist-high modeling stands. Plaster casts lined with rubbery silicone await assembly. When I visited the space, I was enchanted by this crowd of figures and solemn heads that seemed to dance around and pay rapt attention to the larger-than-life-size figure that rose effortlessly in the room's center. All of these

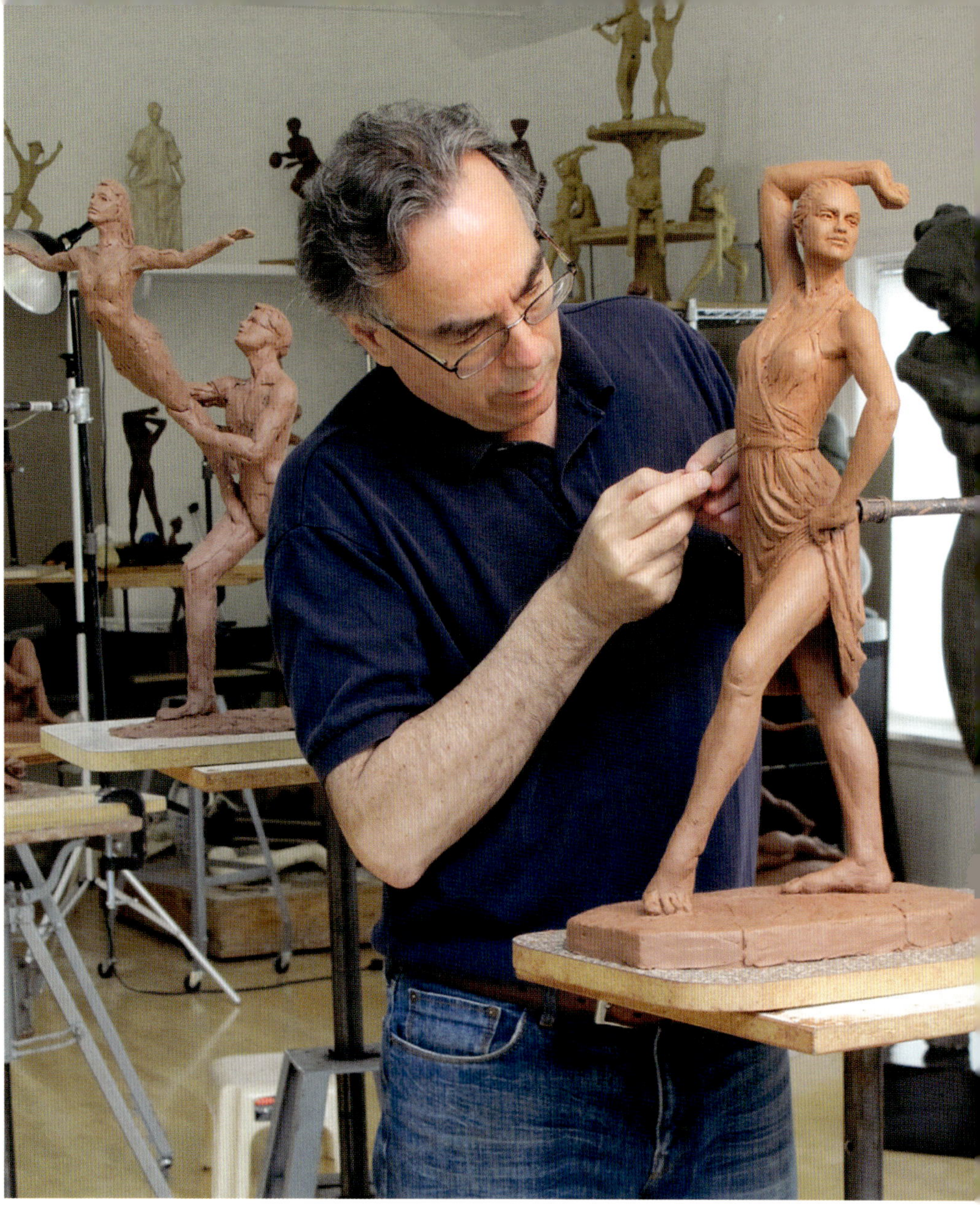

Mellon working on his clay study of a model.

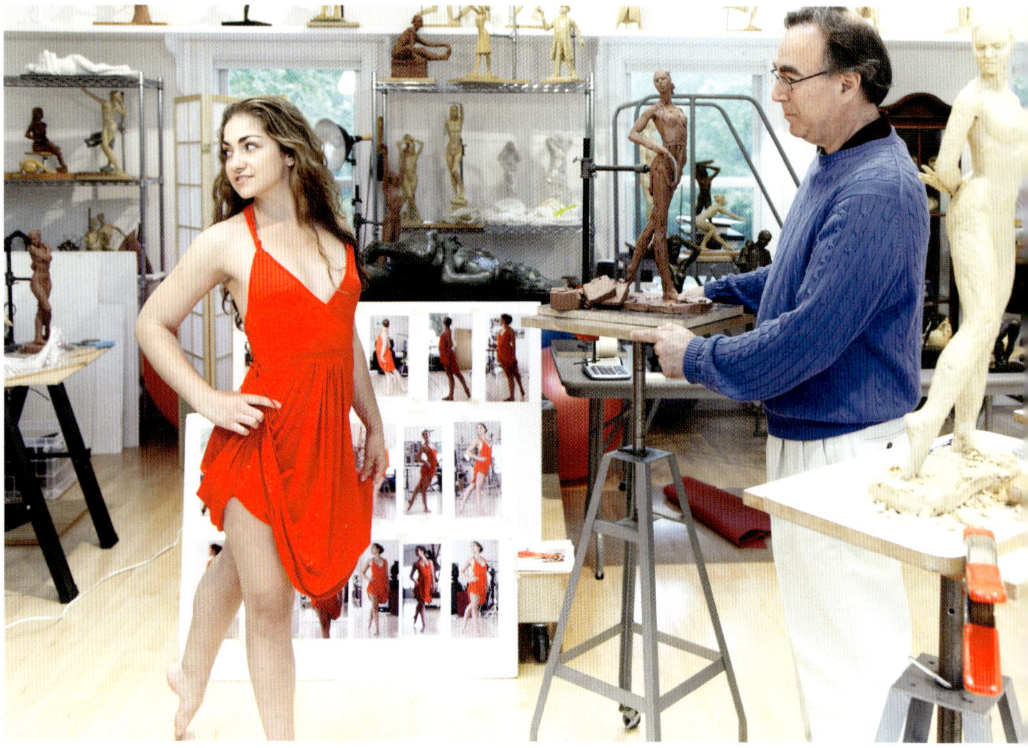

Mellon working with a model in his studio.

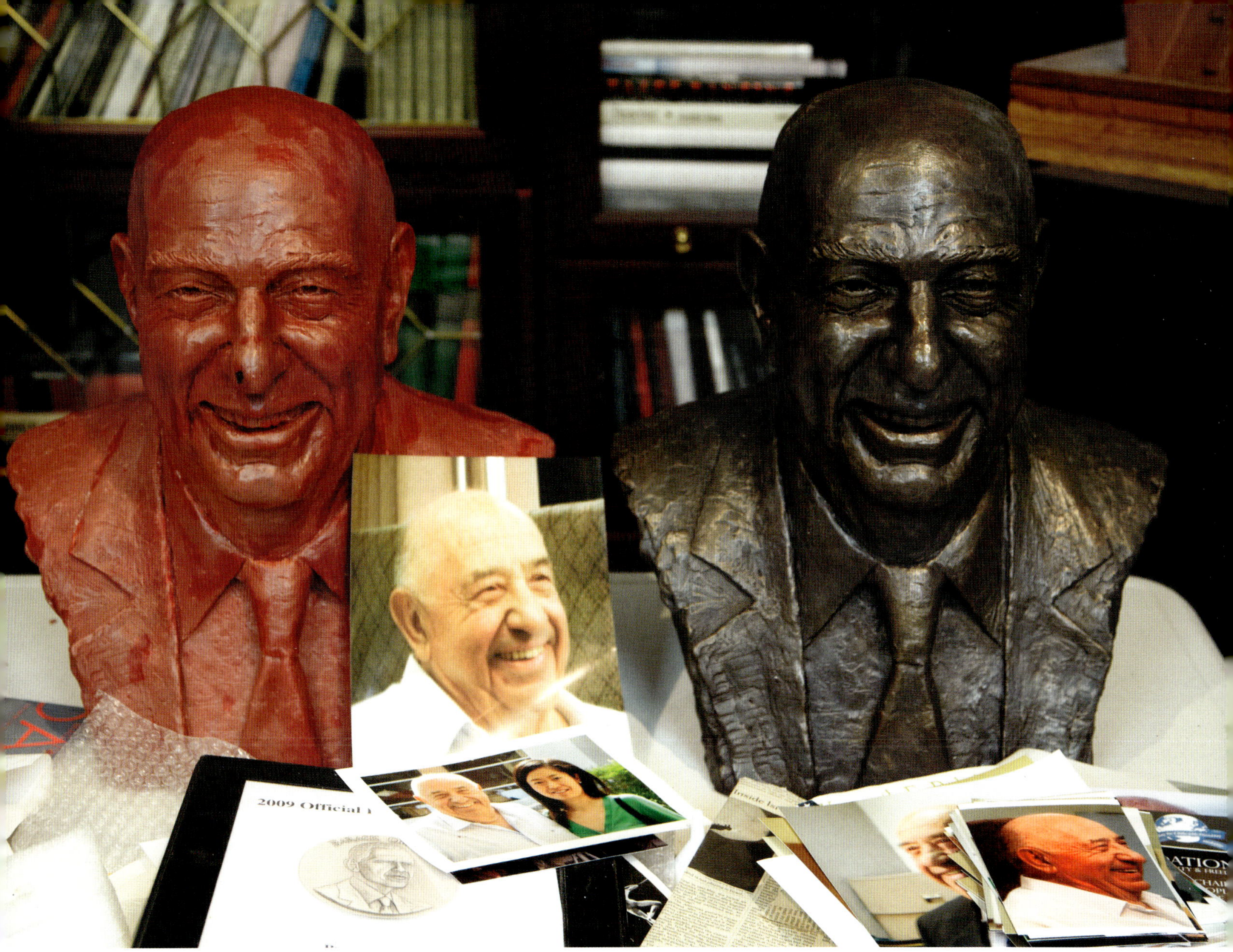

↑ A wax and bronze cast, with photo references, of developer and philanthropist Kenneth E. Behring. This portrait bust was commissioned by the National Museum of American History, part of the Smithsonian Institution, for which Behring is a major donor.

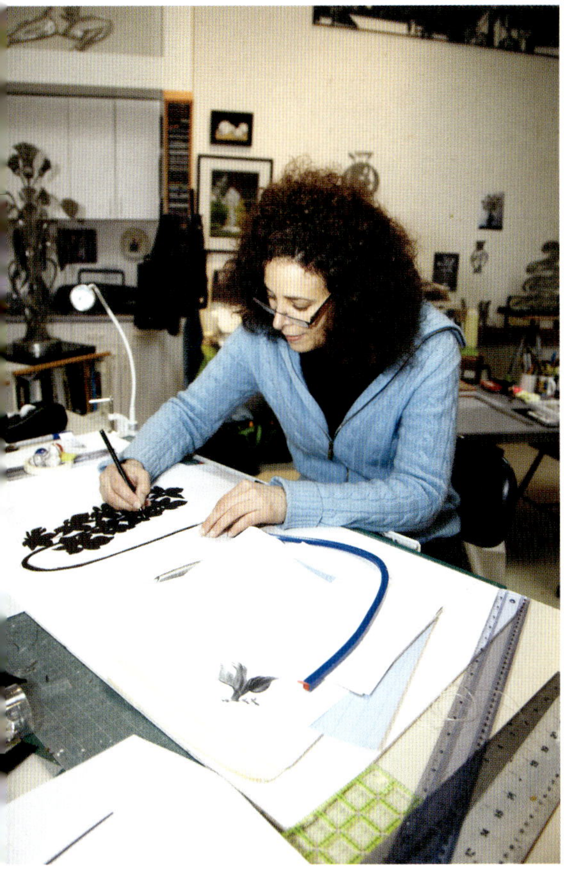

← Bloch at work in her studio.

works evince a sustained study of life and an earnest search for expressive form and gesture. Mellon's studies of dancers—with their expressive displays of movement, grace, and poise—most clearly signify his embrace of classical form. While viewing Mellon's nudes, one is reminded of the great American sculptor Augustus Saint-Gaudens, whose embrace of humanist principles and classical ideals informed the founding of the Art Students League of New York, which was Mellon's training ground.

Although she has explored various materials during her artistic career, Babette Bloch now works primarily with heavy-gauge stainless steel. The steel is fabricated according to her specifications into three-dimensional pieces based on paper models and drawings. The steel pieces are first laser-cut, then

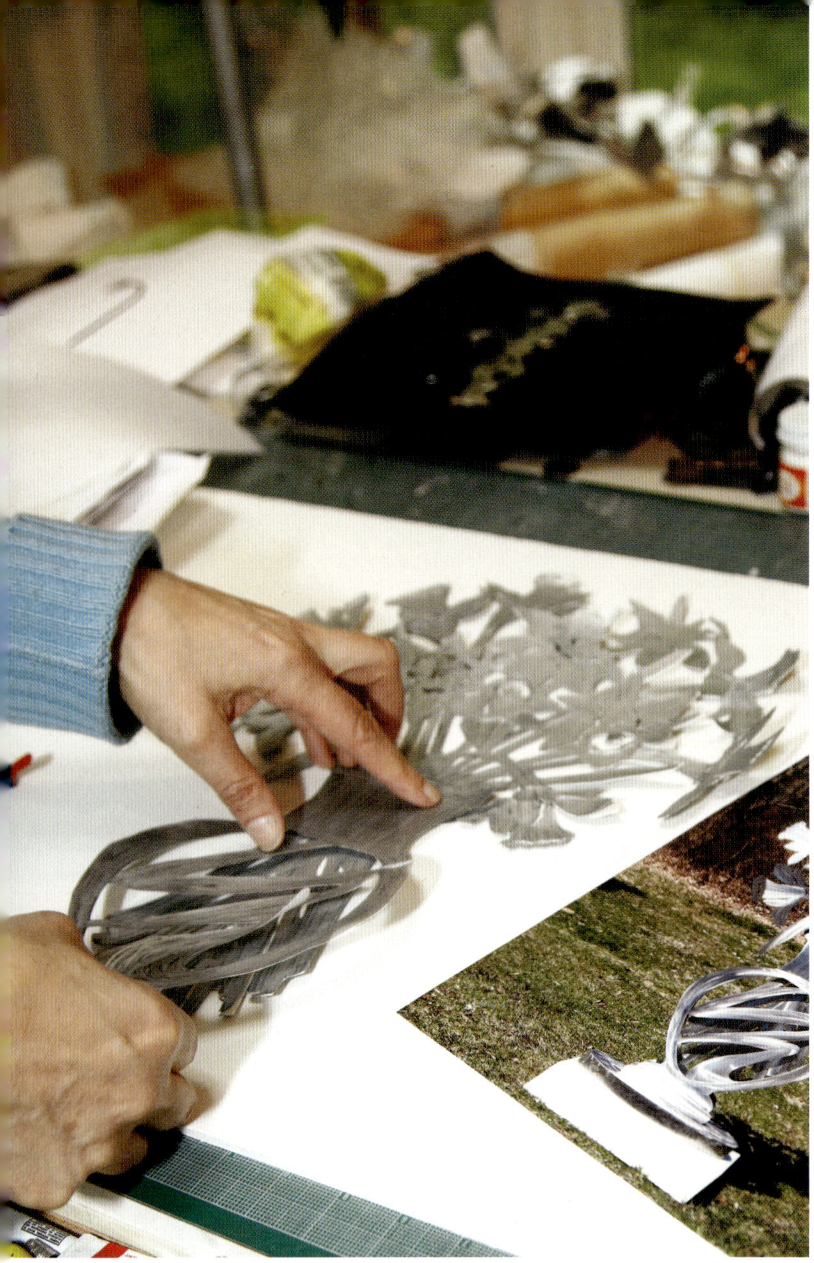

Bloch assembles a paper model showing her planned composition.

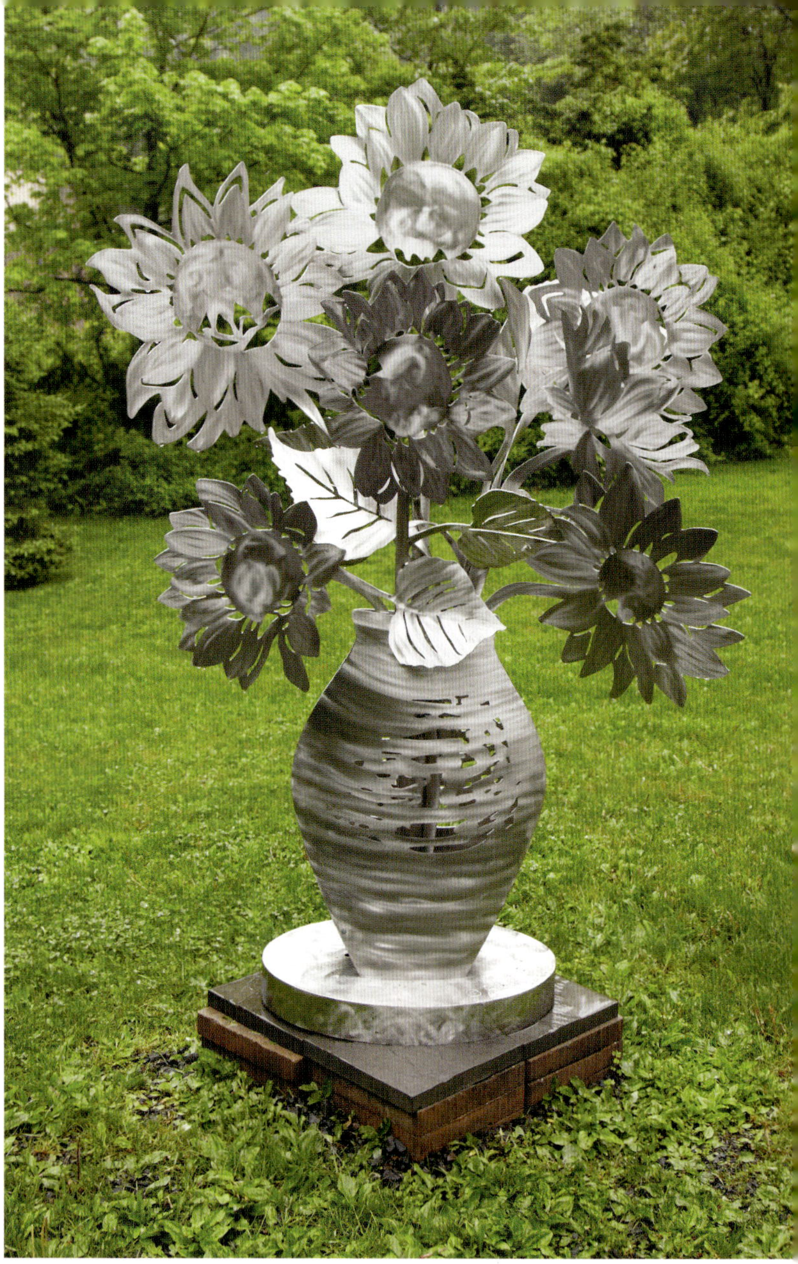

Vase
by Babette Bloch, stainless steel, 69" (175cm). Collection of the artist.

the cut edges are smoothed and the surfaces ground. Some final pieces, such as those from the artist's *Reflecting History* series, remain relatively flat, like silhouettes. Others, such as those comprising her *Vase* series and *Egret* series, are elaborately shaped and assembled.

Bloch walks a fine line by successfully preserving the movement and lightness of these deceptively simple preparatory models and drawings in her final works. The weighty stainless-steel sculptures, punctured by a continuous negative space, are experienced as animated three-dimensional contour drawings. Placed on-site, their open form seeks to incorporate, rather than compete with, surrounding environmental elements.

The sharp contrast of material, scale, and process in Bloch's work offers an insightful foray into contemporary post-colonial and gender theory. The drawings and paper models from which she fabricates heavy metal sculptures reference stencils and silhouettes—traditional home crafts generally associated with women. Large-scale metalwork sculpture, however, has historically been the preserve of men.

Bloch has experimented with numerous surface treatments to further express movement, light, and transparency in her work. Originally she experimented with color; currently she grinds her surfaces with various power tools to manipulate the flow and direction of the steel's reflective surface. The effect, prized by the Impressionists, is one of flickering light. Form and materiality are further dissolved, resulting in works that appear to sculpt light rather than steel.

The additional space Bloch gained in the recent addition greatly helps her work with large sculptures. "The new space made it easy for me to bring large pieces home from the precision metal shops where I construct my sculptures," she says. "I can back my car up to the bay and off-load the piece through a garage door. I can build crates in the space and pack and ship our work from the garage bay. The mess doesn't get into the house, and we do a lot less lifting. Thanks to this addition, I can do any metal grinding and finishing in this space."

Bloch likes the natural light in her studio. She doesn't like to work at night with artificial light. "When we built

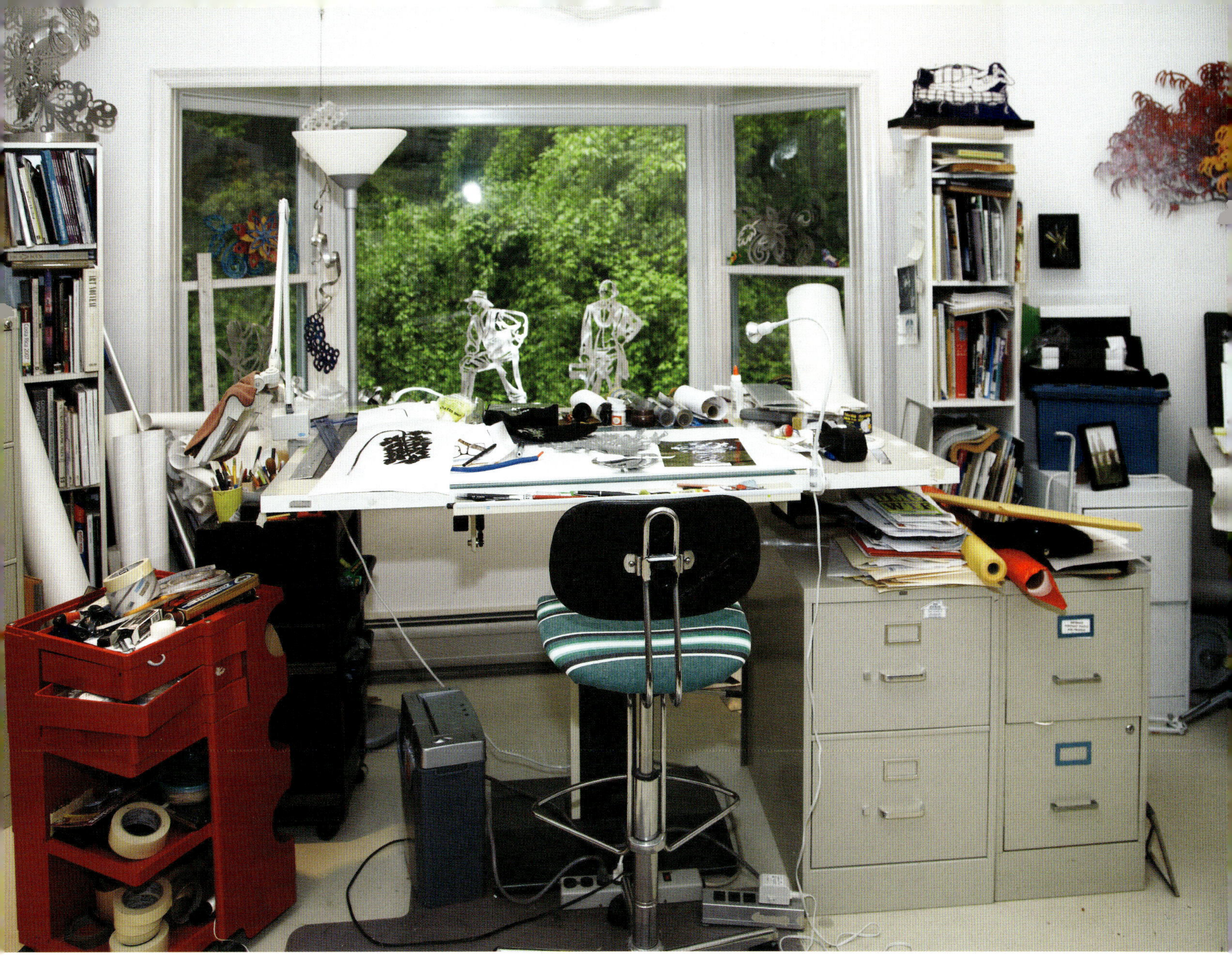

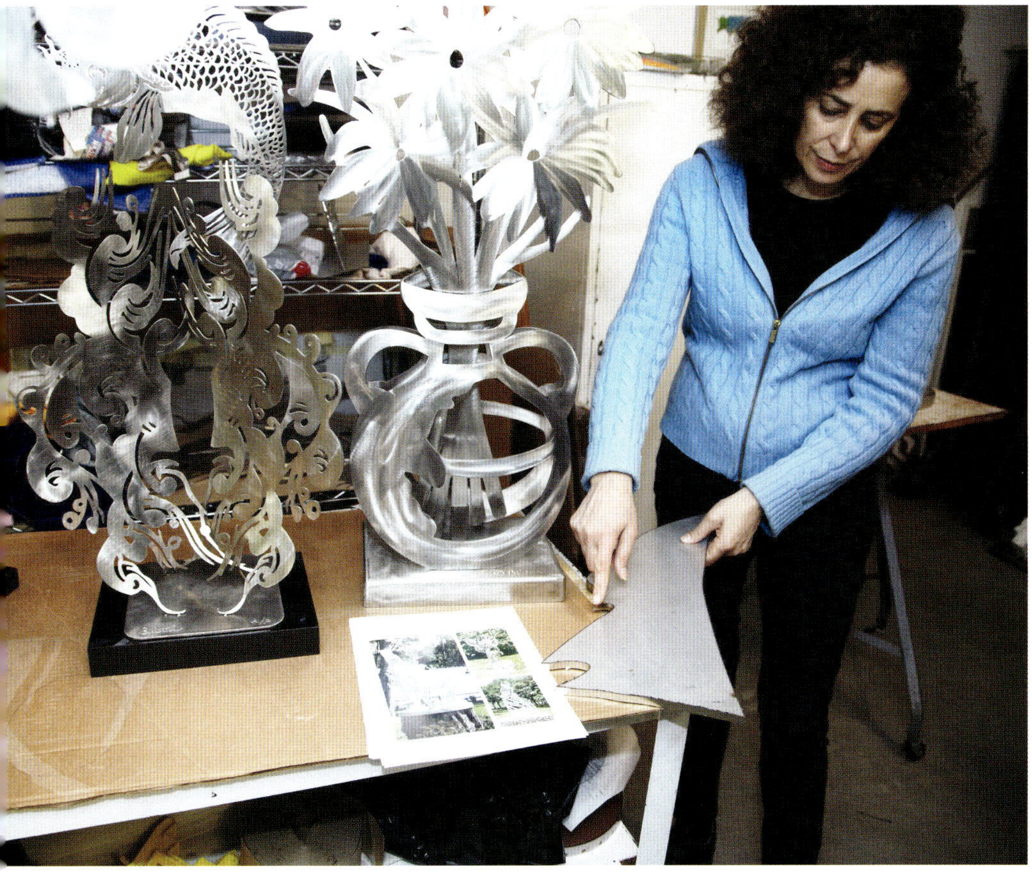

↑ Bloch's second studio, with drawing tables and model-making supplies for research and design.

← Bloch demonstrates machine cuts to heavy-gauge stainless steel suitable for large outdoor or public sculptures.

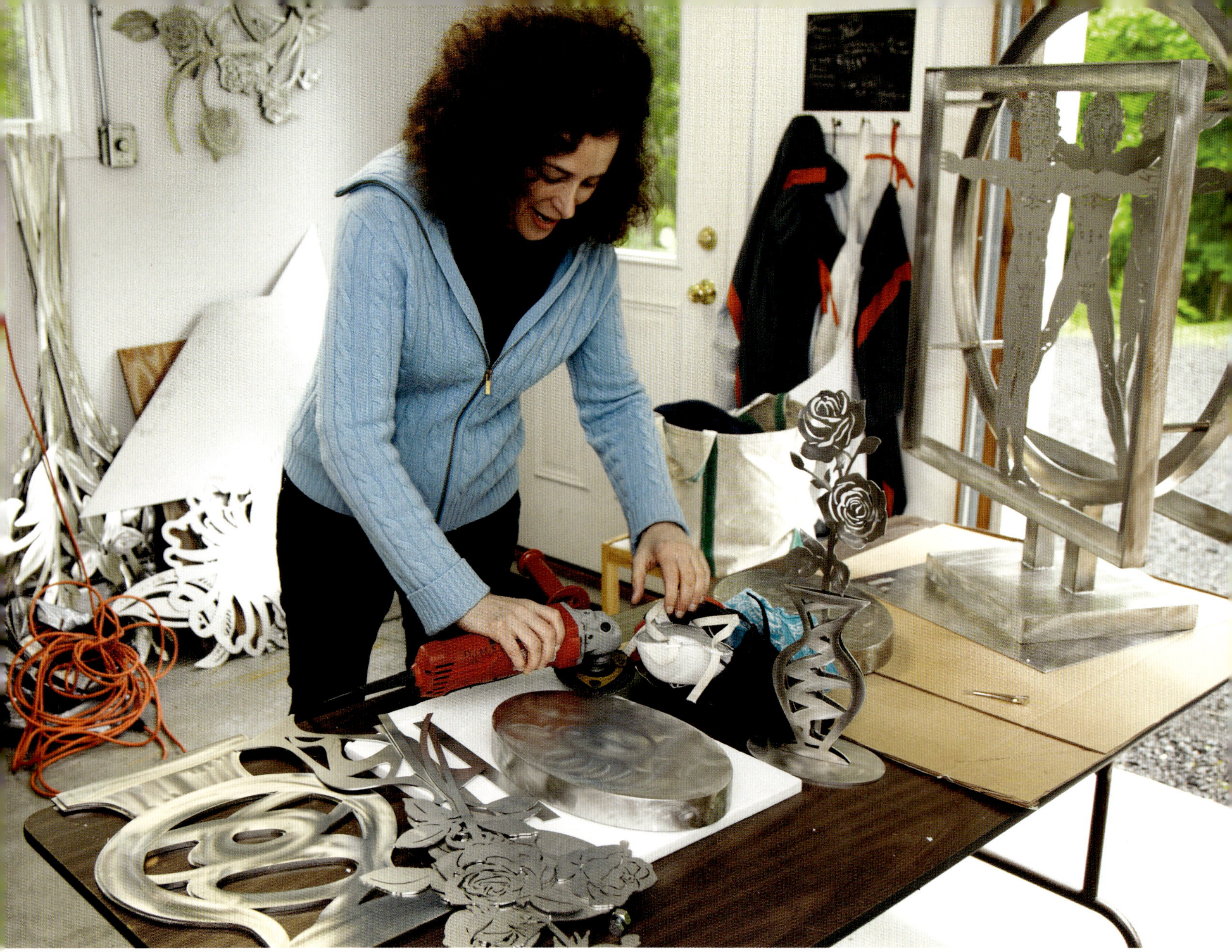

Bloch's garage studio, which she uses for sculpture finishing and staging shipments and deliveries of large works.

the studio, we put a ceiling fan in the peak," she notes. "When I had the lights on, with every turn of the fan I felt like there was a strobe light above me. It is important to make sure that the blades of a fan don't disrupt the light path. I also use a lot of lightweight papers for my drawings, and the fan would blow the papers I was working on, so I got rid of the ceiling-fan blades."

Although both Bloch and Mellon enjoy the proximity of studio and home, both acknowledge the challenges of having home studios and children. "The hardest part is to maintain a separation of housework and studio work," Bloch says. "When my children were small, I had a hard time with this, but not anymore. I am the luckiest gal in the world to have been able to successfully pull off being a mother, wife, and artist and still have the energy to do community service, such as serving as the president of the Artists' Fellowship, Inc. (AF) and co-chairing a committee at the National Arts Club (NAC). With my husband's support and because we have our studios in our home—and are not confined by traditional working hours—we have the flexibility to make all this possible."

Some years after they moved to Redding, Bloch and Mellon's social life and critical feedback came primarily from fellow artists still living in New York City. "We had a strong network of artist friends within the NAC; we didn't really reach out much locally," Mellon says. "But over time, we met some wonderful local artists, including Kathy Anderson (page 20) and Everett Raymond Kinstler (page 36). Everett and I had been friendly colleagues since I moved into the NAC in 1982, but in those early years, I saw him more as mentor and was flattered that he respected my work. He'd offer to critique my projects; his eye is extraordinary, and he was always honest in helping me better see and conceive my portrait projects. He really has teaching in his blood. We had been in Redding about ten years when Everett and his wife, Peggy, moved up; now we are neighbors both in New York and Connecticut. We've become very close friends, and I'm honored that he considers me a colleague. We'll get together, sometimes at Kinstler's home, sometimes at ours, sometimes at the Andersons', and sometimes at the Greene-Caporale home (page 40). It's

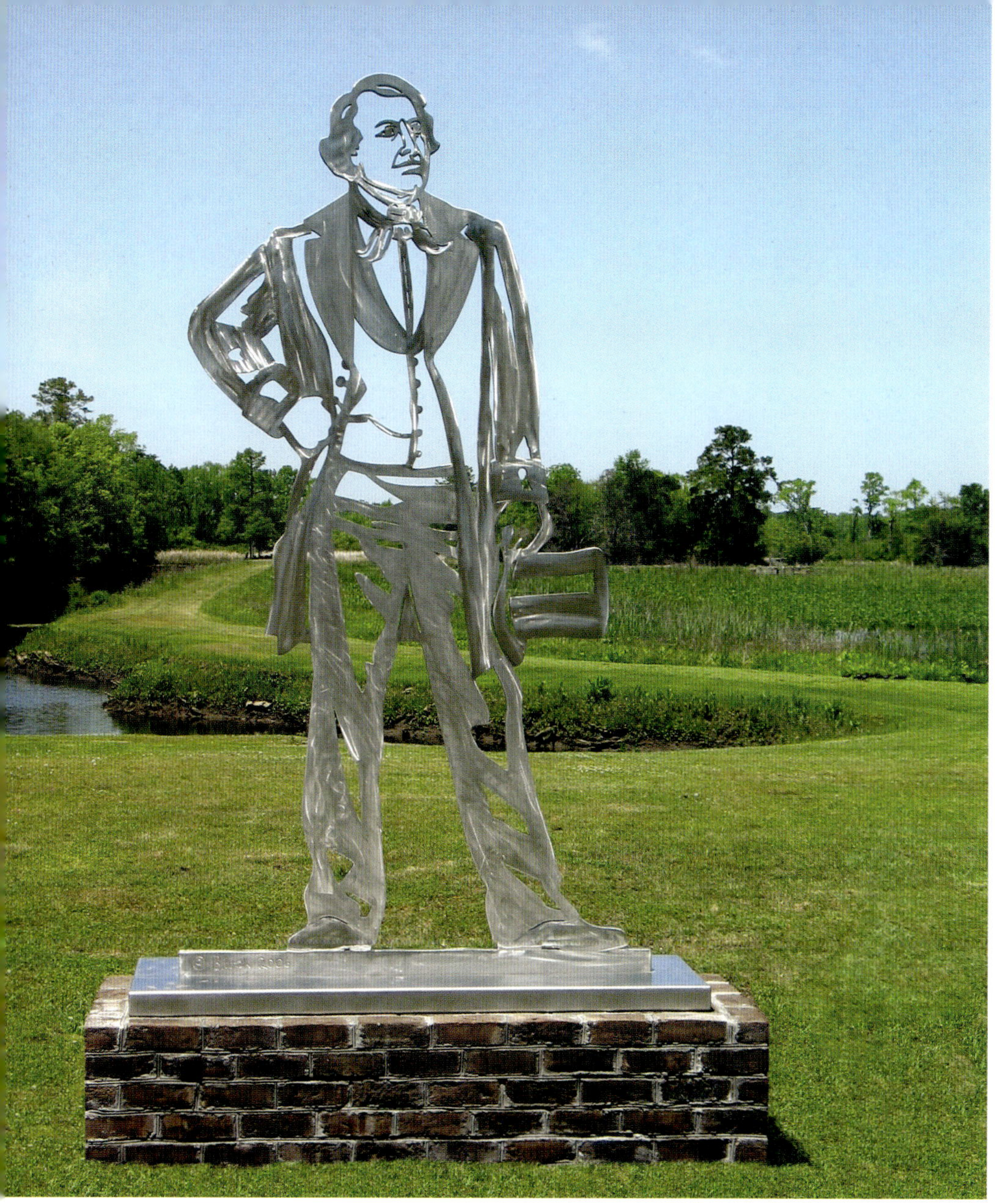

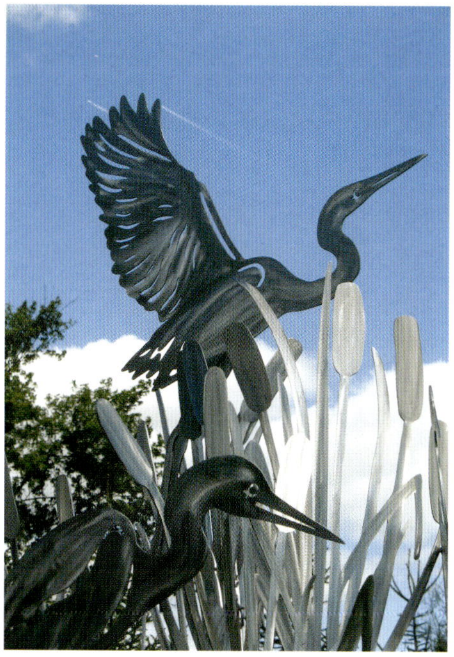

↑ **Egrets (detail)**
by Babette Bloch, stainless steel, 90" (229cm).
Mahopac, New York, and Winter Park, Florida.

← **Brookgreen Gardens Plantation Owner**
by Babette Bloch, stainless steel, 108" (274cm).
Brookgreen Gardens, South Carolina.

nice to share the ups and downs of the artist's life with others who are living it."

"I can really count on my local artist friends and their families," Bloch adds. "The camaraderie and friendship makes living in this beautiful and isolated place not feel lonely. There is always a helping hand if you need it, from critiquing to modeling to helping build something. I've come to depend on that help. Making art requires a lot of heavy lifting—figuratively speaking!"

For more information on Marc Mellon, visit his website at www.marcmellon.com.

For more information on Babette Bloch, visit her website at www.babettebloch.com.

STUDIO TIPS

Bloch notes that when she and Mellon built the new studio, they put the airflow on a different system, and this has kept fumes from their materials from going into the living space. She adds, "The additional 30'-x-16' (9m-x-5m) studio space we built for me attached to our garage has running water, a heat system, a ventilating fan, and a paint spray booth. When I paint my sculptures, I tend to work on the metal with water-based enamels, and they emit an odor and need to be ventilated. The booth has made a big difference.

"The best advice that I can give to an artist for combining a living and working situation is to be very aware of the toxins that you are exposed to with your materials," she continues. "All precautions should be taken to reduce exposure. This is paramount to living a long and healthy life. I have asthma and have had to control our work and living environment from the get-go. Wearing protective gear, using safer alternative materials, ventilating, and using fans correctly should be in the forefront of all artists' thinking."

Everett Raymond Kinstler

Two Studios, Two Locations, One Community

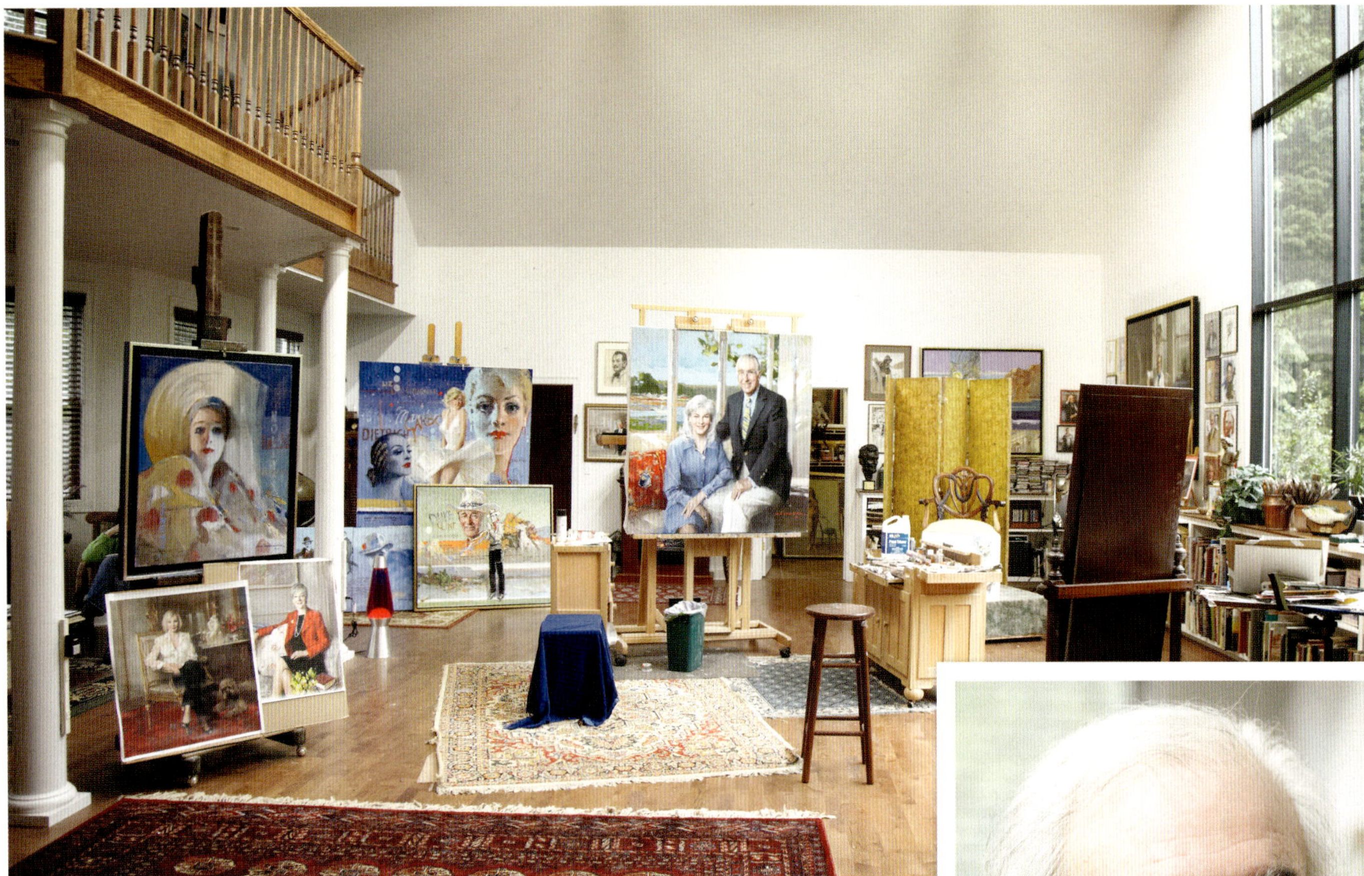

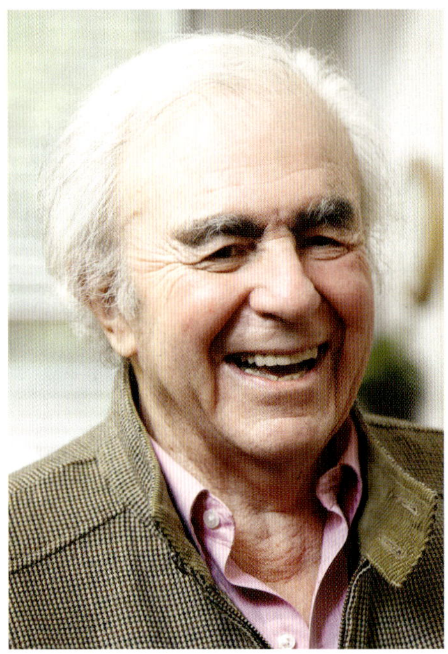

↑ Everett Raymond Kinstler.

Top: Kinstler's studio in Easton, Connecticut.

Everett Raymond Kinstler, a celebrated portraitist, painter, and beloved mentor to scores of artists, maintains two art studios: one in New York City at the National Arts Club (NAC), and the other in Easton, Connecticut. Kinstler moved into the NAC studio more than fifty years ago. He enjoys—along with his colleague, the equally celebrated artist Will Barnet—the status of "tribal elder" at the club. Artists young and old seek out these talented masters, who are always willing to offer a kind word or valuable piece of advice on the practice of painting.

"I have always needed and enjoyed the camaraderie of my artist friends," Kinstler says. "I'm fortunate to have a stimulating, creative group of friends, and I value the interaction and discussion about my work, as well as theirs." In my short visit with Kinstler at his studio, I was struck by the encyclopedic store of information he retains and readily shares about the important people, places, and things that inform current art practice. He is a treasure—a vital link to our collective artistic memory.

In 2006, Kinstler and his wife, Peggy, moved to Easton. They were drawn to the town's rural feel and its close proximity to New York City. The artist wanted a large space with unobstructed north light. His architect delivered just that, by building a 30'-x-40' (9m-x-12m) room with 18-foot (5m) ceilings around

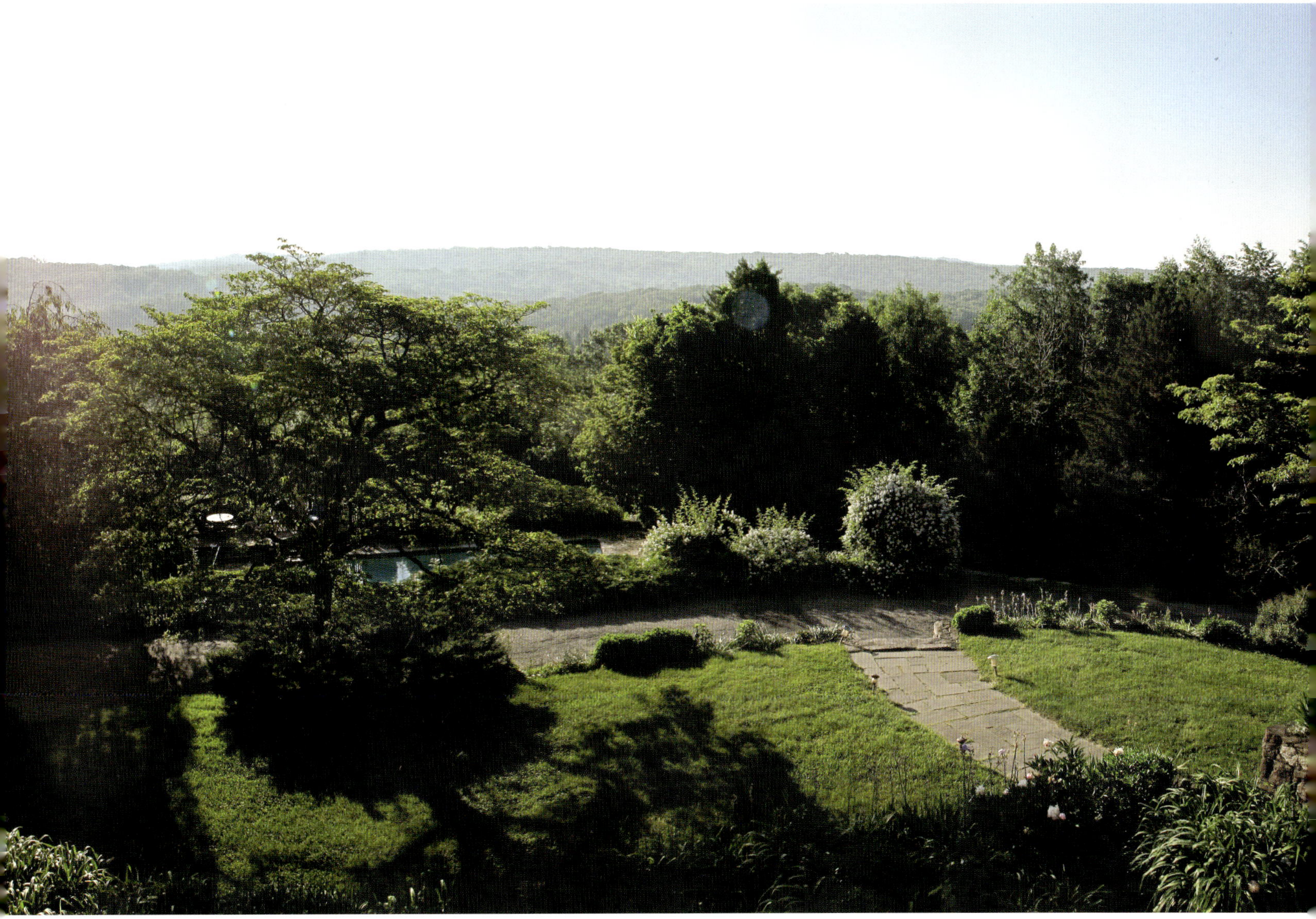

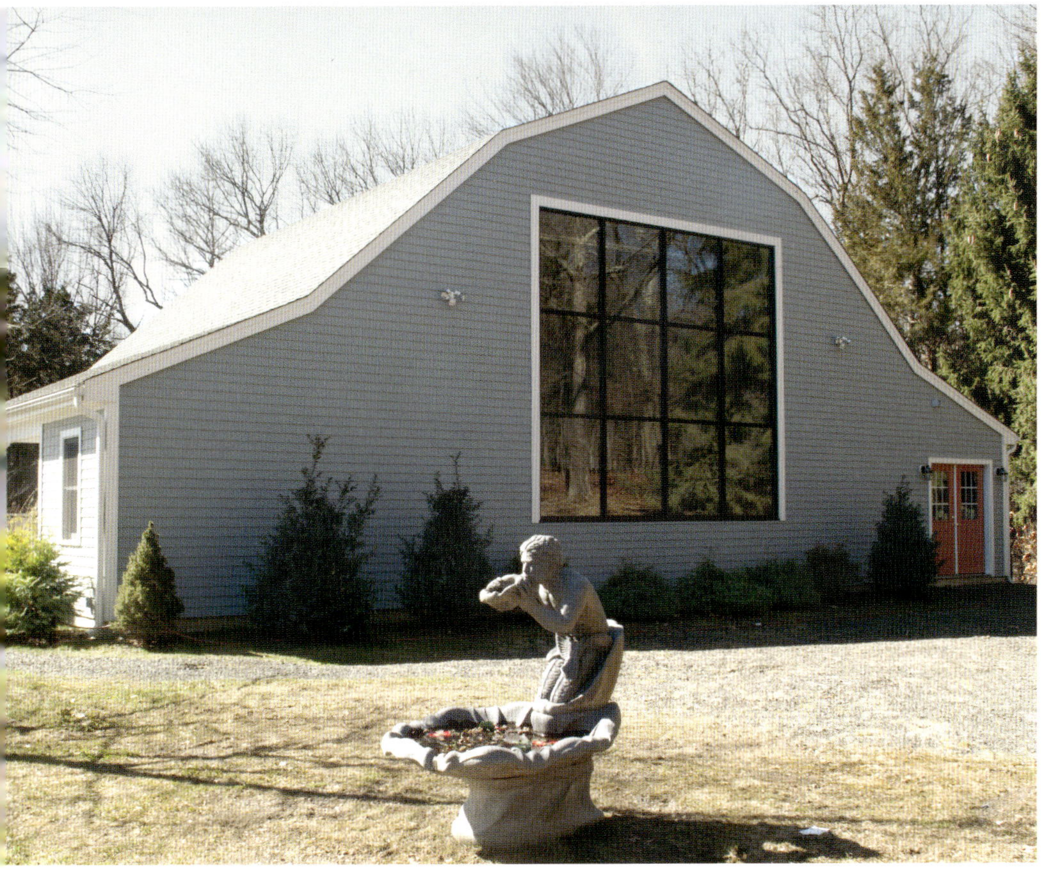

↑ The woodlands of Easton, Connecticut.

← An outside view of Kinstler's studio and its large north-facing window.

a north-facing, sheer expanse of glass. Everything after that was built to be functional and aesthetically appealing.

Kinstler enjoys splitting his work time between his two studios; he finds the periodic change to be refreshing, stimulating, and fun. "I enjoy living and working in the same location," he says. "The NAC studio is contiguous with an apartment on a high floor in a building overlooking Gramercy Park. My Connecticut studio is a separate structure minutes from the main house, and both the house and the studio are situated on high hills with striking views in all directions."

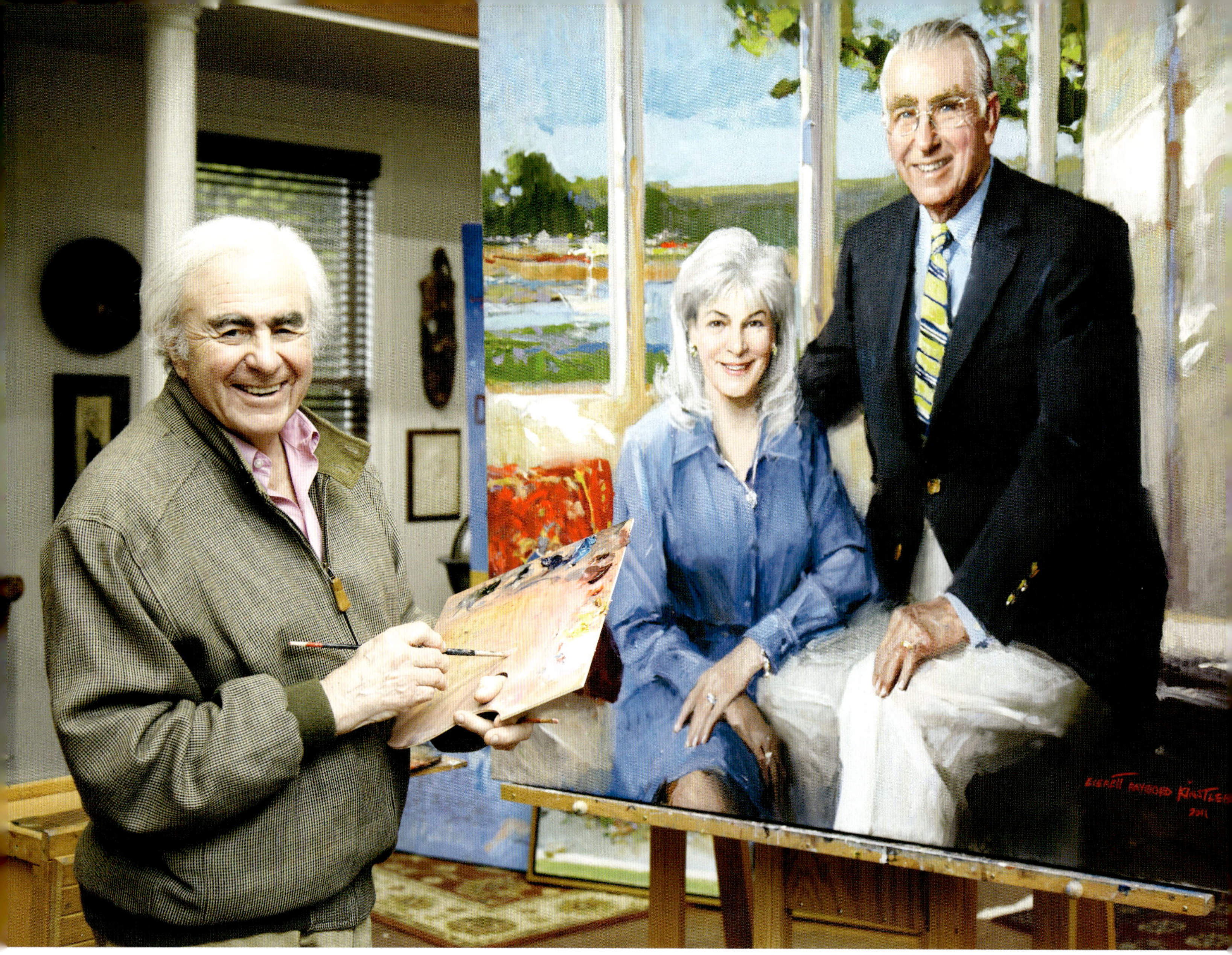

The daylight in Kinstler's NAC studio is very constant, given its unobstructed view, and the light is fantastic. In his Connecticut studio, the daylight is affected by seasonal changes—foliage obstructs some of the light during the summer months. "This is a small price to pay for the privacy and quiet," Kinstler says. "I find the country landscape and sky offer me mental and emotional perspective and a welcome change from the daily pressures of the city."

Kinstler notes that his studios reflect his practical needs and his personality. The studios are quite open, with few furnishings and little clutter. His Connecticut studio contains a few work easels, a taboret for his studio accessories, and a large model stand for his many portraits painted from life. He has a favorite vintage drawing table that he uses for sketching and watercolor painting. An inviting sofa welcomes afternoon naps. Under the north window are bookcases for the artist's extensive library. On the walls he displays both his own artwork and other works from his collection, including pieces by John Singer Sargent, Anders Zorn, James Montgomery Flagg, and Dean Cornwell, as well as the work of friends.

A completed portrait commission was sitting on Kinstler's easel during my visit there. Boldly painted and invitingly sunny, it depicted a world I longed to live in. I saw in one clear moment why this painter remains one of our most sought-after portraitists. He captures much more than a likeness. He captures a beautiful life.

For more on Everett Raymond Kinstler, visit his website at www.everettraymondkinstler.com.

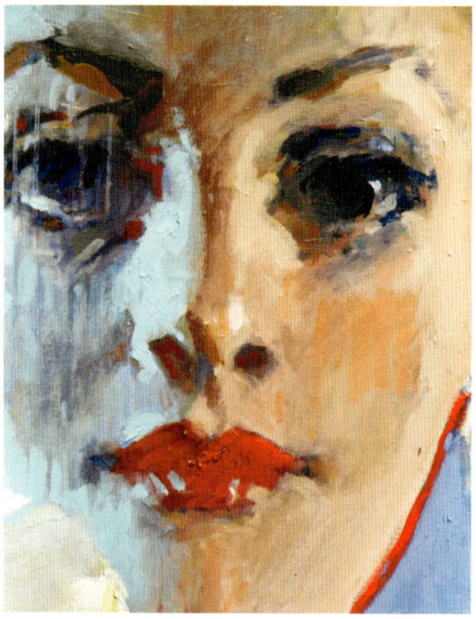

↑ Detail of a new painting.

Top: Kinstler before a portrait of Mr. and Mrs. Ed Shanahan, for the Choate School, in Connecticut.

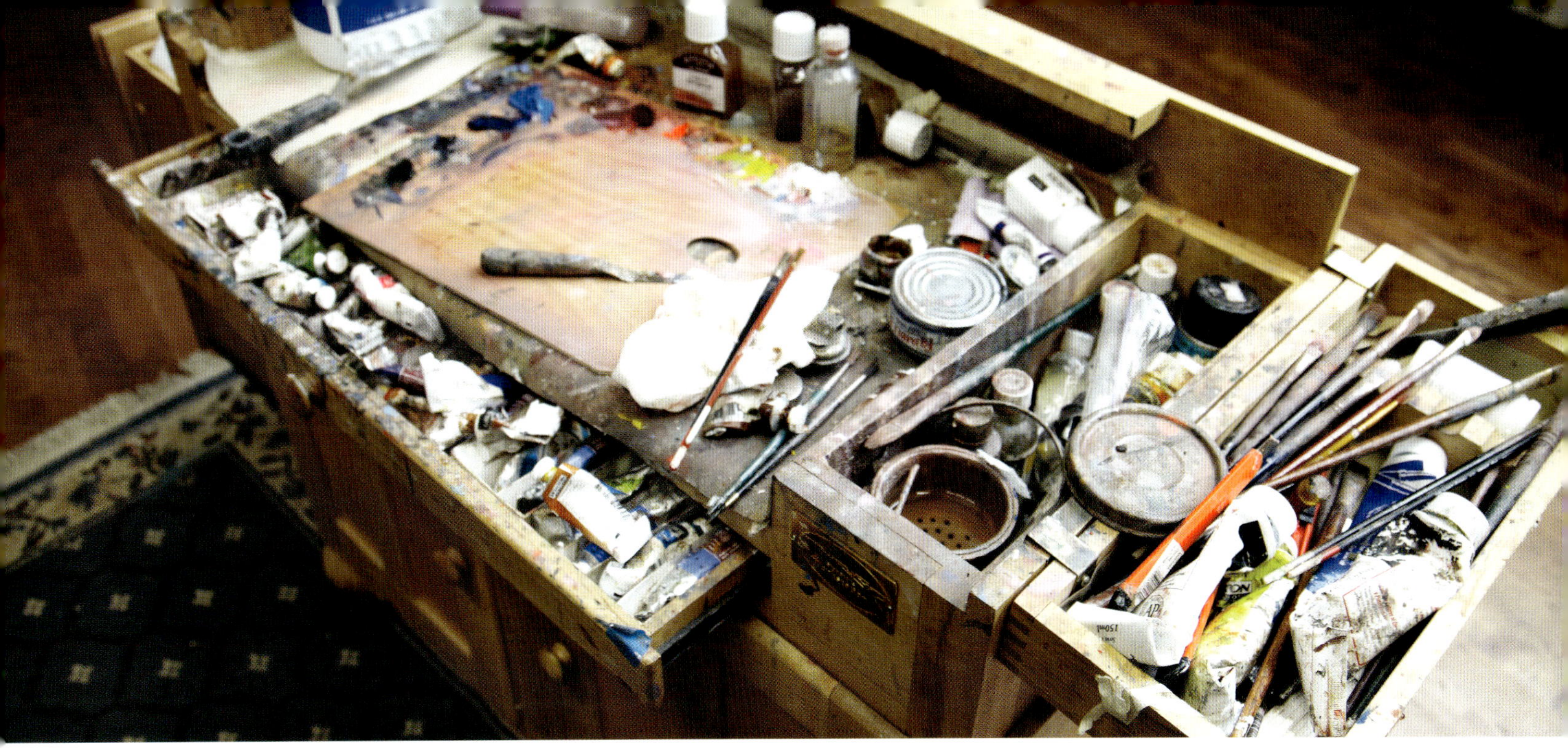

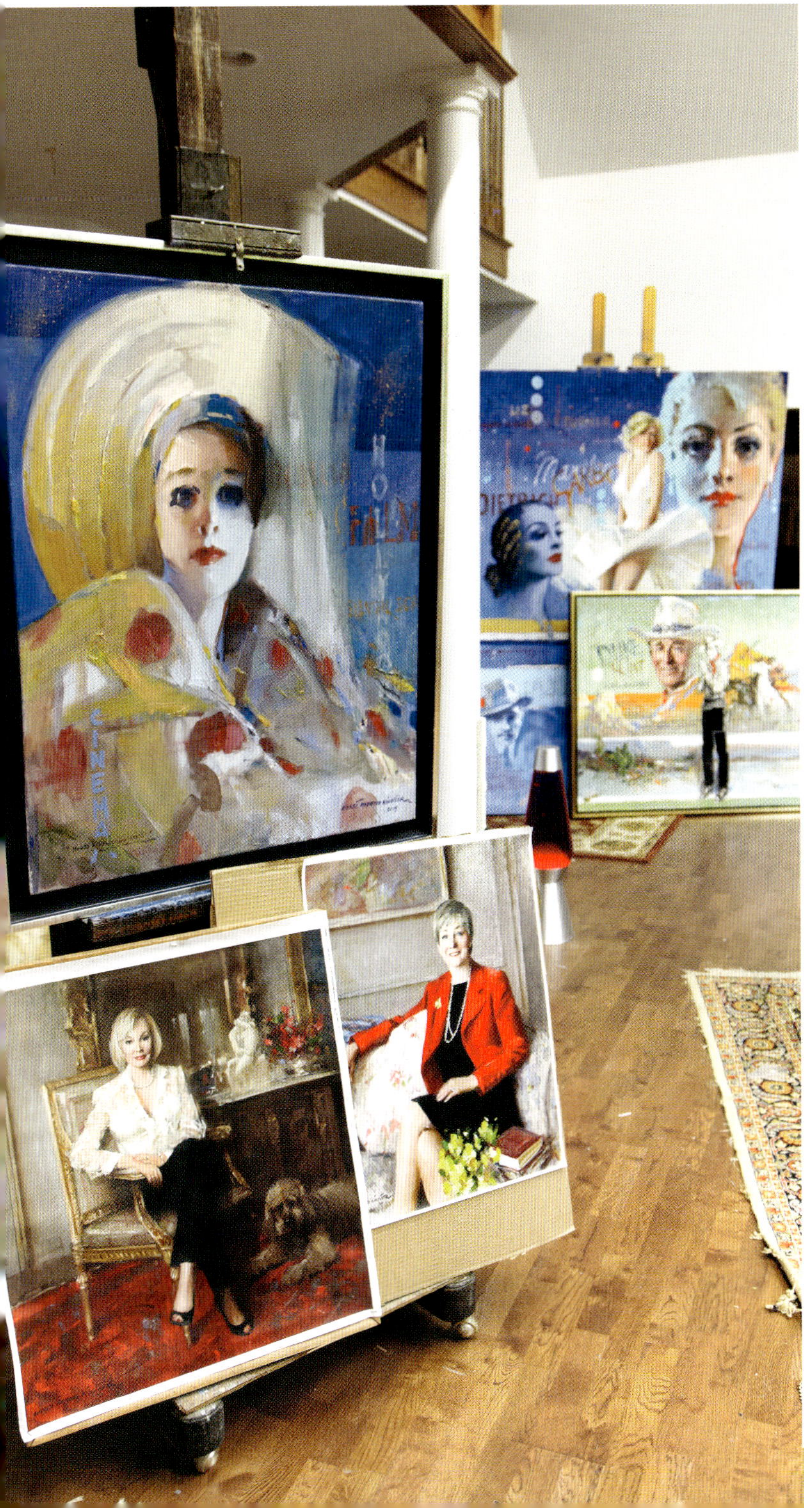

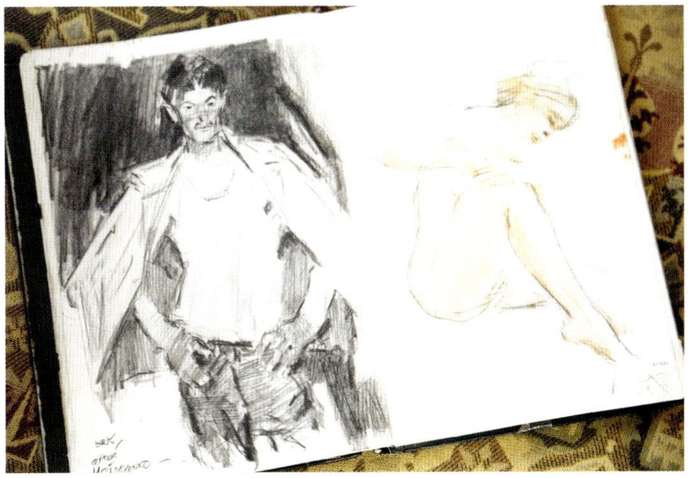

↑ Sketchbook and pose studies.

← Paintings.

Top: The artist's palette and painting supplies.

STUDIO TIPS

Kinstler notes that it is very important to have a light source that can be controlled. "If there is a great deal of natural light, you can reduce it," he says. "The opposite situation can present difficulties, as you need to supplement natural light with artificial light—not an easy condition to remedy. I am very dependent on daylight, and I rarely use my studios at night. For overcast or dark days, I have several fluorescent cool-warm lights that I use to supplement the weakened daylight."

Wende Caporale and Daniel E. Greene

A Barn in North Salem

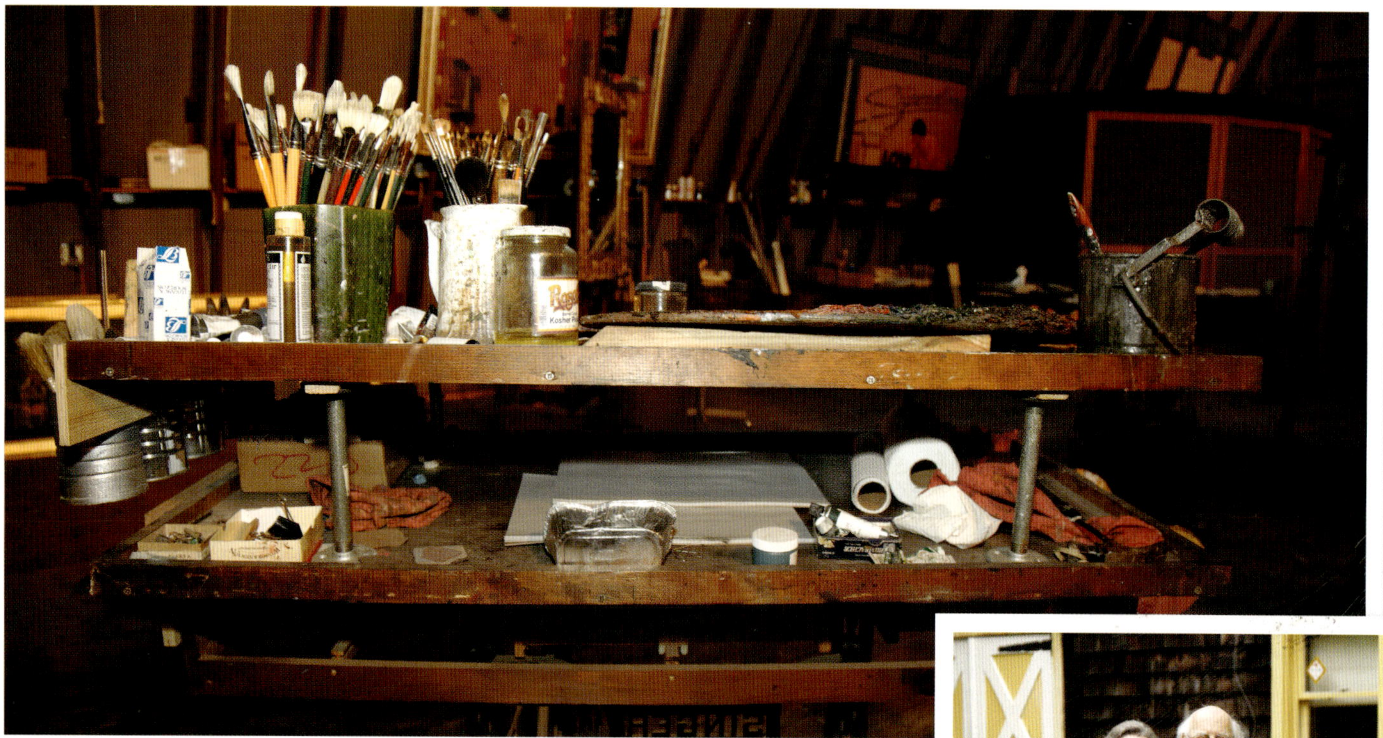

Greene's painting taboret placed on wheels to allow for movement and flexible setups.

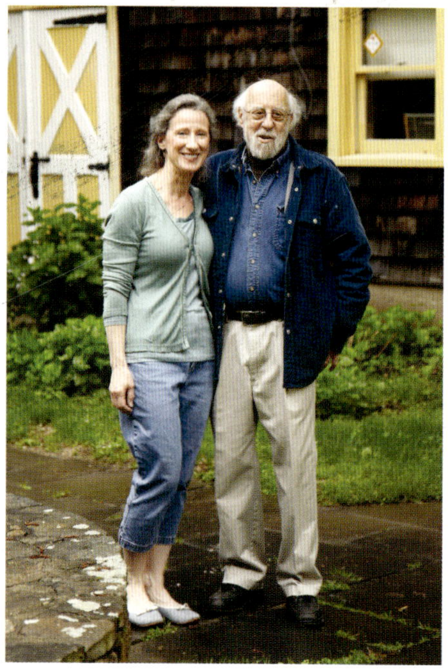

↑ Caporale and Greene in front of the converted barn studio.

The married artists Wende Caporale and Daniel E. Greene live in North Salem, New York, across the state line from Redding and Easton, Connecticut. Greene moved to North Salem in 1980, and Caporale joined him there in 1983 after graduating from Paier College of Art, in Hamden, Connecticut. Prior to coming to North Salem, Greene resided on West 67th Street, in New York City, in a turn-of-the-century building that was designed to provide working artists with live-work spaces. Greene's studio, an artist's dream space, was grand by anyone's standards—a seven-room duplex with north-facing windows and 20-foot (6m) ceilings.

Greene left that apartment, and his search for an affordable live-work studio space led him to North Salem. By this time, Greene had been teaching for more than ten years at the Art Students League of New York and at the National Academy School, and the artist had amassed a large student following. The growing demand for his summer workshops—which averaged forty-five students and had long waiting lists—fueled the artist's hunt for a space large enough to accommodate both his growing teaching practice and his studio work.

Greene notes that he always thought of himself as an urban dweller, until 1979, when he was invited to teach workshops in Gloucester, Massachusetts. "I discovered that I really enjoyed being outside of the city," he says. "I decided to extend my studio search to include a fifty-mile radius of the city."

His space needs were answered when he saw a listing for a country property in North Salem that boasted a

Opposite top: The interior of Greene's studio.

Opposite bottom left: Greene exiting his studio.

Opposite bottom right: Notices and clippings on the artist's bulletin board.

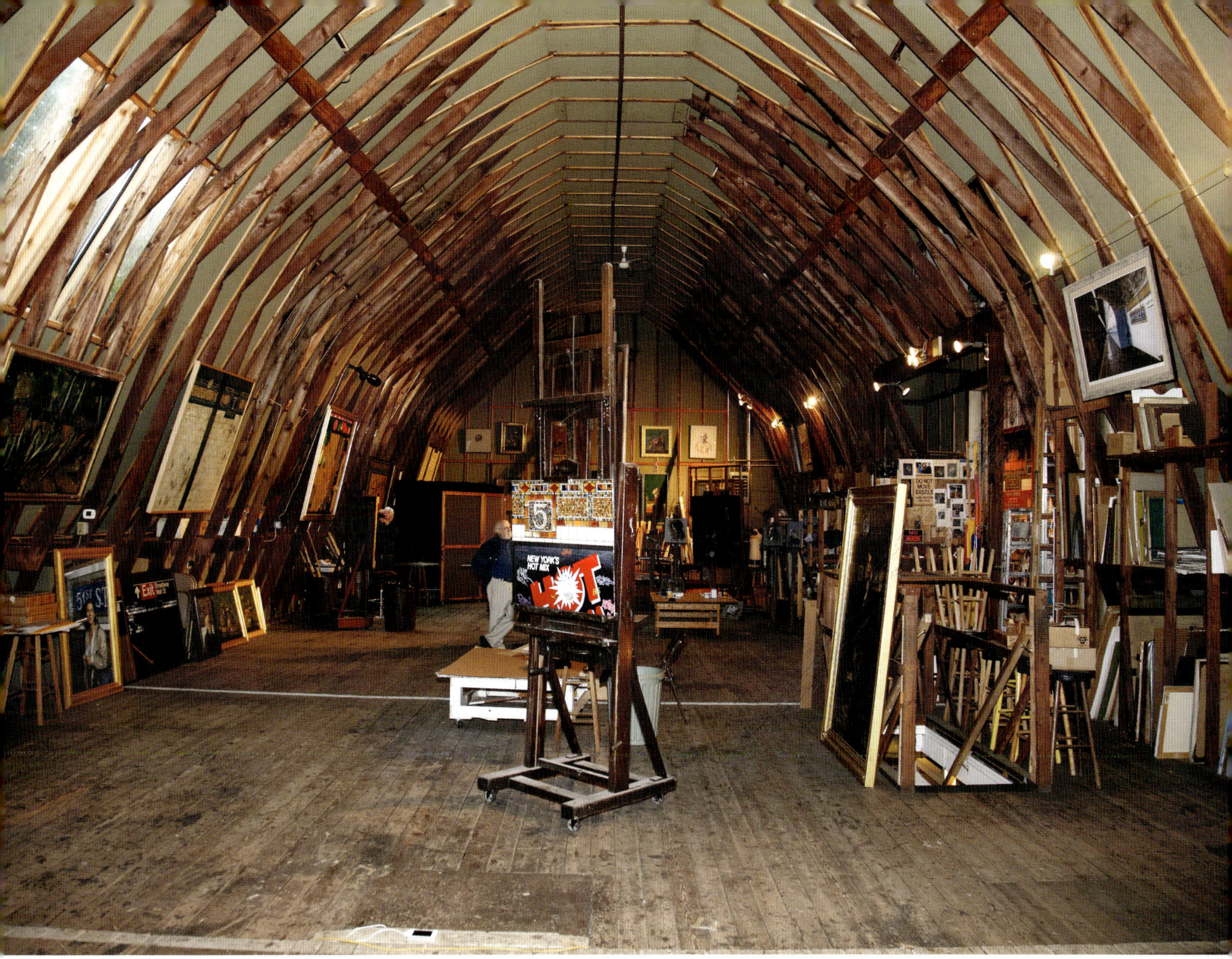
NEW YORK'S
HOT MIX

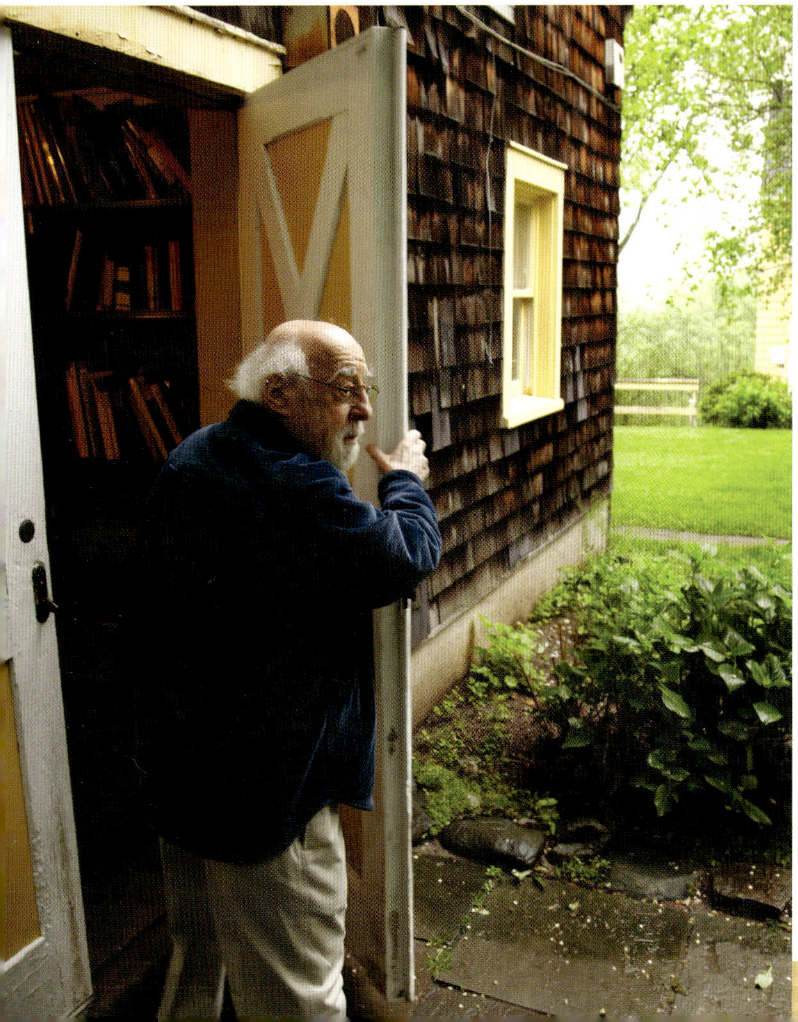

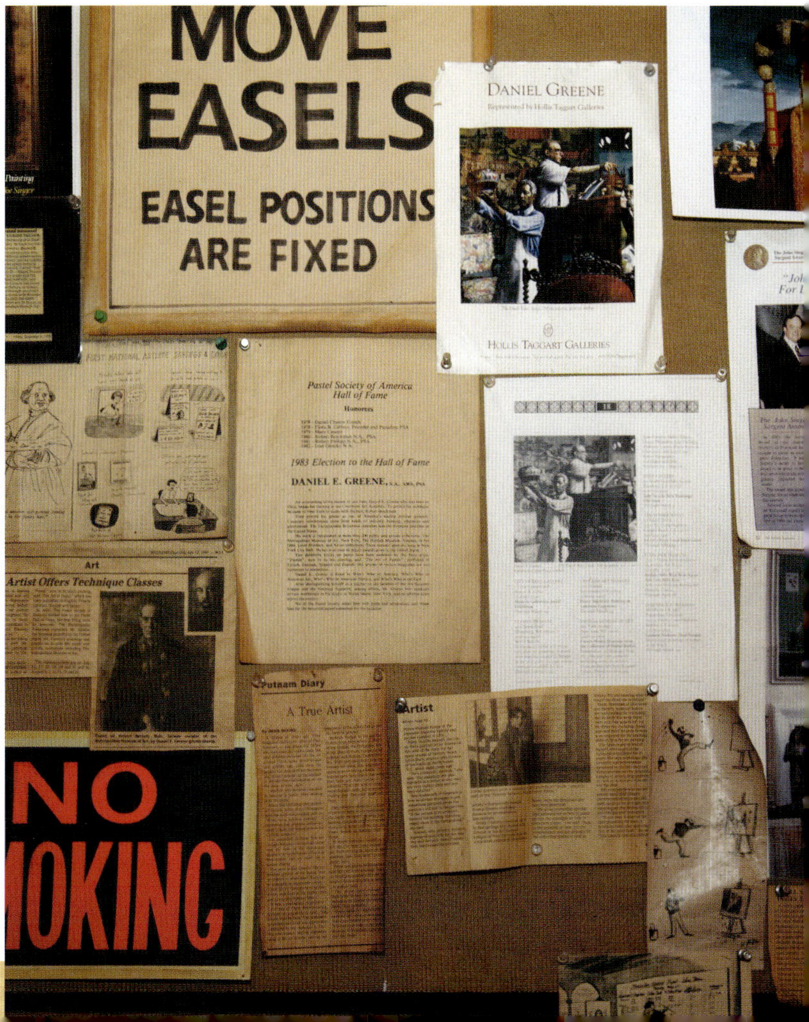
MOVE
EASELS
EASEL POSITIONS
ARE FIXED
DANIEL GREENE
HOLLIS TAGGART GALLERIES
Pastel Society of America
Hall of Fame
1983 Election to the Hall of Fame
DANIEL E. GREENE
Artist Offers Technique Classes
Putnam Diary
A True Artist
Artist
NO

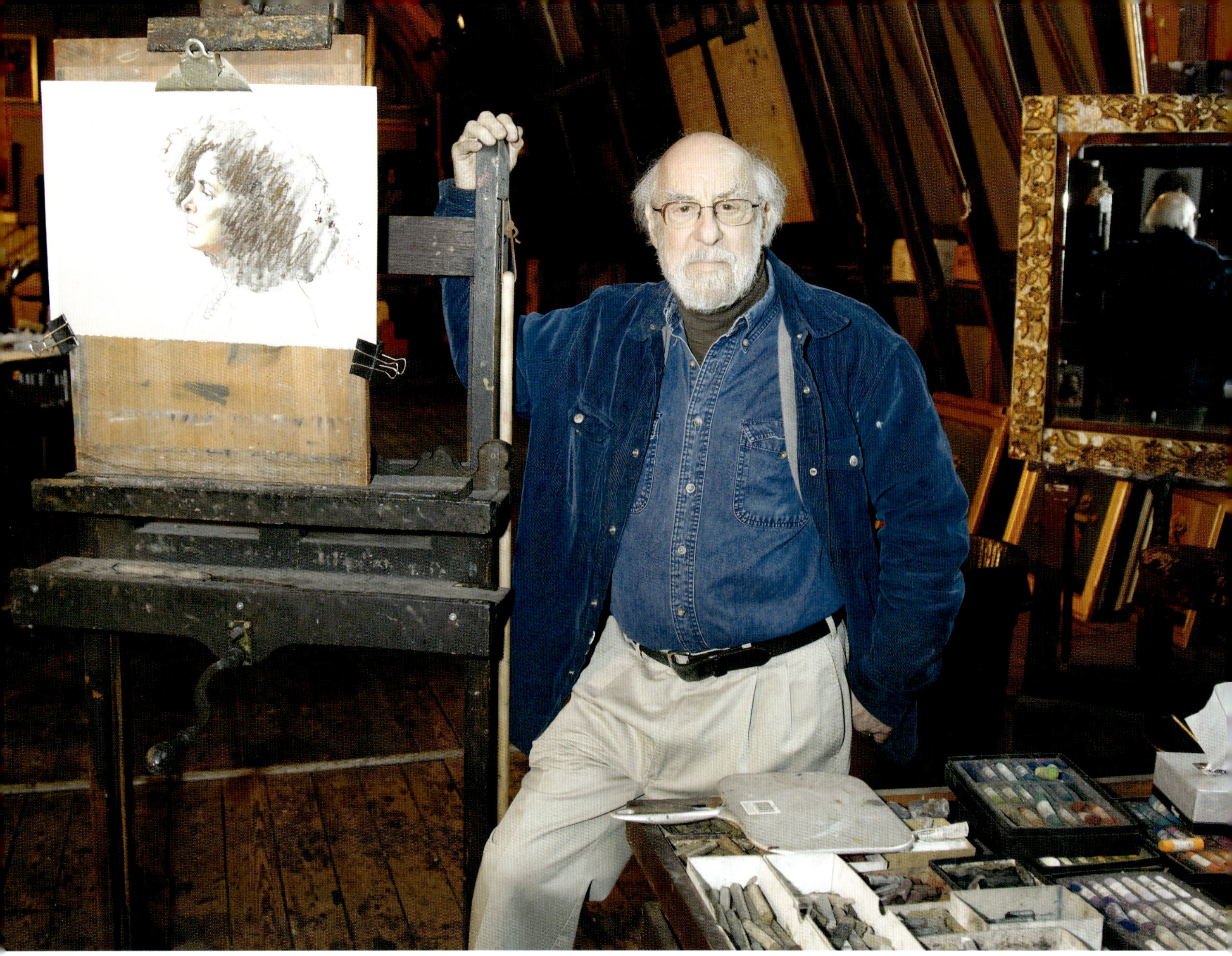

Greene with a pastel study of Babette Bloch. Greene references studies such as this one for his complex figure paintings. The large mirror to the right is an aid for checking composition and proportions. Greene's pastel table is in front. Like all of Greene's studio furnishings, the table is on wheels and can be moved around the studio.

3,000-square-foot (279-square-meter) barn with a soaring cathedral ceiling. "The old barn was perfectly suited for both my teaching and personal work," Greene says. "The 67th Street studio was certainly elegant, but it wasn't the ideal environment for throwing paint around. Here in the barn, I don't worry about messing up the floors. I bought the property, packed up my belongings and studio supplies, and have never looked back."

The barn did require some alterations. Having true north light is essential to Greene's studio practice. He rarely works at night and employs artificial lighting only when it is essential—for example, when he is offering an evening painting demonstration for his workshop students. The barn sits on a northeast axis—not ideal, but workable. Greene's solution was to block all the windows except those facing north and cut three skylights into the roof. The barn was also unheated and unusable during the winters. The artist had to wait out a few years before finally landing a lucrative portrait commission with a builder, who bartered a heating system in exchange for a painting of his mistress. The builder wanted a nude—no heat, no go. Greene got his heaters (wall-mounted forced air blowers), along with insulated walls.

Greene notes that the old masters he most admires—El Greco, Rembrandt, Velázquez, and Vermeer—all preferred working from a single source of north light. In his work, Greene seeks to further develop this master practice through the exploration of tone, value, and mass. Good light is critical to meet this aim, and Greene suggests that any artist looking for studio space check out the lighting situation before moving in, especially an artist who prefers natural light. "Even with a north-facing window, nearby trees and buildings can either obstruct the light or make for unwanted reflections," he observes. "The higher the window, the better. Above eye level is best. Otherwise, the light will reflect onto the wet canvas and cause glare."

Greene notes that his relationships to other artists are important to him, and there are many contemporary artists he

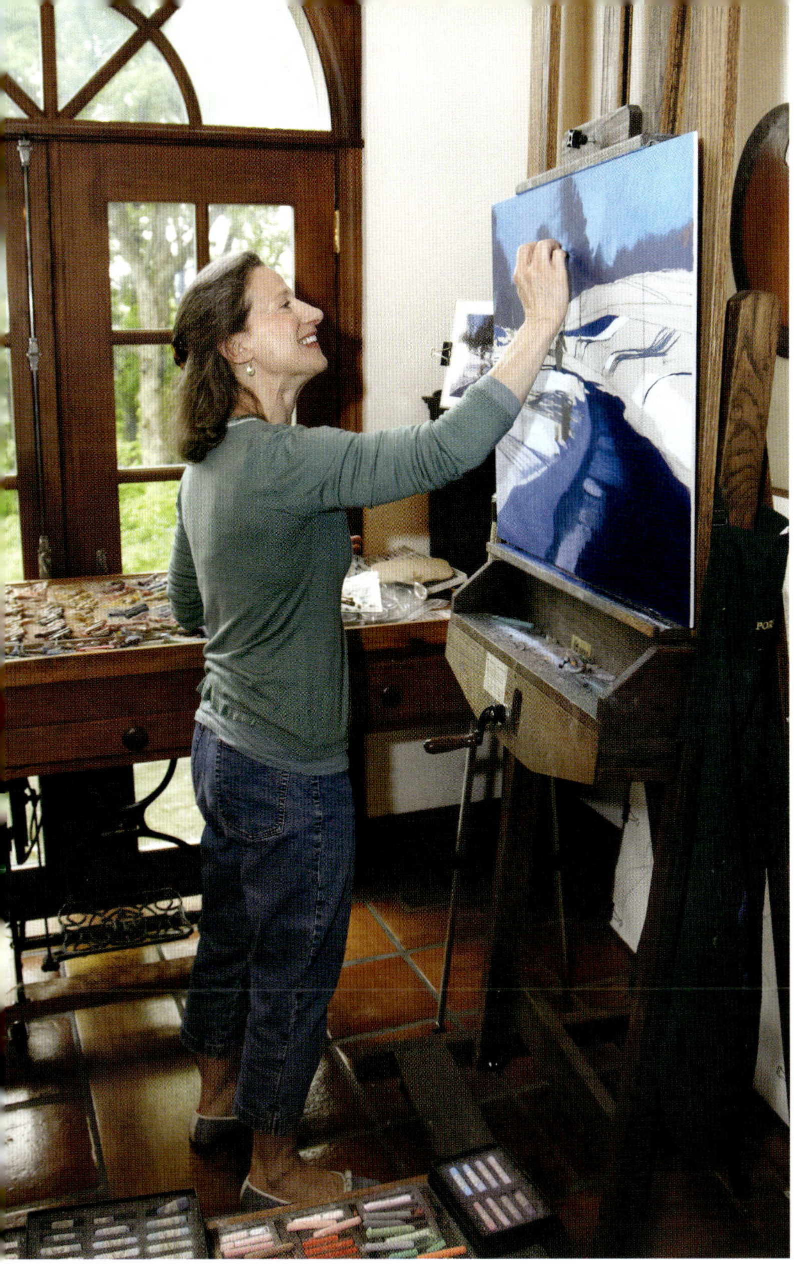

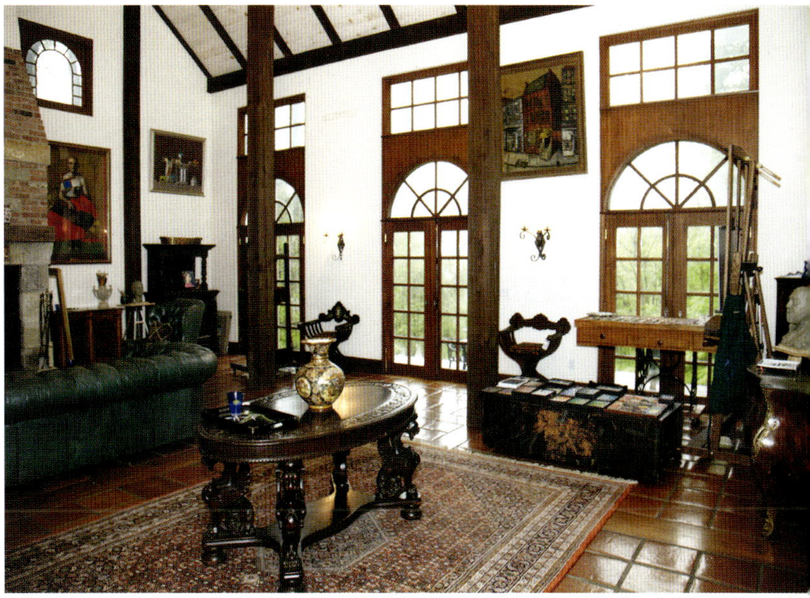

↑ Caporale's studio, with north-facing windows, a work easel, and pastel tables.

← Caporale working on a pastel landscape of her property in winter.

admires. Two close friends are Everrett Raymond Kinstler (page 36) and Burton Silverman. These relationships have a social, rather than a professional, focus. Caporale, though, is not only Greene's wife but also serves as his most trusted artistic confidante.

Caporale was working on a pastel landscape during my visit to her studio. Although a photograph was tacked to the easel for reference, Caporale didn't appear to refer to it as she worked. The winter scene depicts the rolling ground of a winding country lane the artist walks every morning, covered in heavy blue snow. Drifts are crisscrossed with deep, purple shadows, and hints of pink recall the crisp flickering of early morning light. The painting is beautiful. "Beauty is what I look for while I am working," Caporale explains. She succeeds. The work captures more than the physical likeness of a scene; it portrays deep emotion—a treasured connection to a special place.

As she assesses her painting, Caporale remarks that she is a "winter person." In light of this remark, we can view her winter scene not as a landscape painting but as a self-portrait. But is Caporale really a "winter person"? Can someone who exudes such warmth be comfortable in the chill of winter? Perhaps; for certain, Caporale and Greene's North Salem home is near and dear to them in any season. Caporale's current studio is a facsimile of Greene's former space in New York City, and it exists in marked contrast to the adjacent rough-and-tumble studio barn where her husband works. It sits a level below the hallway entrance to the home, and the studio's 18-foot (5m) ceiling soars back to the hallway's height. The walls terminate in balustrades, balconies, and French doors with garden views. Exposed beams and columns punctuate the space, and the overall effect is reminiscent of an aristocratic English country estate.

Prior to working in her current home studio, Caporale had a studio space in the barn that had little natural light. But Caporale was trained as an illustrator—much of her early artwork was commissions for covers of youth novels—and she was accustomed to working under artificial light late into the night to meet publishing deadlines. When computer-generated imagery became popular in the illustration market, Caporale, who prefers to work with traditional media, sought out portrait commissions instead. "Like me, a lot of my illustrator colleagues watched as the market for their work dried up," she recalls. "My

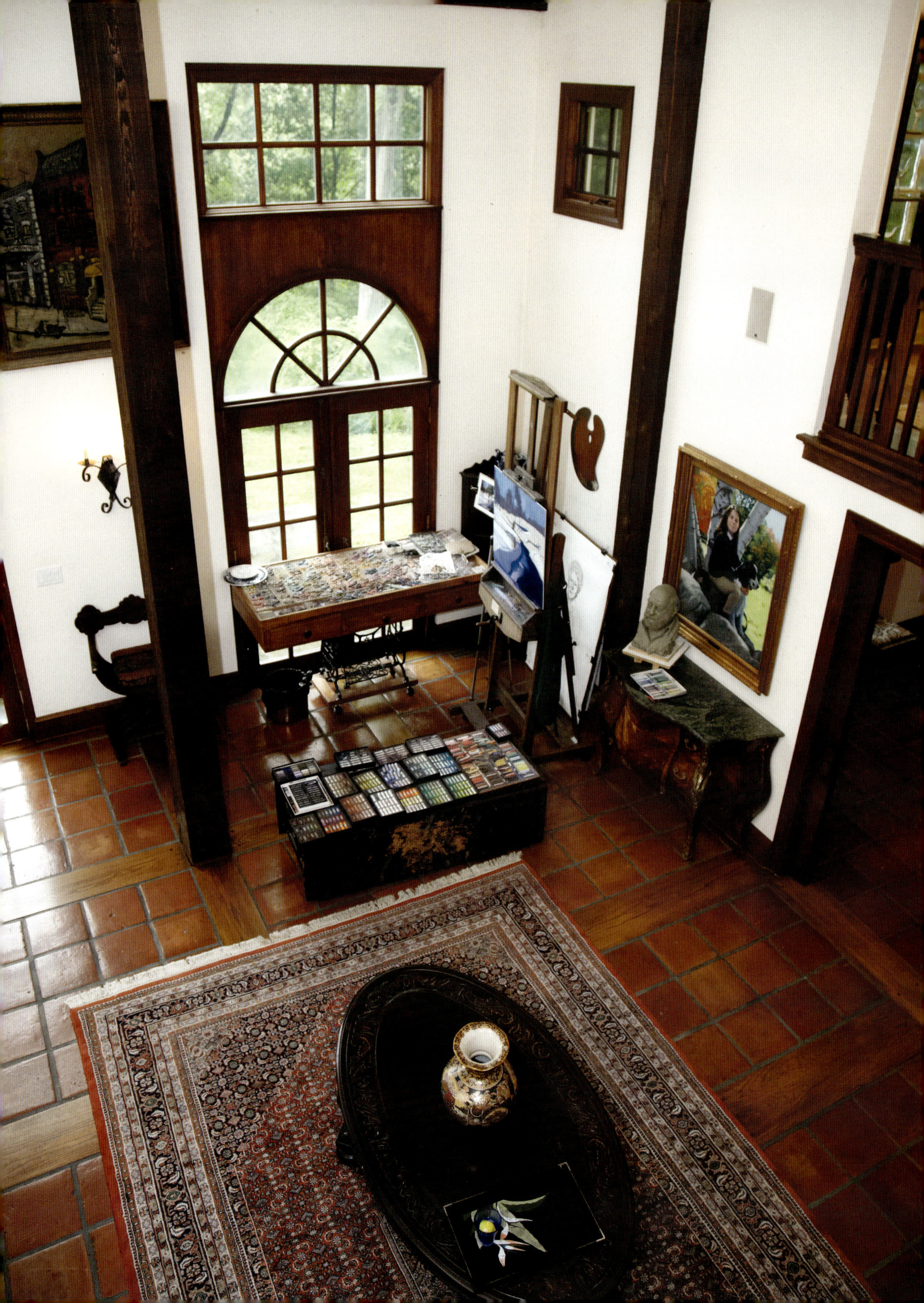

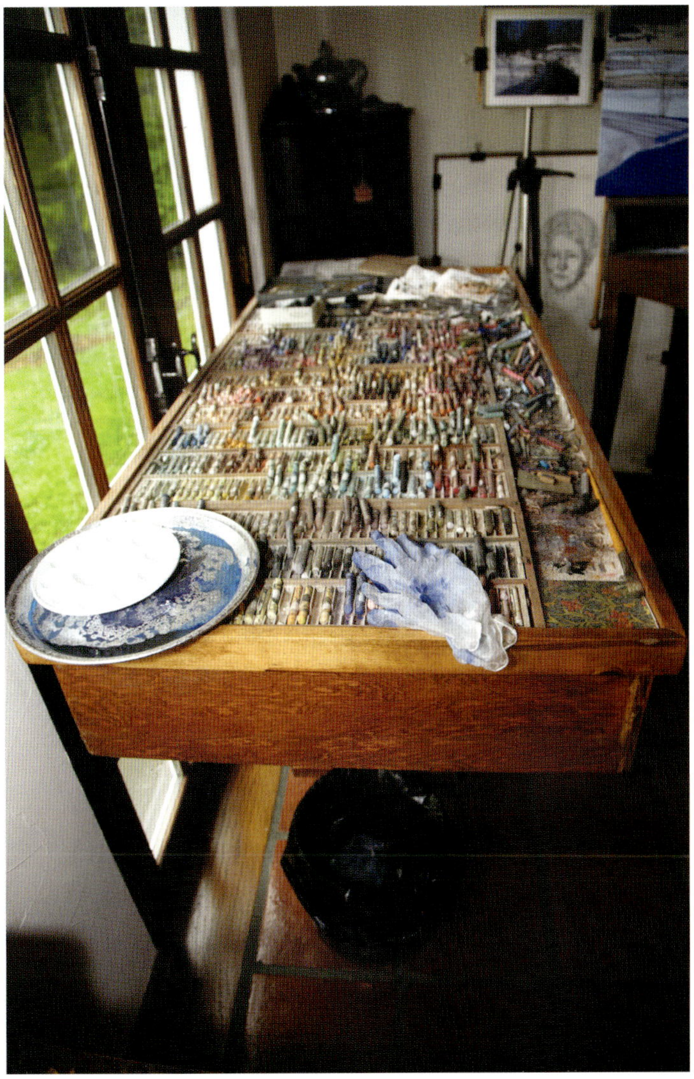

STUDIO TIPS

Greene recommends mounting studio furnishings on rolling canisters, which allows for a flexible use of space. His taborets, worktables, viewing mirrors, model stands, and easels can be rearranged to suit any project he is working on. He adds that adequate storage for the safekeeping of artwork and studio supplies is essential. "Otherwise," he notes, "you will be spending half your time searching for your materials or fighting clutter."

↑ A view of Caporale's pastel table.

← A view into Caporale's studio from the entrance hall.

illustration training was closely tied to fine art—I couldn't give that all up and start working on a computer, although some of my friends did make that transition. I loved drawing and painting from life and often participated in Dan's figure workshops."

Then the mother of a young child, Caporale had community ties to families like her own. Her portrait work, by extension, began to focus on children. "My early training as an illustrator—specifically my ability to combine photographic reference with life sketches—was a real plus when I embarked on this line of work," she says. "Children can't be expected to hold a pose for long. I would schedule an initial sitting for a preparatory drawing, get a good amount of photographic reference, and finish the work in my studio."

Greene and Caporale have close ties to their Connecticut-based friends. Greene's studio is full of in-progress paintings for a show, including studies that Babette Bloch and Marc Mellon (page 28) posed for. And Caporale, Bloch, and Peggy Kinstler often travel together to New York City to attend meetings for the Artists' Fellowship. (Bloch is the president of the organization, and Peggy is a trustee, as well as the organization's historian. Additionally, Mellon and Kinstler are former presidents of the organization.)

Caporale and Greene are looking to relocate to Connecticut to be closer to friends and to help simplify their lives. Greene takes on fewer students in his workshops these days, instead focusing more on his own artwork, which greatly reduces his space needs. Caporale, who has begun to explore sculpture and is working more from life, desires a studio that she needn't worry about getting messy. For the first time in both their practices, they are exploring the possibility of commercial studio spaces outside of their home—an exciting experiment that represents a new chapter in their lives and careers.

For more on Daniel E. Greene, visit his website at www.danielgreeneartist.com.

For more on Wende Caporale, visit her website at www.wendecaporale.com.

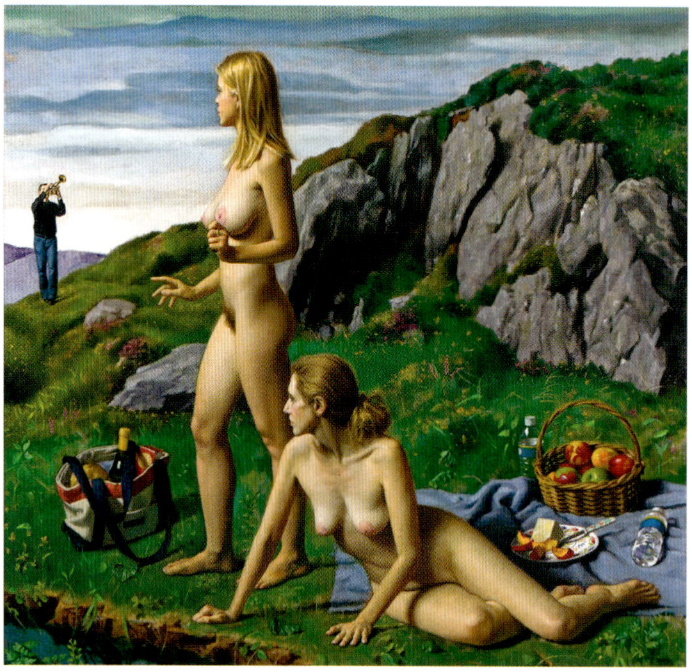

↑ **Afternoon in North Salem**
by Daniel E. Greene, oil, 60" x 60" (152cm x 152cm). Collection of the artist.

→ **Yolande Sculpture**
by Wende Caporale.

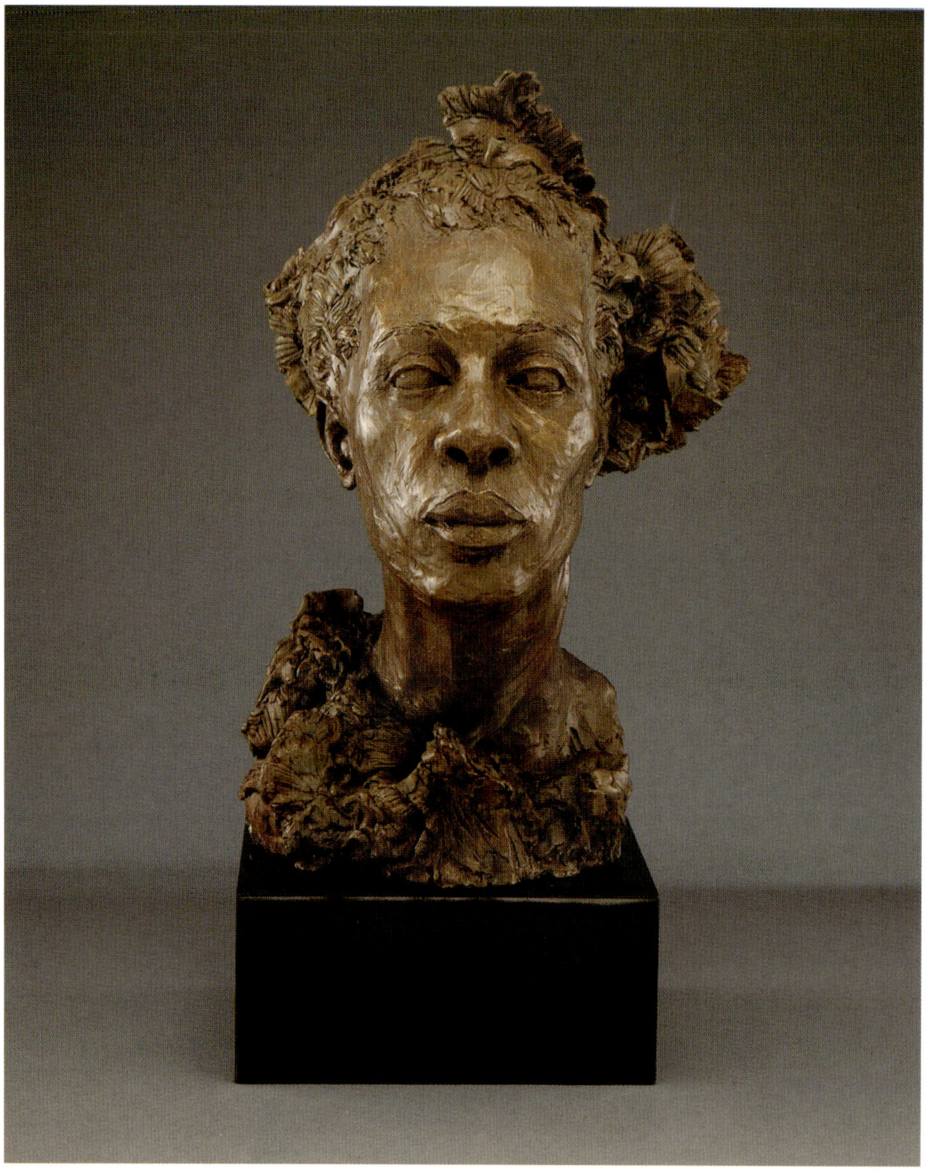

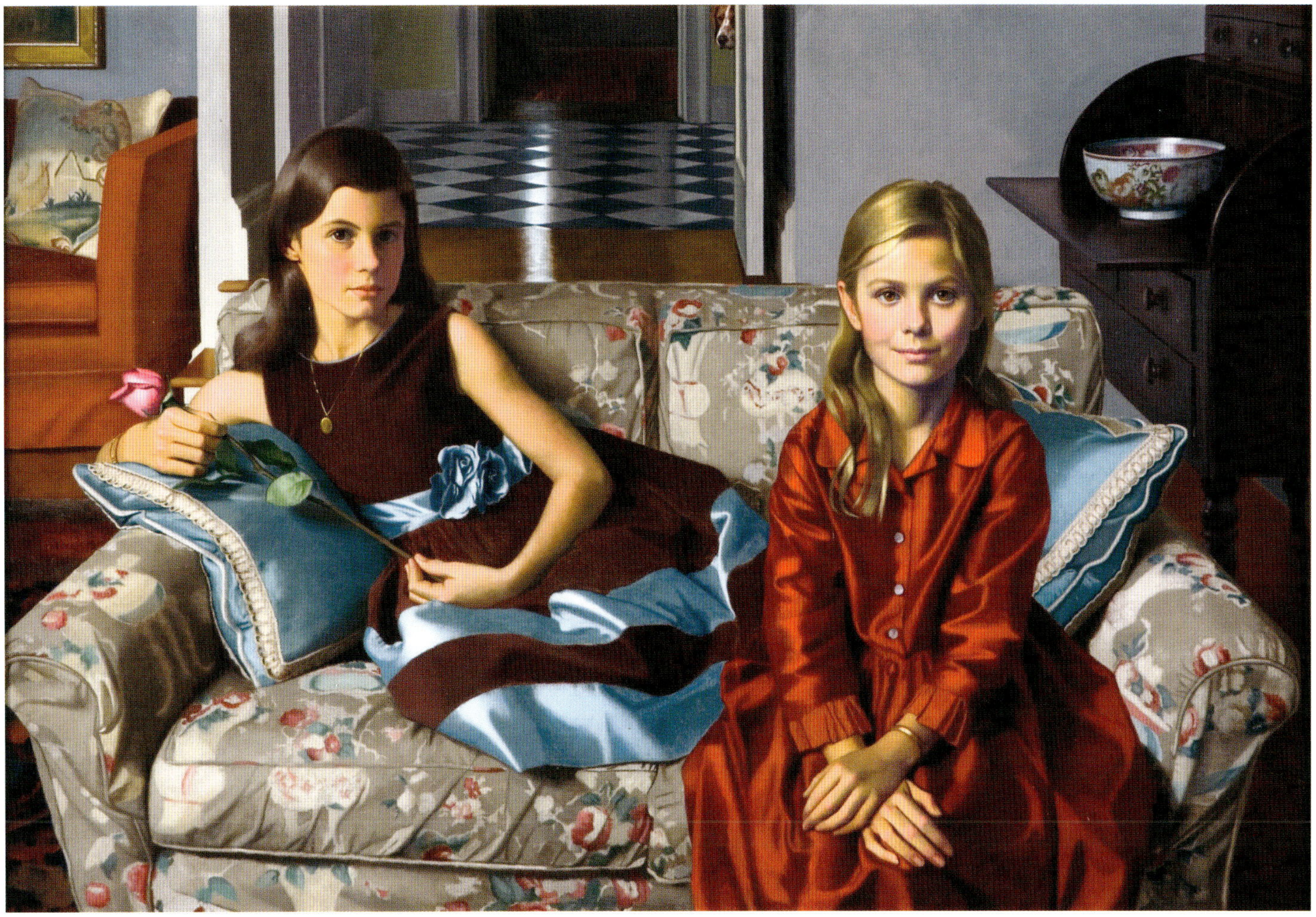

↑ **Lizzy & Daisy Collins**
by Wende Caporale, oil, 48" x 60" (122cm x 152cm). Private collection.

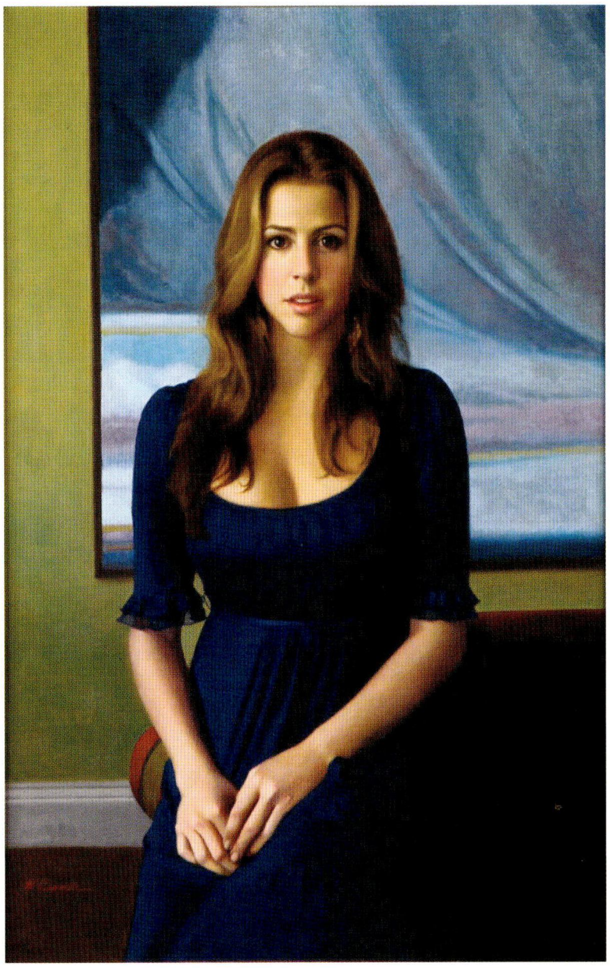

← **Hillary Johnson**
by Wende Caporale, oil, 40" x 30" (102cm x 76cm). Private collection.

Artpost Austin

An Enclave for Visual Artists

"There's a bubble over Austin, and it kind of protects it from the rest of the state," says artist Tina Schweiger. This is a common sentiment among locals and visitors to the capital city, known as the live-music capital of the country and the home of the annual South by Southwest (SXSW) film, music, and interactive festival. Although Austin is home to hundreds of prolific and highly skilled visual artists—many of whom cut their teeth in the University of Texas at Austin's M.F.A. program—it seems they have fewer opportunities for exposure and recognition than those who work in the music industry. Real-estate developer and Texas native James McCurry created Artpost to help address this disparity—and to nurture his own creative spirit.

"Working in commercial real estate for more than thirty years, I had renovated shopping centers, restaurants, and other retail properties," McCurry says. "I worked with great designers and architects, and that began to refine my own visual palette. Going from great architecture to great art wasn't a huge leap for me." While living and working in North Carolina, McCurry fell in with a group of artists and felt they needed a venue for their work. "I got my hands on an old brick building in Charlotte," he recalls, "and I turned it into the Art House Center for Creative Expression, which is still supporting more than twenty artists."

When McCurry returned to Texas in 2005, he wanted to create a similar space but go even further with the idea of creating an enclave for artists. "In North Carolina, it was all under one roof," he says, "but back in Texas, I wanted to work with multiple buildings and create more of an artists' village." During a visit to his home state, he located a 3-acre (1-hectare) vintage World War II-era industrial complex and knew it would meet his needs. Seven buildings dotted the property, including a former

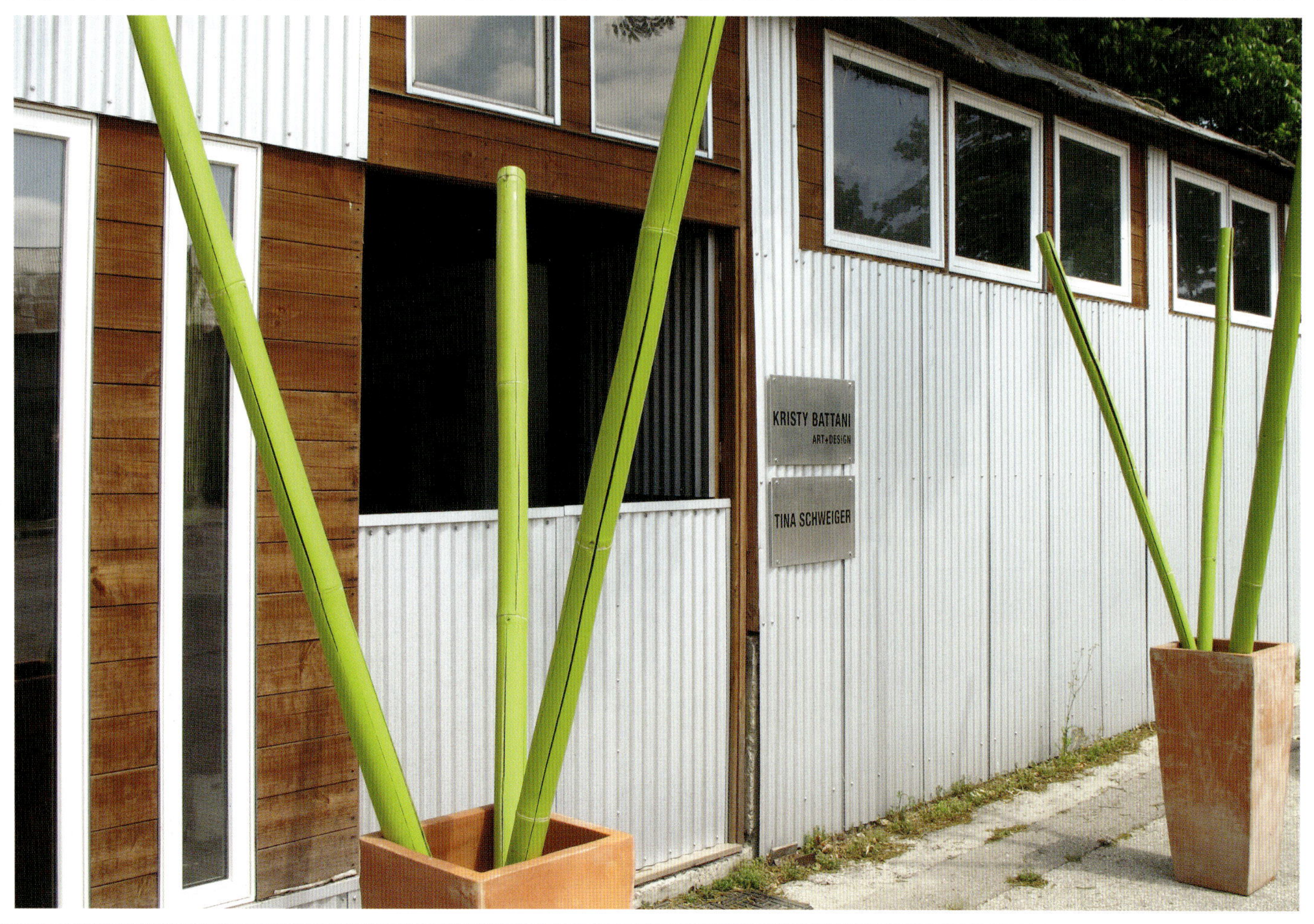

The exterior of Schweiger and Battani's studio.

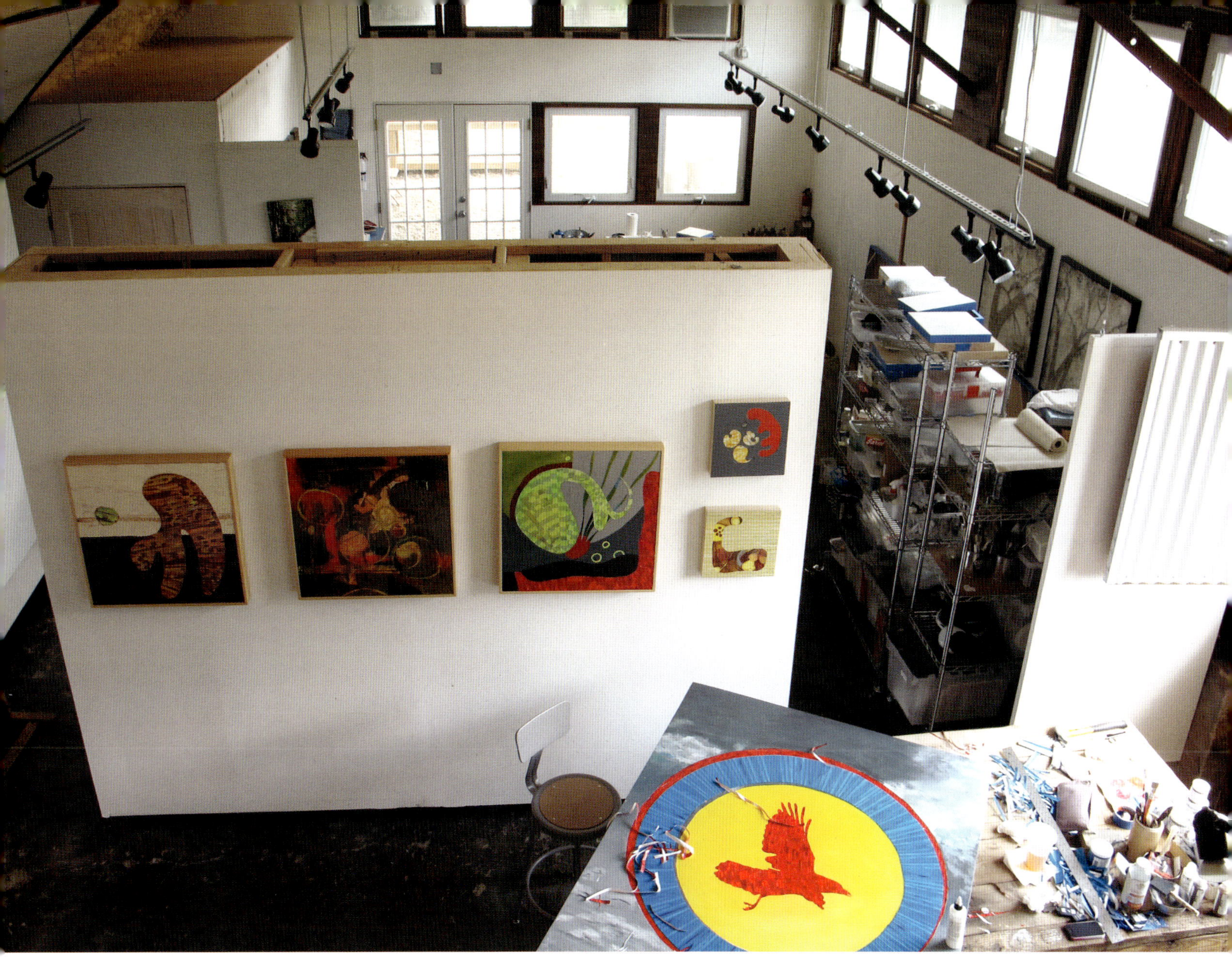

Real-estate developer James McCurry built walls inside the studios to delineate space, but for artists Tina Schweiger and Kristy Battani, who share the space shown here, there's a sense of openness to the studio.

public library and three military-surplus buildings constructed post-World War II. "I knew this array of buildings could support a lot of different kinds of work," McCurry says of the property, which he purchased in 2006. Because the buildings range in size and height, a diverse array of artists can hone their craft, ranging from contemporary abstract painting and sculpture to large-scale installations and jewelry making. The former library, for example, is home to local independent filmmakers, who use the space as an editing and animation lab. Many of the working studios are shared by two artists and also double as an exhibition space.

McCurry secured his first tenant shortly after he purchased the property, and other artists quickly followed. In less than five years, Artpost has become a haven for the creative community, hosting four annual open-studio events each year and housing nearly thirty visiting and resident artists.

Needless to say, getting a studio at Artpost is no simple task. Although the application process is informal, the list of applicants is long. Schweiger, for example, has lived in Austin for more than twenty years but only recently became a full-time artist. After years as an executive of an advertising and marketing agency, she was eager to channel her creativity for her own ends instead of a client's. Once she sold her agency, the only obstacle was finding a place where she could really get down to work. She came across Artpost during a studio tour in 2010 and instantly felt a connection. "I noticed a dramatic difference in the quality of the work," she says. "It was like it was being curated. I introduced myself to Jim at that event and gave him my information, hoping he'd remember to contact me if a studio became available."

For McCurry, a desirable applicant isn't just a prolific or talented artist. "We look for people who want to be part of a community," he says. "It's about the exchange of ideas and support, as well as tools, materials, and skills."

Schweiger, who had been a fixture in the local art scene, filled the bill. "I just really wanted to be around other artists," she says. "I'd always go to openings and

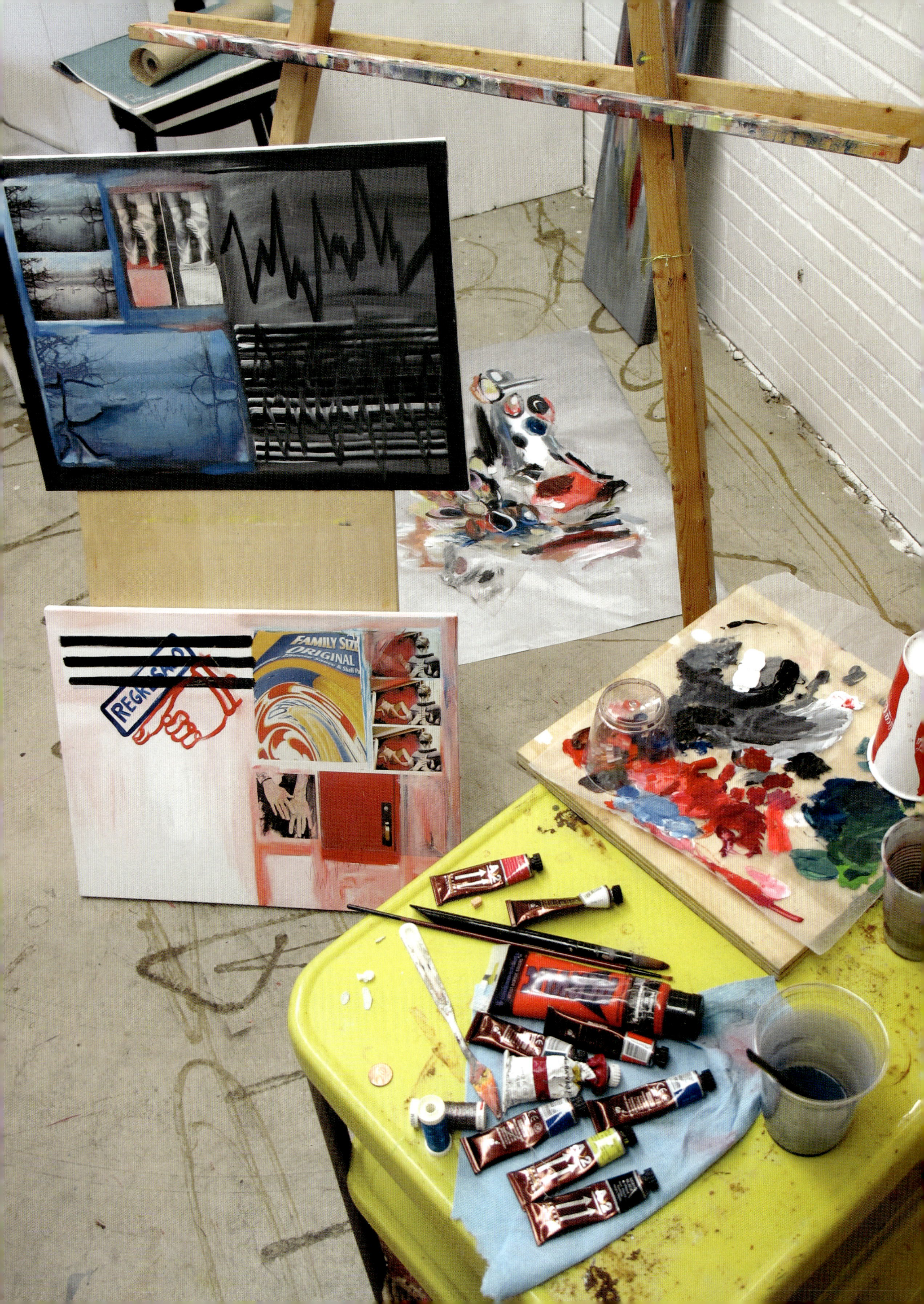
FAMILY
ORIGINAL

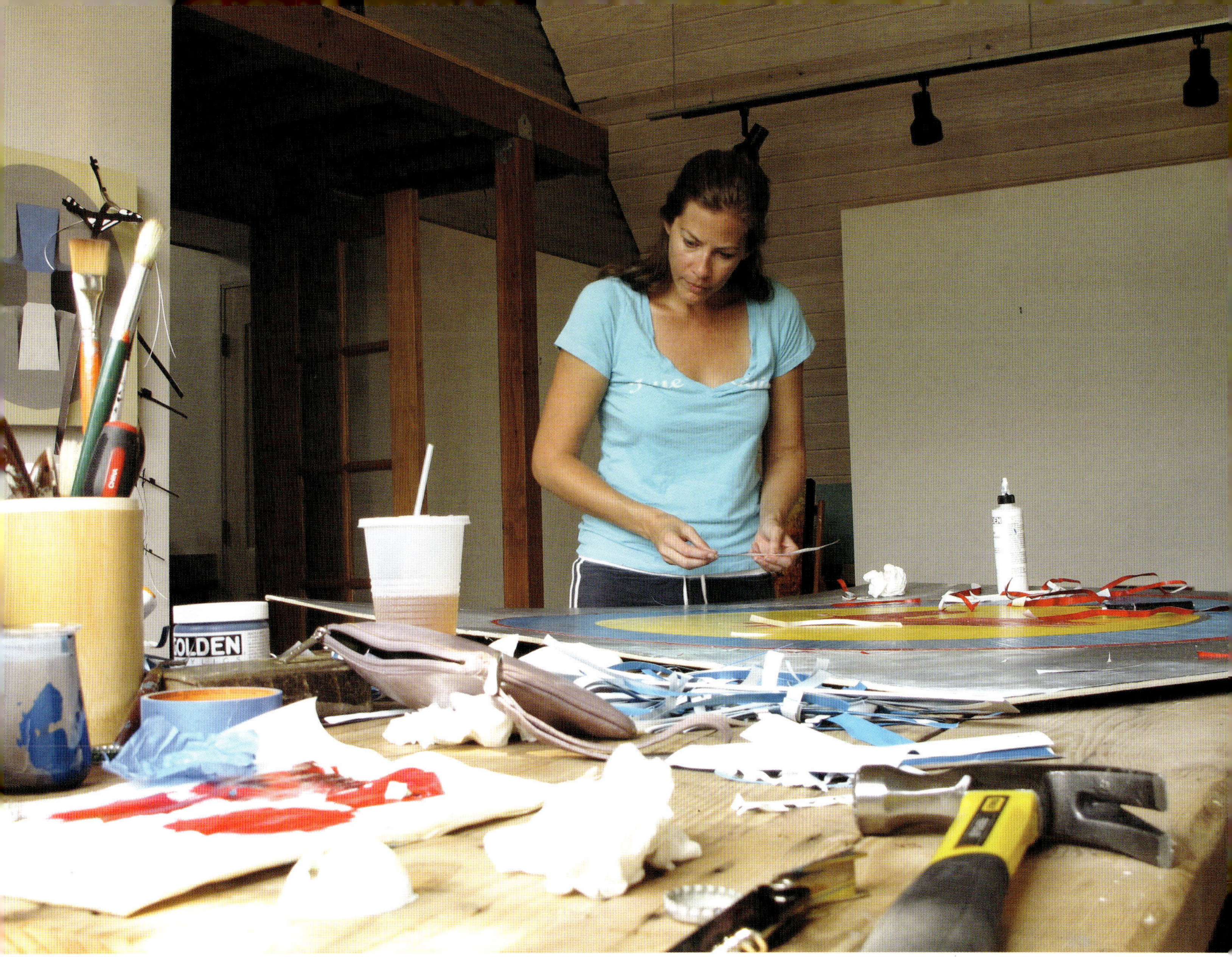

↑ "The table is my all-purpose work surface," Tina Schweiger says. "I'm not into easels. I've got big walls, so when I want to step back, I can lean a painting against the wall, move 20 feet (6m), and nothing gets in my way."

← Lacey Richter's studio.

other art events, but it isn't the same as working in a space with other artists who are equally focused on creating."

And at Artpost, creating is what it's all about—by any means necessary. When McCurry purchased the property, it required a lot of renovation and refitting, but the developer was up to the task, doing much of the work himself. "My first goal was creating studios for painters," he recalls. "That meant cutting in more natural light, creating proper ventilation, and creating exhibition-style walls." The original metal walls of the post-World War II Quonset huts were covered with sheetrock to reduce visual clutter. Old windows were replaced with new double-paned versions that could be opened and closed to create a free flow of air throughout the space. Given the Texas heat, cooling was also a priority, and McCurry found that it wasn't as much of a financial burden as one might assume. "We have wall units in many of the studios," he says, "and the good news is that the current generation of window air-conditiong units are Energy Star-rated and don't cost much to run. The units are also small enough that they don't zap too much electricity."

The artists who create at Artpost share McCurry's hard work, dedication, and generosity. Lacey Richter, an artist who works in abstract painting and drawing, returned to art after working at a local museum. "My small house became an art obstacle course," she recalls of the days before she joined Artpost. "I no longer had a living space. I couldn't get away from my art or materials. I stopped by Artpost on a whim one day, and there was a nice, large space, but I couldn't afford it. But I also saw a charming small space in the rear of the building that used to be the back porch of the library." This space suited her needs, and, taking a page from McCurry's book, she "ripped up the sea-foam green carpet to reveal a glue-stained concrete floor. It then became the Back Porch Studio." Although Richter took

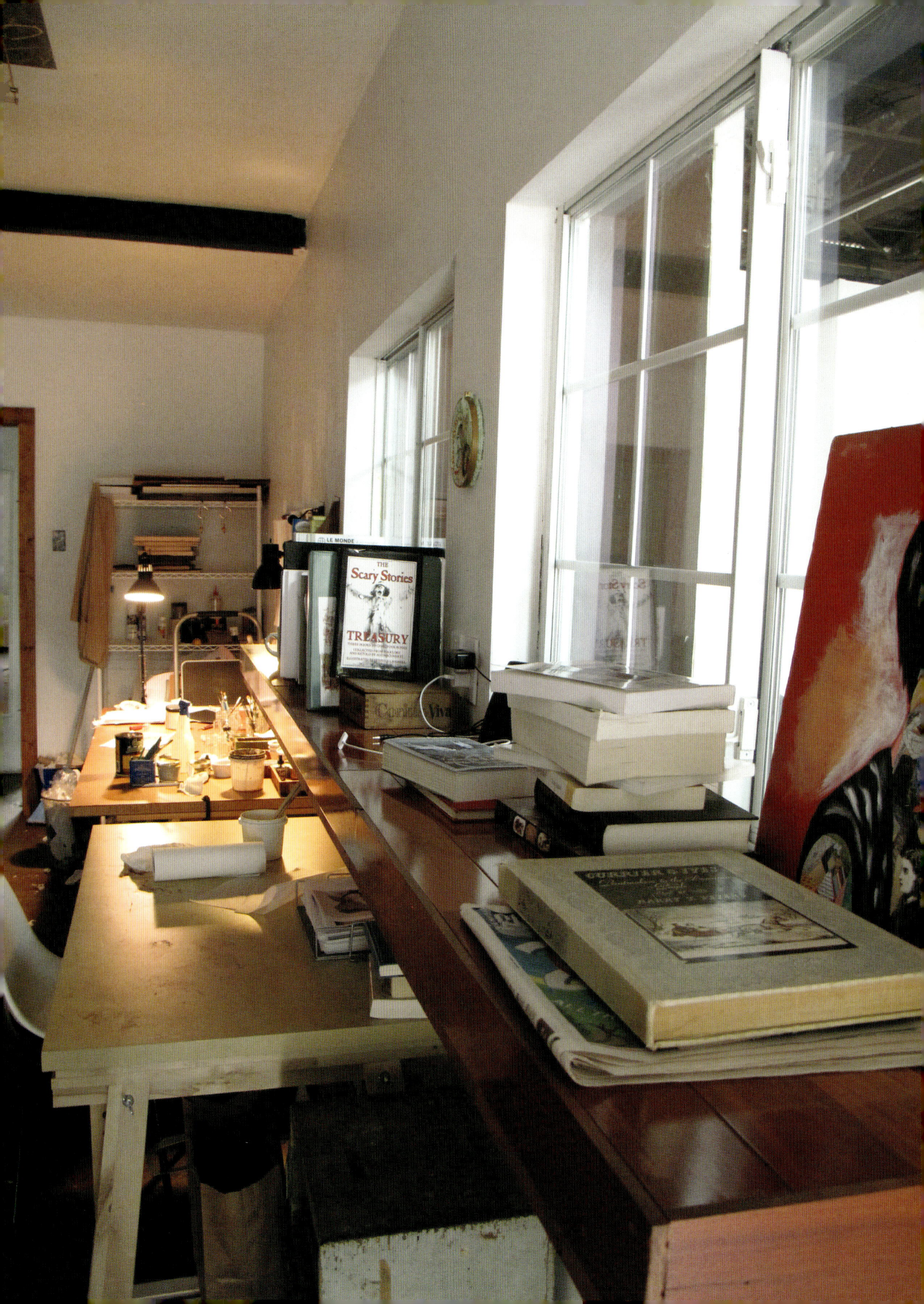
THE
Scary Stories
TREASURY
LE MONDE

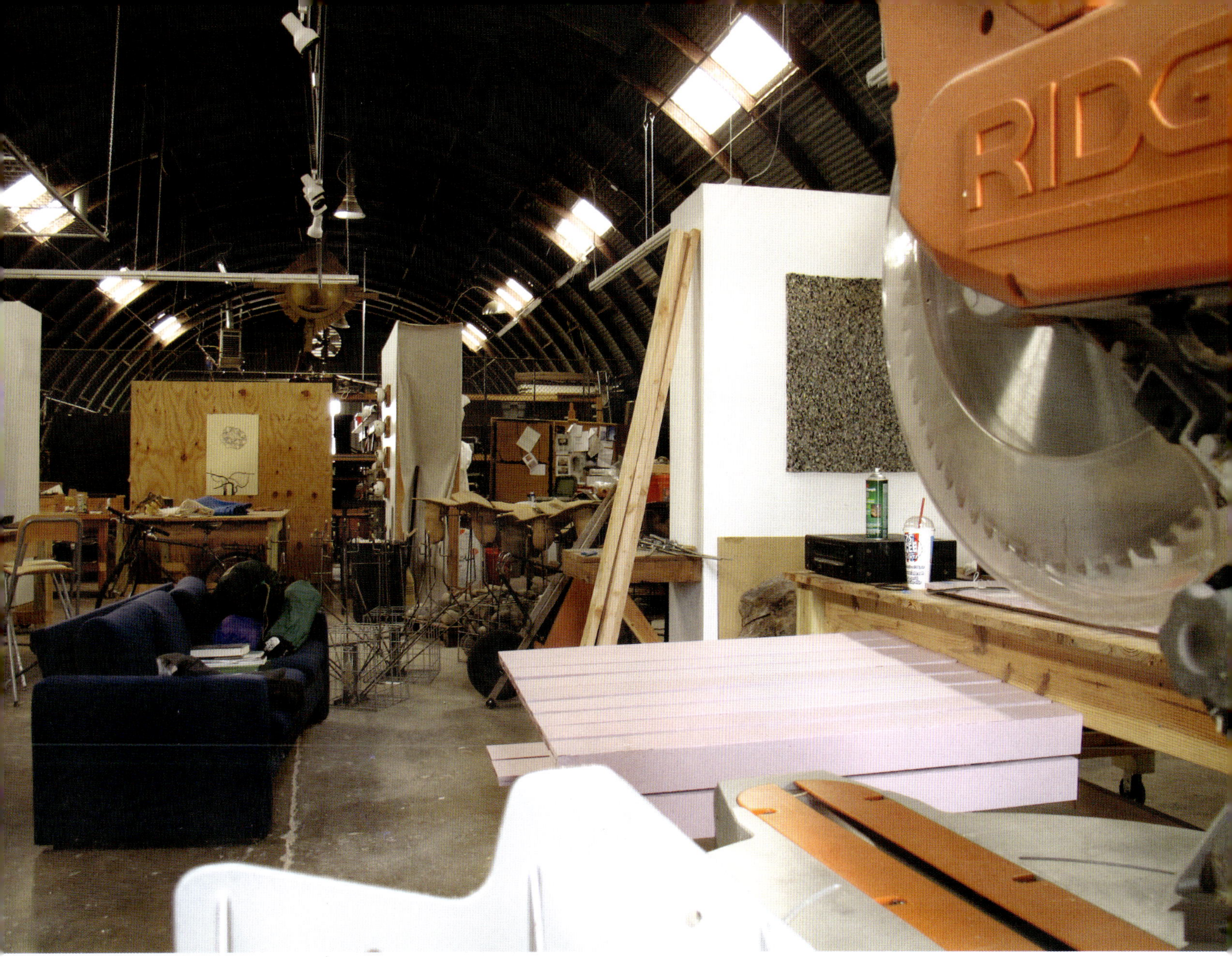

↑ This work space, shared by sculptor Scott Proctor and other artists, is known as the Ultralab. "It's the biggest hut, with a 21-foot (6m) clear height," McCurry explains. "It's ideal for Scott's large-scale installations."

← "I knew I needed a private space, because I like to lose myself in my work," says Artpost resident Katy Horan. "I've had many studios before, but this is the first one that has big windows, and I love it!"

studio art classes as an undergraduate and had her first solo show at a local gallery, she feels that in having her own space, she's really started to arrive as an artist. "I'm still figuring it out—what it means to be an artist," she says. "I can change my mind from one day to the next, but I now have an actual studio space, so I feel more legit."

The larger buildings in the complex are shared by multiple artists, which may seem unappealing, but for those who choose Artpost, it reinforces and nurtures the idea of community. Artists are generally grouped with studio-mates who work in a similar style, subject, or media—and it seems to be working out well. "There's a mutual professional respect and courtesy that you have to extend," McCurry says simply. "It's never really been a problem. It's naturally happened that we have two shifts: those who are full-time working artists, who come in during the day, and those who have day jobs and come into the studio in the evenings." Schweiger shares a studio with encaustic painter Kristy Battani and has found camaraderie and inspiration from her fellow artist. "We both have a background in graphic design, and we both had left-brained careers before focusing on art," Schweiger says. "I've always been interested in encaustics, and I recently found out that Kristy teaches workshops, and I've already signed up for one."

It's this free-flowing exchange of ideas that helps set Artpost apart from other creative communities. Artists may come in with one area of expertise or subject matter, but they quickly develop and sharpen new skills by interacting with their neighbors. "Just about anything you can conceive of, someone else here has the tools to do it," McCurry says.

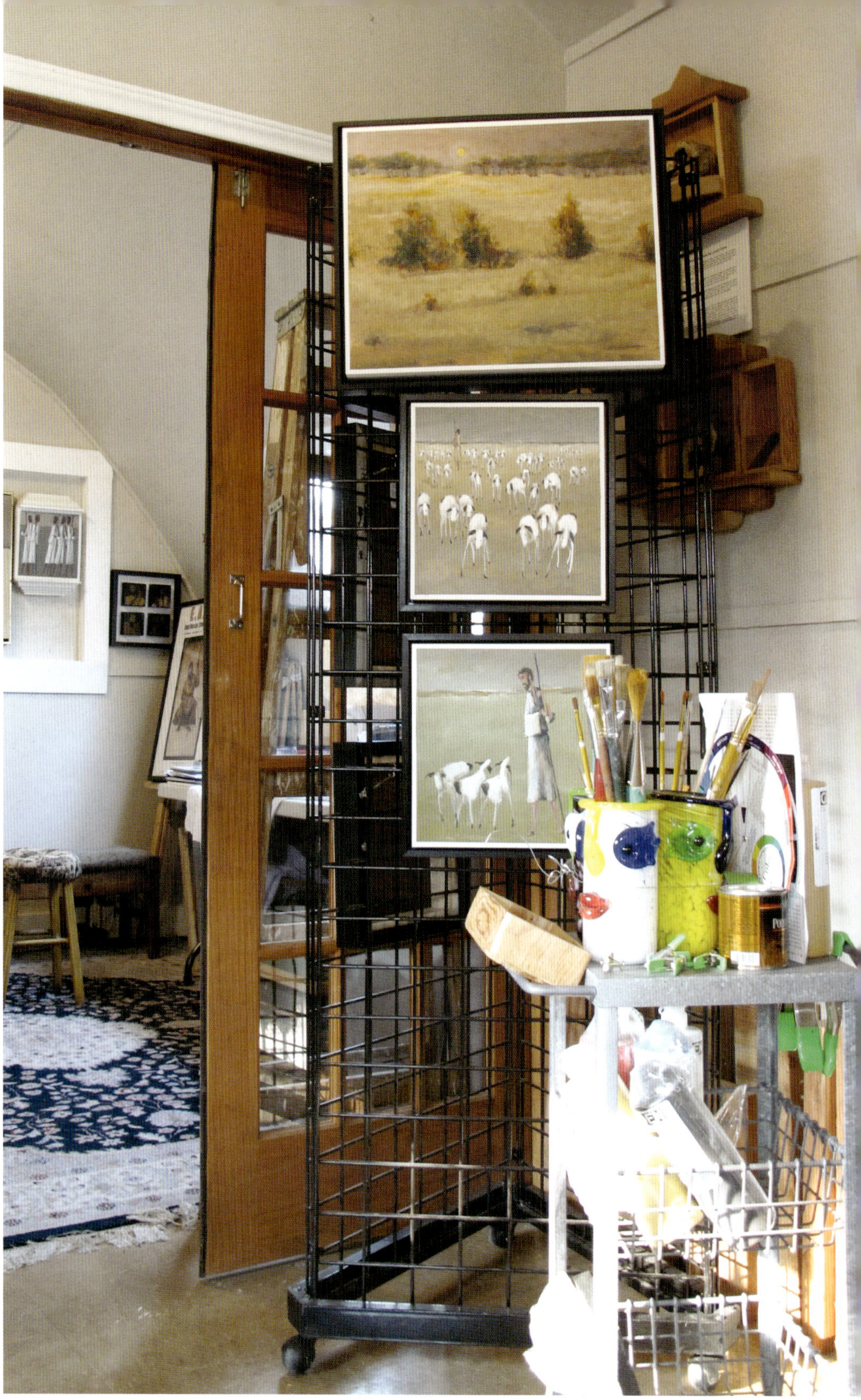

Painter Dan Arredondo's studio.

"If you're in the process of working on something and reach a stopping point—let's say you're a painter, but you decide that you want to cut a piece of metal or stain a portion of a piece—there's someone here who has the experience or the tools to help you get it done."

Because Battani has children, she works daytime hours during the week, when they're in school. Schweiger, on the other hand, tends to work early in the morning, in the evening, and on weekends. "It's a lot like having a roommate in college," she says of sharing the studio. "We don't overlap all that often, but we have to be conscientious. We're naturally respectful of the space and don't really step on each other's toes."

As the landlord, McCurry maintains the exterior grounds, but it's up to each artist to tend to his or her studio space. "It's kind of like having a guest in your home," he says. "The moment you know someone's coming by, you tidy up. Our ongoing events, coupled with the fact that the studios double as galleries, is pretty self-enforcing."

Taking responsibility for and control of one's creative expression is at the core of Artpost's mission—and, one could even say, Austin itself. With the local motto, "Keep Austin Weird," the goal is not simply to maintain a sense of creativity and individuality but also to nurture independent businesses. "There aren't a lot of collectors or established gallery channels here," Schweiger says. "You have to be more independent to live and work as an artist in Austin. It's an intensely entrepreneurial community, and there's a lot of cross-pollination between artists, business owners, and developers. It's all about innovation."

For McCurry, fostering the creative process allows him to support his own independent spirit. "Having been raised in a small town in East Texas, and after attending a conservative university and studying business, it took many years for me to understand and appreciate the value of the creative release for each individual," McCurry says. "There's a mental, physical, and spiritual value in it. Those who have the chance to work on their creative pursuits every day sometimes forget how good they have it. Professional artists often face the challenge of trying to keep up the sense of experimentation and risk taking that they had when they started. I wanted to create a space that encouraged that kind of freedom." For the sculptors, painters, filmmakers, and designers who take advantage of Artpost, McCurry's goals are met every day. "Sometimes I feel a bit guilty," says Schweiger. "Getting up and going to my studio every day is a luxury. When I'm at Artpost, my art is all I'm doing. It's a nice change after years of creating work for other people."

For more on Artpost, visit www.artpostaustin.com.

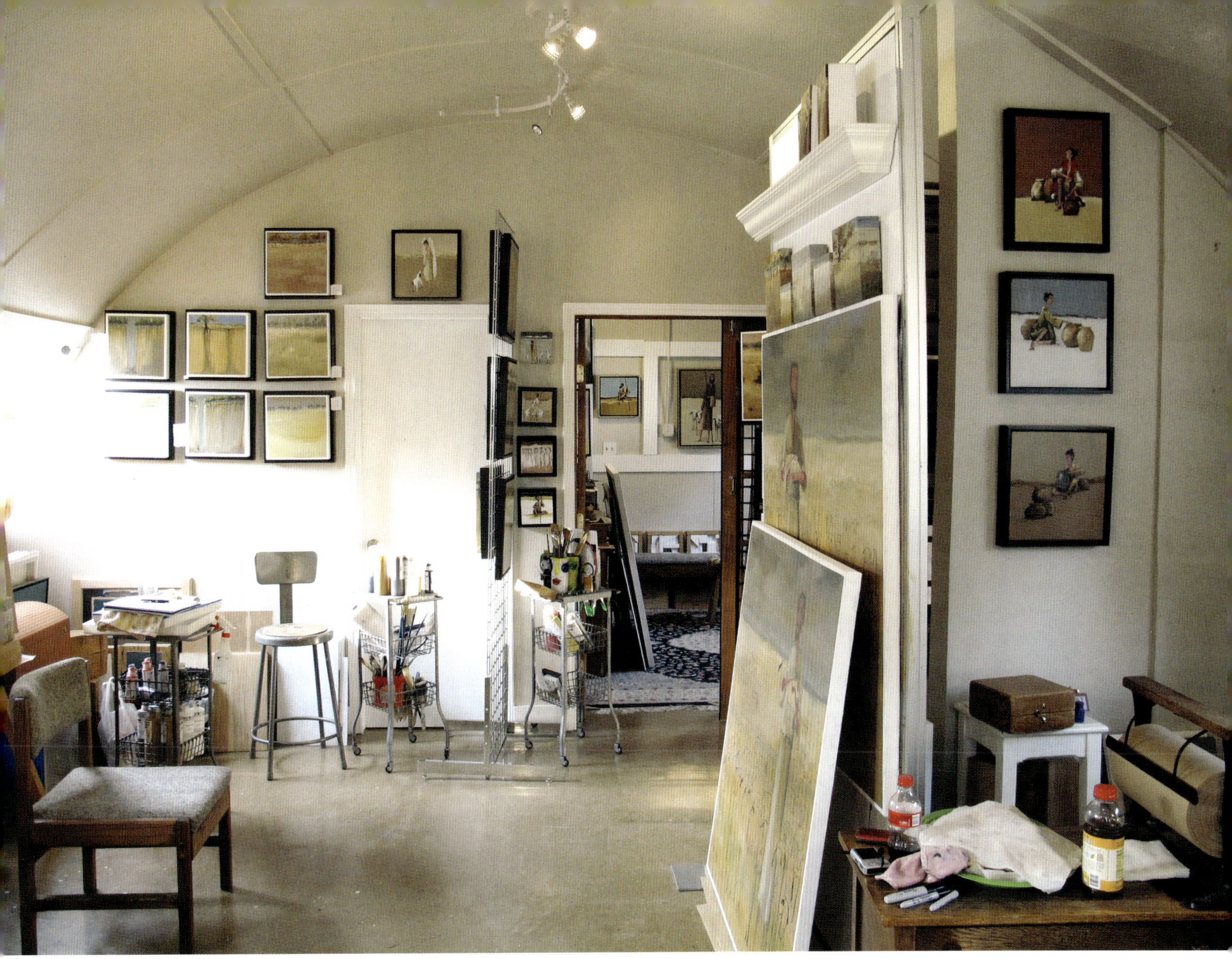

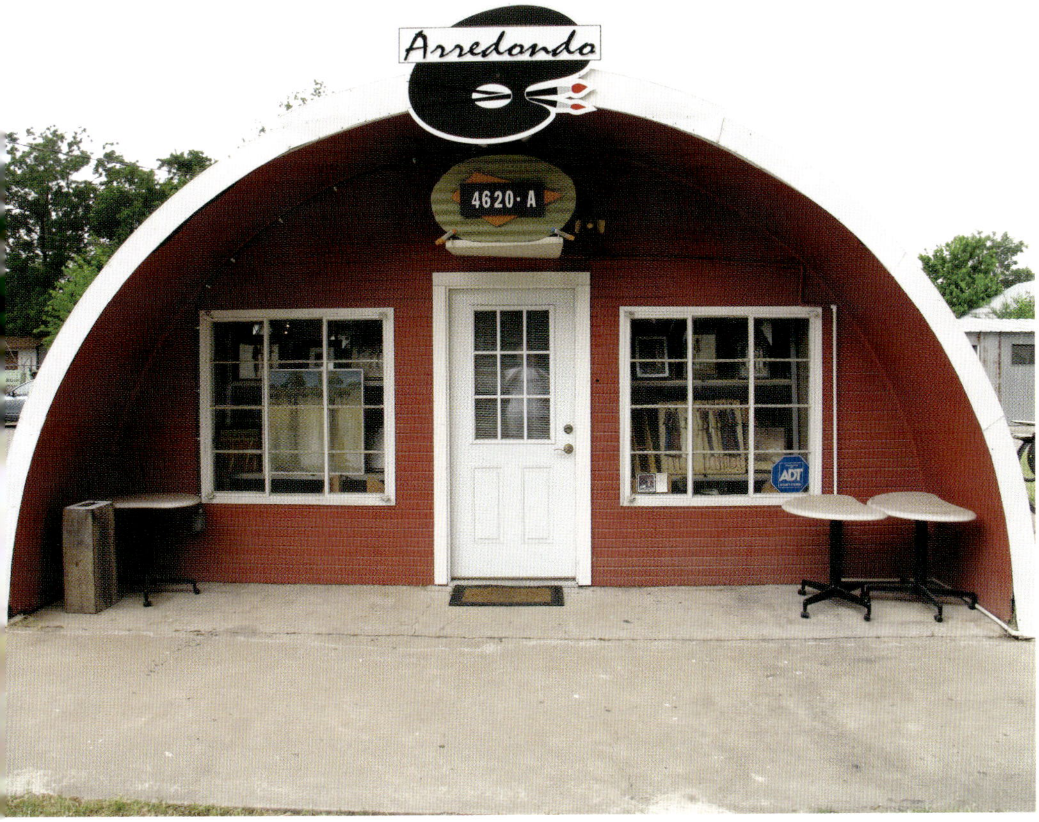

Opposite and above: Painter Dan Arredondo's studio was once a Quonset hut during World War II. One of the most important renovations was the installation of large windows.

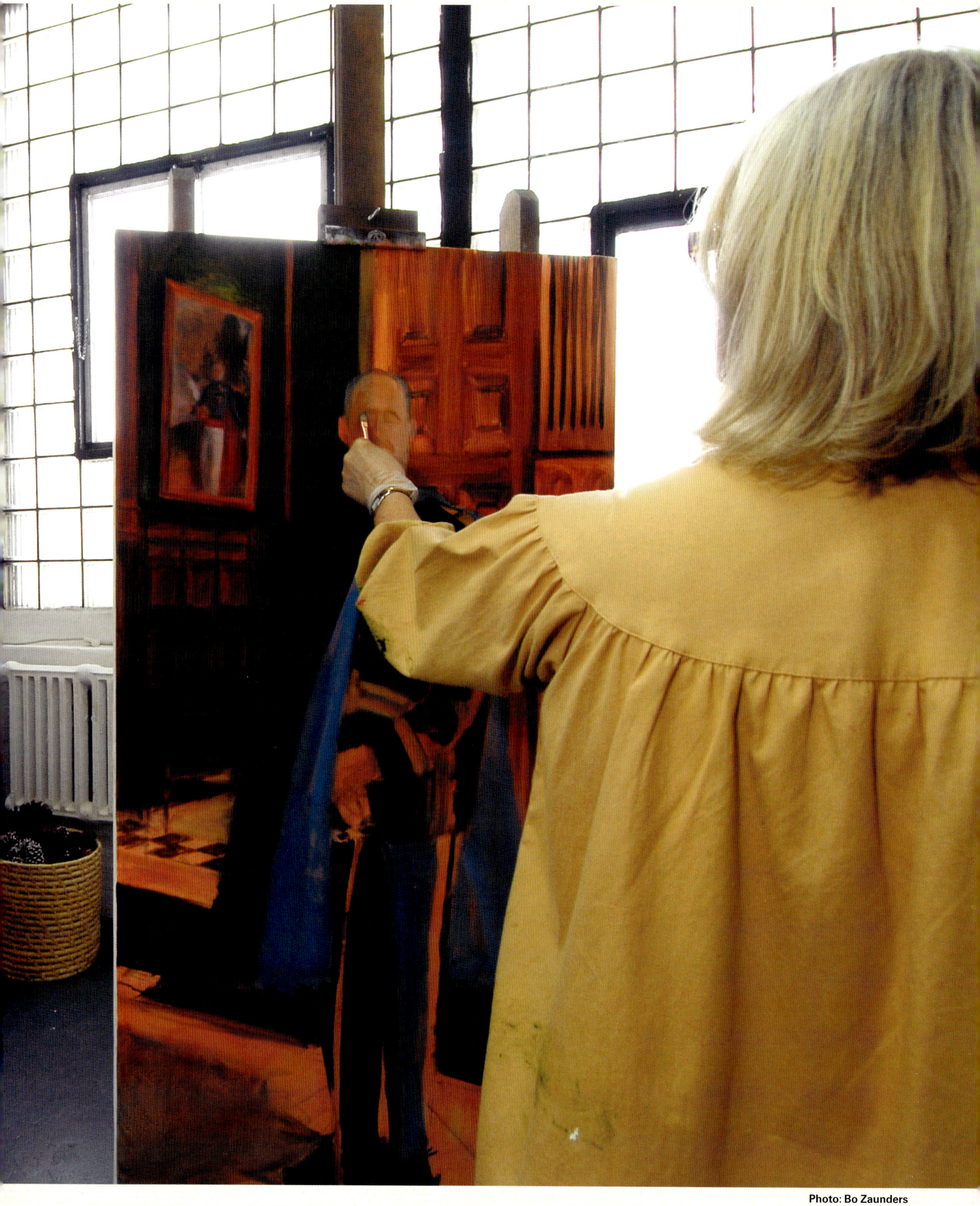

Photo: Bo Zaunders

CHAPTER TWO

Portrait Studios

"Some will not recognize the truthfulness of my mirror. Let them remember that I am not here to reflect the surface . . . but must penetrate inside. My mirror probes down to the heart. I write words on the forehead and around the corners of the mouth. My human faces are truer than the real ones."

—Paul Klee

← Betsy Ashton painting a portrait in her studio in Long Island City, New York.

Wendy Walworth-Schrijver

Creating a Space That Feels Like Home

Portraitist Wendy Walworth-Schrijver believes in engaging with her sitters to capture the subtle nuances of their personality and demeanor. She has been painting commissioned portraits for more than twenty years and has developed a working method that helps her to create dynamic compositions while capturing a genuine response to her subjects and an accurate likeness. A visit to her studio outside of Manhattan shows that part of her success comes from her working environment itself.

There is a refinement to Walworth-Schrijver's manner that is immediately apparent upon meeting her—her sense of calm permeates the entire studio. Situated on the third floor of a red-brick factory built around 1940, her space is part of a block of artists' studios carved out of large factory workrooms. As she explains the numerous renovations she made upon acquiring the 500-square-foot (46-square-meter) space, one can see the dedication and discipline that informs every painting she creates. To say that the studio needed improvement would be an understatement. The windows were cracked; the ceiling had sustained some damage from several bad storms the previous winter; some of the wooden floors had been ripped up; and there were only two electrical sockets in the room. As she approached her first winter in the space, she also discovered that the radiator had been installed backwards, making it not only nonfunctional but also extremely hazardous. "For days there was only a trickle of heat for limited hours at best," she recalls. "I siliconed and caulked the

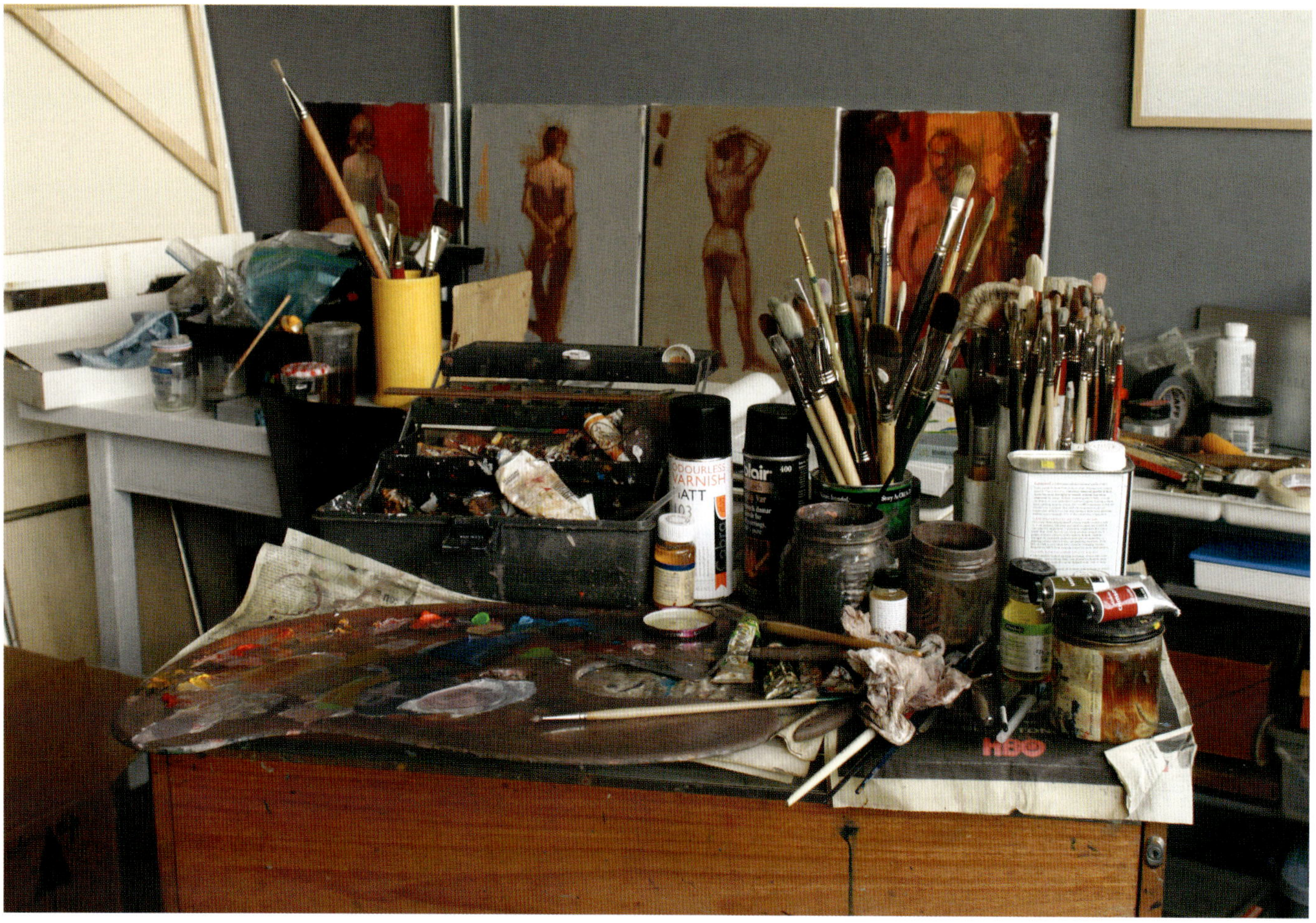

The artist's taboret.

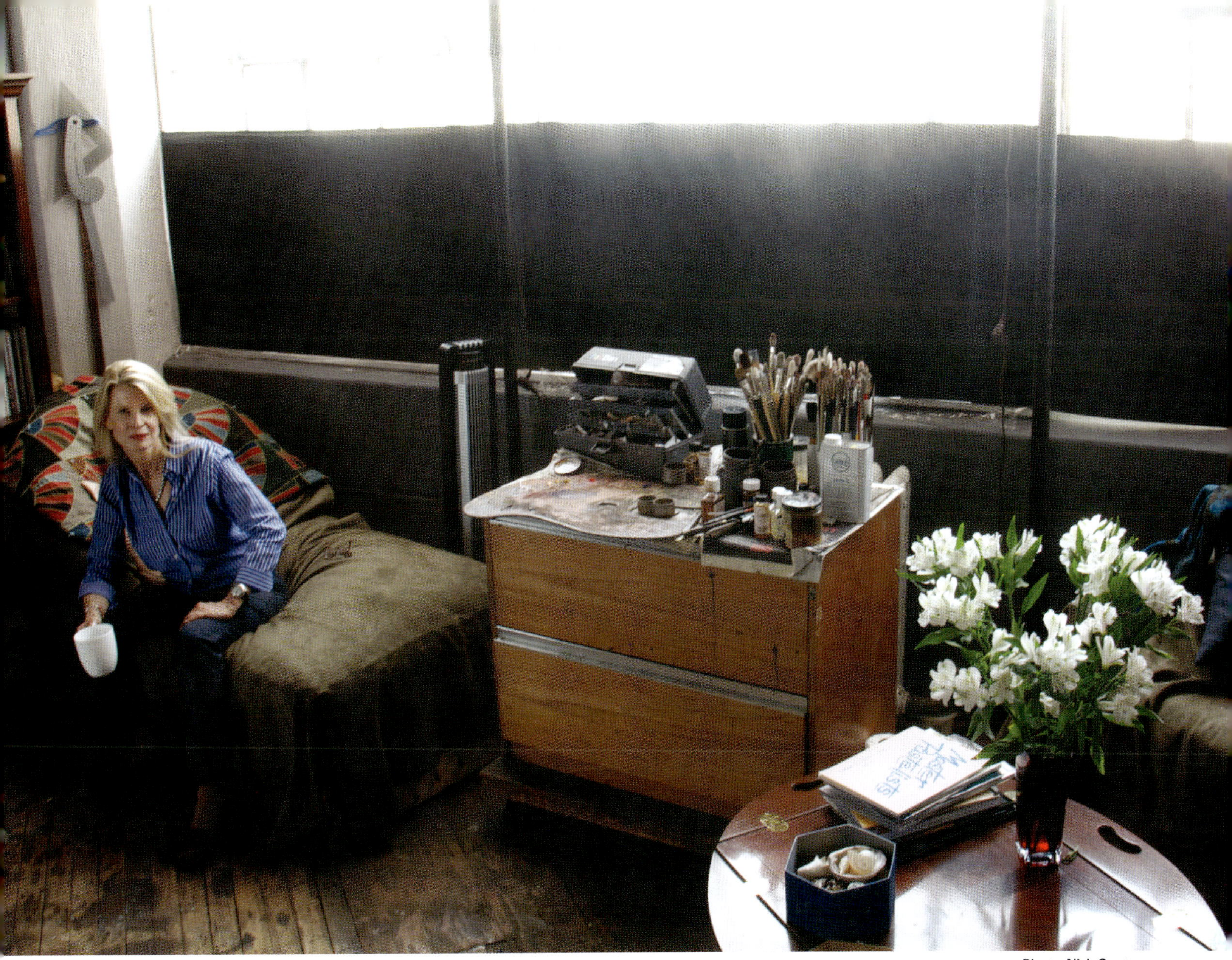

Photo: Nick Gupta

Walworth-Schrijver in her studio.

windows, covered them in a wooden frame wrapped in plastic, and prayed that the temperature outside would drop below the 40s [40° F/ 4°C] to receive the mandated allotment of heat supplied by the building."

One of the other issues that Walworth-Schrijver had to address was the lighting. The artist is accustomed to working by natural north light, and her current space gets both north and northeast illumination. Even with this ideal lighting, she did need to make some adjustments to the interior to strengthen the light that came into the space. "I painted the walls a gunship gray to cut down on the glare and intensify the cool light," she explains. "I also patched up the walls and repainted the ceiling white—it was originally black. I ordered extra-thick black mat board from New York Central Art Supply and covered the lower half of the windows to cut the glare from the two-story building across the street. The black cardboard panels are removable, and the light spills in 6 feet (2m) up from the floor, which cuts down on ledge glare." Recently, after much consideration and research, the artist bought six tubes of natural-spectrum lighting made by Verilux and installed them above the windows to bolster the light where needed. "I'm still exploring additional light sources," the artist says, "such as fluorescent cool and warm combinations with hanging mounts and fixtures, to provide more areas for painting in other parts of the studio."

Halfway into Walworth-Schrijver's studio hangs a 10-foot-high (4m) draped screen inspired by John Singer Sargent's tall screen, and a model stand on wheels that can be pulled up and stored in the corner, creating more space if needed. "I have three easels that I use constantly," the artist explains. "One is a very old, medium-size wooden easel. I recently purchased an Abiquiu easel by Richardson from Wisconsin; New York Central Art Supply was the liaison for this transaction because it took a bit of extra work to arrange for a delivery. I had an even harder time finding a painting rack that was not for lighter works, fewer works, or a hobbyist. Finally I found a solid white one through Utrecht, which can hold canvases of any height and width—and plenty of them. I was not in the market for an expensive veneered or polished wooden unit for an industrial space, but at the time the elaborate, sleek, and well-designed customized storage was very appealing."

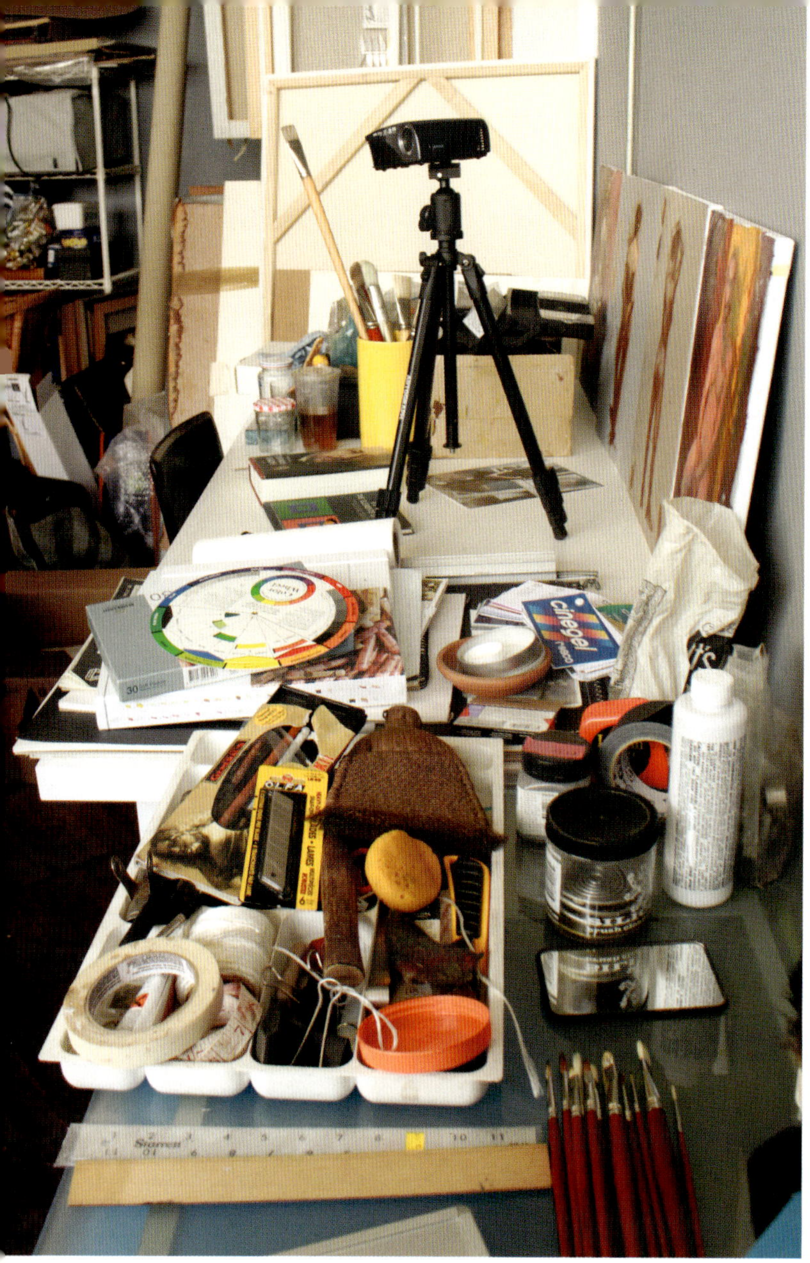

Photo: Ben Berlin

← The artist makes use of a portable projector when she needs to focus on details.

→ Walworth-Schrijver at work on a painting of President Eisenhower, commissioned by The Players Club, in New York City.

↓ This draped screen provides a neutral background for her subjects. The padded chair provides comfortable support and also has elegant detailing that aids her poses.

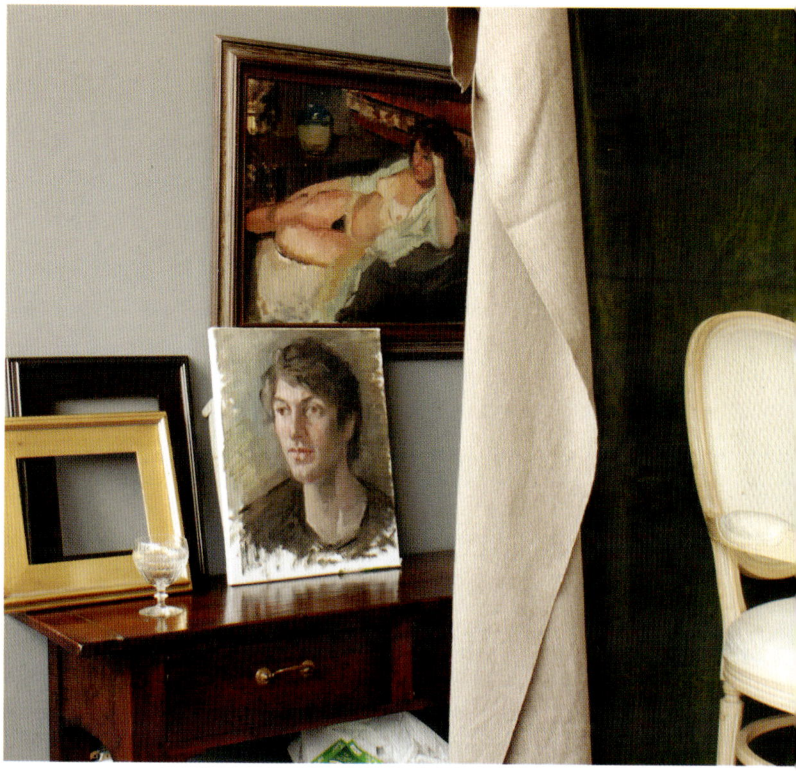

Photo: Ben Berlin

Because there are no real views from the windows, Walworth-Schrijver likes to arrange small displays of inexpensive flowers, which she purchases from a local market on her way to the studio. During my visit, the artist talked about some of the special touches and useful resources that make her studio feel like home—for both her and those who sit for a portrait. "I wanted to make it as inviting as possible so that sitters feel comfortable," she says. "I installed an air conditioner, a space heater, and generally made it more attractive and livable." For her own comfort, she keeps favorite shells and small pieces, along with magazines, a coffee maker, a chaise longue, throws, reading lamps, and plenty of bookcases filled with art books. "These touches make it an appealing place to be for eight hours a day," she says. "I also like to play my favorite jazz artists such as Charles Mingus or John Coltrane, as well as Steely Dan and the Allman Brothers. Having a studio that reflects my identity is essential. It enables me to center myself and focus on what is important and what I want to accomplish."

For more information on Wendy Walworth-Schrijver, visit her website at www.wendywalworth.com.

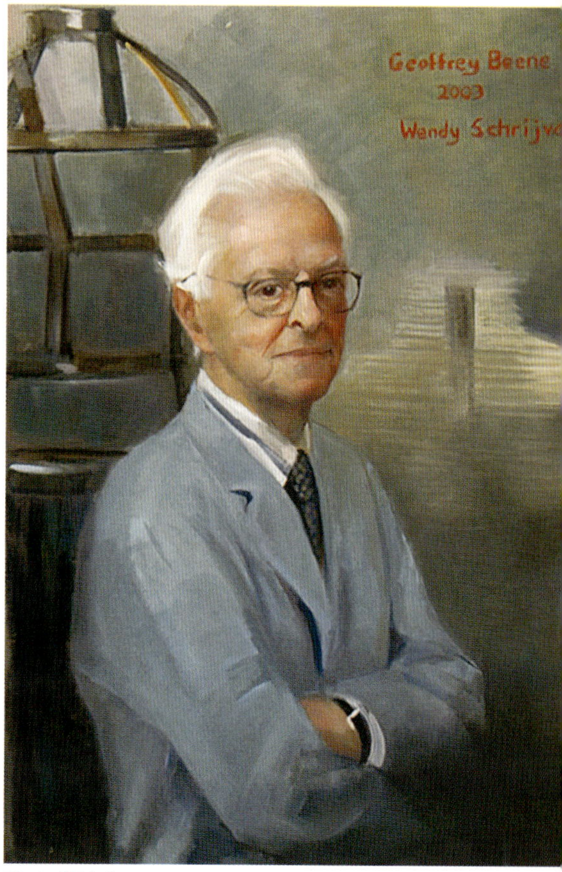

Geoffrey Beene
by Wendy Walworth-Schrijver, 2003, oil, 36" x 24" (91cm x 61cm). Private collection.

Photo: Nick Gupta

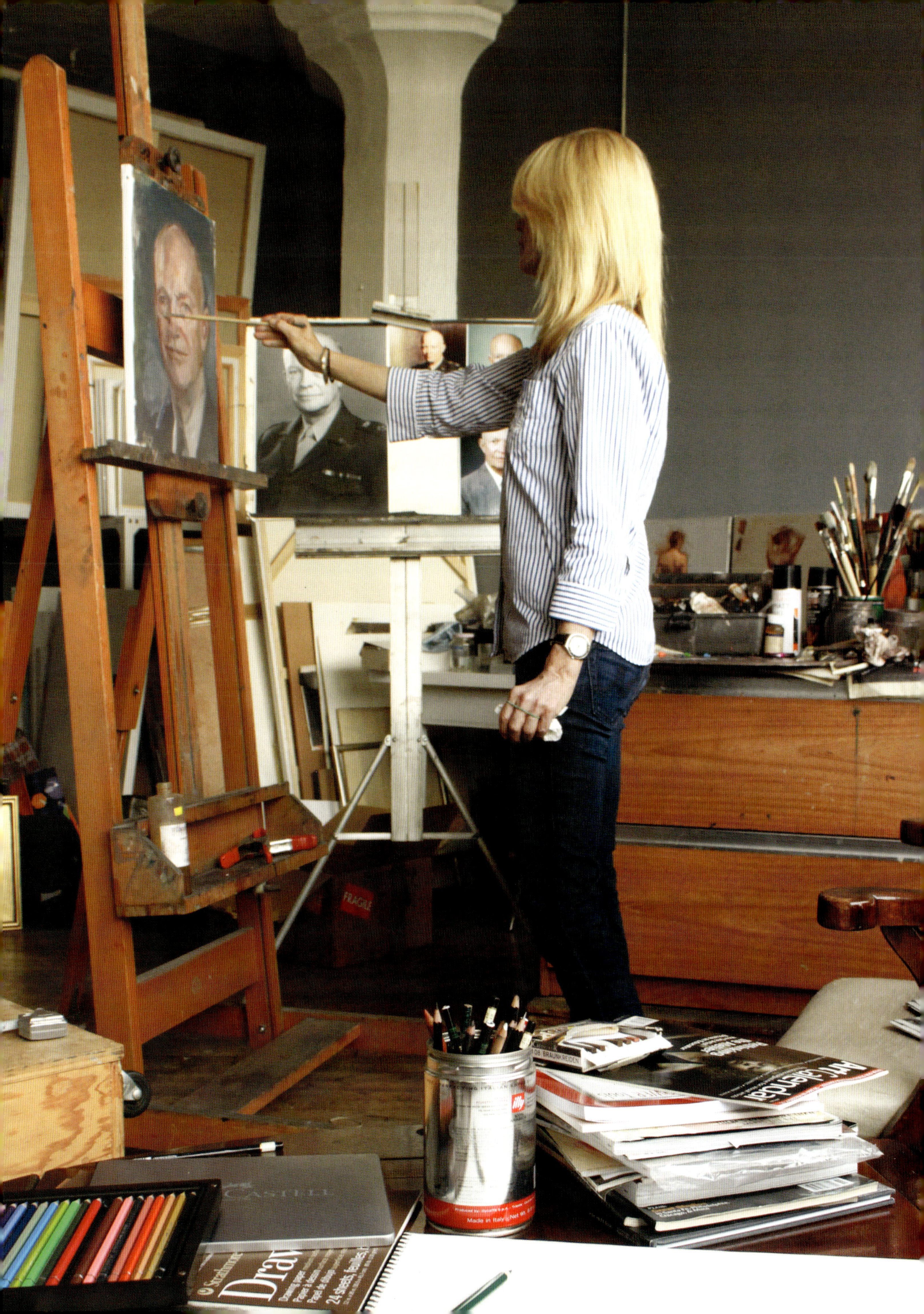
FRAGILE
Art Calendar
Strathmore

Betsy Ashton

Creating a Space You Won't Want to Leave

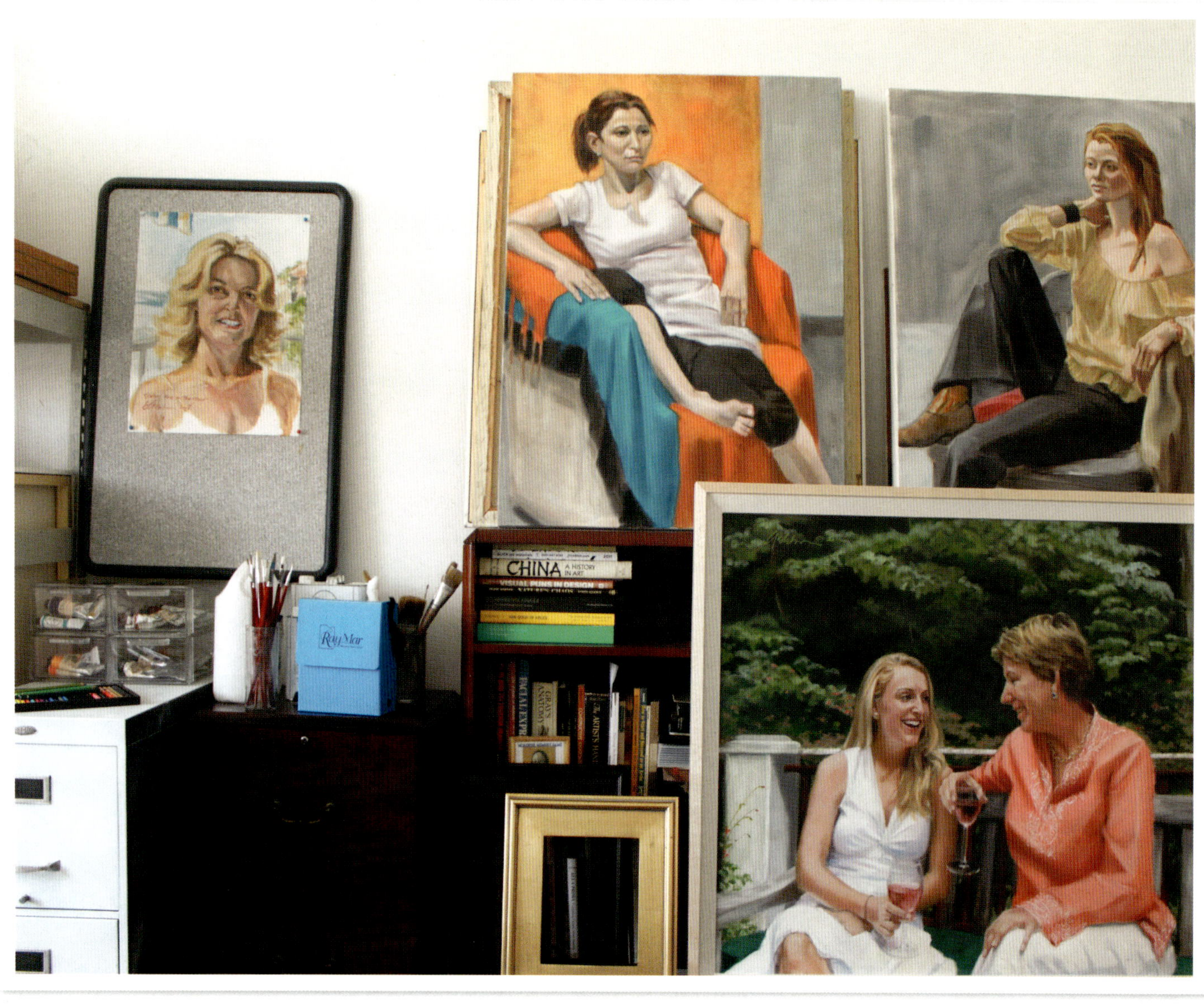

Photo: Ben Berlin

Before becoming a full-time artist, Betsy Ashton was a radio and television news reporter and anchor in Washington, D.C., and later in New York City. "That was an insatiable, lucrative, and fun career that lasted twenty years," Ashton says. "I returned to painting in 2006, and after two years of 'tuning up' my dormant skills at the National Academy School of Fine Arts and the Art Students League of New York, I went out on my own."

Ashton first rented a small studio space at the Women's Studio Center, in Long Island City, New York, but she mostly used it as a storage space for her old art supplies and canvases. When the center dissolved three years ago, "I moved across the street into Reis Studios. Reis Studios is a community of artists located in an old factory building in what used to be a manufacturing district. Last spring I moved to a slightly larger space with north light, brought in some of my old home-office furniture, rigged up a very portable stand for models, and I couldn't be happier."

As with many artists, the layout of Ashton's studio evolved organically. Through another painter, she bought old easels, a file cabinet, a rolling computer stand that she uses as a taboret, a desk and chair, a bookcase, some wonderful art books, a small refrigerator, and other useful items at "fire-sale prices," she says. She was able to create an office

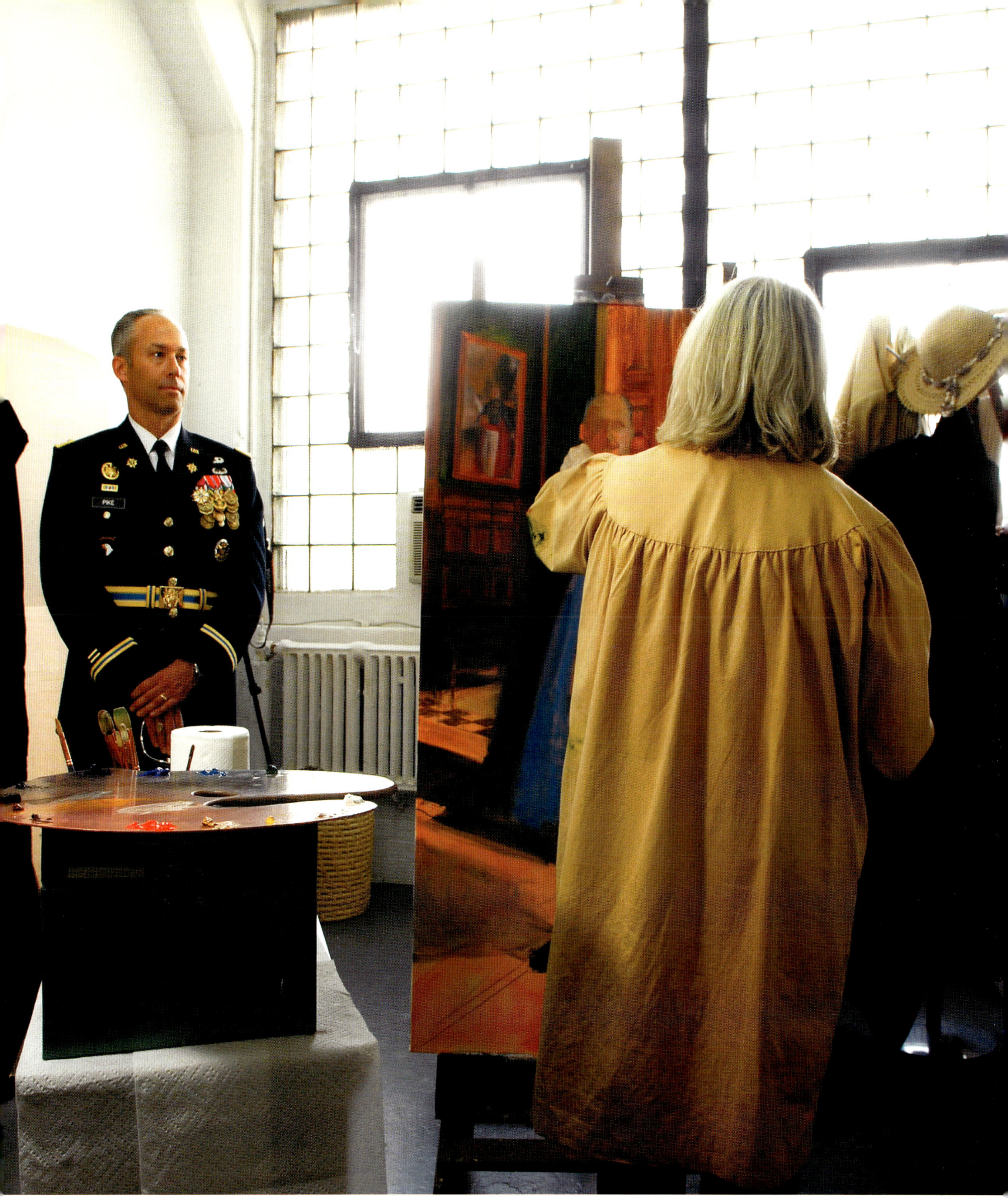

Photo: Bo Zaunders

Ashton's studio provides ample natural light through large windows. To make sure her tools are easily accessible, she keeps her palette on a makeshift stand that reaches hip height. "I use what was a rolling computer stand," she says. "I place my large palette on top of the stand and have a roll of paper towels and brushes spread out beside it. The stand also has a niche for legroom that perfectly holds my lidded garbage can—very handy for tossing paint-filled paper towels."

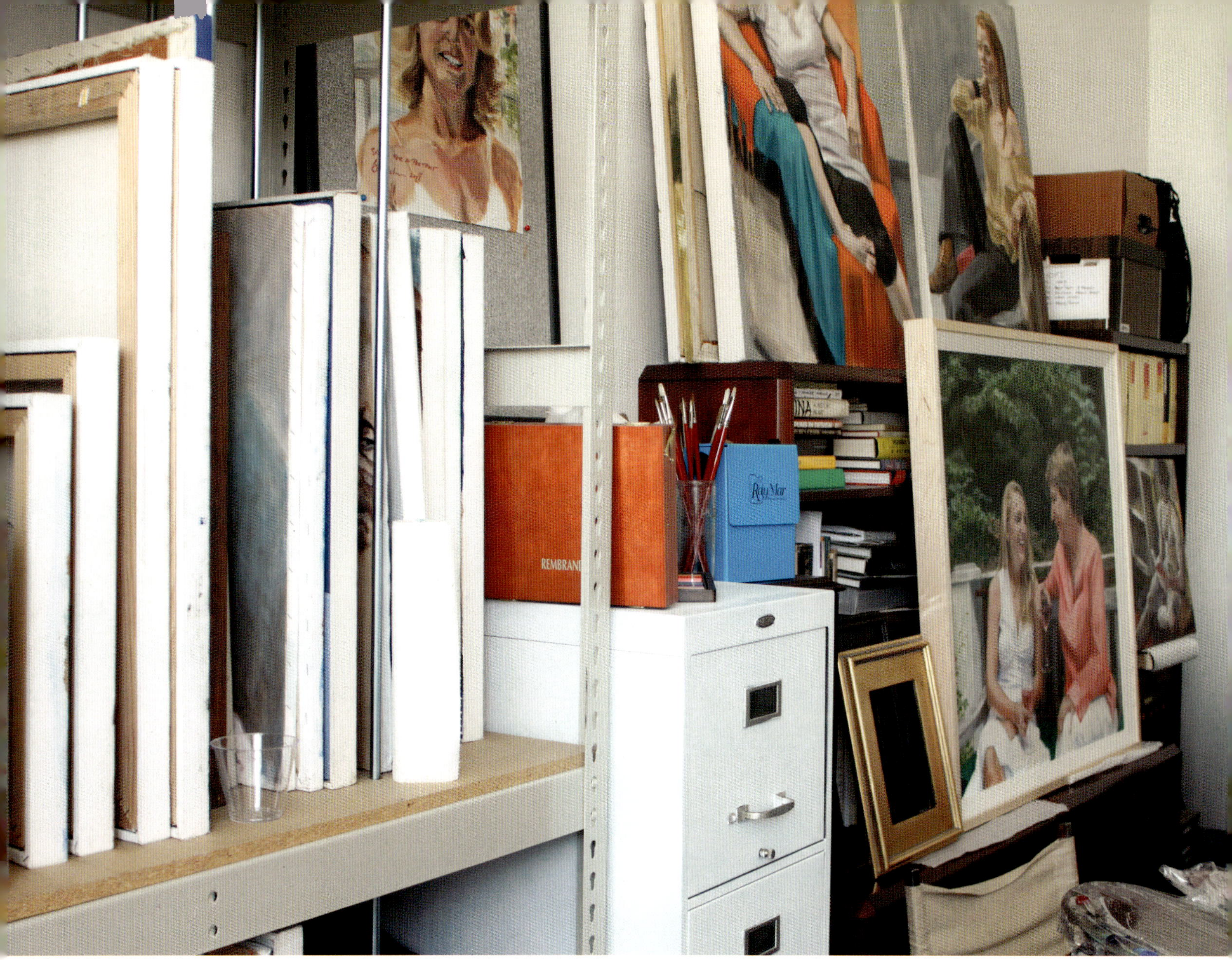

↑ Ashton has several racks for storing canvases.

Photo: Ben Berlin

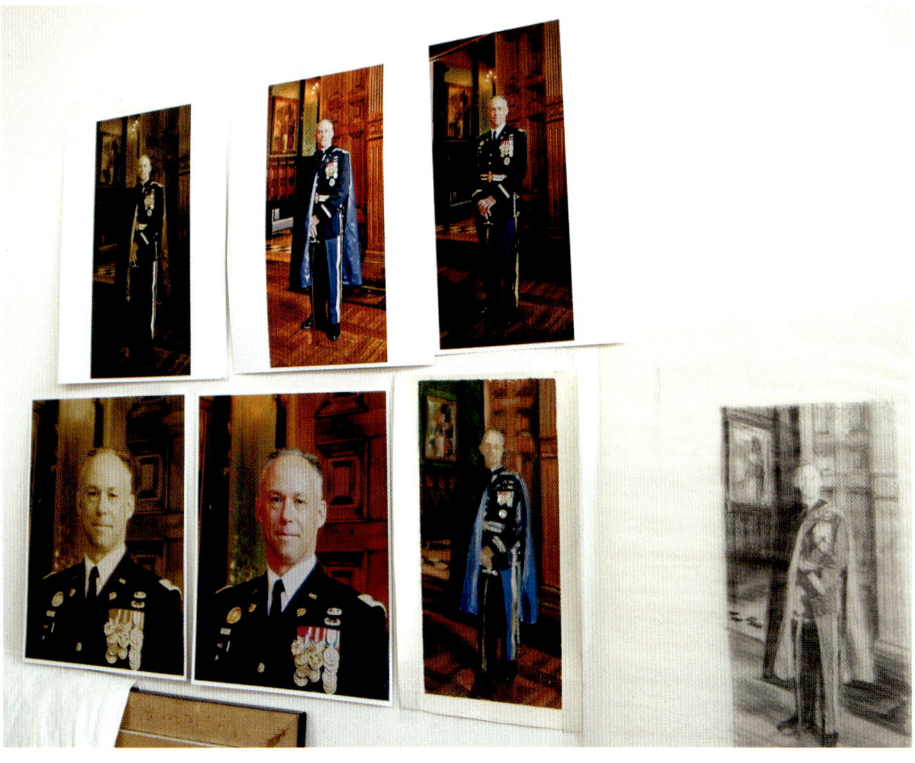

Photo: Bo Zaunders

For her portrait of U.S. Army Lieutenant Colonel Thomas Pike Jr., Ashton took several reference photographs and created detailed drawings to help her determine the best composition.

area, a painting area, and a storage area. "My first real purchase was a metal rack of warehouse shelving for the canvases, and I got a handyman to help me put it up. Planning was mainly a question of what would fit along the wall space and away from the old radiator that runs full-length under glass brick windows. Gradually, I replaced the desk, files, and bookcases with solid cherry pieces from my old home office and put the old stuff out in the hall for someone else to make use of."

Every year Ashton participates in the Long Island City Arts Open festival, during which she opens her studio to the public for a weekend. "I send e-mail invitations to a long list of friends, family, clients, and potential clients, and

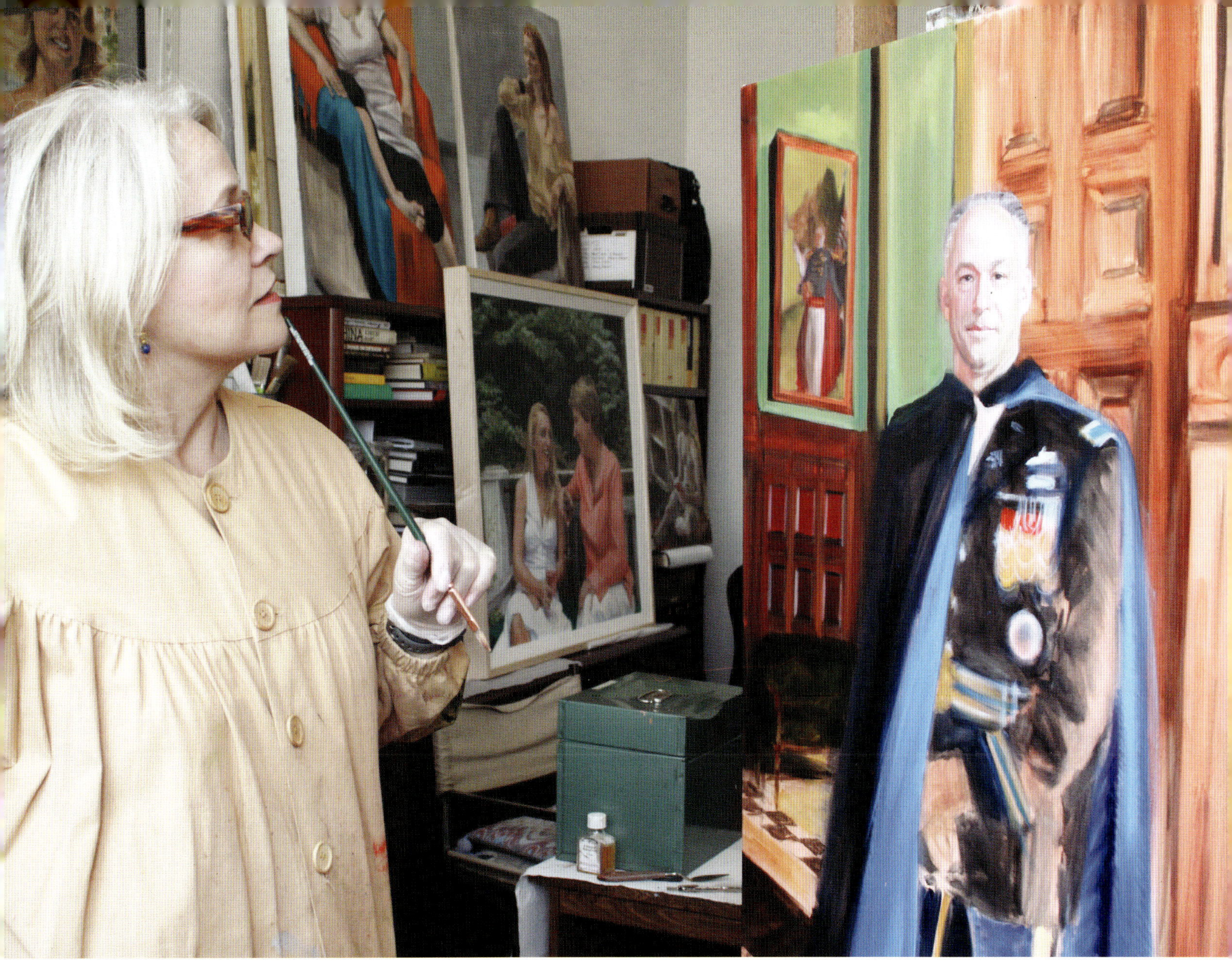

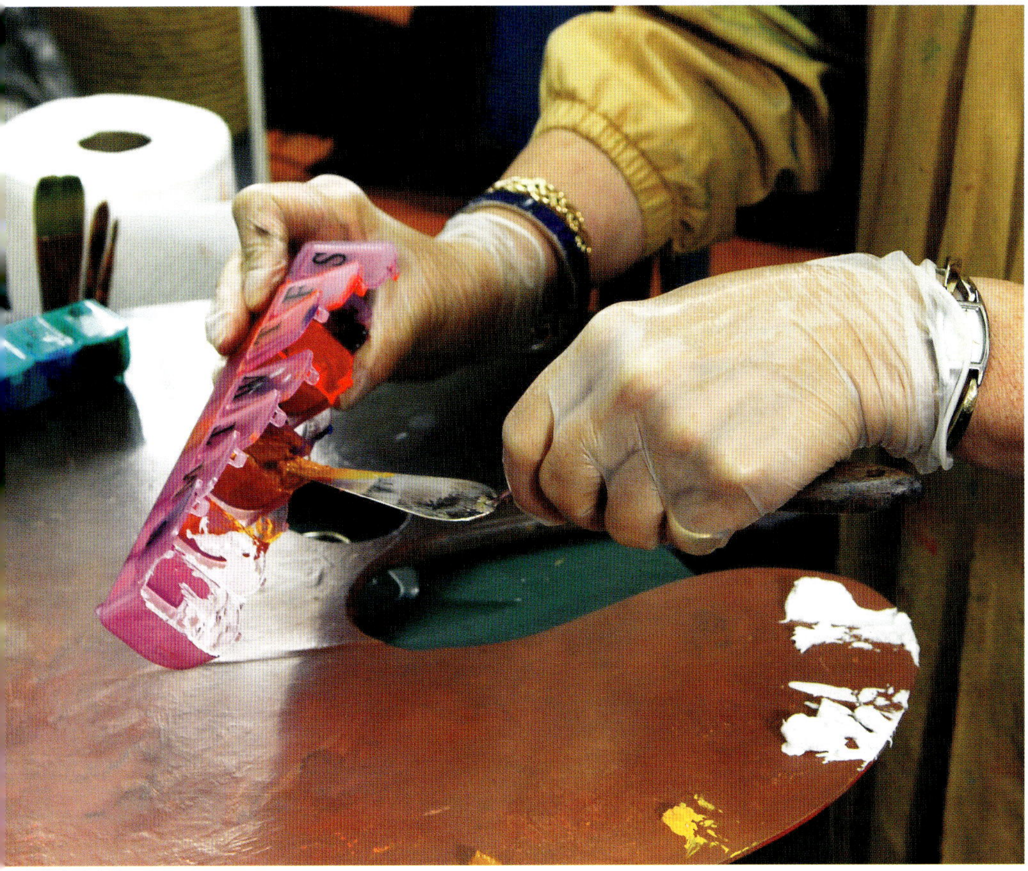

Photo: Bo Zaunders

↑ "I interview my subjects extensively, watching their natural gestures and poses, and listening to what they say about spaces and places that have special meaning for them," the artist explains. "Then we go to that location, and I do an extensive photo shoot on-site."

Photo: Ben Berlin

← The artist stores her paints in pill containers in the freezer in between sessions.

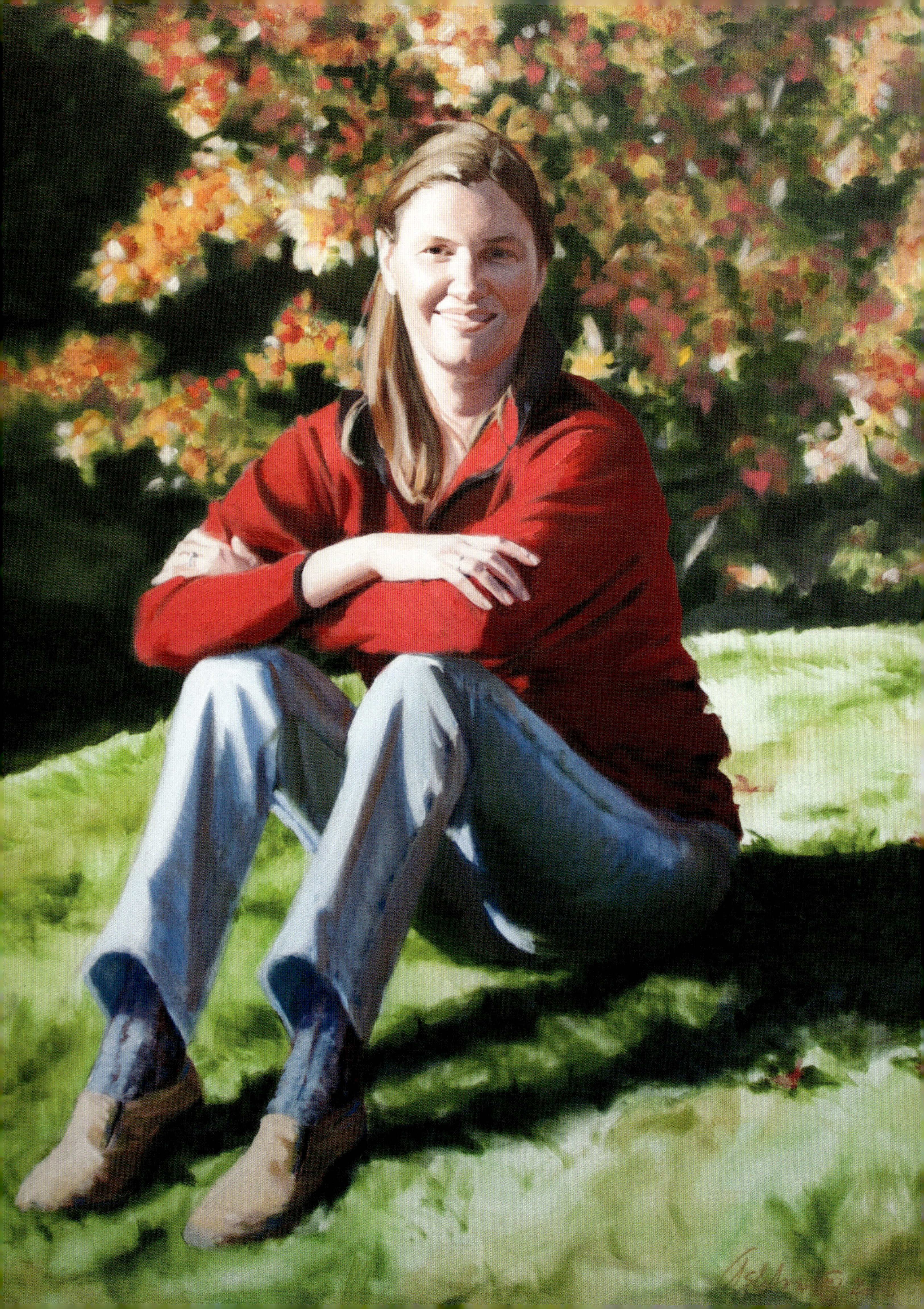

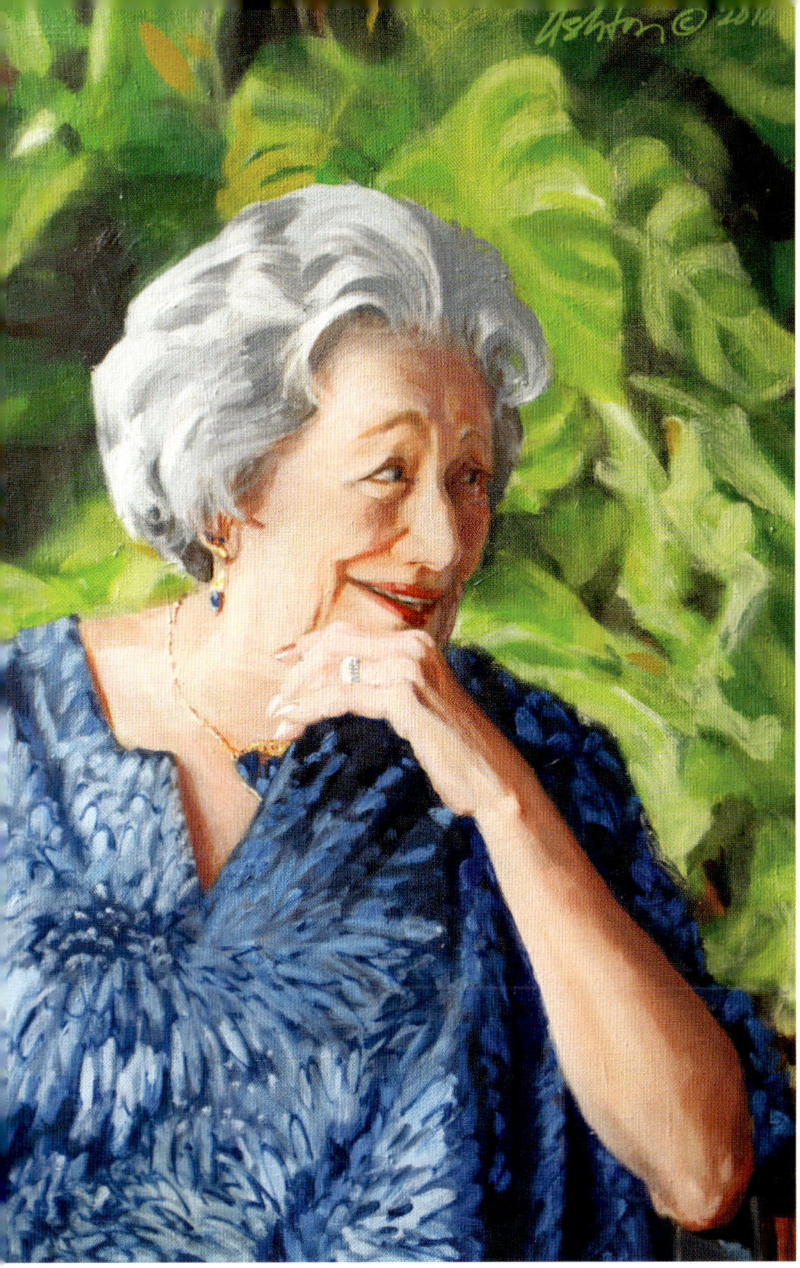

Photo: Bo Zaunders

↑ **Connie Shaland Rabinowitz**
by Betsy Ashton, 2010, oil on linen, 24" x 18" (61cm x 46cm). Private collection.

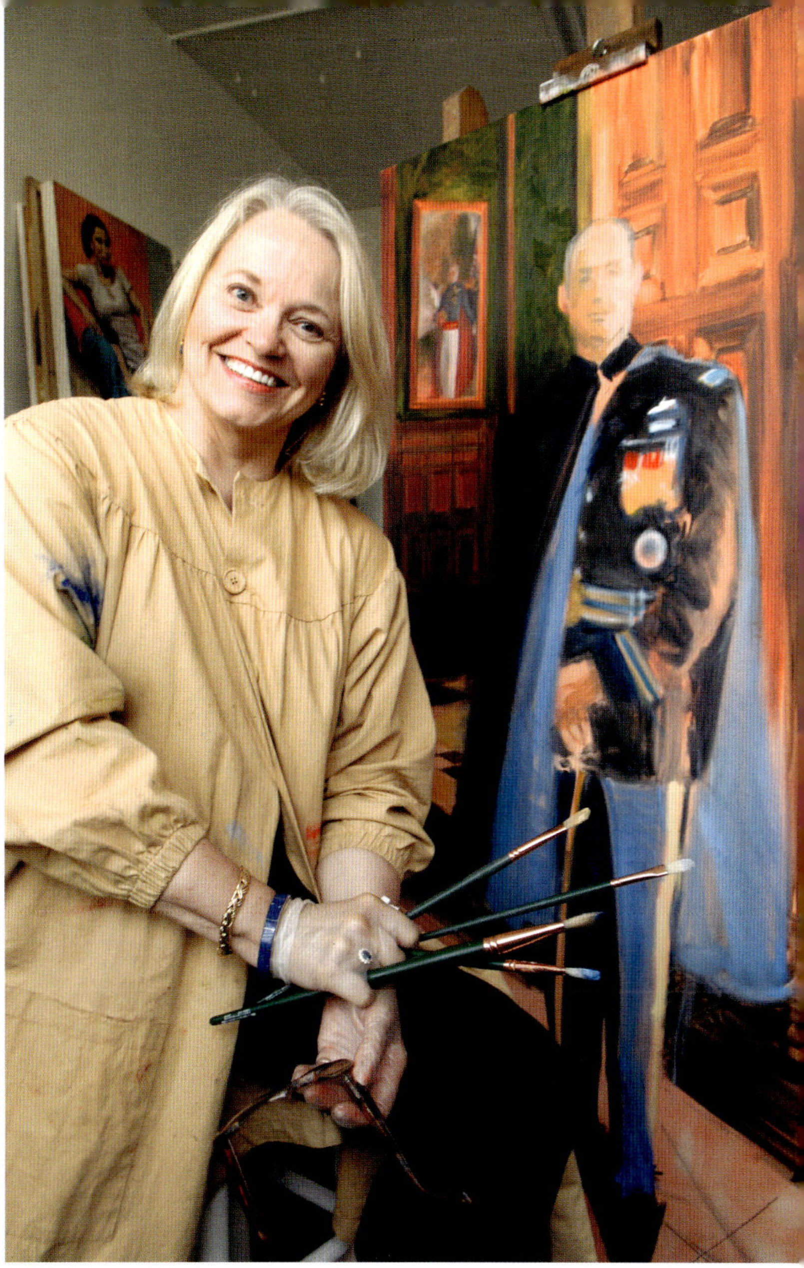

Photo: Bo Zaunders

After twenty years as a news reporter and anchor, Ashton returned to art full-time in 2006.

← **Portrait of Susan Tveekrem**
by Betsy Ashton, 2010, oil, 48" x 36" (122cm x 91cm). Private collection.

then I clean up the studio for the event," she says. "This involves picking up the model platform, arranging recent paintings on easels, and placing my portfolio and guest book on stands where visitors can peruse all of my work, procedures, and prices and leave comments and their contact information for future events. And, of course, my partner, Jim, comes in and sets up a wine bar and serves nuts, cheese, and nibbles—we all have a great time."

"I love the time I spend in my studio," she continues. "It is my space alone, not shared with anyone else or for any other purposes. I feel wonderfully peaceful and productive there, even when a painting needs a lot of work." For many artists, having a home studio is the ideal setup to foster creativity and prevent procrastination. Ashton, on the other hand, has found that distance makes the heart grow fonder—even if it is only a four-block commute. "I think the fact that my studio is outside my home is very important," she says. "I have to get up in the morning and go somewhere to work, just as I used to do when I worked in television news. There are three floors of studios in my building, filled with working artists of all ages. It's great to be in a totally quiet space near other artists who are working behind closed doors. It's not a place for dabblers, and the atmospheric energy, aspirations, and professionalism rub off on all of us and keep us going on those otherwise uninspired days."

For more on Betsy Ashton, visit her website at www.ashtonportraits.com.

John Howard Sanden
A Studio Visit

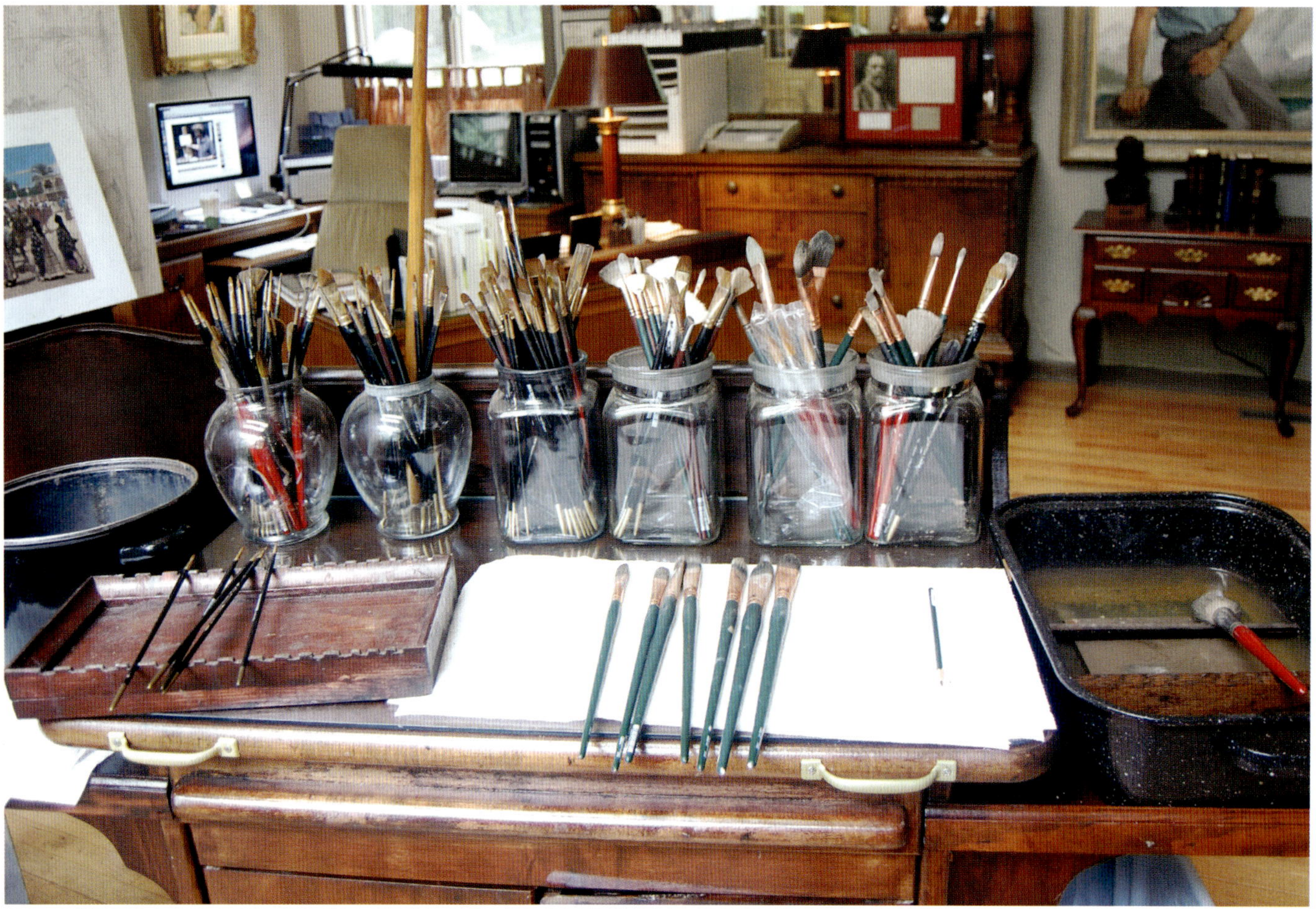

The brush table stands to the right of the artist's easel. The tray on the right contains mineral spirits, and the pot on the left is a brush cleaner.

For the last several decades, John Howard Sanden has reigned as one of the finest and most admired portrait painters in the United States. His pictures brilliantly combine acute observational skills with rich color and lively, open brushing. But Sanden's real strength is finding warmth and accessibility in his sitters, even when the nature of the commission demands a sense of decorum and formality. In his portraits, one can find a smile playing around the mouth of the CEO of a great company; the state governor with a twinkle in his eye; or a socialite in a ravishing gown who seems to be enjoying life to the full. It is certainly this sense of powerful human connection that accounts for the artist's extraordinary success. His client list of cabinet members, university presidents, and business magnates also includes African kings, cowboys, and evangelists, as well as family and friends. Already showered with professional awards and wide recognition, the artist recently received the most coveted commission in his field, an official White House portrait, this one of former President George W. Bush.

As a top professional, it is hardly surprising that Sanden works in a highly organized setting. His studio is custom-built onto the side of his home in Ridgefield, Connecticut, a space that is open and gracious in proportion without being in any way overwhelming or ostentatious. "I made it exactly the same size as Norman Rockwell's studio," says the artist. "I visited him several times, and I actually went out there and measured the building. It's 24 feet x 24 feet (7m x 7m) and 16 feet (5m) high at the apex of the ceiling." The bulk of the daylight in the space comes from a generous stretch of north-facing windows. The floor is made of finished hardwood, and it's spotless, even under the artist's easel. "I used to say to people that a tube

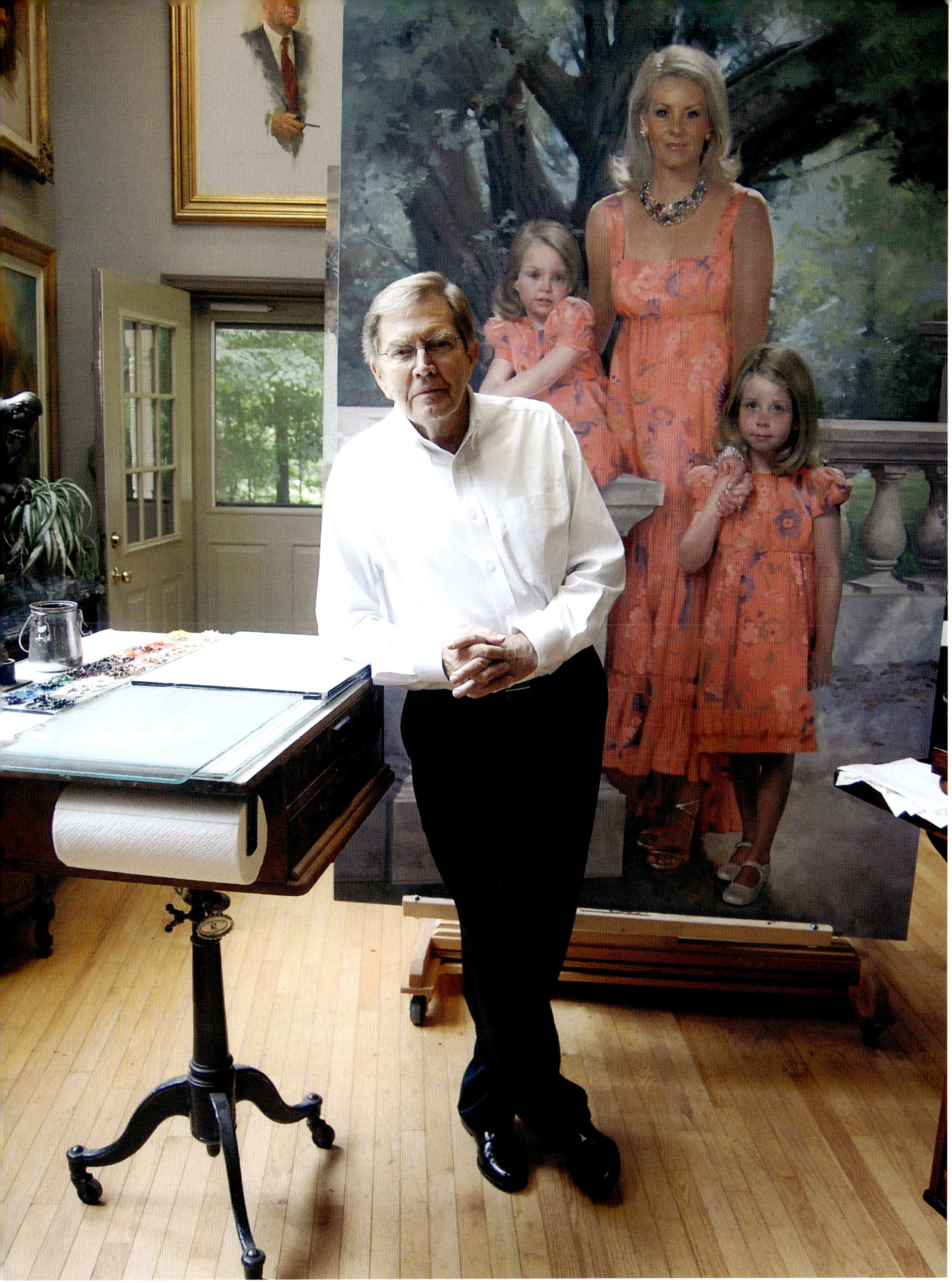

Sanden in his studio. The table is equipped with two glass palettes. Another long piece of glass carries two lines of paint—regular colors and Sanden's own Pro-Mix line of colors.

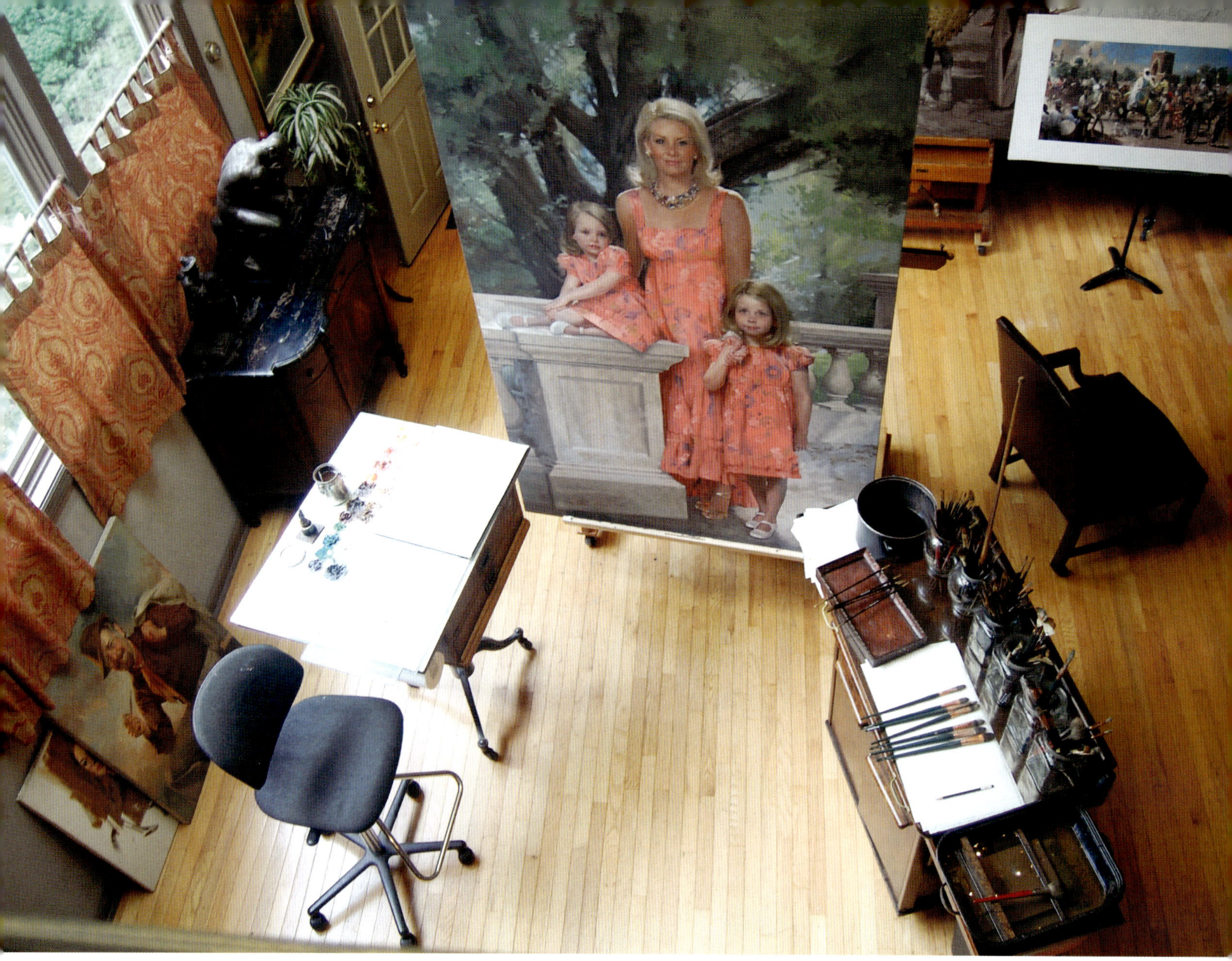

The studio from above.

of cadmium red costs thirty-two dollars, so I can't afford to put the paint anywhere else but on the canvas," the artist says with a smile.

Hanging from the ceiling is a large gold chandelier that adds a note of luxury to what is largely a utilitarian setting. A railed gallery, accessible from a bedroom in the house, looks down onto the space from the west side, contributing a further grace note. Beneath it, a pair of doors leads into a modest storage room and a small sitting room. The storage room is equipped with a line of painting racks, although Sanden says—like almost every artist—that there is never enough storage space.

The main studio area is dominated by a large Hughes easel, an ingenious device that allows the artist to raise and lower the canvas at the touch of a finger. The daylight coming from the north-facing windows on the left can be supplemented by two large fluorescent fixtures to provide even illumination across the canvas. To the left of the easel, a small paint table is equipped with a glass palette on which the artist has laid out two lines of color. On the outer edge is a standard selection of colors, such as cadmium red and yellow and ultramarine blue. Alongside these is a line of colors that the artist has had manufactured: the Sanden Pro-Mix colors, a set of premixed combinations that the artist repeatedly finds useful in painting flesh and that are now available commercially. These are joined by a small container of clove oil, which the artist adds to each pile of paint to slow its drying time. A bracket at the side of the table holds a roll of paper towels, and two small drawers hold tubes of paint.

To the right of the easel stands an old wooden kitchen cart that Sanden has customized with an extra shelf to hold his brush storage pan. The surface is covered with glass on which is placed a line of jars holding a wealth of brushes and a mahlstick. Next to them stand a large container for cleaning brushes and a tray containing mineral oil, on which the artist lays brushes for storage while painting. The cupboard below provides storage for cans of mineral spirits, the only medium the artist ever adds to his paint. A short distance in front of the large easel, a smaller easel holds a mirror, which the artist uses to view his painting with fresh eyes from time to time.

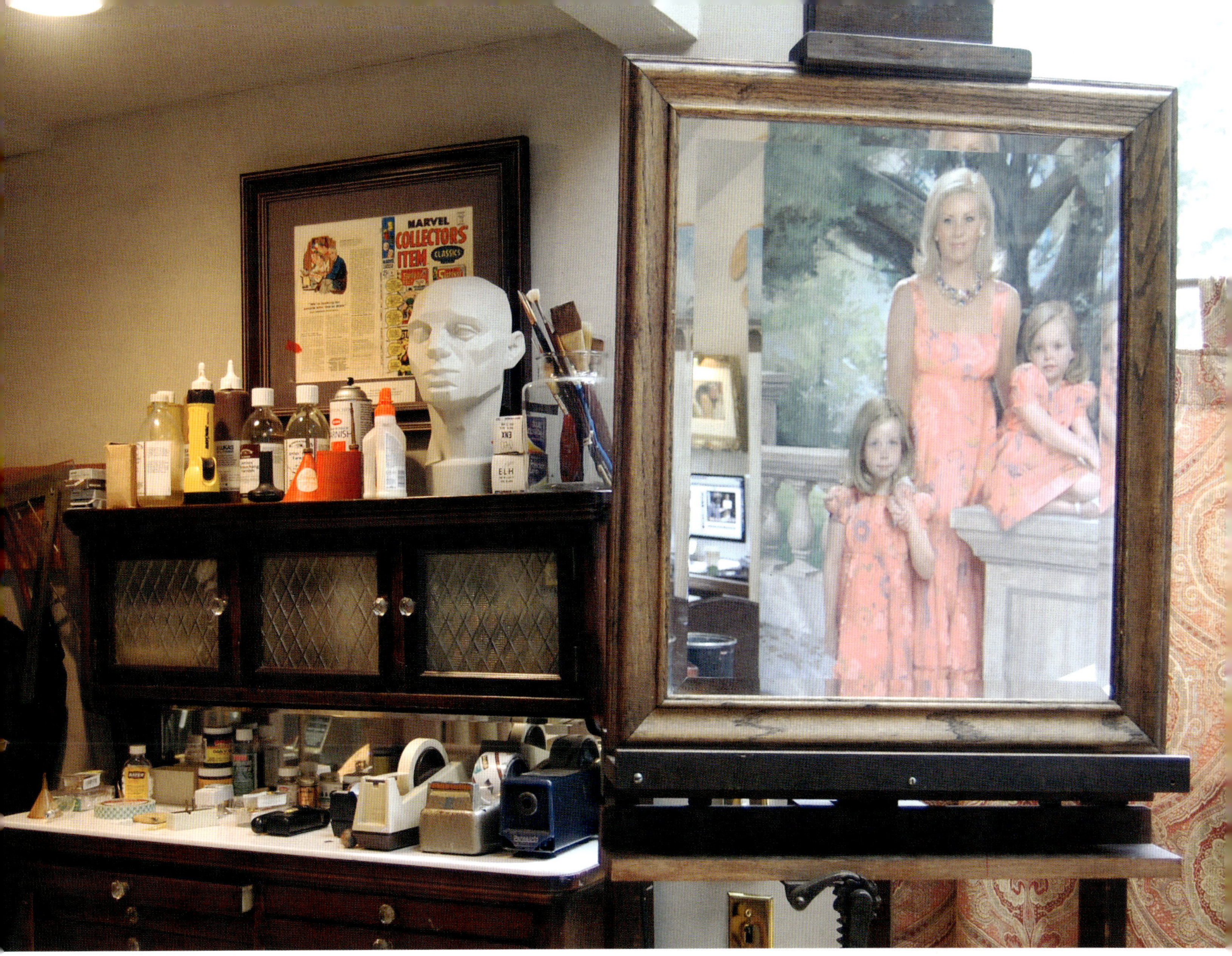

↑ A mirror allows the artist to view his work with fresh eyes. Behind it an antique dentist's cabinet holds miscellaneous supplies.

→ Fresh tubes of paint are carefully stacked in a custom dispenser.

↓ Shelving in Sanden's storage room.

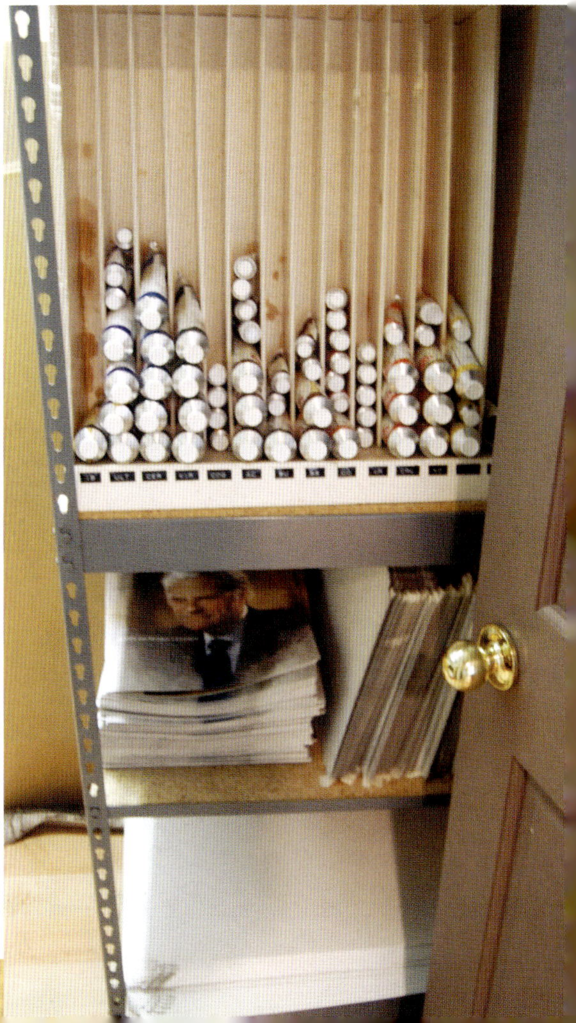

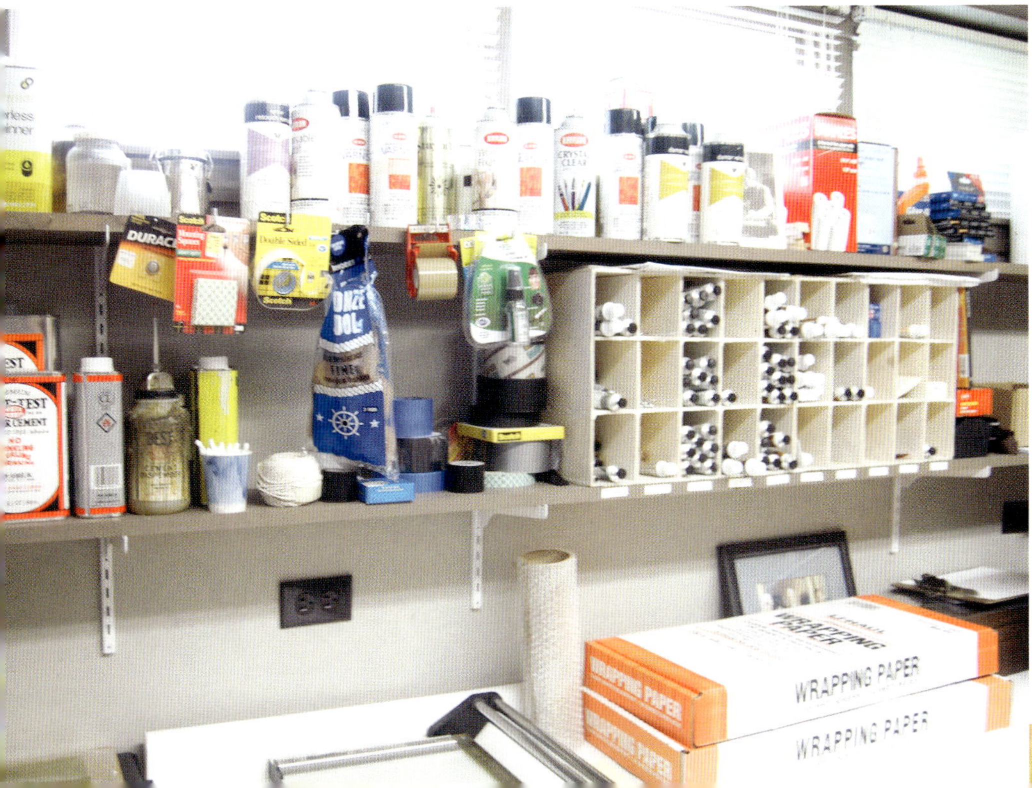

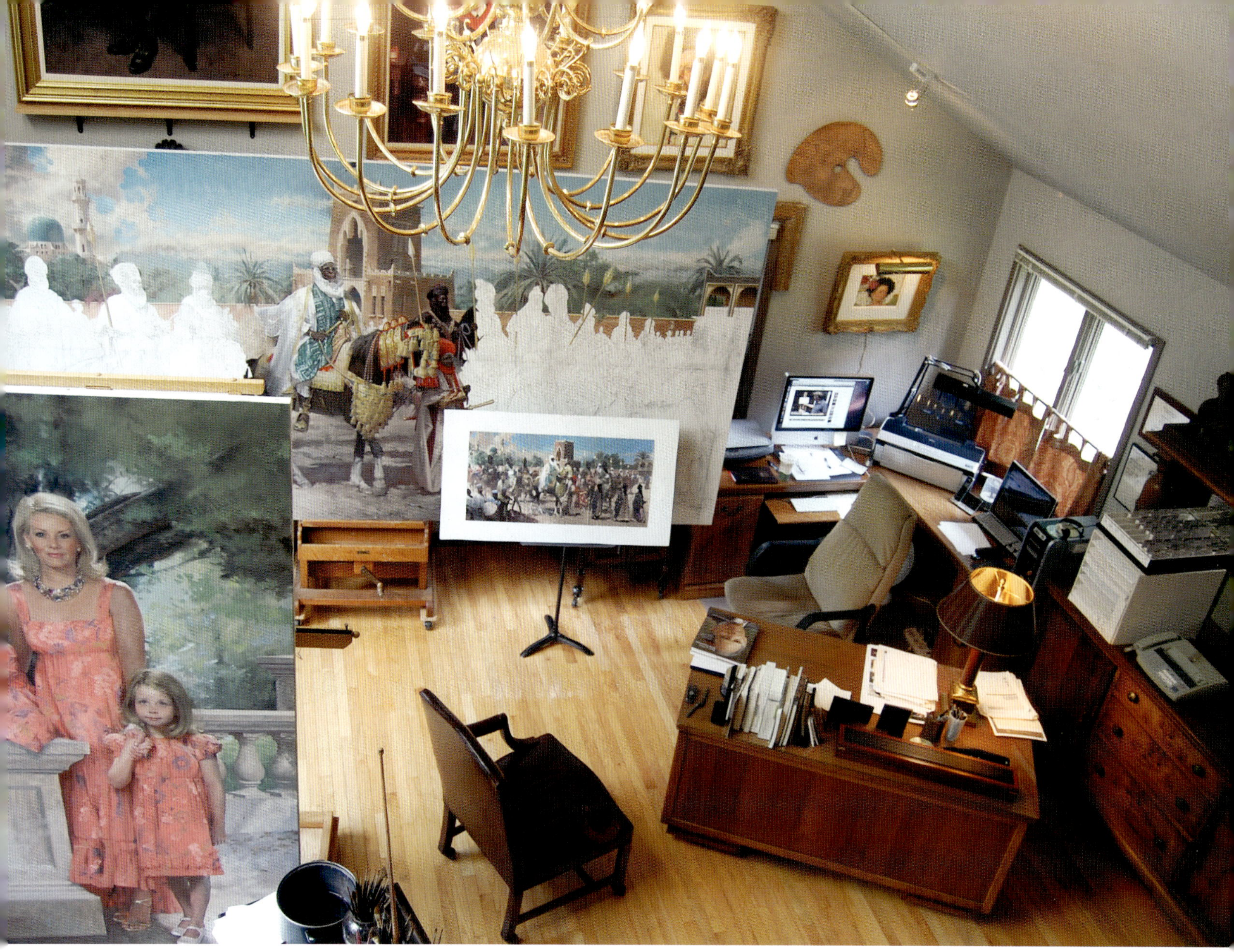

One corner of Sanden's studio serves as an office and computer area, with an Apple computer, a scanner, and a large format inkjet printer. Although he prefers to paint from life, the artist has found digital photography to be indispensable, especially with clients who have busy schedules. The small portrait in the corner is by Sanden's most influential teacher, Samuel Edmund Oppenheim.

All these furnishings are on wheels so that they can be moved around as required. An adjustable-height drafting chair allows the artist all the sitting options that he needs. In a nearby corner, an old dentist's cabinet is used to store tubes of paint, as well as pencils, erasers, and all the smaller paraphernalia of the artist's craft. Across the room, bookshelves display a wealth of art books that the artist continually combs through for inspiration and ideas. John Singer Sargent and Diego Velázquez feature prominently in Sanden's conversation on art.

Further inspiration is provided by various small sculptures placed on shelves around the room, including a copy of Rodin's *The Thinker*. In addition to Rodin, Sanden also greatly admires the sculpture of Daniel Chester French. "Although he worked within a conventional framework, he produced artwork of extraordinary power," says Sanden. This same statement could reflect, perhaps, an ambition for his own work. The walls of the studio are hung with a mixture of Sanden's own paintings and those of artists he has known or admired, including a piece by John Stobart, the marine painter, who once took a course with the artist, and a painting by Samuel Edmund Oppenheim, Sanden's most influential teacher.

Although the bulk of the main studio is given over to painting, one corner serves as an office and computer station, featuring a large desktop Apple computer and a high-end color printer. Sanden is forthright about his embrace of digital photography and computer software in preparing for his portraits. "I never got involved in the photography-versus-direct-painting debate," he says. "I originally trained as an illustrator and have always been comfortable using photographic reference. Years ago I worked in the same building as Charles Baskerville, who was an old-school portrait painter and never owned a camera in his life. He wouldn't dream of

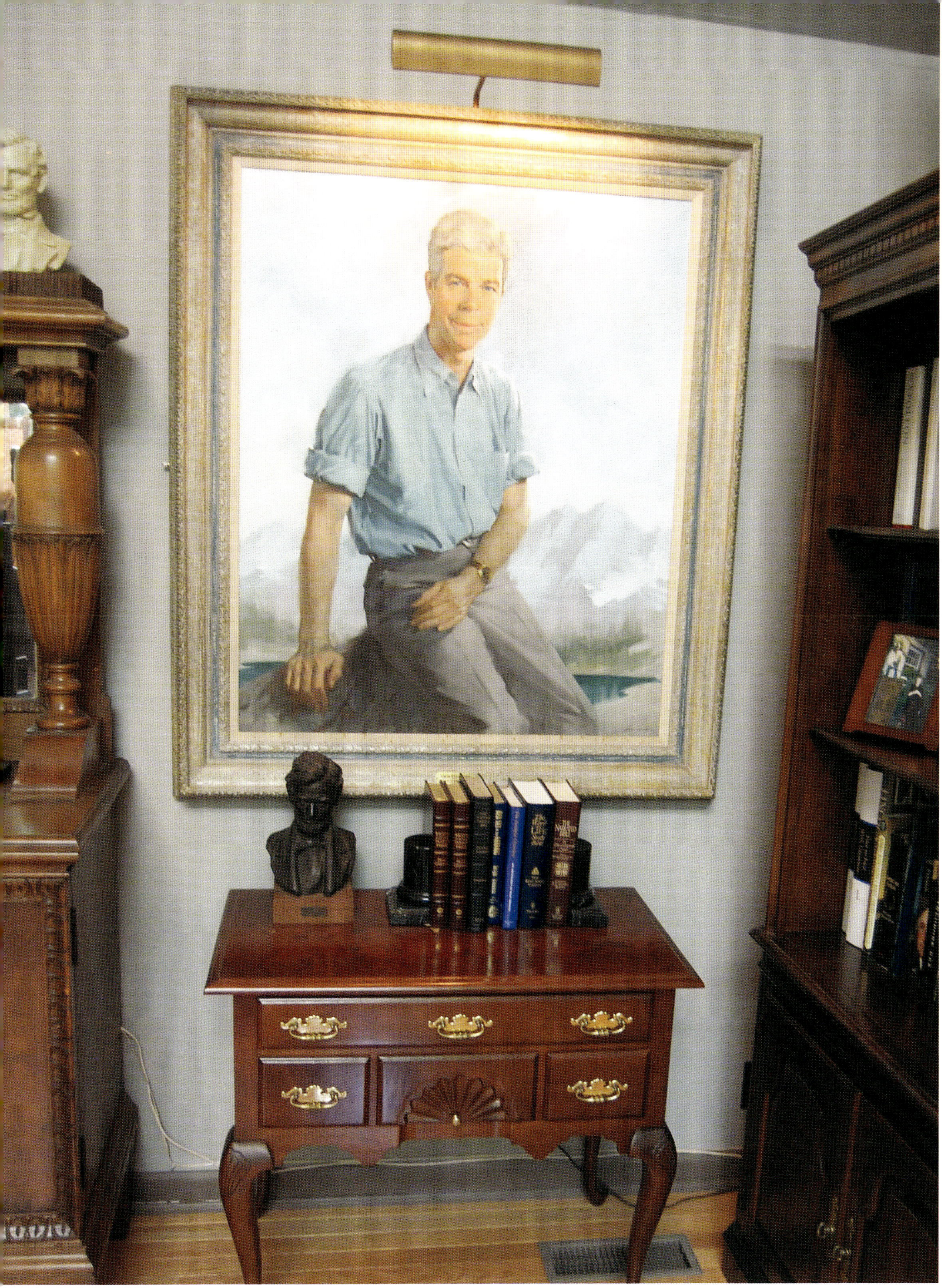

A sketch of Peter H. Dominick, a former U.S. senator for Colorado, and Sanden's first major portrait commission.

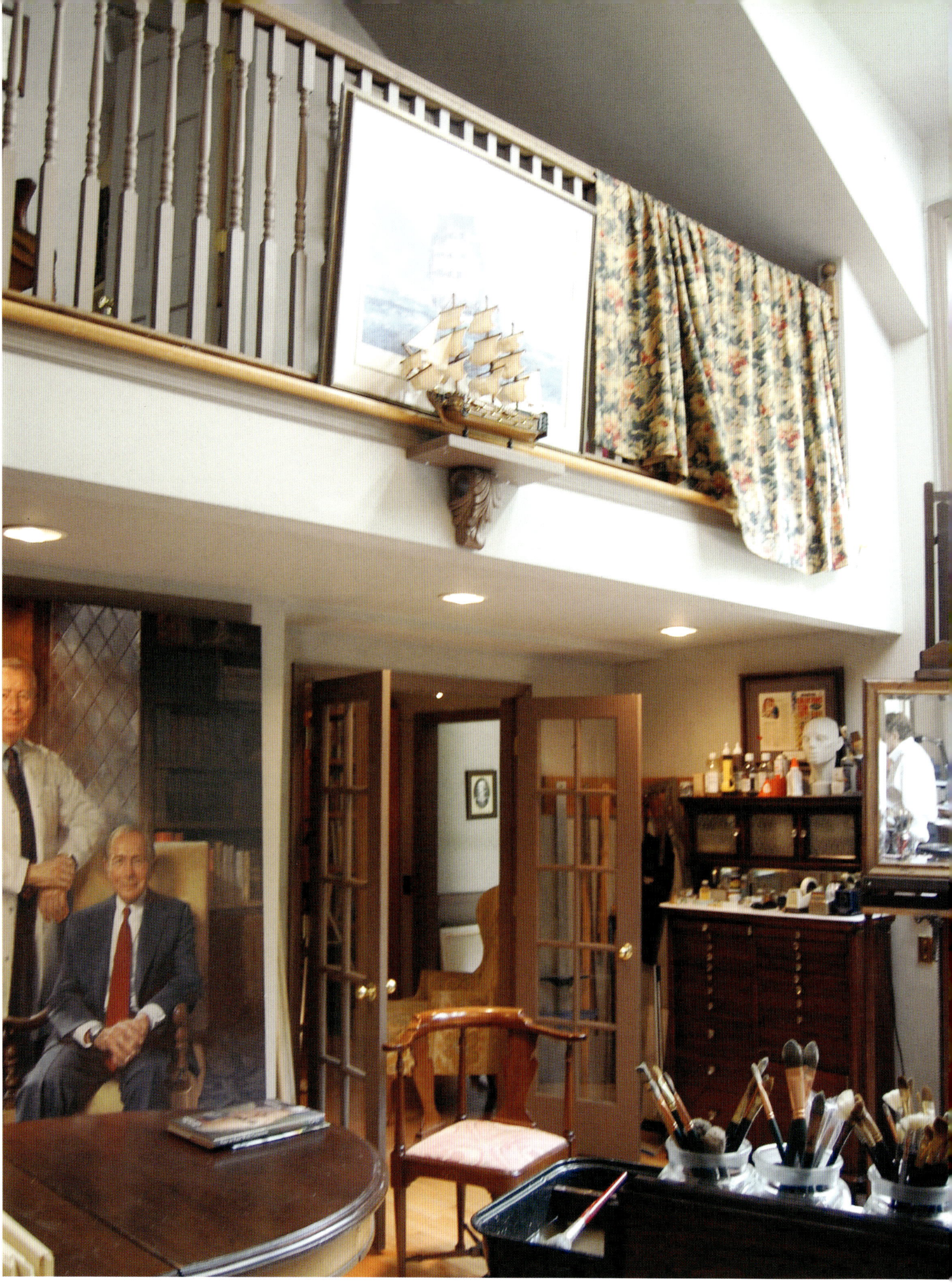

A balcony opens up the studio's space. The maritime painting is by John Stobart, who once took a class with Sanden. A large double portrait stands unfinished, awaiting the artist's final touches. The double doors lead into the sitting room.

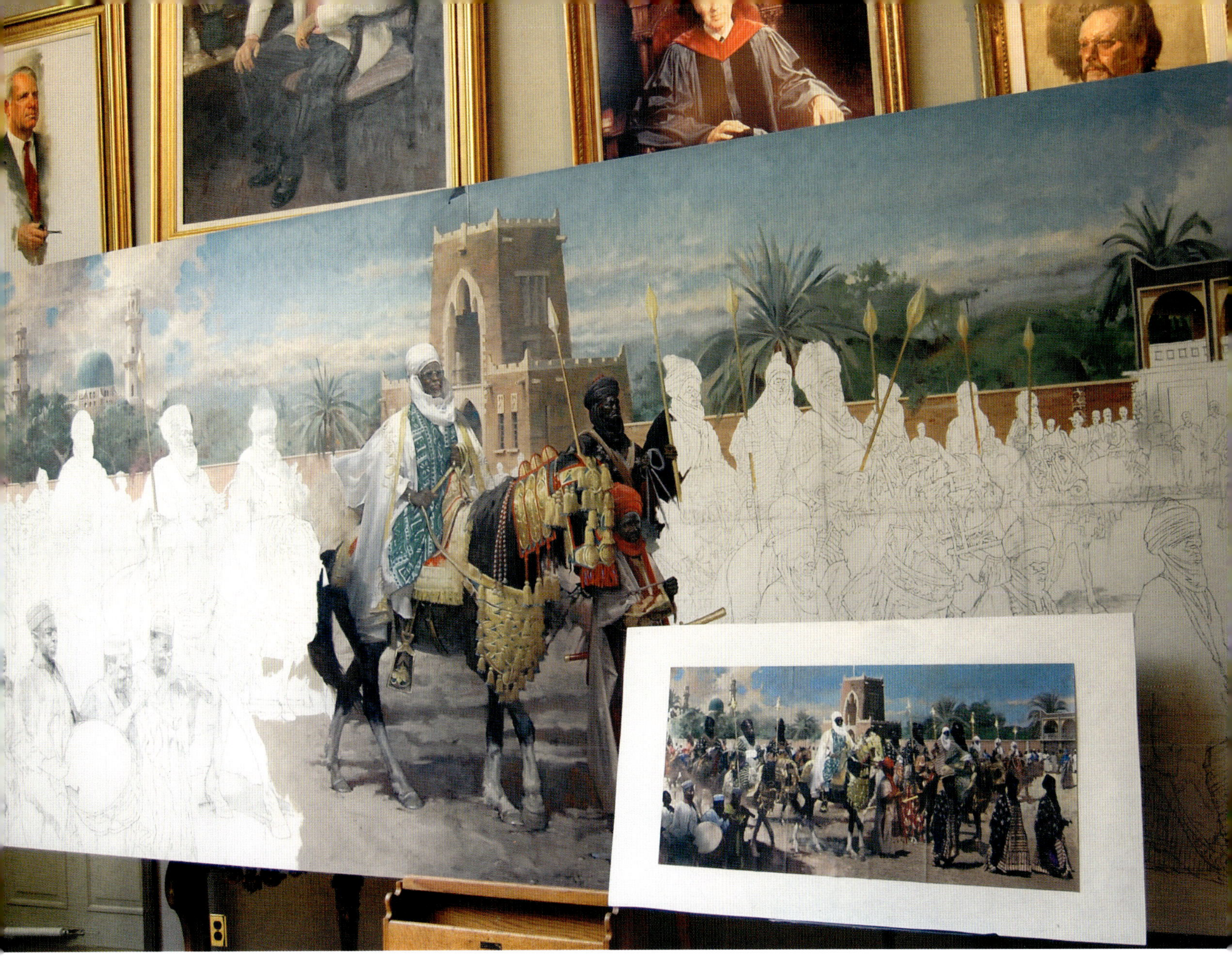

The smaller painting is the complete oil sketch for the larger picture. The scene is an official procession in Kano, Nigeria, which took place in honor of one of Sanden's clients. He is pictured on horseback in the center of the composition.

using one. If he was painting you, he'd have you come back for thirty sessions. I told him to invest in a camera, that he'd get more fun out of life and that his work would be better. But he never did. Digital photography is so brilliant and foolproof. You don't have to run to the lab; you go right to work and get your results."

For all his embrace of photography, Sanden is a formidable painter when it comes to working from life, and for many years he began his portraits by having the clients sit for color sketches. Several years ago, however, he decided to dispense with this stage and simply begin with photography. "I realized that the sketches were actually making the clients nervous," he says. "They'd worry whether that was how the finished portrait was going to look. And then it took me a whole day of work to complete the sketches, only to find that when I got back to the studio I didn't really trust them anyway, except in some cases when they could tell me something about the color. In the end I'd always be working from the photographs."

Sanden happily makes use of Photoshop to adjust his photos, cropping compositions, tweaking color and contrast, and experimenting with alternative backgrounds. He makes further use of the computer when it comes to communicating with clients during the painting process. In the old, days the artist would often travel to a client's home in the late stages of a painting to make final adjustments in person, a time-consuming and sometimes harrowing experience. "Now I try and do everything here in the studio," he says. "I have a really good high-resolution digital camera. I photograph the painting, add a frame to it in Photoshop, and print out a large high-quality print. I send it overnight to the client, and they can e-mail me with any comments or requests for adjustments."

One thing missing in Sanden's studio is a model stand. "These days I don't have clients come to the studio for sittings," he says. "For thirty-five years I was privileged to have a wonderful studio in Carnegie Hall. It had 14-foot (4m) windows looking north to Central Park. It was a perfect location for clients to come to and a very creative environment to be in." Also working in the building were the veteran *New York Times* fashion photographer Bill Cunningham, the fashion designer Bert Geiger, and the fine-art photographer David Hamilton. Two years ago, Carnegie Hall took over the space for use as rehearsal and teaching areas, displacing the group of artists who had lived and worked there for decades. "I searched for alternative space in the area," says Sanden, "but the rents in midtown Manhattan are extraordinary, and I could find nothing suitable." He now has an arrangement whereby he rents a large room at the New York Athletic Club by the day. "It's a good space, although it doesn't have north light," he says. "And I have to take all my equipment over there and set up each time. But it is very convenient for clients, the building is elegant, and the service and staff are wonderful. So all in all it works out fairly well."

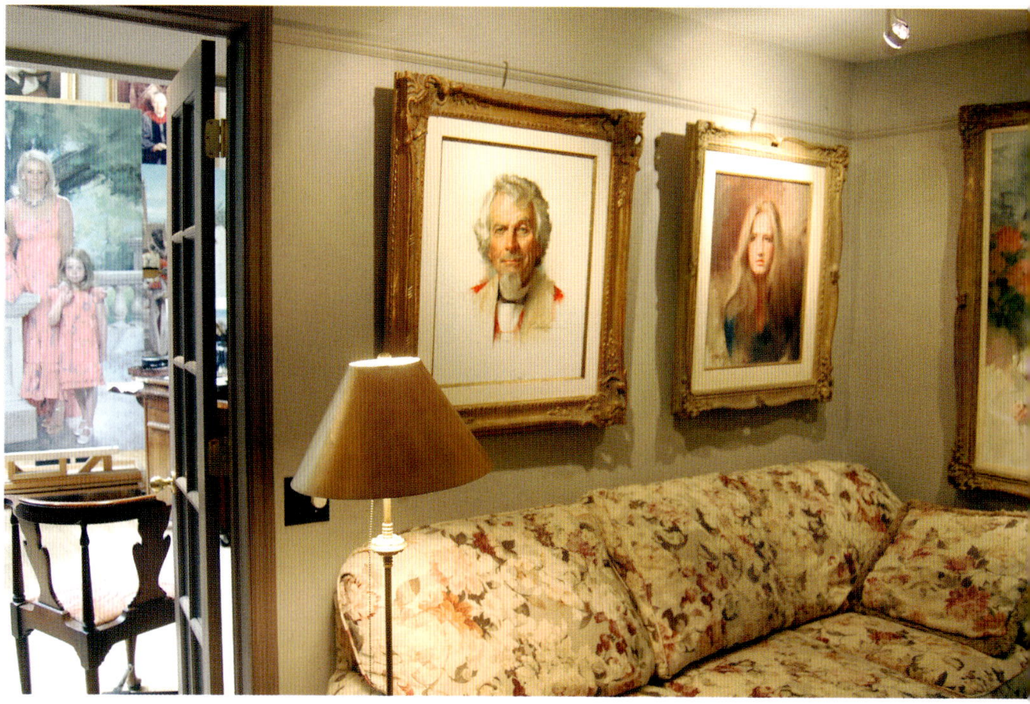

A small sitting room off the studio.

Standing in the studio on the day of my visit were two enormous uncompleted projects. One is a grand panoramic view of a parade of horsemen in Africa; the other a large family portrait showing a woman with her two daughters. Of the vast African painting, Sanden jokes, "I don't know if I'm ever going to finish it. The figure in the center is a man I have painted many times. He was given an honorary title in a ceremony in Kano, in Northern Nigeria, and he asked me to do a painting re-creating the official procession. I wasn't there for the actual event, but my wife and I flew out, and I had all these people pose for the painting." A full-color sketch standing next to the canvas shows the highly complex composition. The rich color of the costumes and settings and the almost cinematic drama of the scene promise a finished painting that will be a considerable eyeful and quite a tour de force.

Seeing the canvas in this incomplete stage allows us to take look at Sanden's painting process. He always begins with a clear and decisive line using a 4B pencil that he then thoroughly fixes so that the graphite won't lift up into the paint. The artist then starts painting on top of this drawing, beginning with the darks, which are generally established in warms of browns or brown violets. He then works up to the lights in graduated stages using a directly brushed approach that yields an almost mosaic-like appearance. In fact, in these early stages, he uses no blending at all. Later in the process, when he finally begins to blend areas together, he keeps the process to a minimum. In this way the color remains as fresh and active as possible, and the surface retains its life and a delightful sense of touch.

Meanwhile, the portrait of the woman and her two daughters stands on the easel in what appears to be a state of completion. However, the artist explains that he is involved in a last period of back-and-forth with the client concerning one of the daughter's faces. "I've already painted it several times," he says. "One problem in working with clients is that sometimes the way they see themselves is not necessarily the way they actually appear. So on occasion it takes a little while to arrive at a solution that satisfies the client. I don't object to this process. I love pleasing the client. I'm a professional, and I'm trying to bring pleasure to these people."

Certainly the artist's close consultation with his clients has contributed to his remarkable track record. Of the many hundreds of commissions he has completed, he can only recall one or two that were rejected. And although his clients are demanding, the artist is even more so. It is not unusual for him to make more than one version of the finished painting if the first attempt does not satisfy him.

Now in his seventies, Sanden allows himself to look back on his career with some warm memories. He did not emerge as a portrait painter until relatively late in life. "I grew up in the South, where my father was a Presbyterian minister," he says. "I studied illustration in college and then got a job working for Billy Graham. I sat at a desk and did work for book covers and other publications—it was the only real job I've ever had. But after nine years of this, I was getting itchy. I began to think that there must be something more. I was married, and for three years my wife and I debated the idea of going to New York. Eventually we did." The couple moved first to Ossining and then into Manhattan. "I had just enough money for the first month's rent," he recalls, "so I had to scramble."

While supporting himself through a monthly illustration for *Reader's Digest* and freelance work from the Billy

Graham organization, Sanden decided to acquire some better painting skills by enrolling at the Art Students League of New York. "Apart from marriage, that was the most important decision in my life," he says. He was intrigued by the paintings of Samuel Oppenheim, a former fashion illustrator whose work displayed a stylish brush handling and variety of edges that was new and attractive to the young Sanden. "It was the class of classes," says the artist, who still brims with admiration for his old teacher. "We were only allowed to work for one session on each portrait. Everything was based on direct observation and truth. Oppenheim was very thin on theory—everything was about the doing of it. We were told to look at an area, consider it, mix the color, look again, and then place the stroke. If you wanted to make a second stroke, you had to look at the model again before doing so."

Oppenheim's insistence on the primacy of direct and careful observation was combined with an appreciation of economy of means. He insisted that the student always use the largest brush possible for a task and was fond of telling them to try to get things right the first time. "The worst sin was to put something in the picture that you did not see," says Sanden. "Oppenheim absolutely wouldn't stand for it. He wouldn't accept anything except what you saw. It's a pretty elementary truth, but if you understand it, then you understand Sargent." Sanden made such strides in the class that when Oppenheim retired two years later, he named Sanden to take over his position. Even at this stage of his career, Sanden still hoped to become a successful illustrator, but his growing understanding of portraiture led him to present his work to Portraits Inc., the gallery that represented most of the leading portraitists in the country. He immediately secured a commission to paint a U.S. senator. Other commissions quickly followed, and the artist never looked back.

For many years Sanden combined a busy teaching schedule with continual production of portrait commissions. In addition to his work at the Art Students League of New York, he founded The Portrait Institute, for which he conducted a highly successful program of seminars, teaching to large audiences at a variety of locations around the country. He shared this operation with Elizabeth, his wife of thirty-eight years, to whose tireless support and encouragement he credits much of his success. The institute also provides resources for professional portrait painters in the form of literature, teaching, art materials, and videos. These days Sanden concentrates solely on his portrait commissions with an enthusiasm, energy, and sheer professionalism that is in itself an inspiration.

For more on John Howard Sanden, visit his website at www.johnhowardsanden.com.

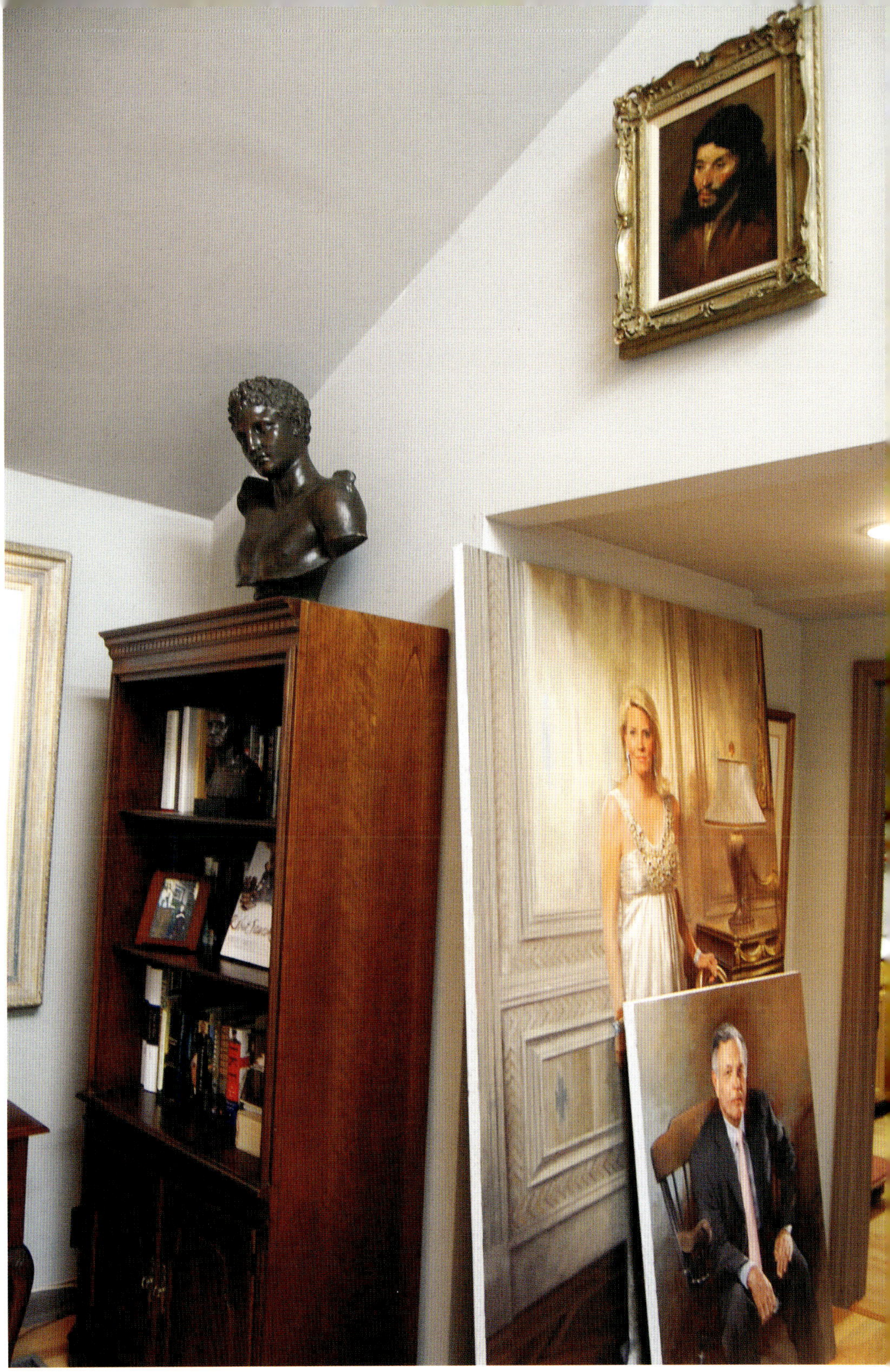

Two nearly completed portraits next to a large bookcase containing works on art and European history.

William Chambers

Adding a Portrait Studio to a Home

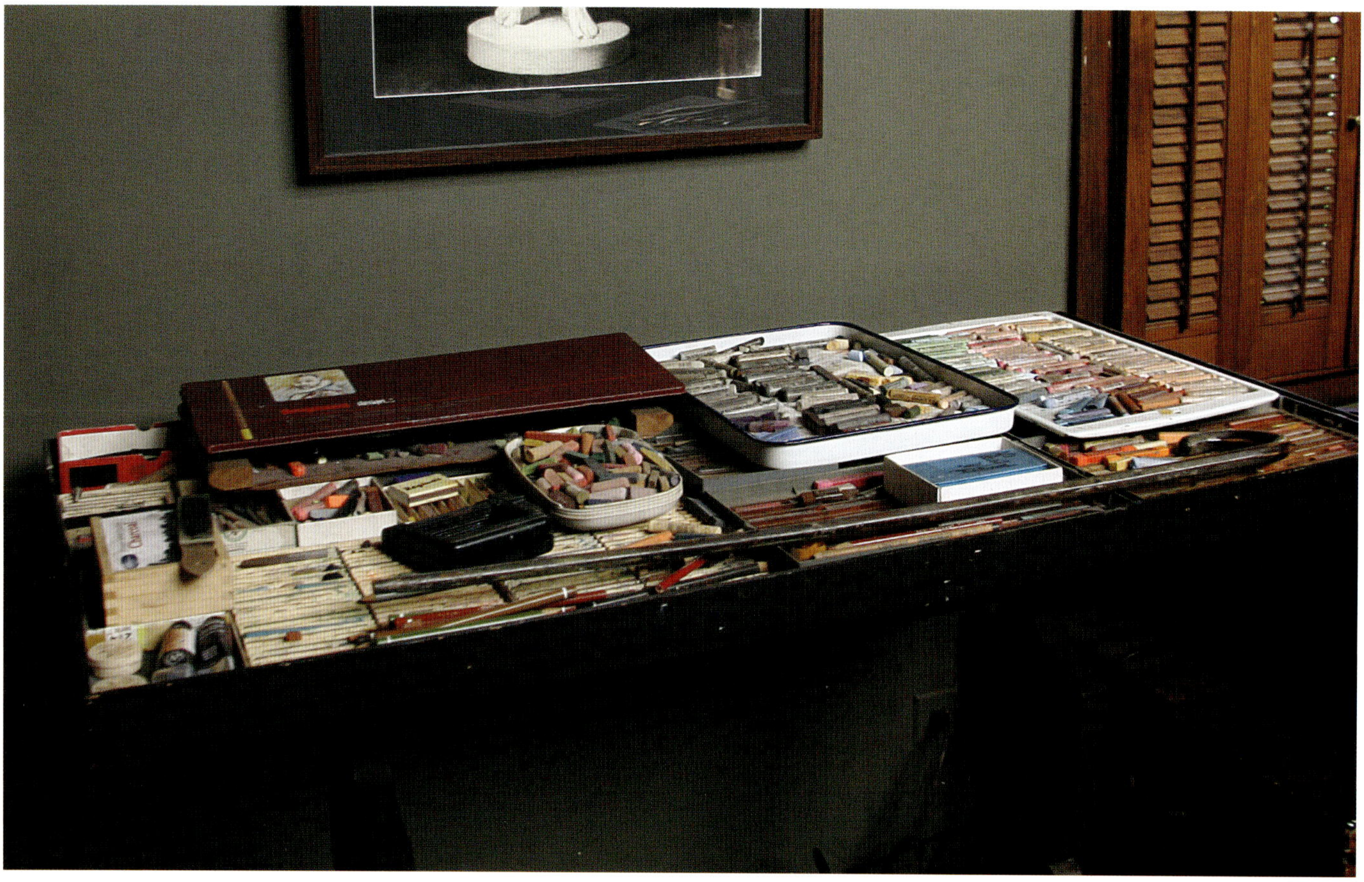

A table full of pastels in Chambers' studio.

Andrew Wyeth used to laugh at himself when he talked about how careless he was in handling his drawings and paintings. "A collector called me to say a framed watercolor painting had fallen off the wall of his home, and when the glass broke, it cut a hole in the paper," the famed artist once recalled. "When I went to see if I could repair it, I realized the damage hadn't been caused by the glass at all. I stepped on the watercolor paper when it fell to the floor of my studio, and in the process I put a hole right through it. I left it alone because I thought the cut and my footprint actually improved the painting."

Wyeth, like many artists, didn't worry about the cleanliness or organization of his studio. Even though his art is worth hundreds of thousands of dollars, he tossed drawings and paintings around the various barns and residences he used as work spaces. If his wife, Betsy, had been allowed to bring collectors or curators into the studios, Wyeth might have been forced to be more tidy and organized.

If you flip through the pages of this book, you can quickly tell something about the working habits of the featured artists and the ways in which their space is used on a daily basis. Some are well-organized and efficient gathering places for students, clients, and family members; others are cluttered and hazardous retreats that are only used by one painter.

Whatever an artist's preferred working habits and standards of cleanliness, he or she doesn't have a choice but to be neat when the studio is an extension of a family's living quarters or when it serves as a place for meeting collectors, business associates, or portrait clients. That has

→ The view toward the Hughes easel in Chambers' studio in Arlington Heights, Illinois.

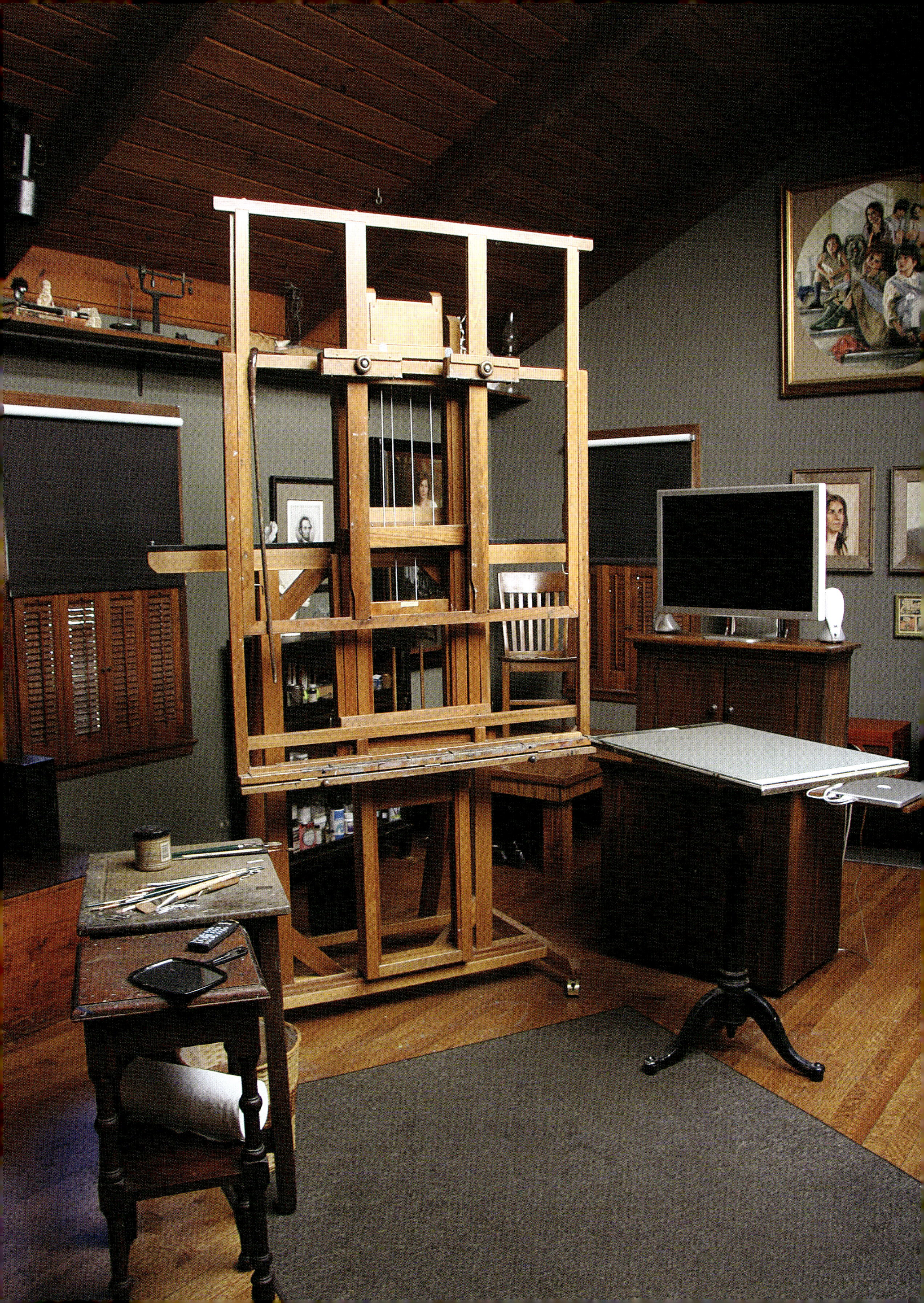

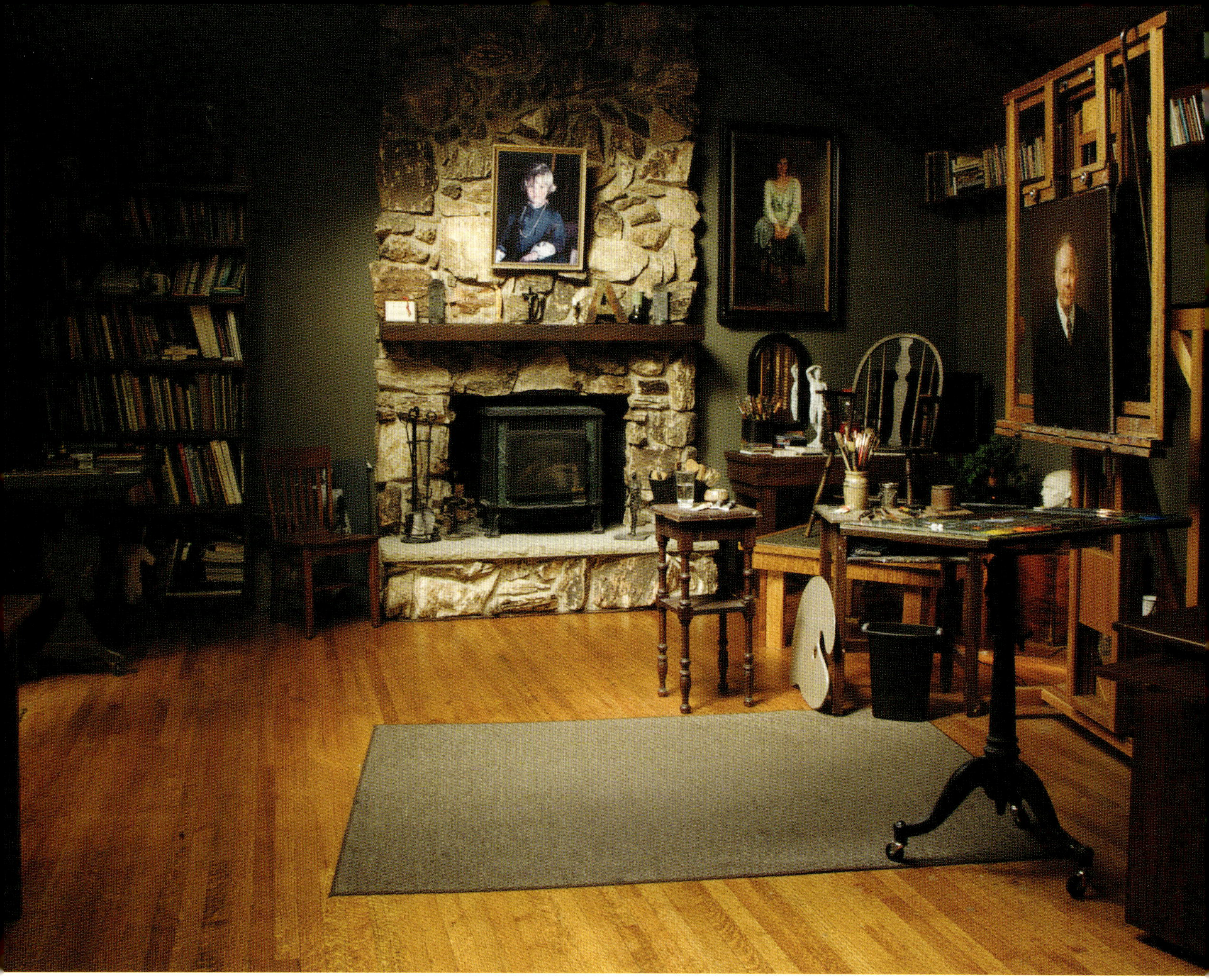

The view from the living area of Chambers' home into the studio, with the fireplace on the eastern wall.

been true for artist William Chambers, who works in a 23'-x-18½' (7m-x-6m) studio that is connected to the living area of his Illinois studio.

Chambers worked as an illustrator and used his studio to create artwork for commercial accounts, publishers, and companies that produced collectable items; but in recent years he has distinguished himself as one of the top portrait painters in the country. Many of his commissions require him to travel to meet his clients, but he also hosts them in his studio. "I built the studio in 1976 when my four children were still around, so for the past thirty-four years, my family and professional life have been seamlessly connected," the artist explains. "I designed it and had it constructed to be better appointed than a studio really needs to be, but from the beginning I had to think about it being part of the home we would live in and would eventually sell to someone else."

Although Chambers prefers to work from life, he is experienced with working from photographs. Those are stored in an Apple computer and viewed on a large matte glass display unit on a portable table near his large Hughes easel. The artist installed two large skylights in the roof of the studio angled to the north, and he added sliding glass doors from the work space into the backyard. "I seldom use the doors, and the blinds are usually drawn to block the light, but I needed to install the glass doors for potential resale," he explains. "There are also more windows in the room than I would want for a studio, but that was also necessary since the next owner is not likely to be an artist." Because Chambers often works in the evening, he installed Vita-Lite fluorescent fixtures with 550 Kelvin north-light-balanced bulbs.

For more on William Chambers, visit his website at www.williamchambers.com.

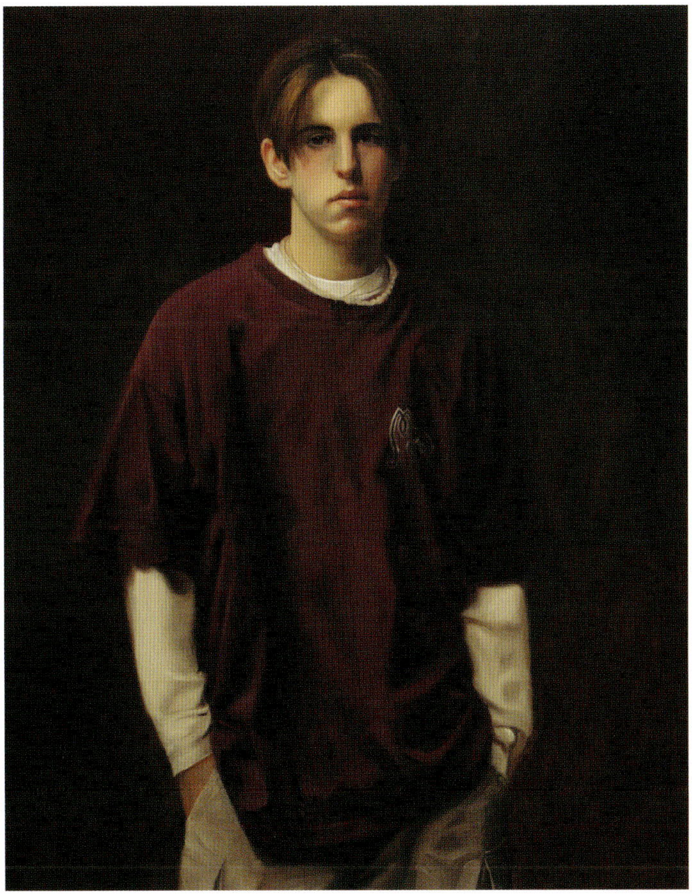

Portrait of Patrick
by William Chambers, 1999, oil, 40" x 30" (102cm x 76cm). Collection of the artist.

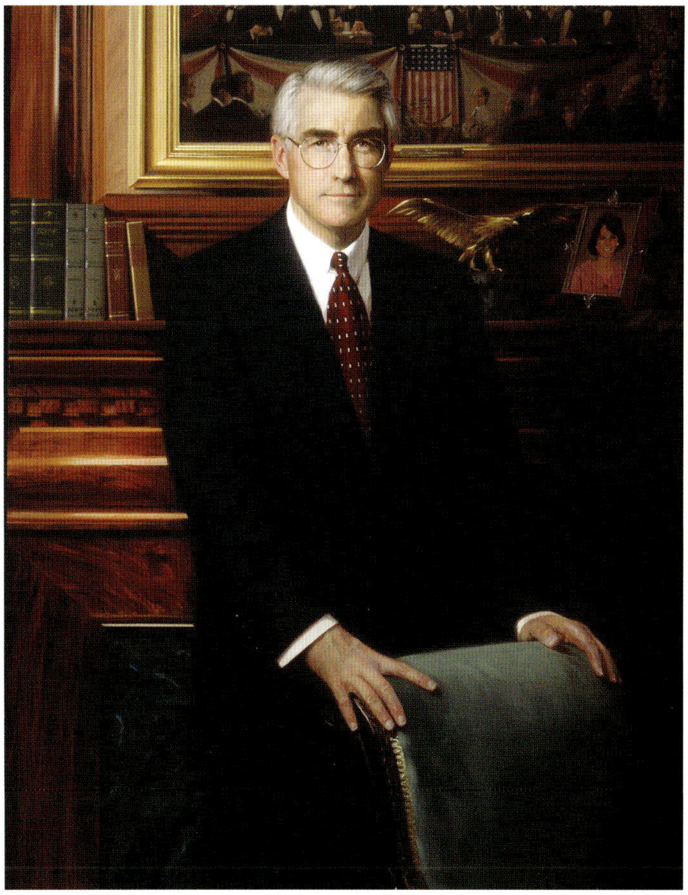

Governor Jim Edgar
by William Chambers, 1999, oil, 55" x 45" (140cm x 114cm). Collection of the State of Illinois.

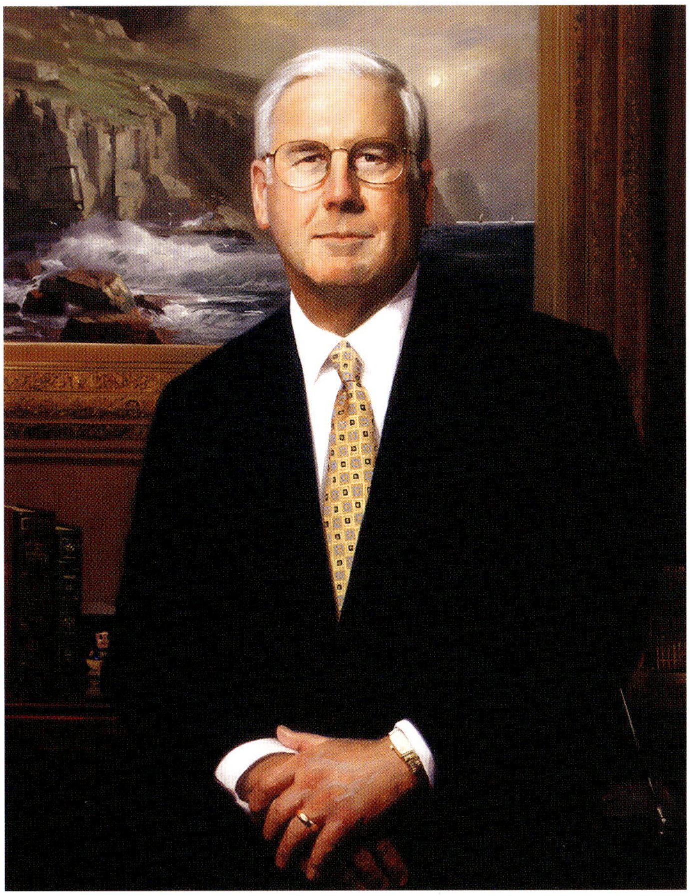

Portrait of Verne Istock
by William Chambers, 2009, oil, 32" x 31" (81cm x 79cm). Private collection.

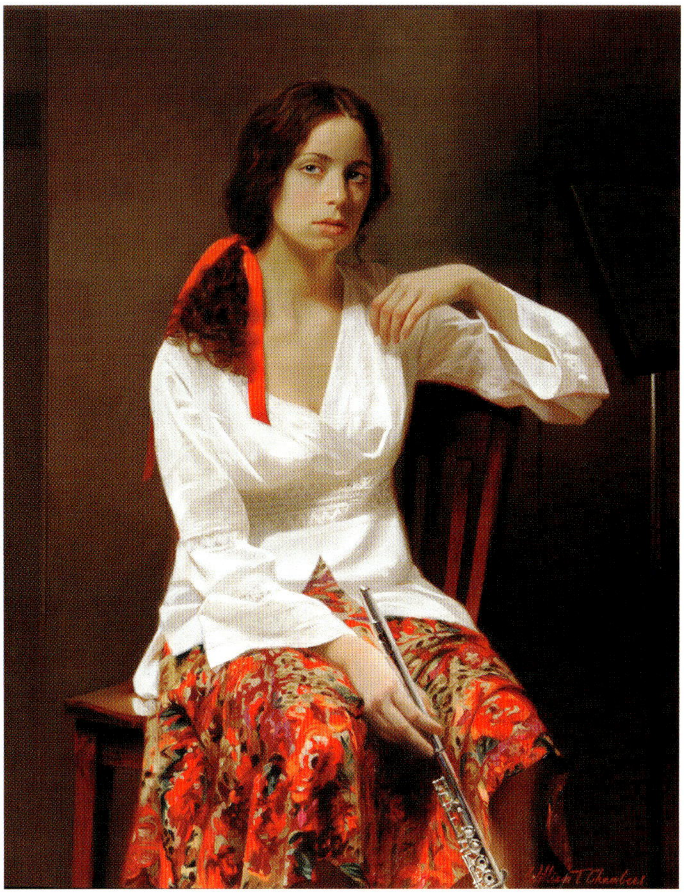

Portrait of Alyse
by William Chambers, 2008, oil, 40" x 32" (102cm x 81cm). Collection of the artist.

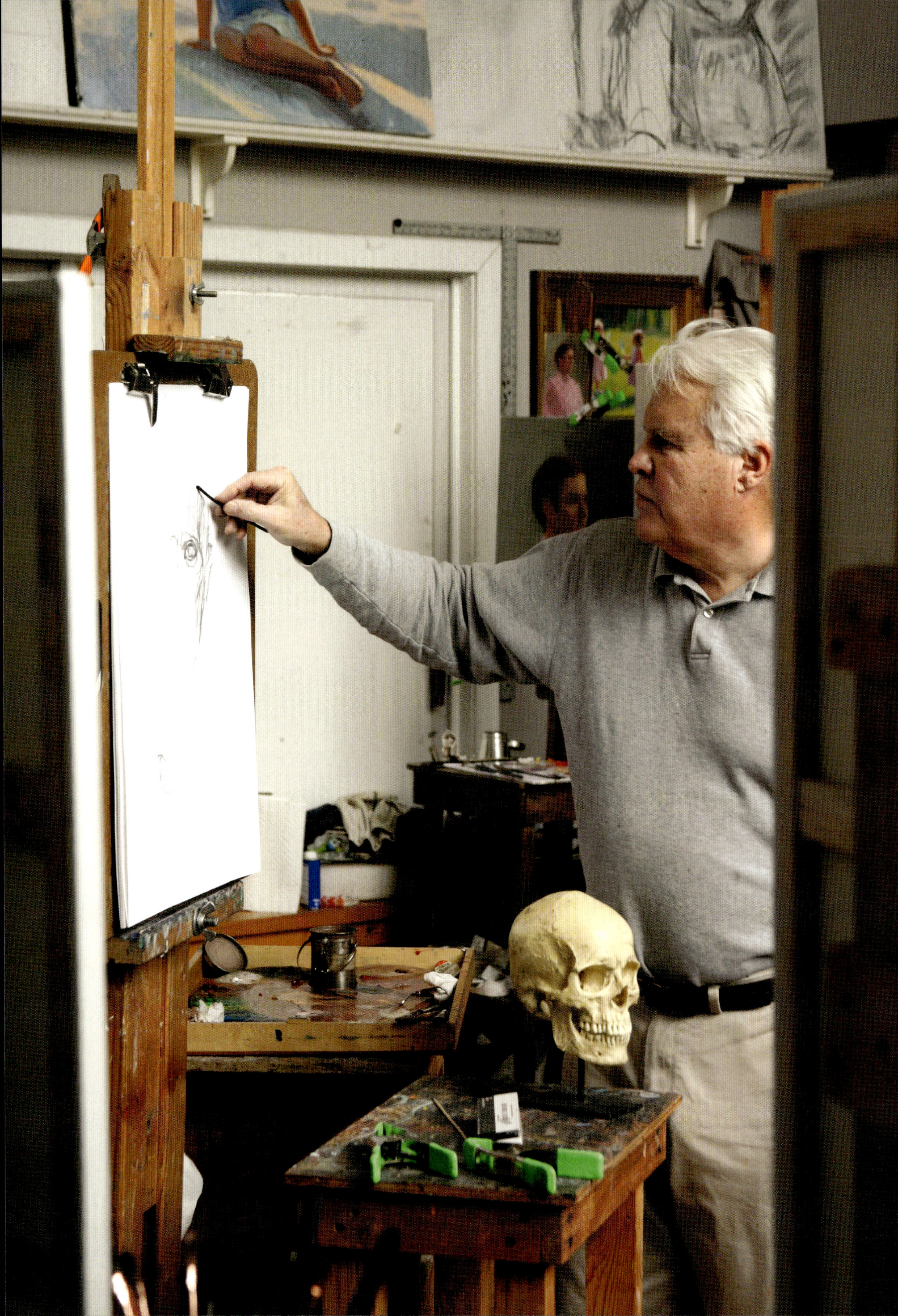

CHAPTER THREE

Educational Studios

"In places like universities, where everyone talks too rationally, it is necessary for a kind of enchanter to appear."

—Joseph Beuys

← Cedric Egeli encourages students to study a variety of painting subjects.

Joanette and Cedric Egeli
A Studio With a Practical Focus

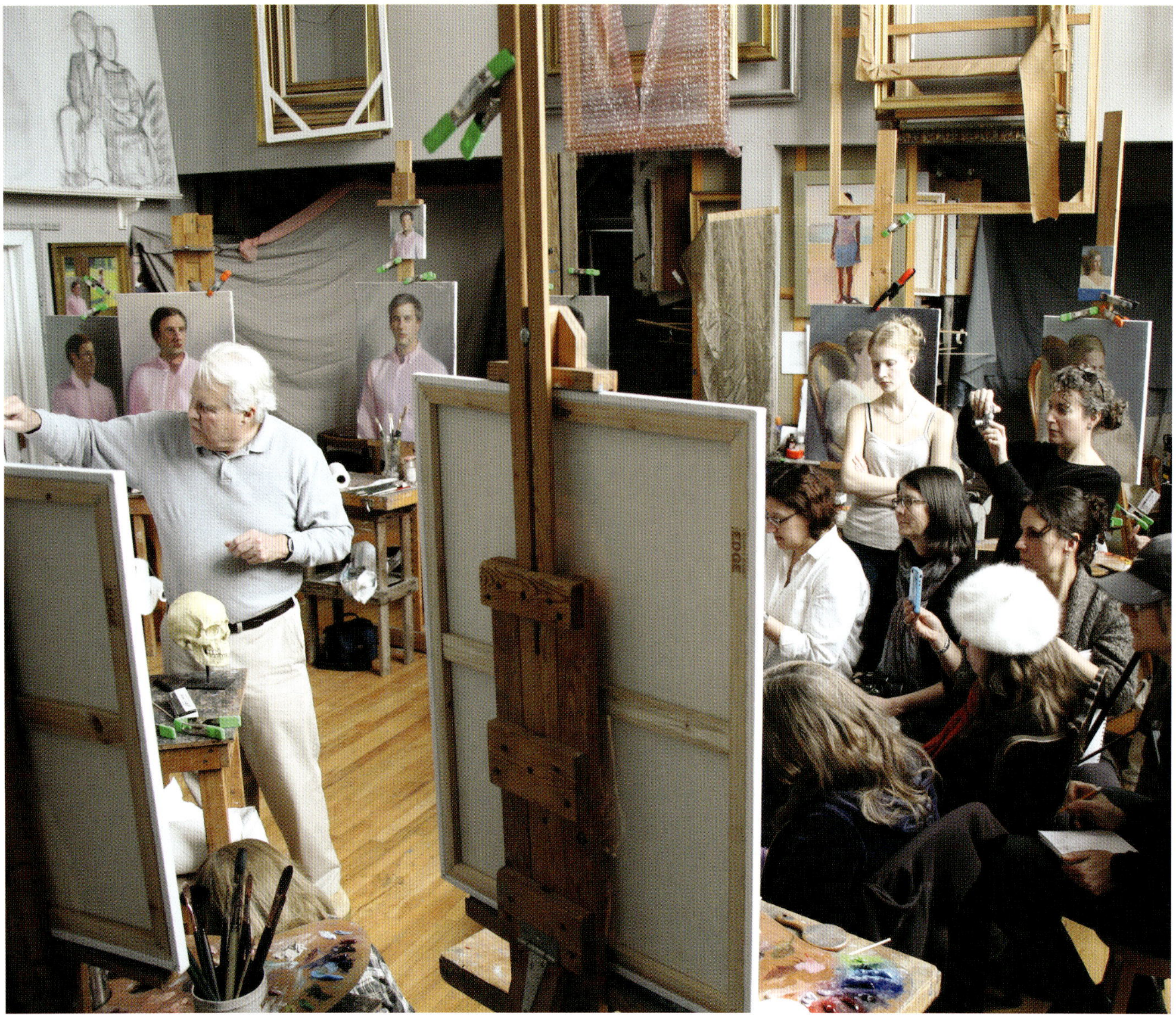

↑ Cedric Egeli conducts demonstrations throughout his monthlong workshop.

→ **Dinah**
by Cedric Egeli, 2011, oil, 20" x 16" (51cm x 41cm).
Collection of the artist.

Joanette and Cedric Egeli have been teaching and inspiring artists for decades, and many of their former students have gone on to win major awards and establish successful careers as painters. Currently they teach one monthlong workshop every January in their studio in Edgewater, Maryland, as well as several shorter workshops in Provincetown, Massachusetts, during the summer. During their January workshop, students learn alongside both artists in a space that was originally built for Joanette and two of the couple's children, who are also artists. It's a large space, measuring approximately 32' x 28' (10m x 9m), and it can accommodate more than twenty students. Every day during the workshop, students work for two three-hour sessions, when the

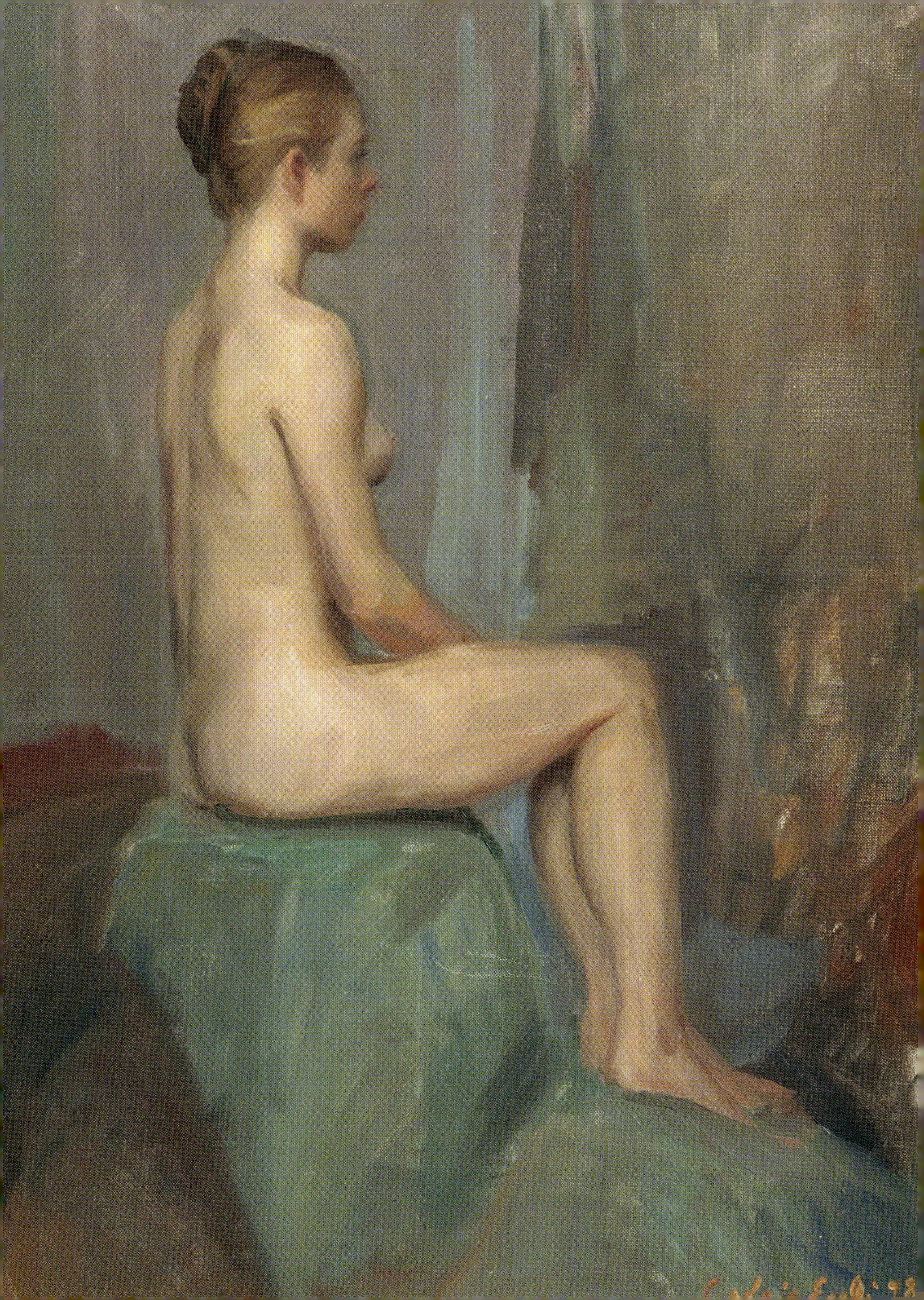

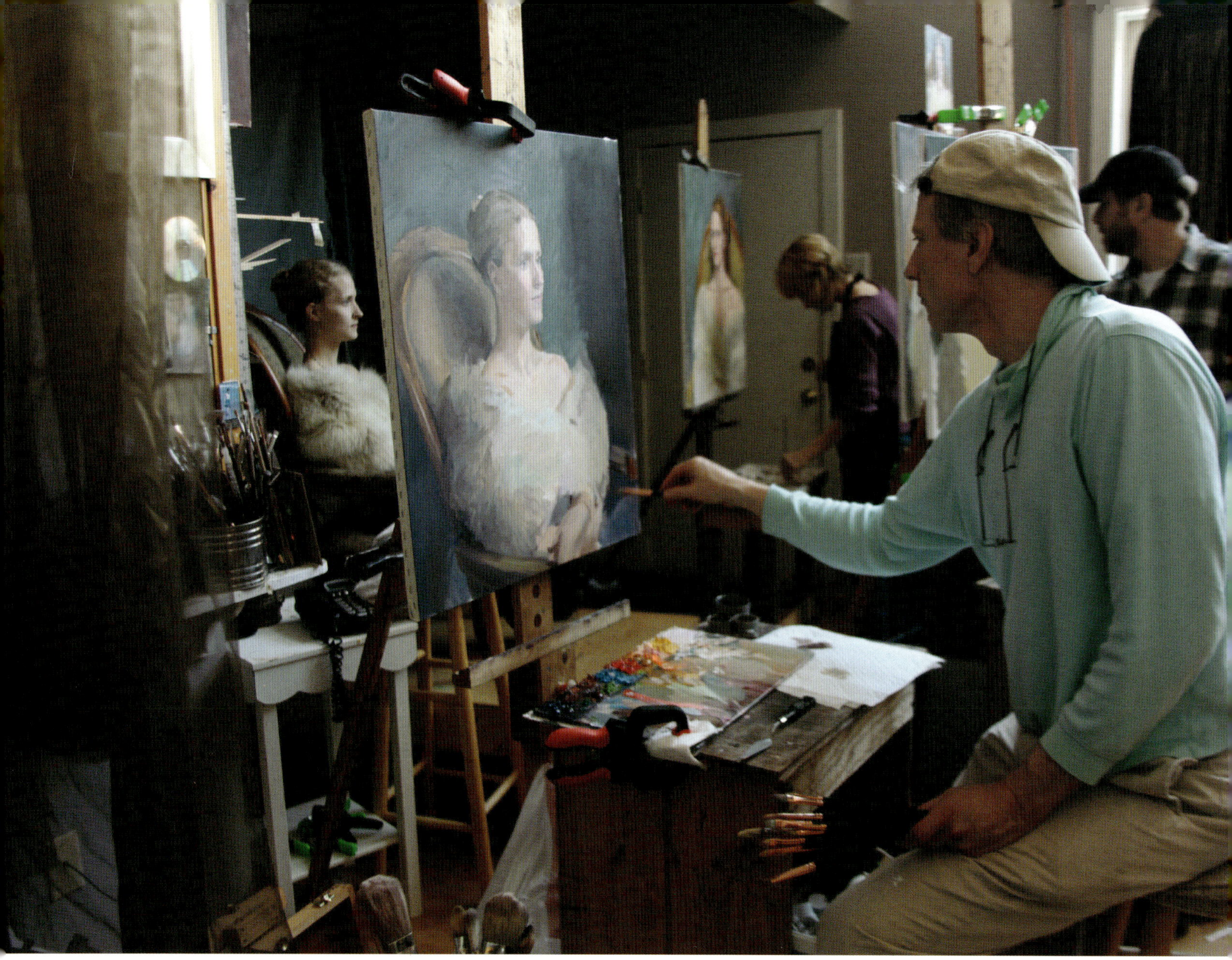

Students work on portraits during the afternoon.

studio is filled with north light from its large windows. Most mornings the focus is on figure drawing, and afternoons are devoted to portrait painting. "These workshops help to precisely develop my ideas," Cedric says, noting that many of the workshop participants are already professional artists. "And they serve as a mecca for artists." Adds Joanette, "January is the perfect time to spend honing your skills."

Founded more than thirty years ago, the Egeli studio has a steady stream of students and an ever-growing waiting list. The family's property is extensive, containing ample space for both working and living. In addition to their monthlong workshop, they also invite young artists to live in their home and work alongside them in the studio. Apprentices have a private dwelling that allows them to feel autonomous and also a part of the family—undoubtedly fostering a confidence that helps them improve their practice. For example, artist Rick Casali served as an apprentice at the estate from 2004 until 2007, shortly after graduating high school. He has since gone on to teach at the Maryland Hall for Creative Arts, and is represented by the Egeli Gallery, in Provincetown.

One thing that sets the Egelis' training apart from others is an added emphasis on the practical challenges faced by working painters and portraitists. "When you get out of art school and into the world, conditions aren't perfect for creating art anymore, and it's easy to be lost," Cedric says. "It's very important when the students get to a certain level to show them ways of existing as an artist. My wife is very good at showing people how to approach making a living."

Indeed, the workshop started when three of Cedric and Joanette's children were attending art school but weren't learning any of the necessary skills or professional practices that would help them succeed after college. The parents took matters into their own hands by organizing a two-month workshop for their children and other local artists. "We needed them to be able to make a living when they got out of school!" Joanette recalls.

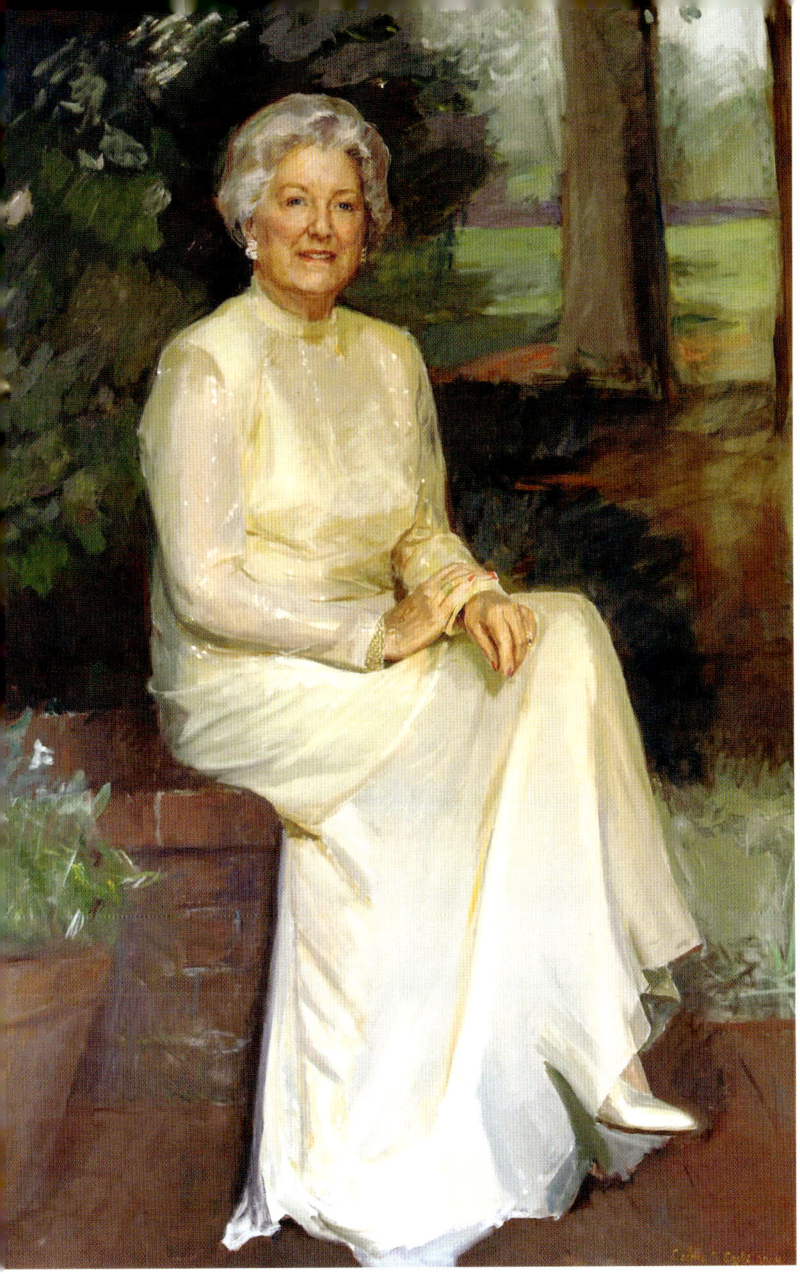

Sarah Bissell
by Cedric Egeli, oil, 70" x 40" (178cm x 102cm).
Private collection.

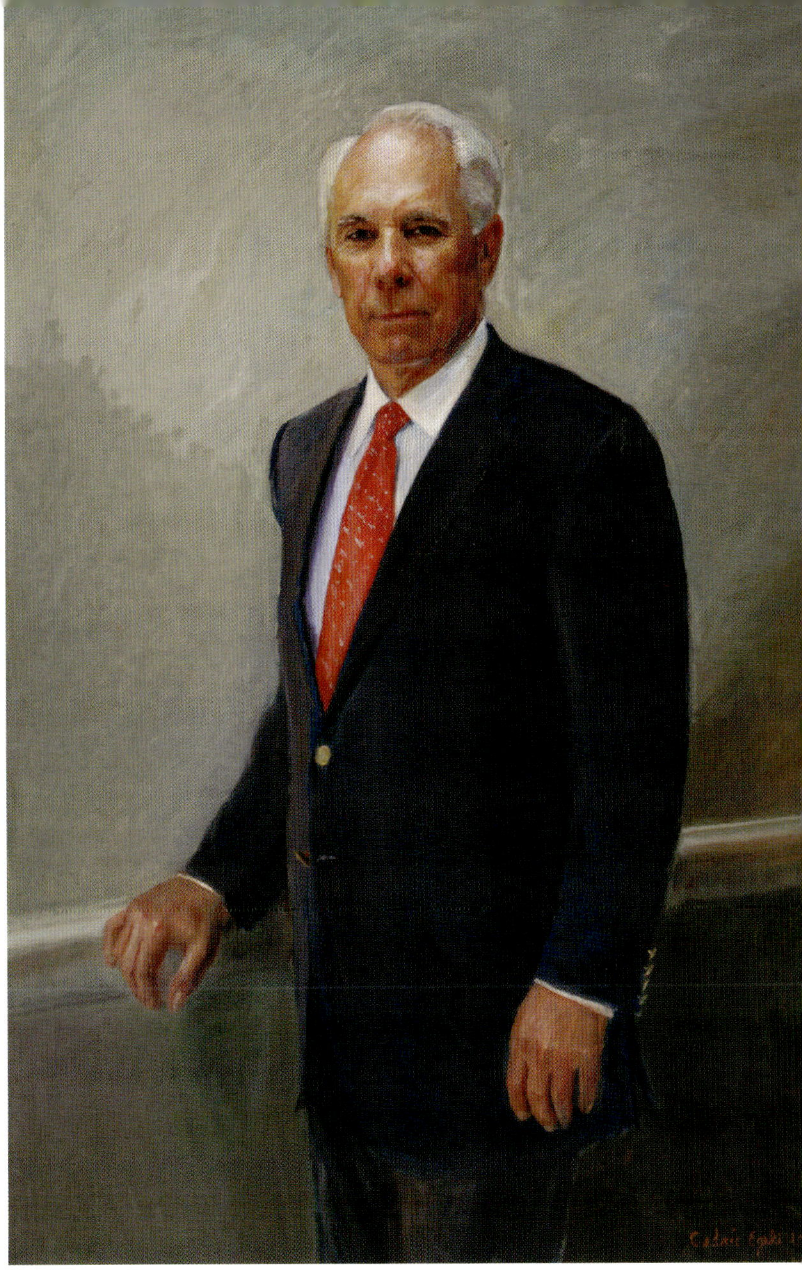

Dr. Dan Spengler
by Cedric Egeli, oil, 70" x 40" (178cm x 102cm).
Collection of Vanderbilt University Medical Center, Nashville, Tennessee.

The Egelis' practical focus manifests itself in numerous ways during their workshops. For example, by having students invite friends to pose for portraits, they get practice painting members of the general public instead of models who are accustomed to sitting still for paintings. Cedric encourages students to study different types of painting and work under different sorts of natural light. "I'm a portrait painter, so all my life I've had to study things that would help portraits, which is everything—landscapes, still life, outdoor painting," he says. "You have to learn how to work in all types of light—how often do you find perfect north light in a client's home?"

The Egelis are key instructors in the great line of art instruction based around the Cape School of Art, in Provincetown, founded by Charles Hawthorne and later run by Henry Hensche. Cedric and Joanette taught together there for years, and they still teach three summer workshops where students learn to see light, color, and form as they paint on the beach. At the Arts Students League of New York, Cedric studied under Frank Reilly, Frank Mason, and Sidney Dickinson. He credits his father with helping him make the transition to professional portraiture. Joanette received her B.F.A. from the University of the Arts and trained with Bjorn and Cedric Egeli. All the Egelis' students—whether they study in Maryland or Massachusetts, winter or summer—benefit from the experience of learning from artists who have decades of experience teaching as a team and who know the importance of coaching students in how to master the art and profession of painting.

For more on their workshops in Provincetown and on Cedric Egeli, visit their website at www.egelistudio.com.

NYK Academy

Creating an Intimate Atelier

For many artists—especially representational painters interested in following in the paths of master European artists—a more ordered, structured course of study is often necessary. Perhaps the best-known curriculum designed to raise students to the high standards of traditional drawing and painting is Charles Bargue's nineteenth-century drawing course. For more than a century, this program has been a cornerstone of the academic tradition in art, and variations on Bargue's method are taught in ateliers and art schools throughout the world.

One such school is the NYK Academy, which was founded in New York City in 2002 by Judith Pond Kudlow and Andrea J. Smith as the Harlem Studio of Art. Kudlow now acts as the primary instructor at the school, which is inspired by the classical atelier model, in particular the curriculum of the Florence Academy of Art, in Italy. Kudlow's students begin their program by drawing Bargue plates in graphite, followed by cast drawings in charcoal, a grisaille painting, and eventually painting with a limited palette.

Overall, Kudlow says, "It's a pretty highly controlled atmosphere." Students are taught to draw and paint using the sight-size method—a precise system of measurement in which students stand at a fixed distance from their subject and easel to be able to make accurate judgments. Students also have the opportunity to draw from a live model twice a week and can elect to complete a color course, based on the Munsell color system.

The NYK Academy is located in a loft building in Spanish Harlem, a Manhattan neighborhood that's currently undergoing a renaissance. "When Andrea went to Rome to open Atelier Canova, I planned on closing the school," Kudlow recalls, "but there were still students who wanted to keep working, so I continued teaching. That's when I moved to the second floor of the build-

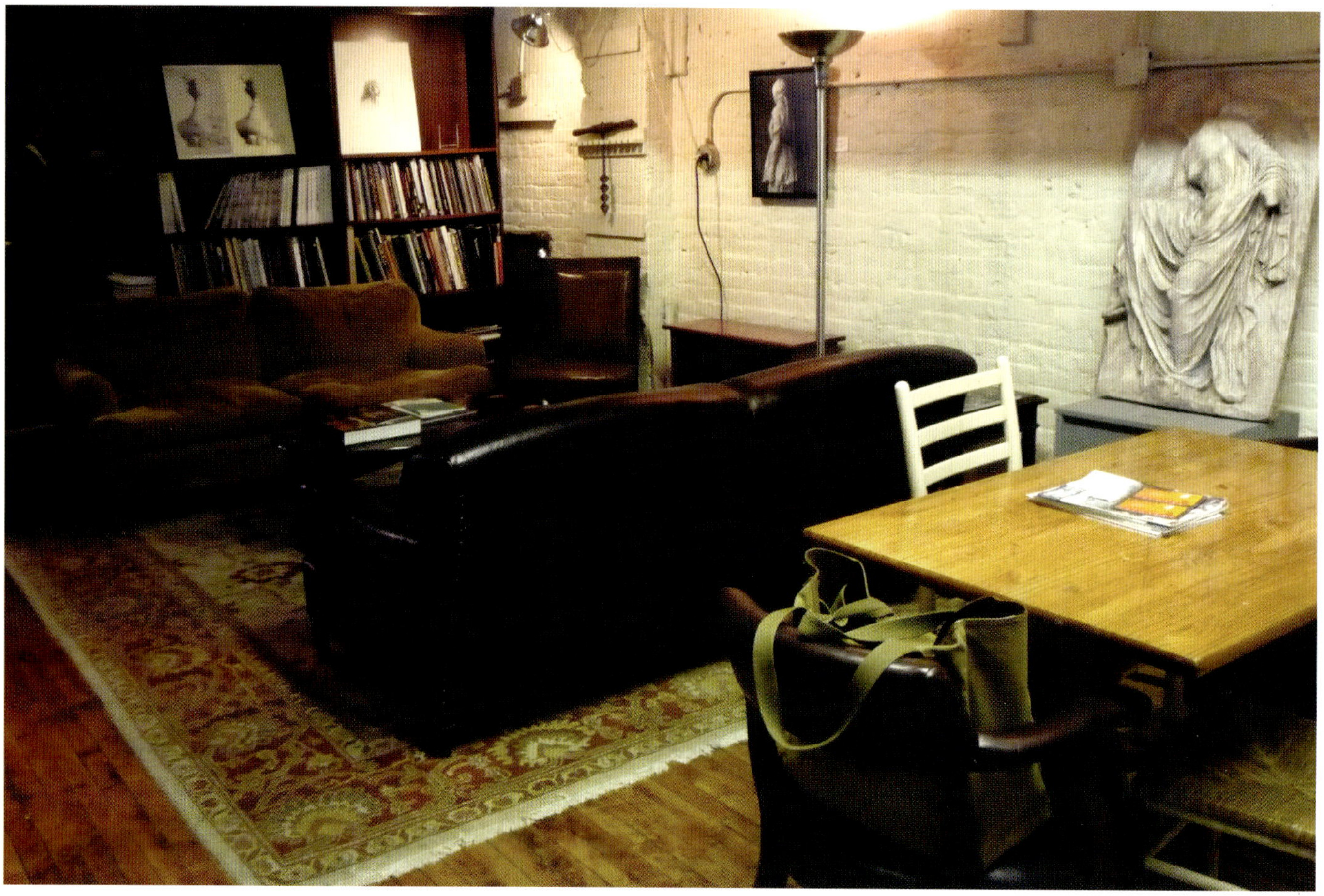

The NYK Academy studio has a lounge and workroom where students can take breaks and have informal discussions.

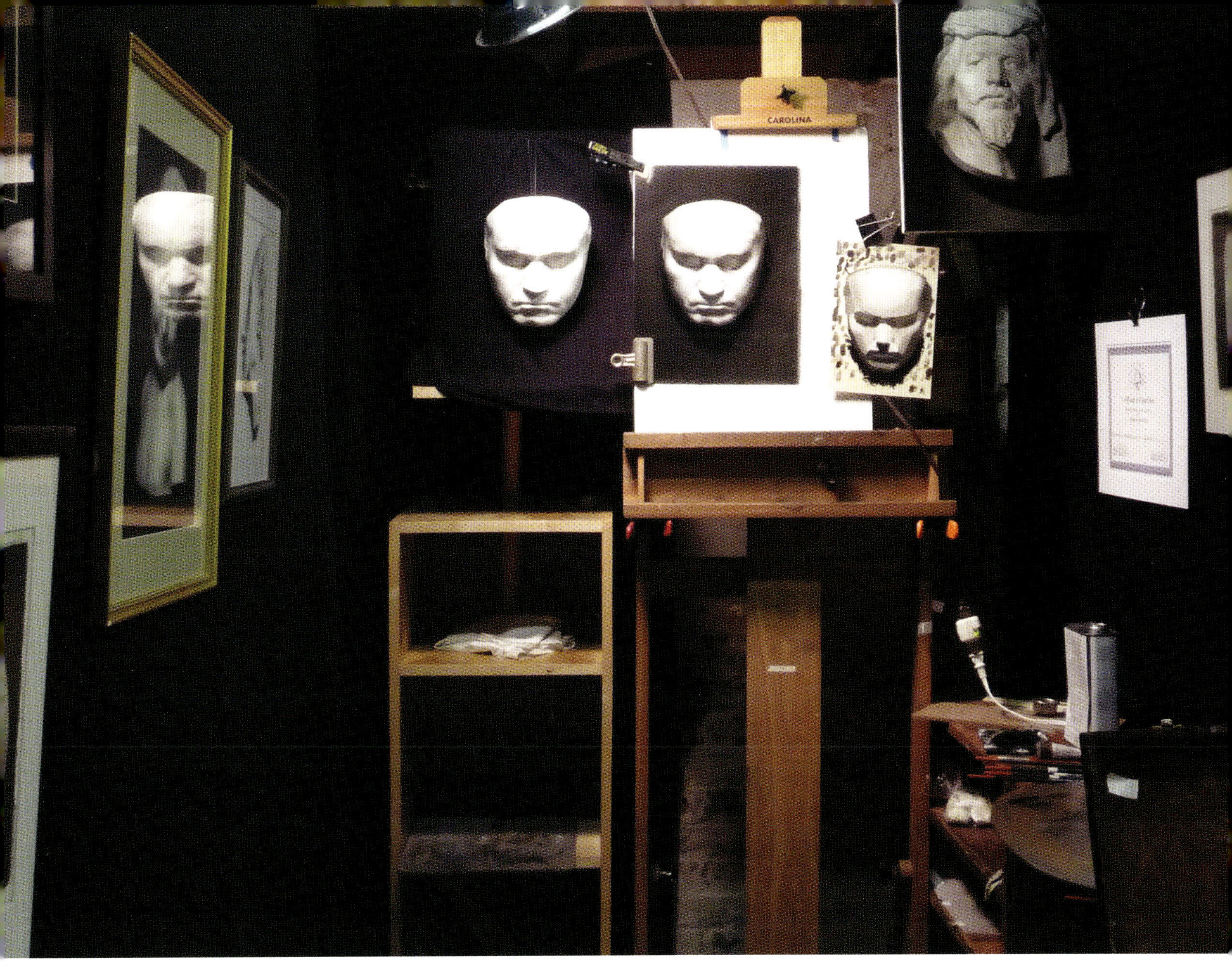

Each student workstation allows artists to work at their own pace and control their desired lighting conditions. For a cast drawing, such as the one shown here, this is of the utmost importance.

ing." Part of the appeal of the new space was the large north-facing windows and two skylights that provide ample illumination. Kudlow designed the 1,800-square-foot (167-square-meter) space so that the student work areas are next to hers, giving them the opportunity to watch their instructors work, as well as share their advice and insights in a communal environment.

The instruction at NYK Academy is focused on helping artists meet long-term goals. "I'm looking for people who want to make a career as a painter," Kudlow says. "I can pretty much assure students that if they follow the course here, they will become a painter. I also give them career guidance and help them make the transition from being a student to being a gallery-represented painter—that's something I find lacking in a lot of art schools." To help meet this long-term objective, the NYK Academy has what Kudlow calls her "masters program" (not an M.F.A. program), in which students can work on their own projects at the academy under Kudlow's supervision. "This way, they can't get too far lost," she says. "If you have the right supervision, you can overcome getting too discouraged. Those moments of frustration are always there for an artist, and they are always difficult. But they don't have to be devastating."

At any given time, the school has a relatively small number of students—ranging from about four to ten artists—ensuring that everyone receives both individualized attention and personal space. Each artist is assigned his or her own station divided by screens and covered with black fabric. The dividers are tall enough to block light from other workstations, which is a critical factor when drawing from casts. The stations allow students to pursue the curriculum independently and at their own pace.

Kudlow also maintains a small store at the school, where she sells several unique materials that she's found singularly helpful for both herself and students. Among them are mirrors, black mirrors, plumb lines, levels, and custom-made viewfinders and palettes.

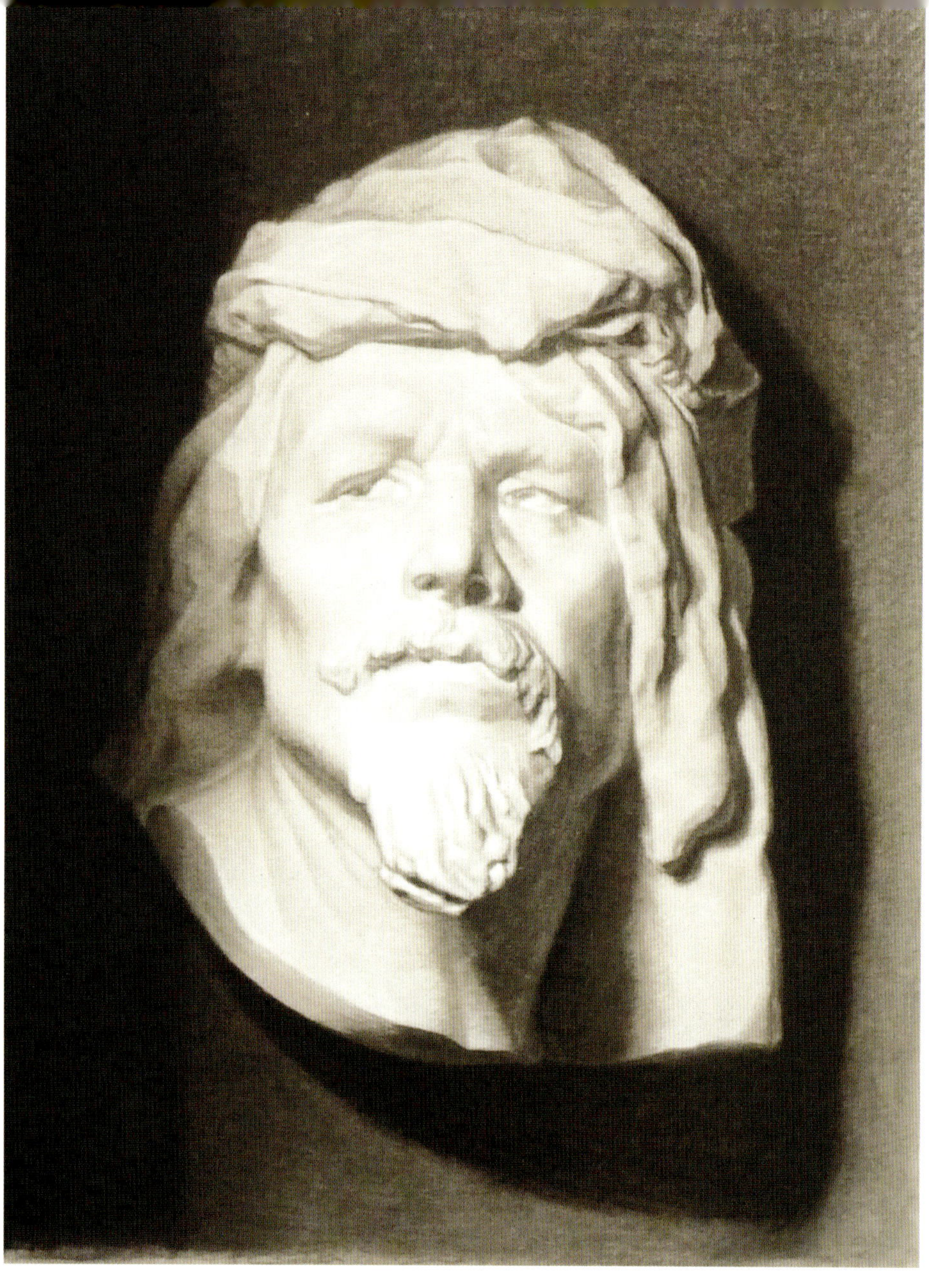

← This drawing is based on the many casts in Judith Kudlow's extensive collection. "I purchased most of them from the Giust Gallery, outside of Boston," she says.

→ Although students have delineated work areas, for Kudlow, it was the large north-facing windows that made this second-floor studio so appealing.

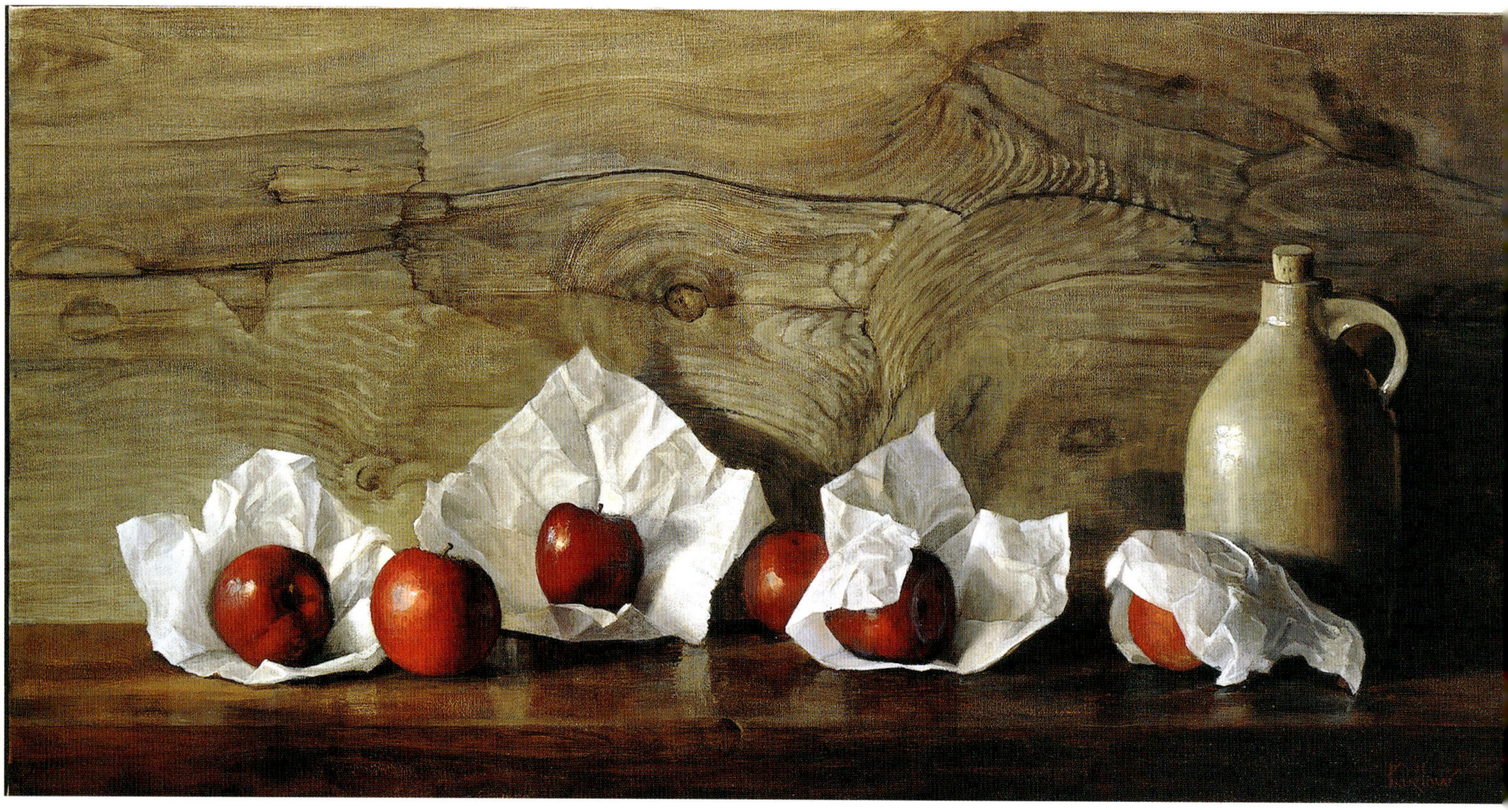

Cider
by Judith Kudlow, 2003, oil, 18" x 36" (46cm x 91cm). Private collection.

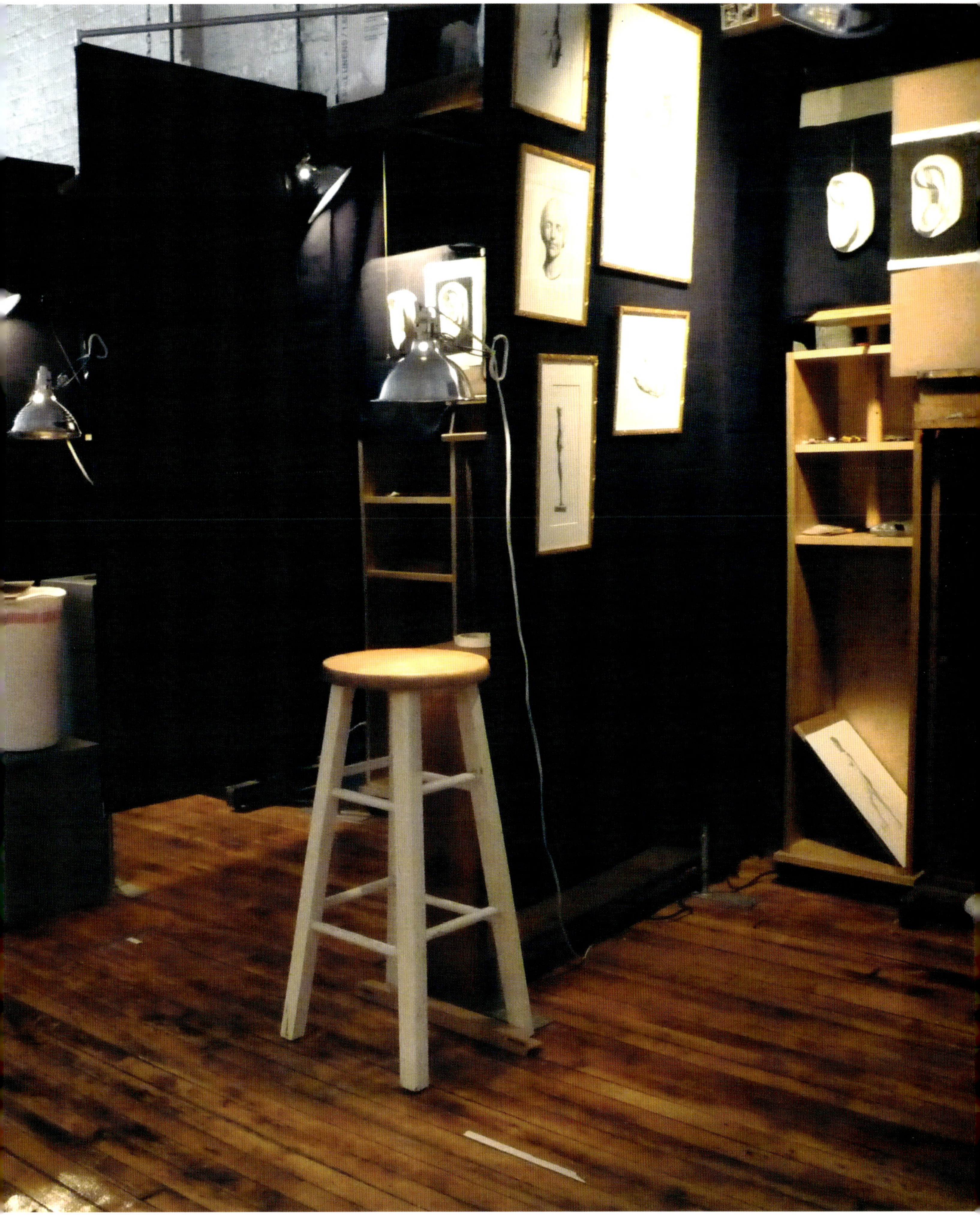

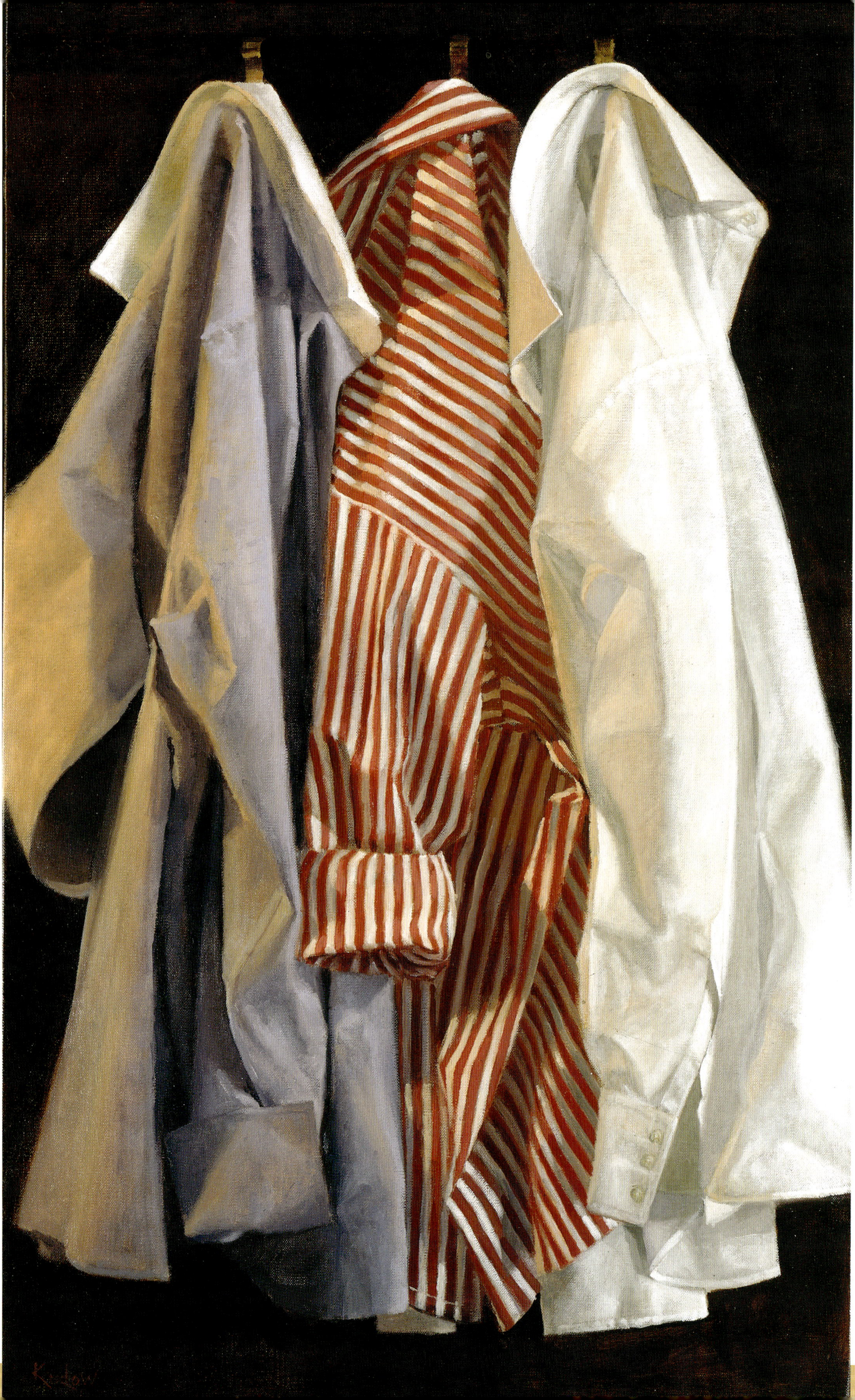

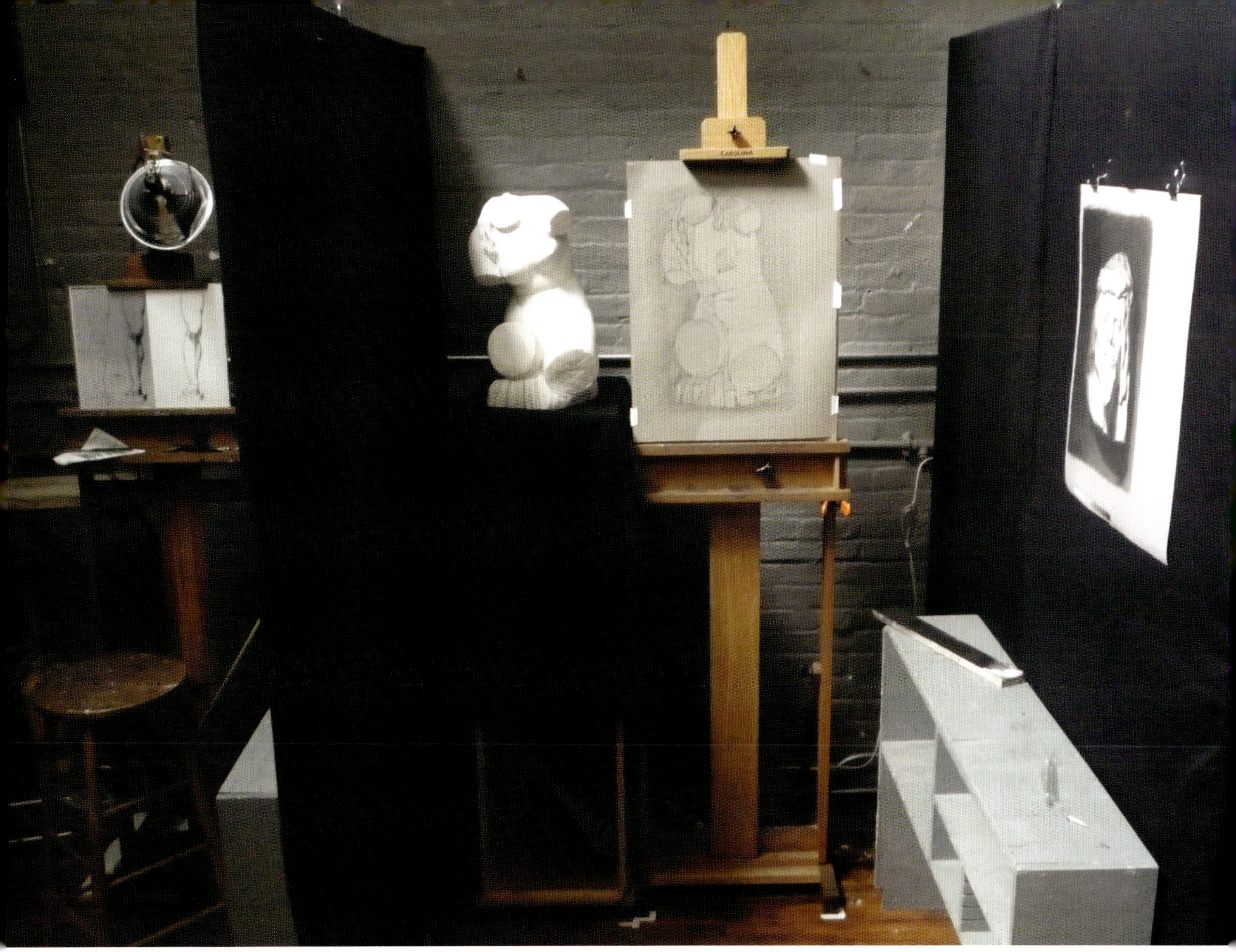

Students at the NYK Academy can maintain the same workstation throughout their course of study, which begins with copying Bargue's drawings and then copying plaster casts in graphite and then charcoal.

← **American Shirts**
by Judith Kudlow, 2004, oil, 33" x 19" (84cm x 48cm). Private collection.

"The level is important because students need to be sure their easels are plumb," Kudlow explains. "The viewfinder comes into play once students start composing their drawings. This happens at the cast-drawing stage; students need to know where to crop them. Andrea Smith had invented a viewfinder made out of wood—about 10 inches (25cm) square with a slide in the middle that moves flat up and down."

Kudlow is also a strong believer that an artist should have a comfortable palette that suits his or her working style. "When you work with the sight-size method, you're walking all the time," she says. "Having a stationary palette is not practical. I've always found that commercially available palettes are too heavy. But my woodworker, who also builds airplanes, suggested using aviation plywood, which is very strong and light. The resulting palette is extremely light, it fits the curves of the body, and the thumbhold is comfortable. It also features a metal plate on the side closest to your body, which you can add magnets to in order to balance the weight of the palette so that you can hold it without any effort. It just floats there on your arm."

These unique, useful materials are just one more compelling aspect of NYK Academy's instruction. Between the time-tested course of study, the high amount of individual attention students receive, and the intimate environment for the creation of art, this is certainly a school where students can learn to master a classical tradition.

To learn more about Judith Kudlow and the NYK Academy, visit her website at www.judithpondkudlow.com.

The Teaching Studios of Art

Excellence Without Rigidity

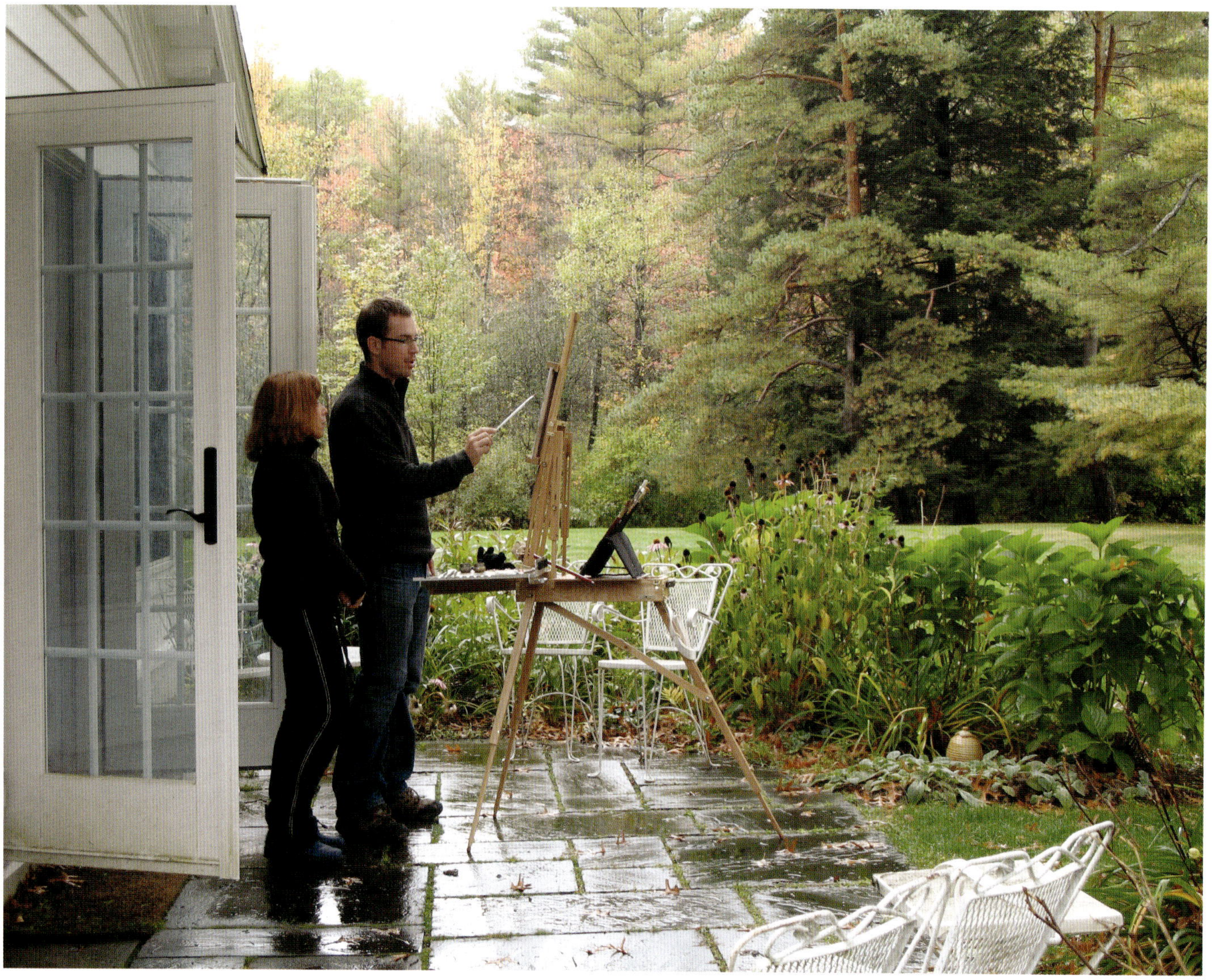

Instructor Bennett Vadnais helping a student with her plein air landscape at a Teaching Studios of Art workshop in the Berkshires.

The Teaching Studios of Art (TSA), in New York, offers a wide variety of instructional options in terms of subject matter, style of teaching, and structure of classes. The school, founded and run by artist-instructor Rob Zeller, currently has two campuses. One is in the coastal town of Oyster Bay, on the North Shore of Long Island, less than an hour's drive from New York City; the other is located in the Bushwick neighborhood of Brooklyn, an area becoming increasingly known as an incubator for contemporary art in New York City.

The rotating faculty is largely the same at both locations, but the subjects they teach are often different. For example, instructor Bennett Vadnais teaches plein air landscape painting at Oyster Bay and figure drawing and painting in Brooklyn. Some faculty may teach a semester-long class at one location and teach short workshops at the other. Oyster Bay is the more established of TSA's two campuses, and it is situated in a much more affluent community in the heart of Long Island's famed Gold Coast. Among the facilities are twelve individual workstations for drawing or painting from casts or still lifes, a large studio space for a class to work from a model, a gallery space, a small kitchen, and a student lounge. Landscape painters need merely to step outside to find beautiful views of Oyster Bay Harbor

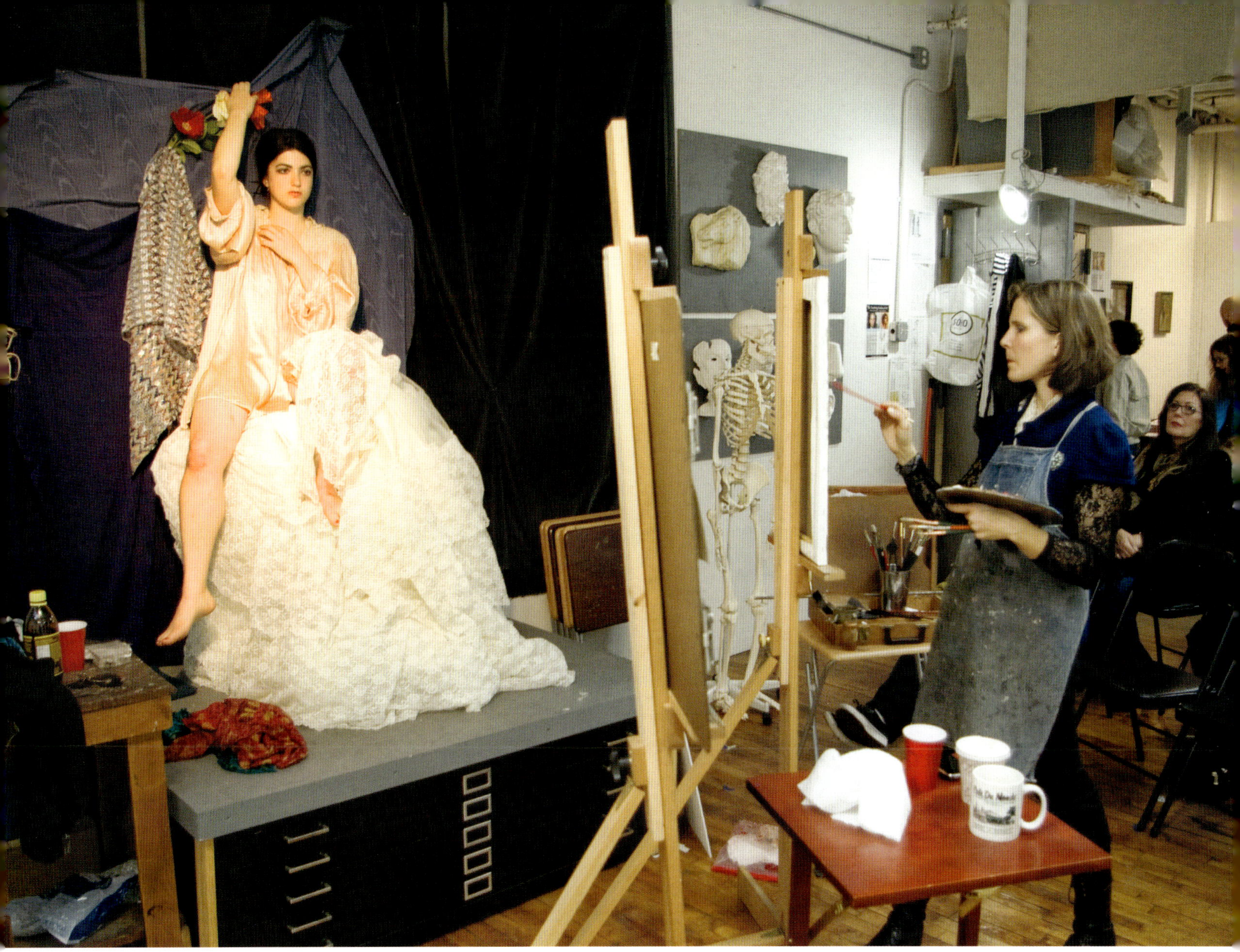

Instructor Patricia Watwood conducting a narrative portrait demonstration at the Brooklyn school.

and Long Island Sound, as well as greenery in nearby nature preserves.

In contrast, the Brooklyn campus is surrounded by the things young contemporary artists crave: urban decay, hip bars, coffee shops, and an exciting batch of new art galleries. The school features a large space for drawing and painting from a model, twelve individual workstations mounted along one wall, and Zeller's personal studio. One of the exciting advantages of the Brooklyn location is its close proximity to the private studios of some of the most exciting young realist painters working today. Workshops such as Adam Miller's Venetian Method often include a visit to the instructor's own studio. "Students need to see that we are all working artists who are trying to get our artwork out there and make a difference," Zeller explains. "It gives them inspiration."

The cultures and clientele of the two spaces are also different. The Bushwick campus is attended by a decidedly younger group who tend to come from a background in art. The Oyster Bay location attracts a wide range of students, from those learning the fundamentals to those returning to art making after many years.

Both campuses, though, are united by Zeller's instructional philosophy, which, in its flexibility and inclusivity, differs from that of many other small art schools and ateliers. "Many art schools revolve around one artist and his or her instructional philosophy," Zeller explains. "The Teaching Studios, though, follows a model set by jazz teachers. In Harlem in the 1950s, music studios would be rented for lessons with different musicians holding court. All the instructors were excellent, but because the maestros were constantly changing, there was no philosophy of 'my way or the highway.' That diversity is the philosophy of the Teaching Studios. We've added variety to the atelier model, and we are extremely fortunate to have such a talented faculty."

The TSA faculty are all working, professional artists in addition to being teachers. Among the many instructors who have taught at the school are Patricia Watwood, Chris Pugliese, Adam Miller, and Kristin Künc. All are representational artists who employ traditional techniques and subjects in their work. But the instructors' artistic

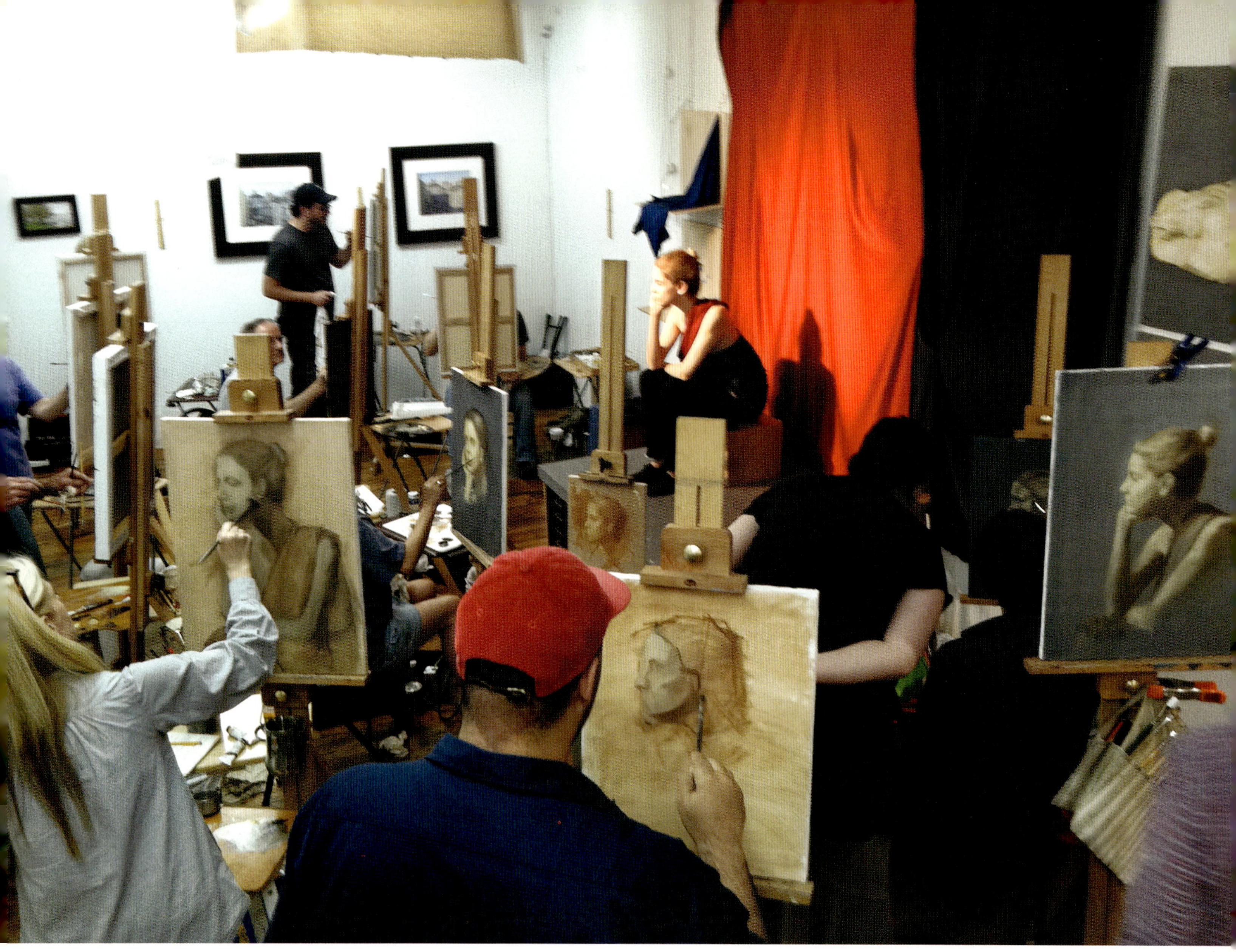

↑ During the four-week figure program in Brooklyn, the instructors rotate, but the model and pose stay the same.

→ Instructor Adam Miller critiques a student's underpainting during a Brooklyn workshop.

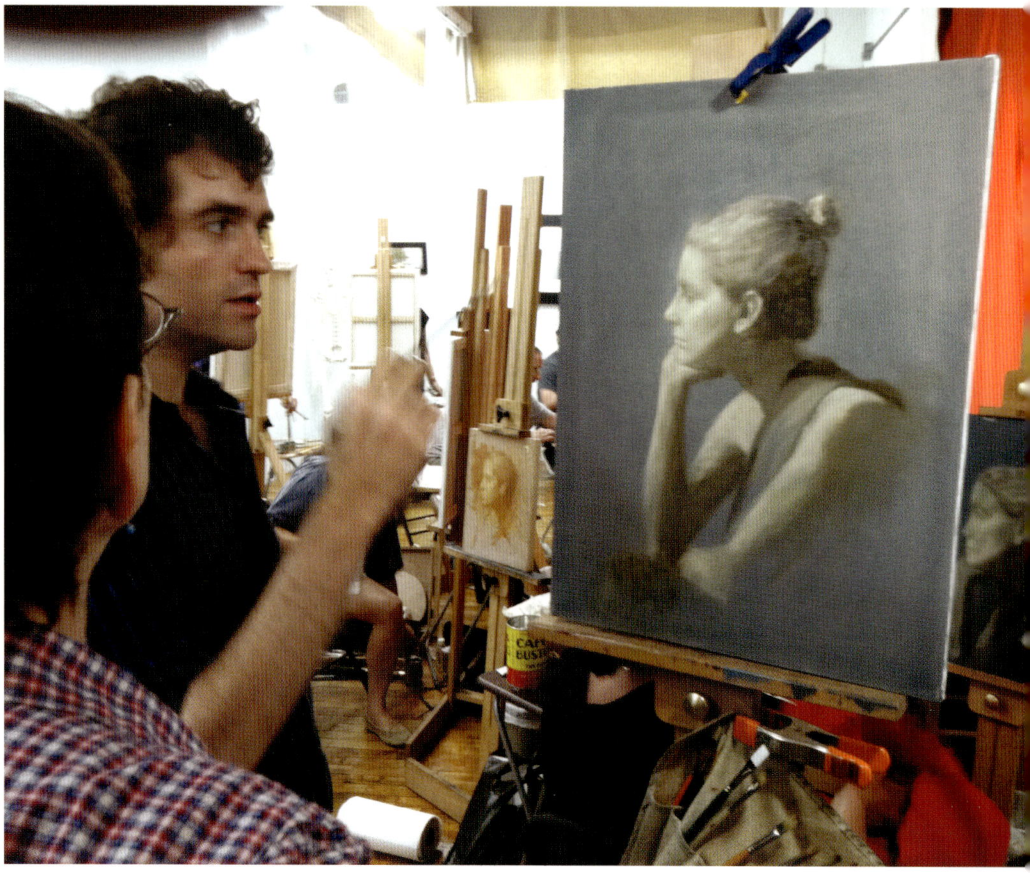

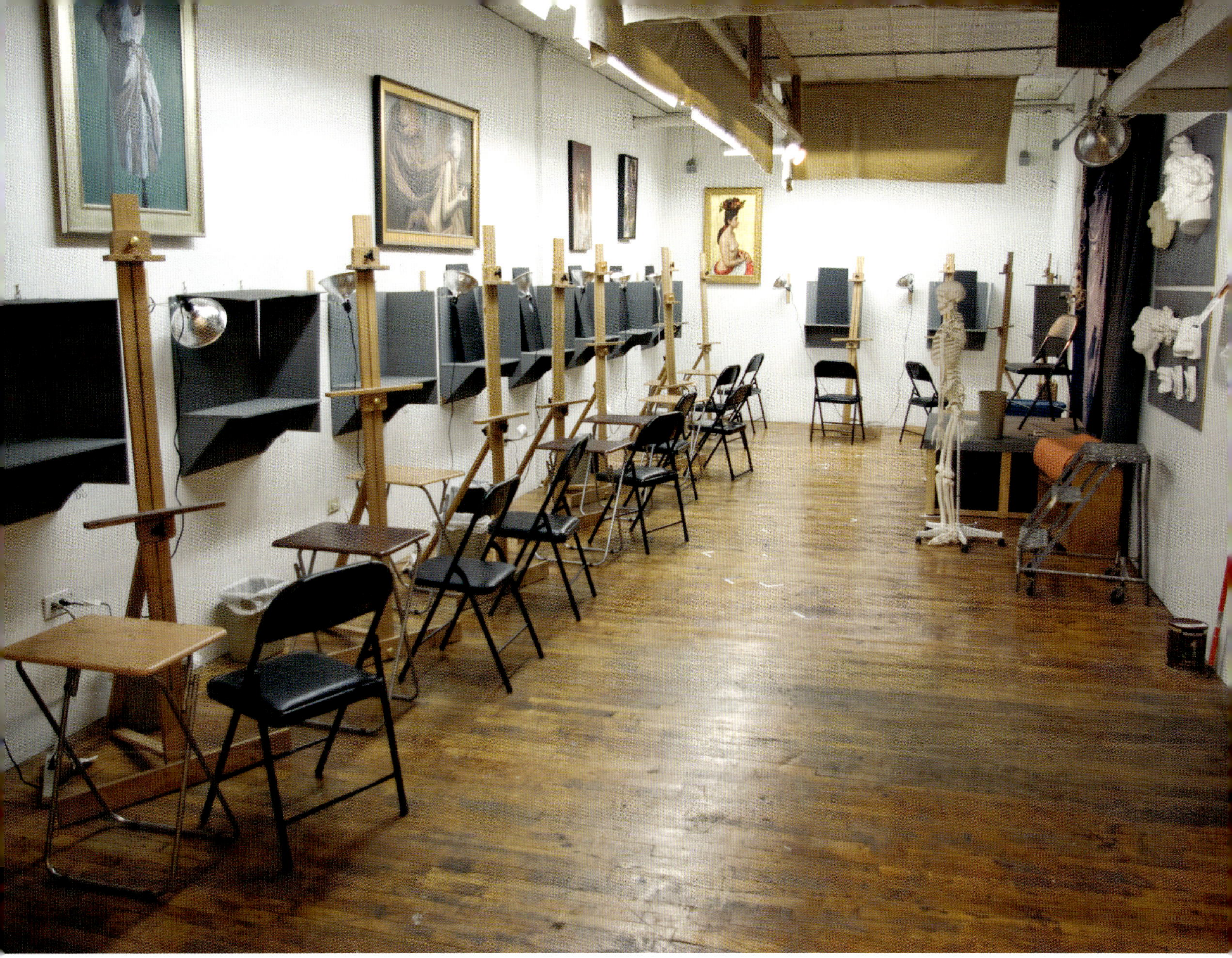

Cast drawing is a major part of the curriculum at the Teaching Studios of Art.

focuses and instructional philosophies vary, and students are free to gravitate to one or several teachers, depending on their interests and which instructional styles they respond to best. "We want excellence without rigidity," Zeller says.

This mission is largely informed by the founder's own varied art education. Zeller earned a B.F.A. from the Boston Museum School of Fine Arts and an M.F.A. from the New York Academy of Art, and he studied for two years with Jacob Collins at the Water Street Atelier, in New York City. He is the winner of a Pollock-Krasner Foundation grant—an award not often given to representational artists. TSA was born out of landscape workshops that Zeller taught in New York City's Central Park in 2008. He soon after began teaching in his Brooklyn studio, and the following year he opened a school.

Like many other art schools, TSA pays careful attention to lighting and uses a combination of light sources, which Zeller believes allows for more accurate value judgments than starker setups. The Oyster Bay studio is lit by daylight-corrected fluorescent lights, as well as a limited amount of natural light. The Brooklyn campus features both warm and cool bulbs pointed toward the model and daylight-corrected fluorescent lights on the easels. In addition, the rooms' white walls create ambient light that leads to softer shadows and a more naturalistic look.

The individual workstations in which students can work from a still life or plaster cast are a key element of TSA's instructional practice. Each station consists of a neutral-gray shelf and backdrop hung along the wall, accompanied by an easel and a side table. Although the workstations are identical in their construction—offering students a degree of uniformity and consistency—artists are free to arrange themselves and their lighting as they wish. In this way, these workstations are much like the Teaching Studios: devoted to classical techniques but built with freedom and flexibility in mind. How appropriate for a school that strives to teach its students classical skills through uniquely individual learning experiences.

To learn more on the Teaching Studios of Art, visit the school's website at www.teachingstudios.com.

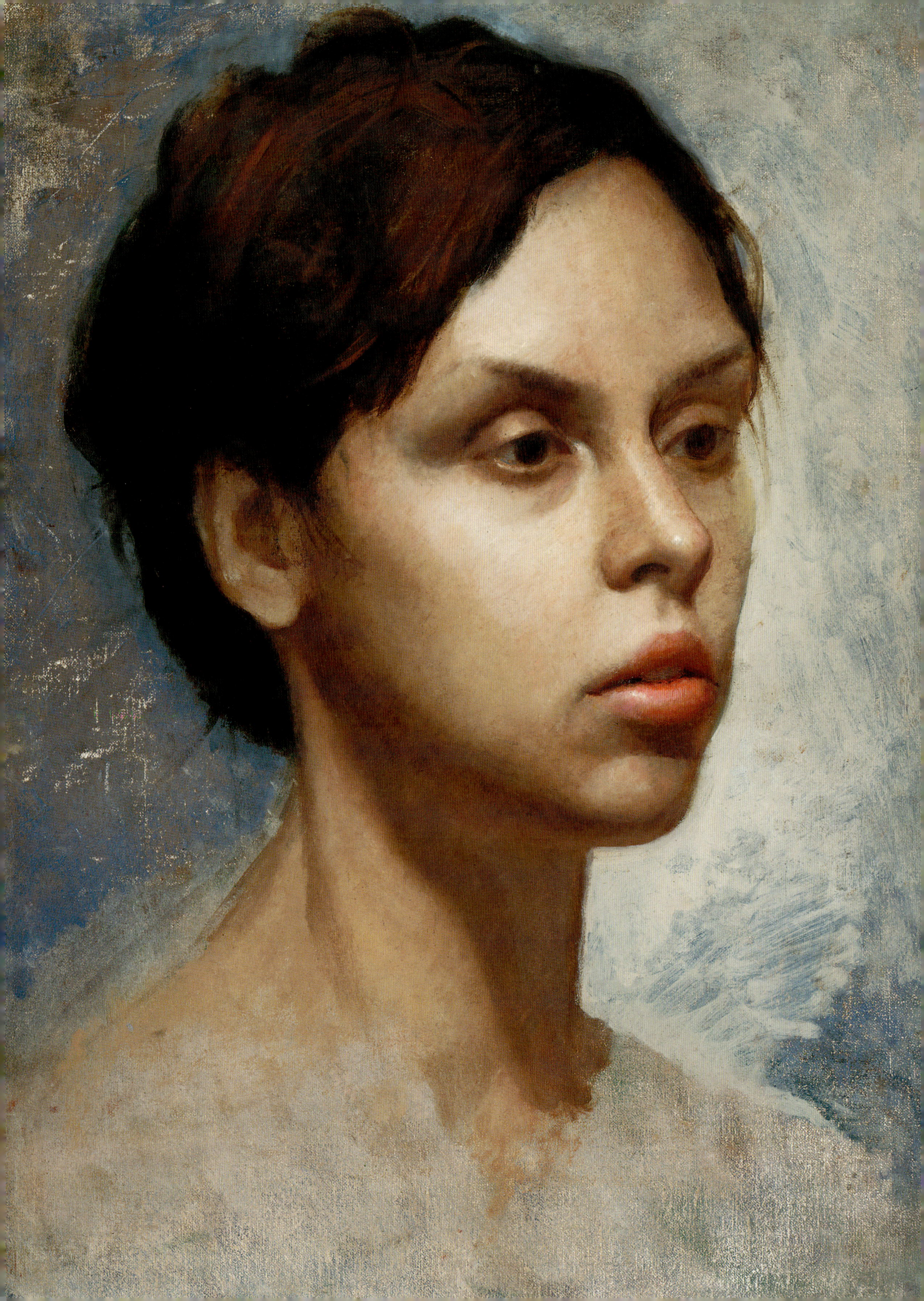

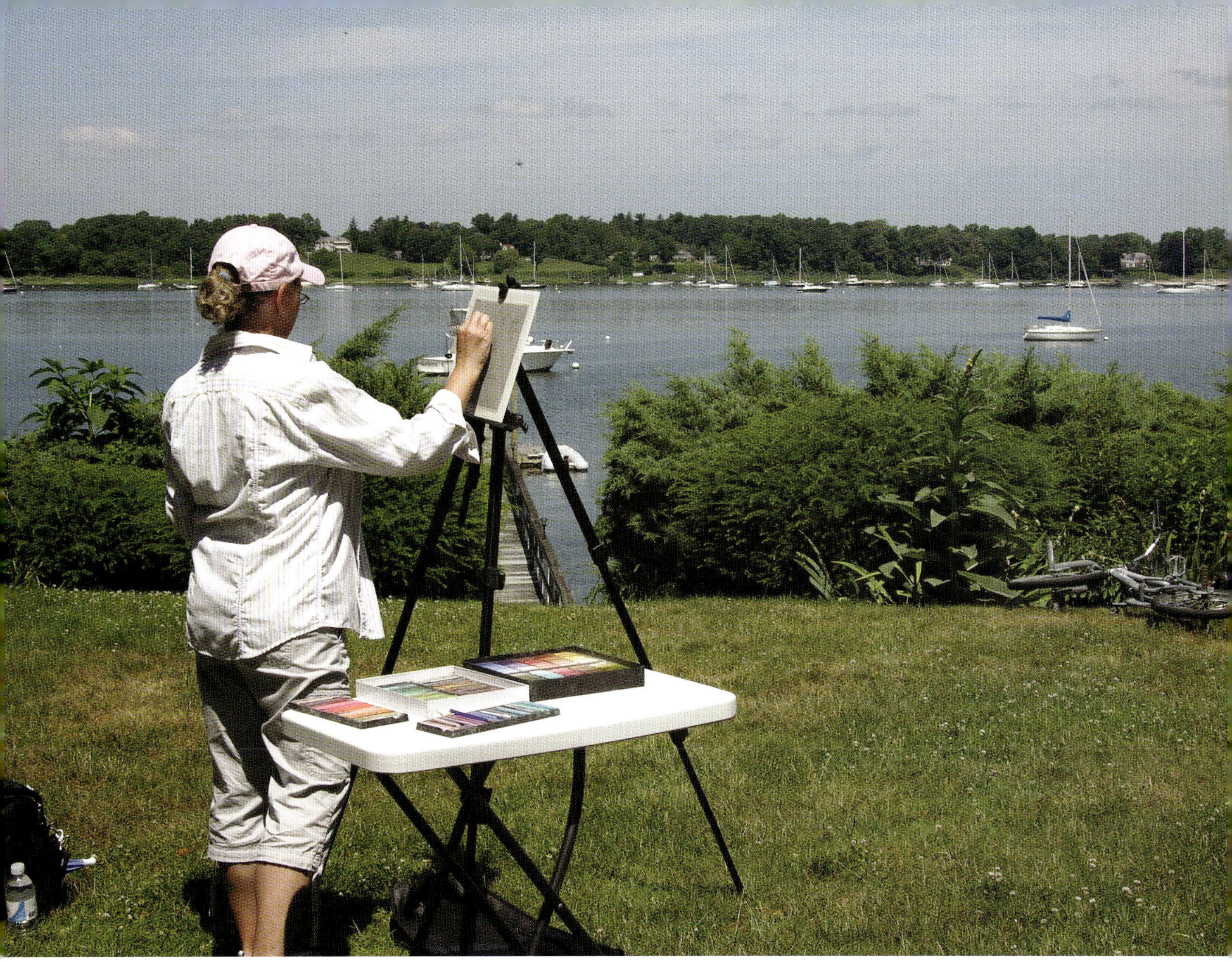

↑ The Oyster Bay location offers scenic harbor views.

→ The Teaching Studios' figure program in Brooklyn features one long pose for four weeks.

← **Cecily**
by Robert Zeller, 2012, oil on linen panel, 11" x 14" (28cm x 36cm).

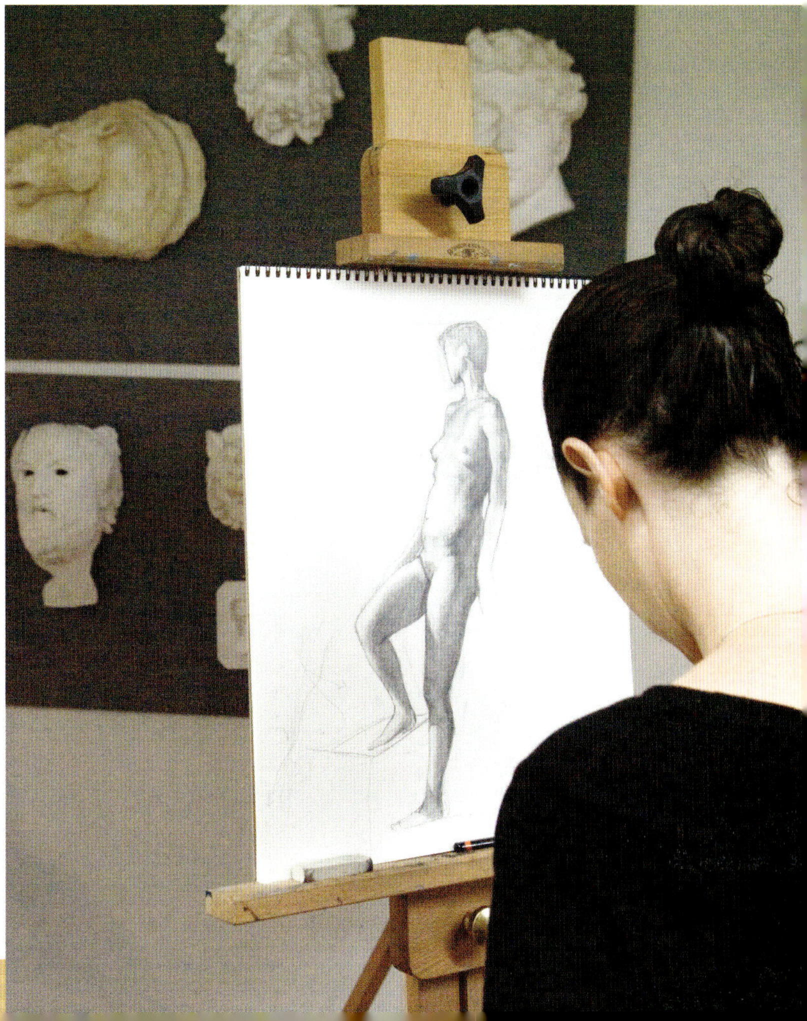

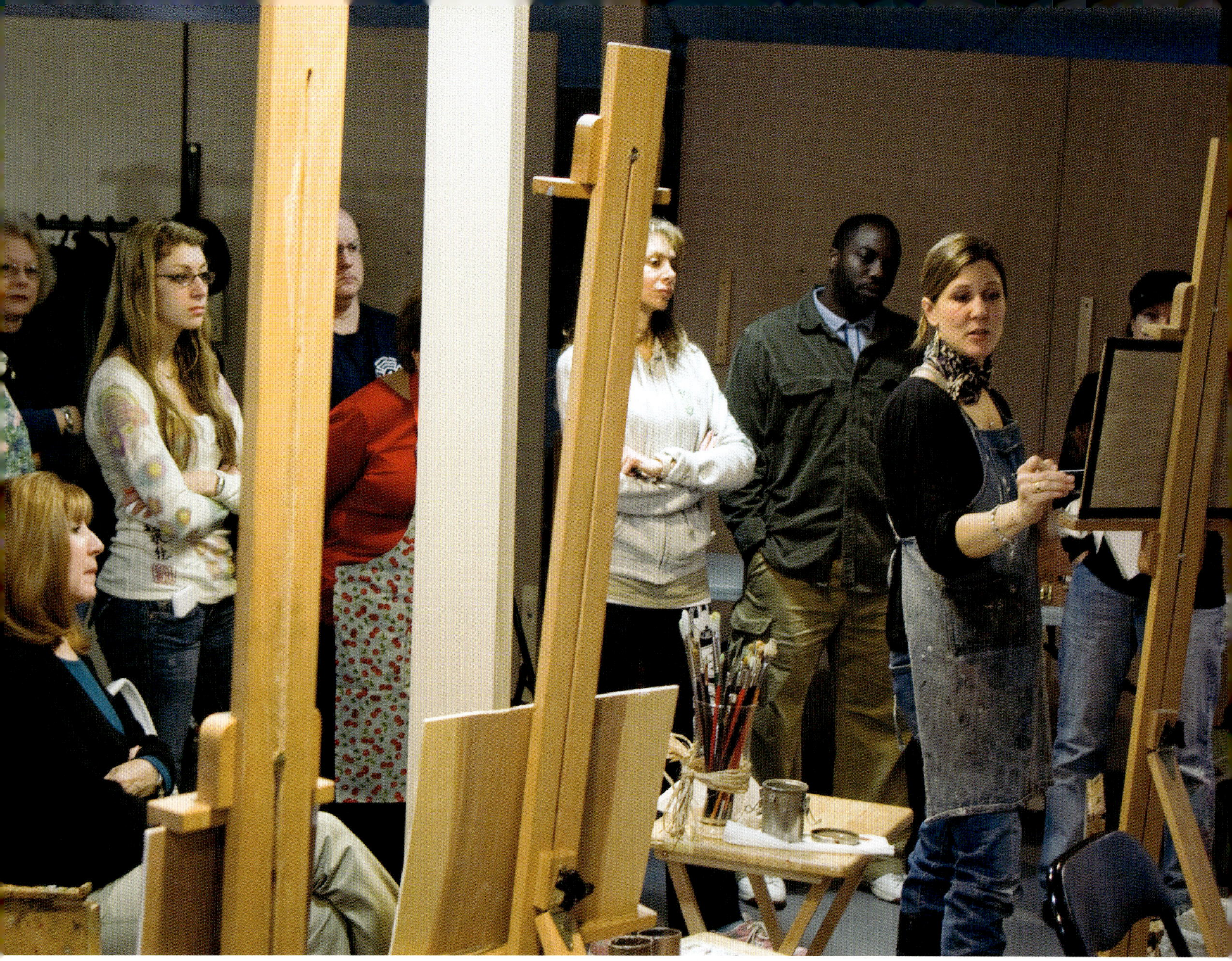

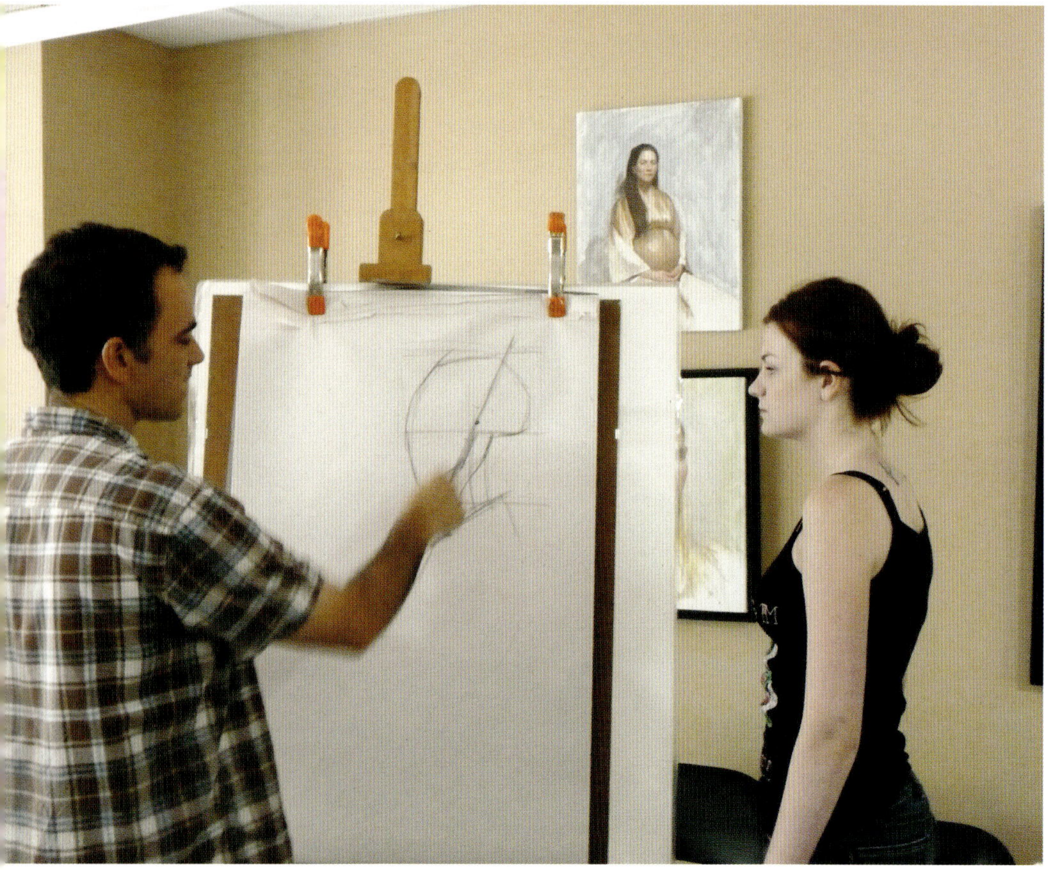

↑ Patricia Watwood conducts a painting demonstration for students in Oyster Bay.

← Rob Zeller demonstrates anatomical structure for his portrait class in Oyster Bay.

→ Instructor Chris Pugliese demonstrates a color-glazing technique in an Oyster Bay workshop.

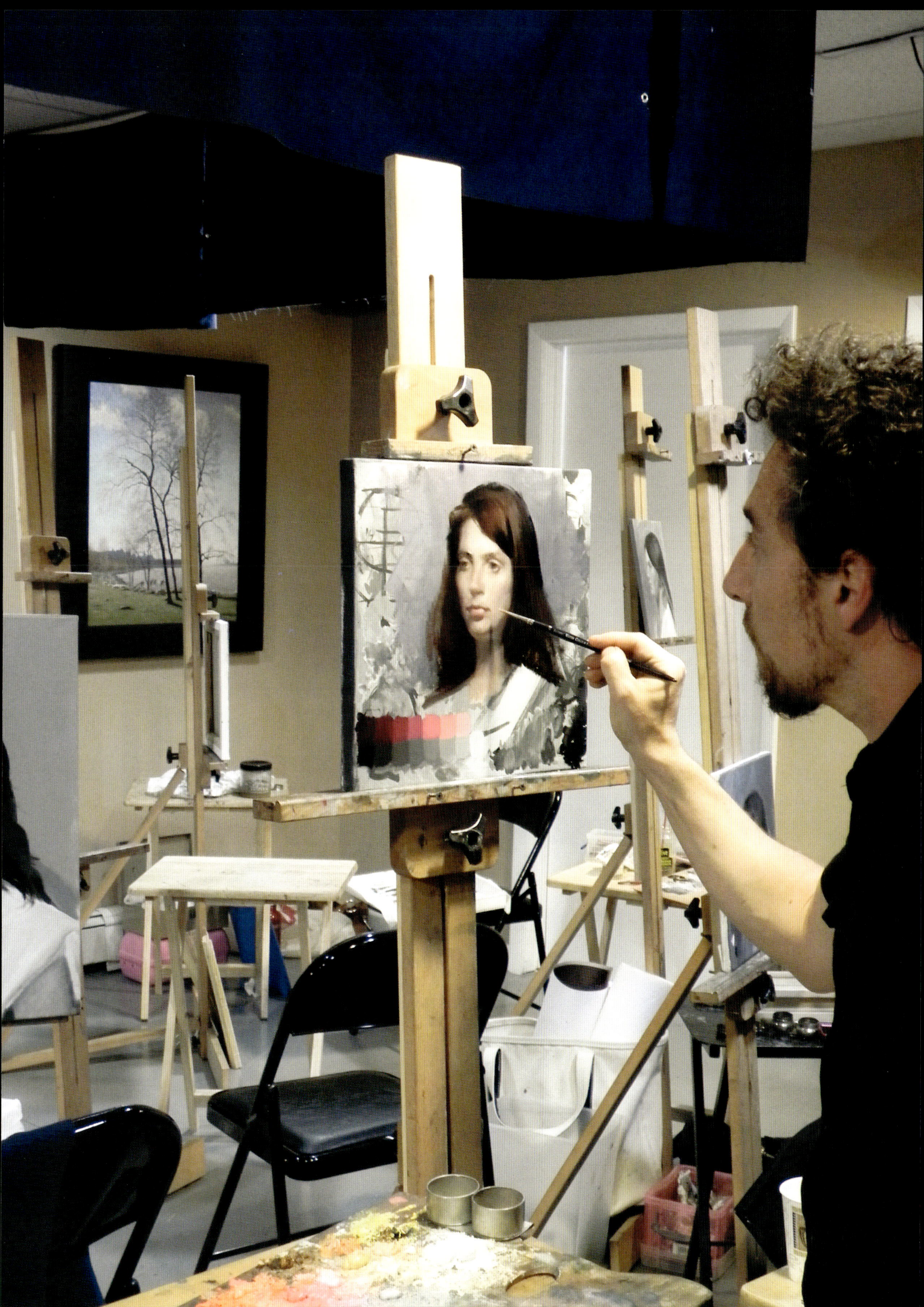

Ryder Studio School

Studios for the Serious Pursuit of Art Education

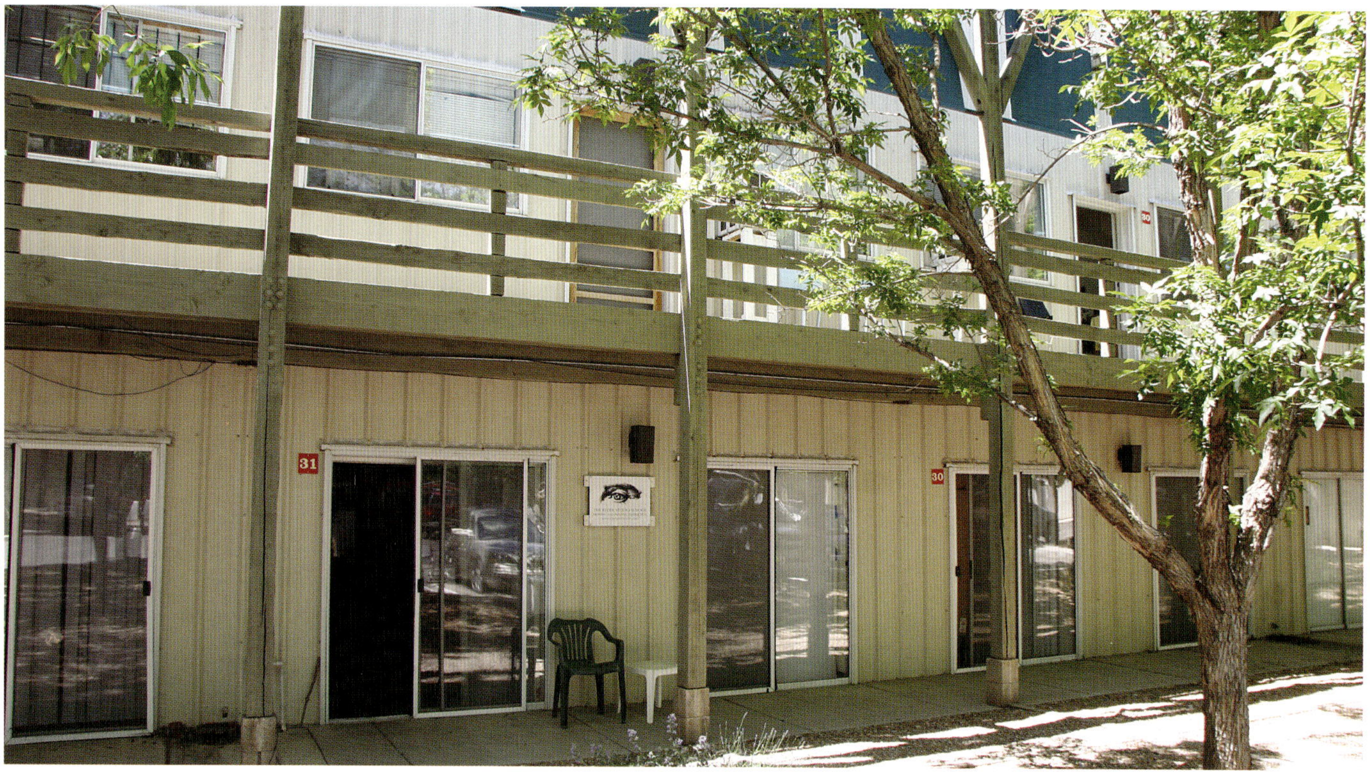

↑ The exterior of the Second Street Studios building in Santa Fe, which houses the Ryder Studio School.

→ Anthony Ryder standing in one of the ground-floor studios in the Second Street Studios development, in Santa Fe.

Across the country, real-estate developers and civic groups have converted abandoned buildings into artists' studios, and some forward-thinking individuals have built new, low-cost complexes of studios and living quarters. Anthony Ryder found one such energy-efficient space in Santa Fe, New Mexico, where he now operates an art school. "I was teaching drawing and painting in New York, Seattle, San Francisco, and Santa Fe for fifteen years, and my wife, Celeste, and I decided it was finally time to put down roots and offer a more comprehensive, sequential art-education program," Ryder explains. "I was renting a space in the Second Street Studios complex on the south side of town and liked the location and the community of creative people, so I decided to also rent a larger space in the same location for my school."

Second Street Studios is a complex of thirteen new and renovated buildings that began offering working and living spaces to artists in 1990. It now markets a variety of rental space from 600 to 2,280 square feet (56 to 212 square meters), with tenants having off-street parking and a landscaped courtyard between the various structures. In recent years, tenants have included painters, florists, craftsmen, and sculptors.

Ryder chose Santa Fe as the location of his school in part because he had been teaching in the city for a number of years and because he first came to know the city in 1979, after spending seven weeks riding his bike there from Rhode Island. "I dropped out of the Rhode Island School of Design after one year, worked as a machinist in Rhode Island, and then I decided to ride my bike to New Mexico where a friend had a job in construction," Ryder remembers. "While working there, I spent most of my free time learning to draw, and eventually I moved to New York to attend the Art Students League, where I studied with Ted Seth Jacobs."

Much of the success of Ryder's school is based on the reputation he developed after writing *The Artist's Complete Guide to Figure Drawing*. The book has sold

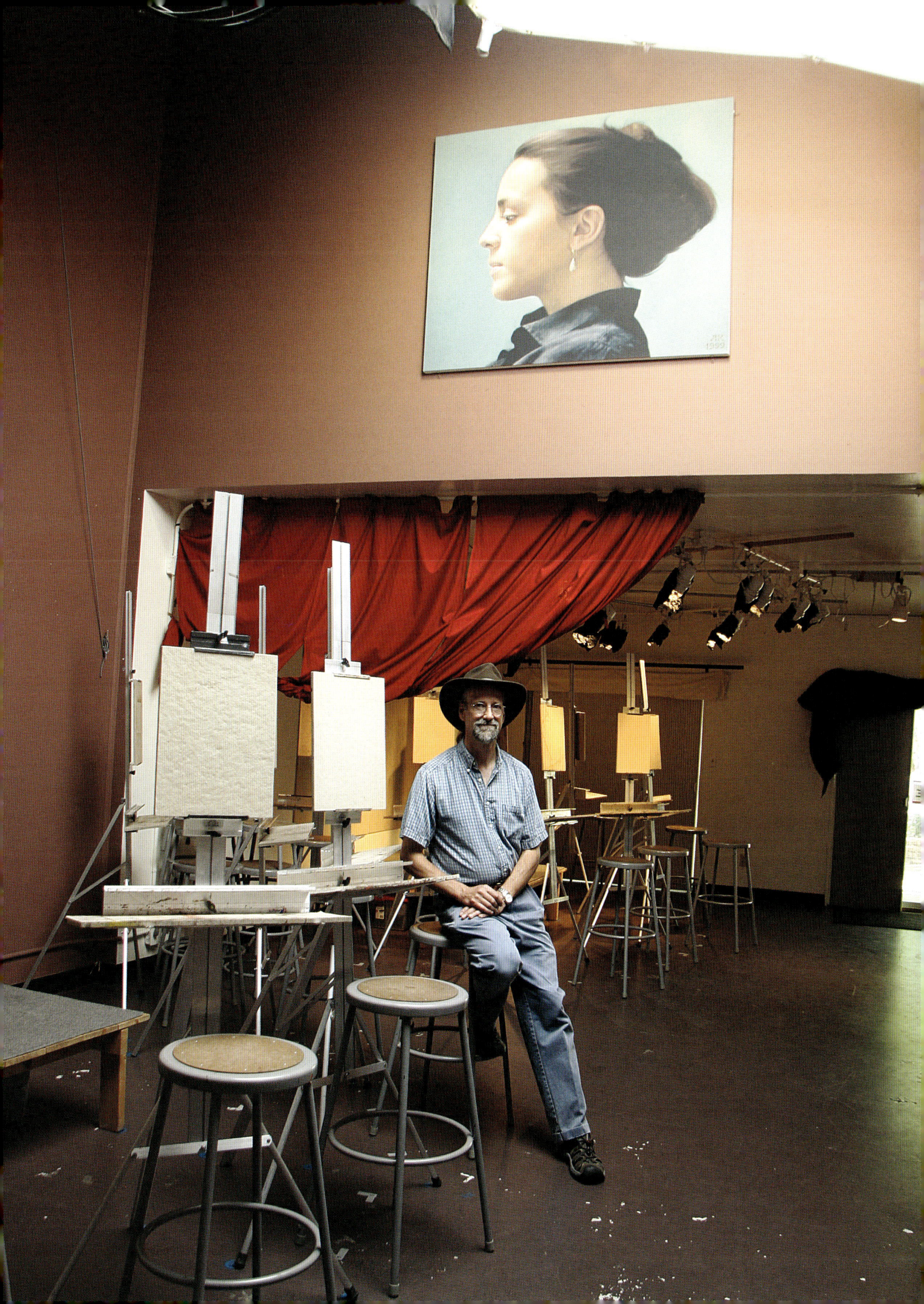

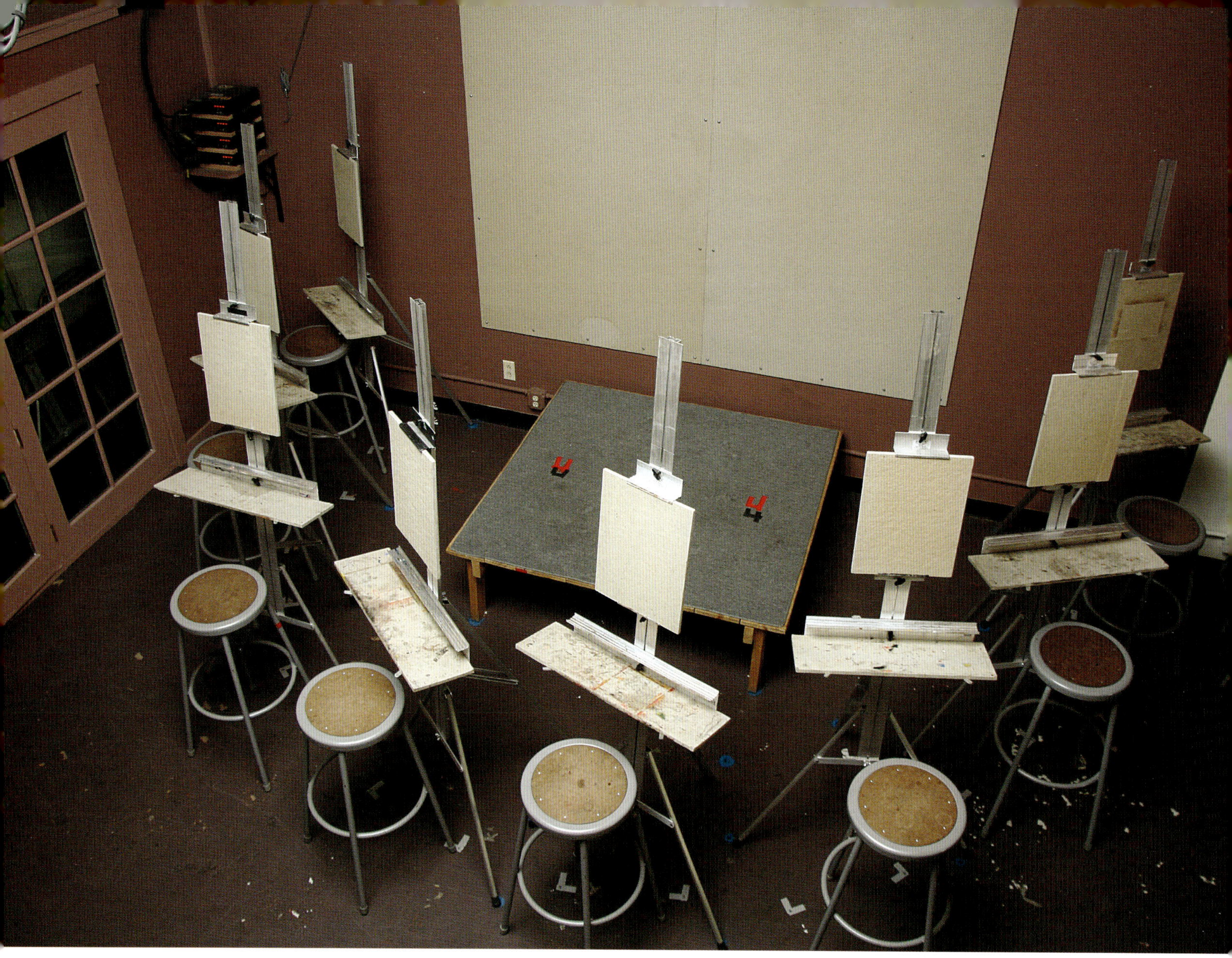

A view of the Ryder School studios with the model stand and easels.

more than 50,000 copies since it was first published in 1998, and the well-written explanations of Ryder's intensive approach to figure drawing have brought many students to his workshops and classes.

The facility of the Ryder Studio School has 800 square feet (74 square meters) of space on the main floor of the building, divided into two large studios—one with a ceiling angled to 14 feet (4m), the other with a lower ceiling because it sits under the 400-square-foot (37-square-meter) second-floor office, bathroom, lounge, and skylit still-life studio. Ryder installed a 6'-x-6' (2m-x-2m) Kino Flo fluorescent fixture in the studio with the higher ceiling, and it provides abundant soft, cool (5,500 Kelvin) light on both the model and easels. In the other space, under the lower ceiling, Ryder put in a halogen track-light system with individual fixtures for the model stand and for each easel. The halogen light is warm (3,000 Kelvin) and intense, with dark, hard-edged shadows. Ryder believes that exposing his students to different lighting situations helps them to better see and understand color, and prepares them to paint under various circumstances.

"Although we've had more than sixteen students working here at one time, I'd say the average class size is closer to a dozen or so," Ryder says. "Notwithstanding the intensive approach to drawing and painting that I teach, it's really just the basics. When I was a student, Ted Seth Jacobs said that what he was teaching us was well-known to artists before the twentieth century: 'Every third-rate nineteenth-century painter knew this stuff,' he commented. These days it's not uncommon to hear students lament the loss of that tradition. At the same time, they want to work from photos, to become masters overnight, and they're looking for quick and easy solutions to the problems of painting. But the tradition hasn't been lost. Neither have the problems become easier to solve. The main thing is practice from life—lots of practice—and sound instruction. As it relates to the former, we provide models, light and a well-furnished, well-organized space. With regard to the latter, I do my best to teach what I learned from Ted."

For more on Anthony Ryder, visit his website at www.tonyryder.com. For more on the Ryder Studio School, visit www.theryderstudio.com.

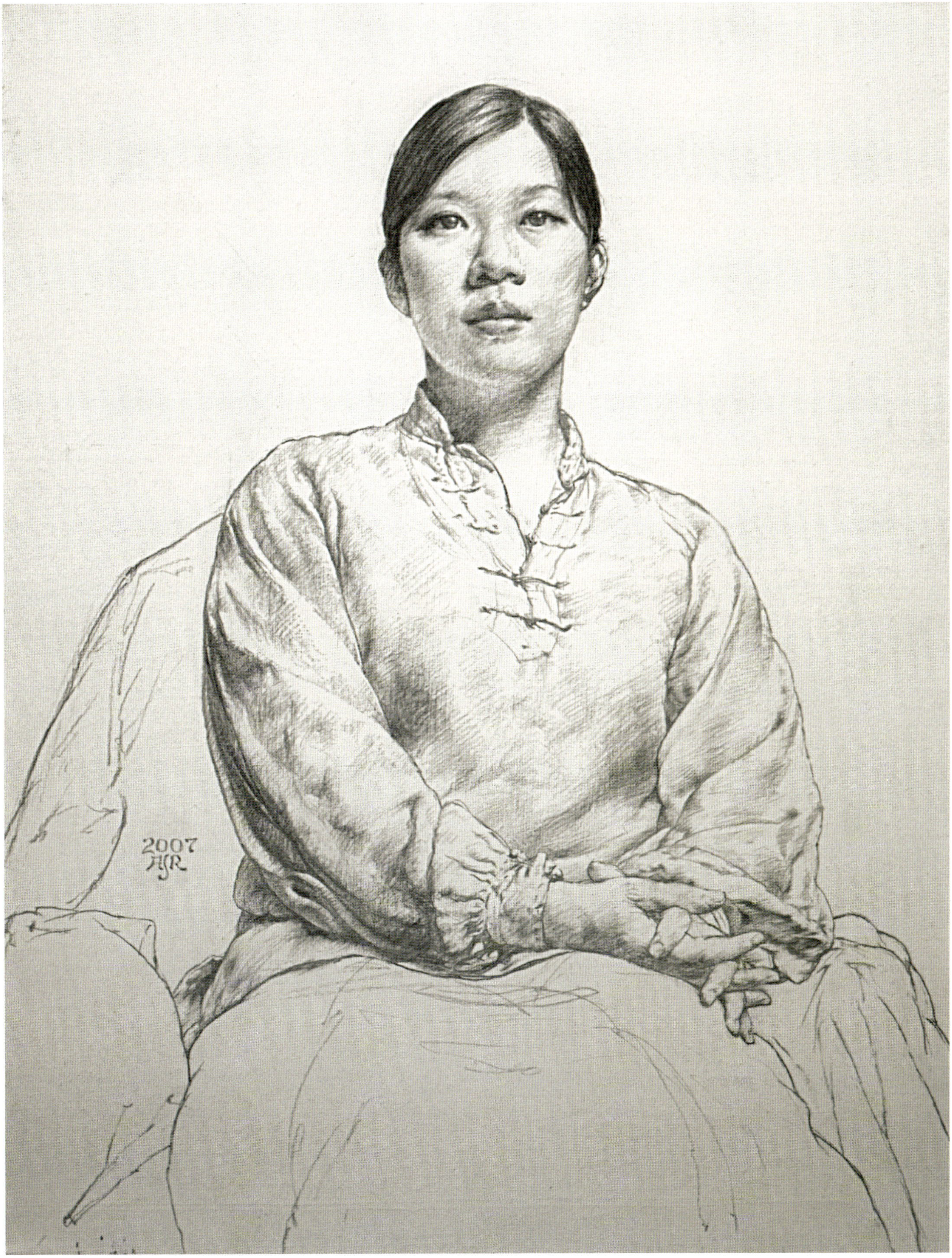

Lai Lin
by Anthony Ryder, 2007, charcoal on primed linen, 18" x 14" (46cm x 36cm). Collection of the artist.

Center for Academic Study & Naturalist Painting

Studios for Academic Study

Ryan S. Brown is a dreamer who somehow makes his dreams come true. Barely thirty years old and the father of four children under the age of ten, he found time to study at the Florence Academy of Art, in Italy, after graduating from Brigham Young University, in Provo, Utah. In 2008, he established his own art school in Springville, Utah. That school, the Center for Academic Study & Naturalist Painting (CAS), moved into a new facility in 2010, where students and faculty members now have ample space on two floors of a building.

"Our previous building had about one-fourth the amount of space and ran out of places for people to work and store their artwork," Brown explains. "Considering that our educational program depends on being able to leave easels and plaster casts in the exact same position for weeks at a time, we didn't have much flexibility. Now we have room to accommodate eighteen to twenty-five full-time students in the painting and drawing program, fifteen

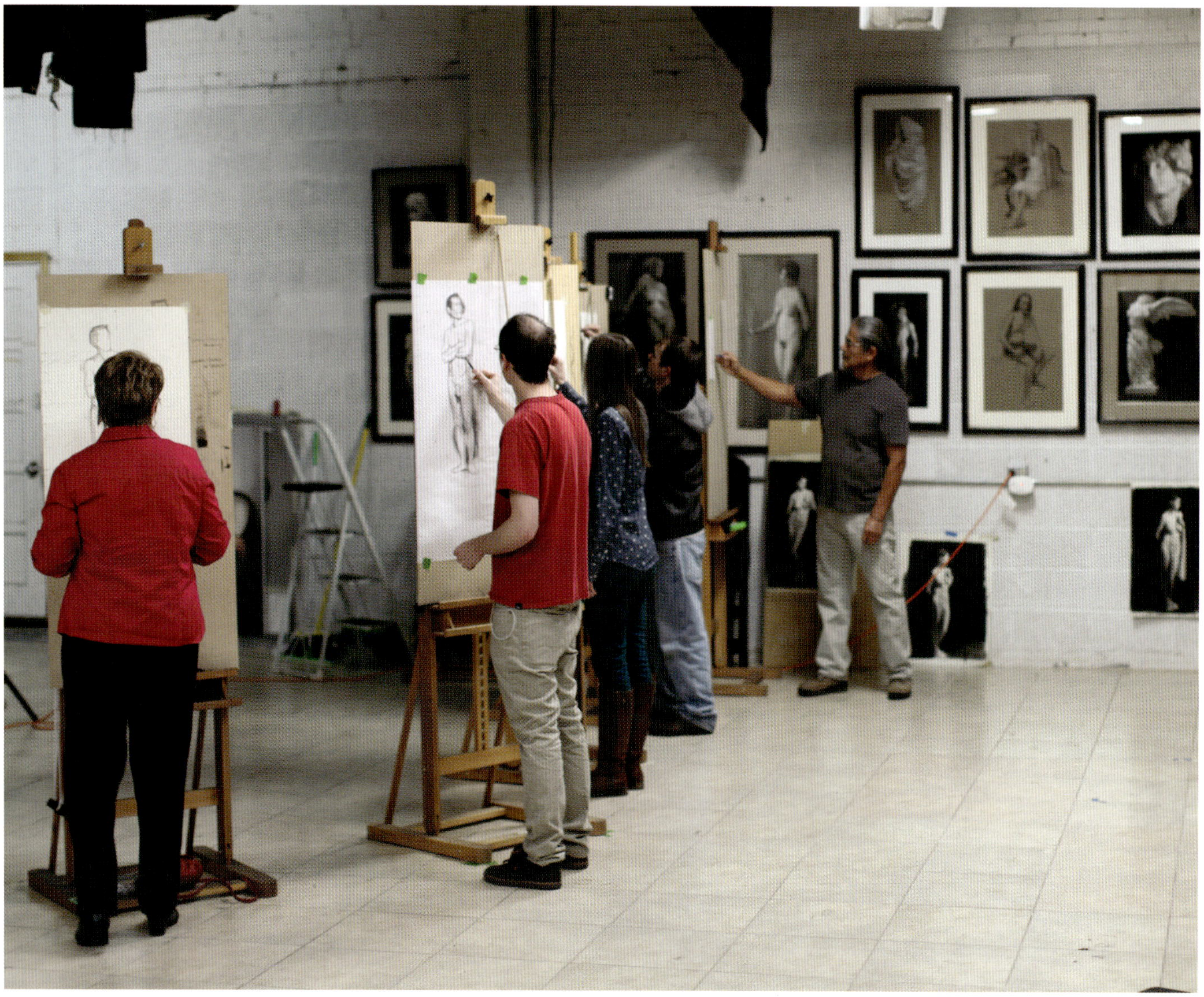

Students working in the large middle studio of the CAS.

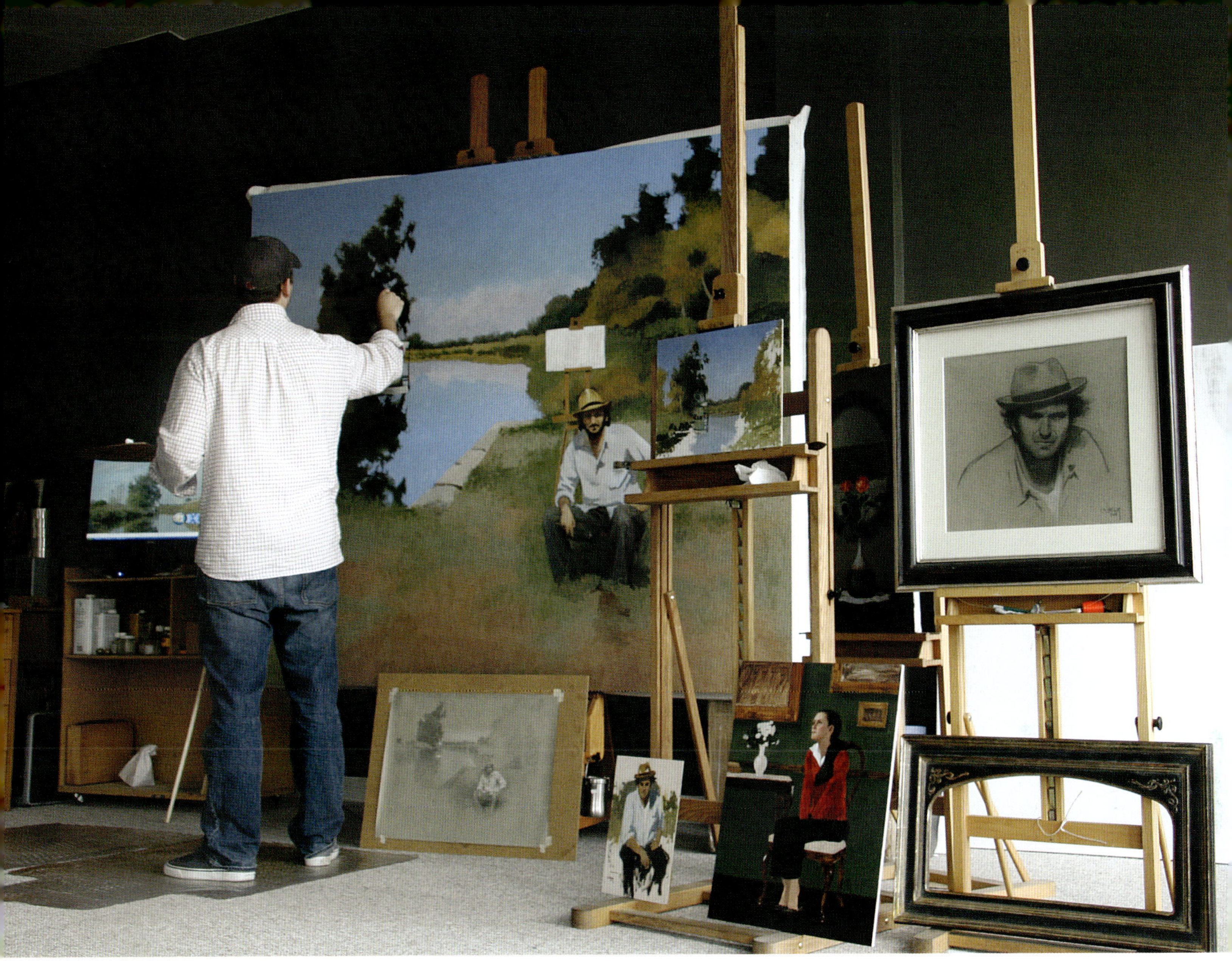

Ryan S. Brown working on a large landscape in the northern studio at the Center for Academic Study & Naturalist Painting (CAS), in Springville, Utah.

area with a computer and microwave oven, and a gallery for displaying our work. We're still making adjustments, but the educational program is thriving in this new facility."

The main floor of the school is divided into three major areas. Brown's studio, where he creates his own paintings and teaches classes in multifigure composition, is on the north end of the building. Also on this floor are a middle room with eastern exposures for cast drawing and working from live models, an entrance gallery section, and two bathrooms. The lower level has a kitchen and storage room, a sculpture studio, a library and lounge, and a bathroom.

In order to convert the industrial building to an atelier, Brown had to block out some of the natural light coming through the windows, install daylight fluorescent light fixtures, add custom daylight fixtures over the model stand, and paint all the walls a neutral green color. He also had to add furniture to accommodate the additional students and prepare for lectures. "We moved some furniture from the old studio, but we had to build additional shelving and storage units," Brown says. "Someone donated a computer, and my grandmother gave us her living room furniture and a freezer. We bought some other items in a surplus sale, including thirty-five chairs priced at two dollars each."

Brown was able to recruit some of his friends from the Florence Academy to teach with him in Utah, including Niki Covington, who last year taught anatomy and écorché sculpting. Brown also travels to teach and work with other young figurative artists, and he recently presented workshops at the Los Angeles Academy of Figurative Art and the Atelier Marchant, both in California.

For more on Ryan S. Brown, visit his website at www.ryansbrownart.com. For more on the Center for Academic Study & Naturalist Painting, visit www.cas-utah.com.

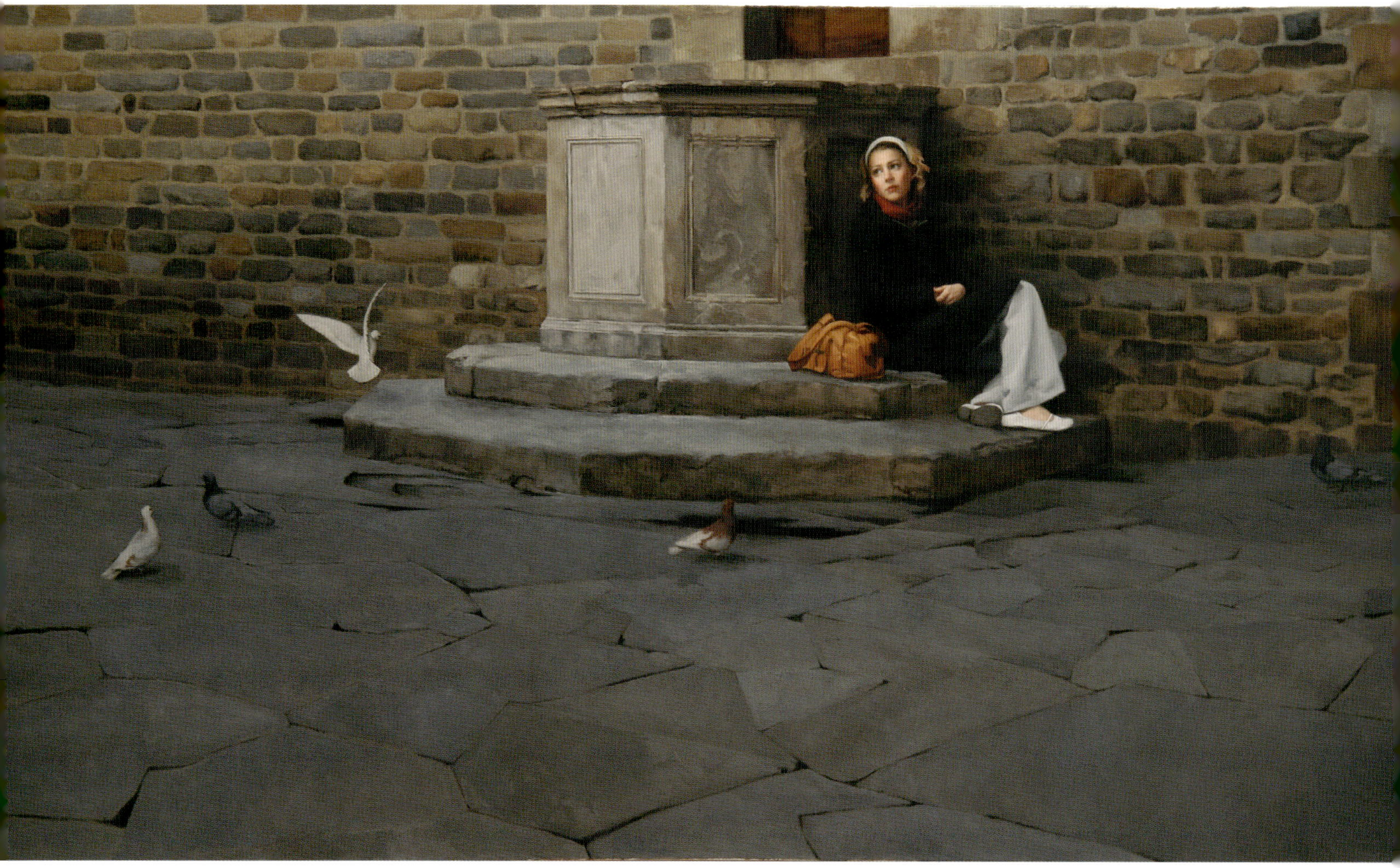

↑ **The Loneliness of Waiting**
by Ryan S. Brown, 2010, oil, 40" x 70" (102cm x 178cm). Courtesy of Astoria Fine Art, Jackson Hole, Wyoming.

→ A storage area where books, plaster casts, and student work is available.

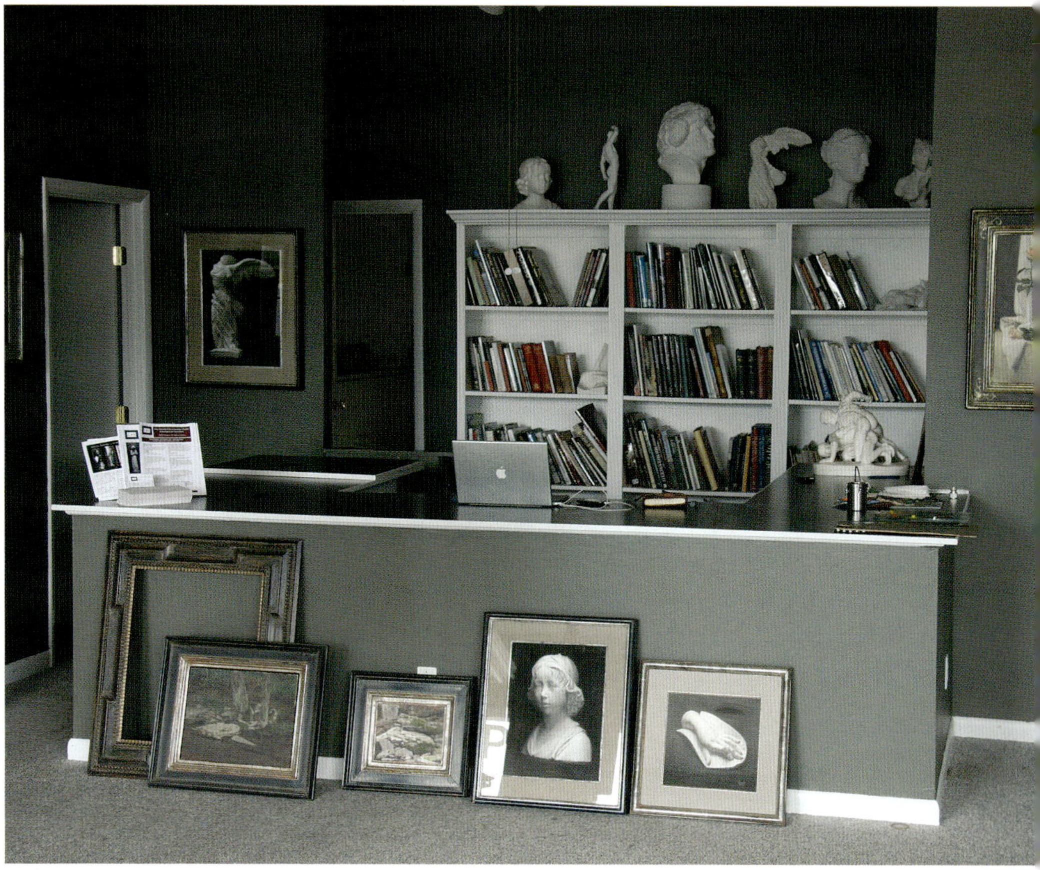

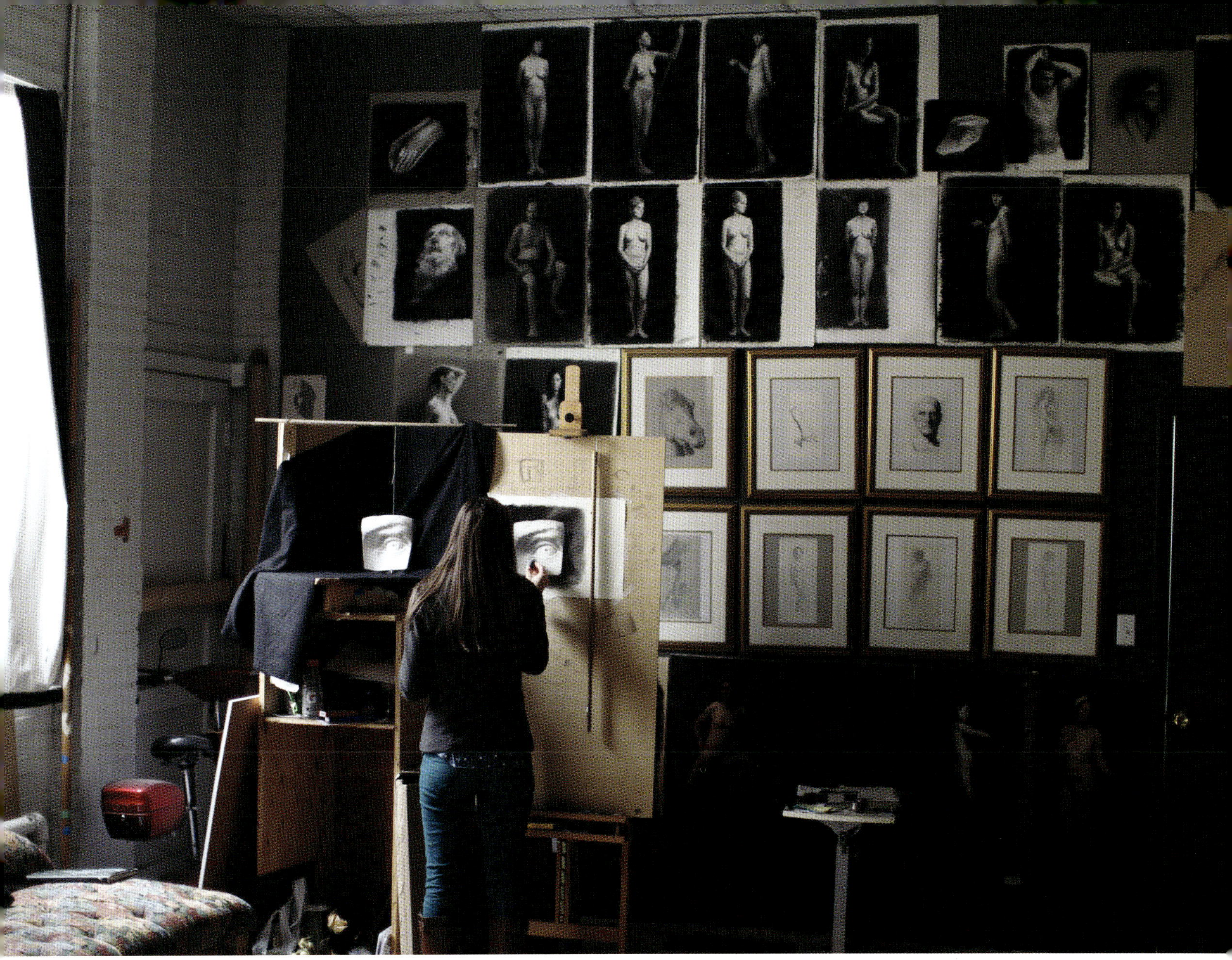

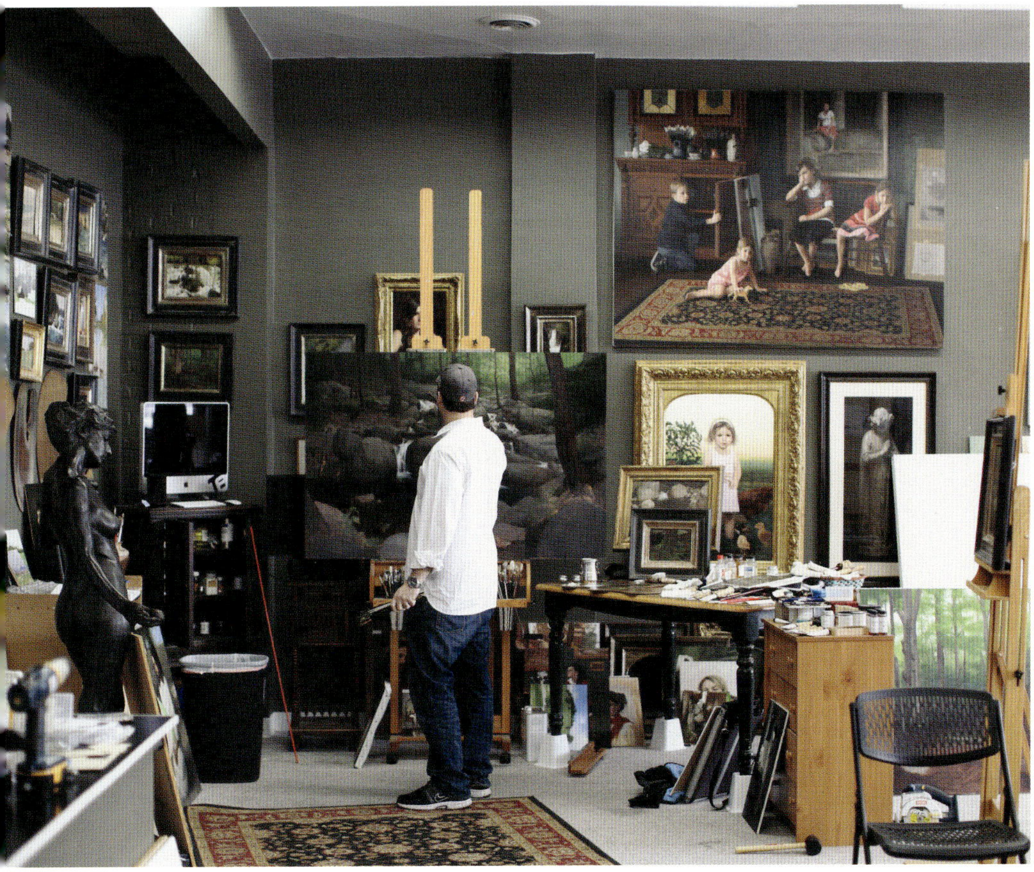

↑ A CAS student working on a cast drawing in natural light.

← Ryan S. Brown in the studio.

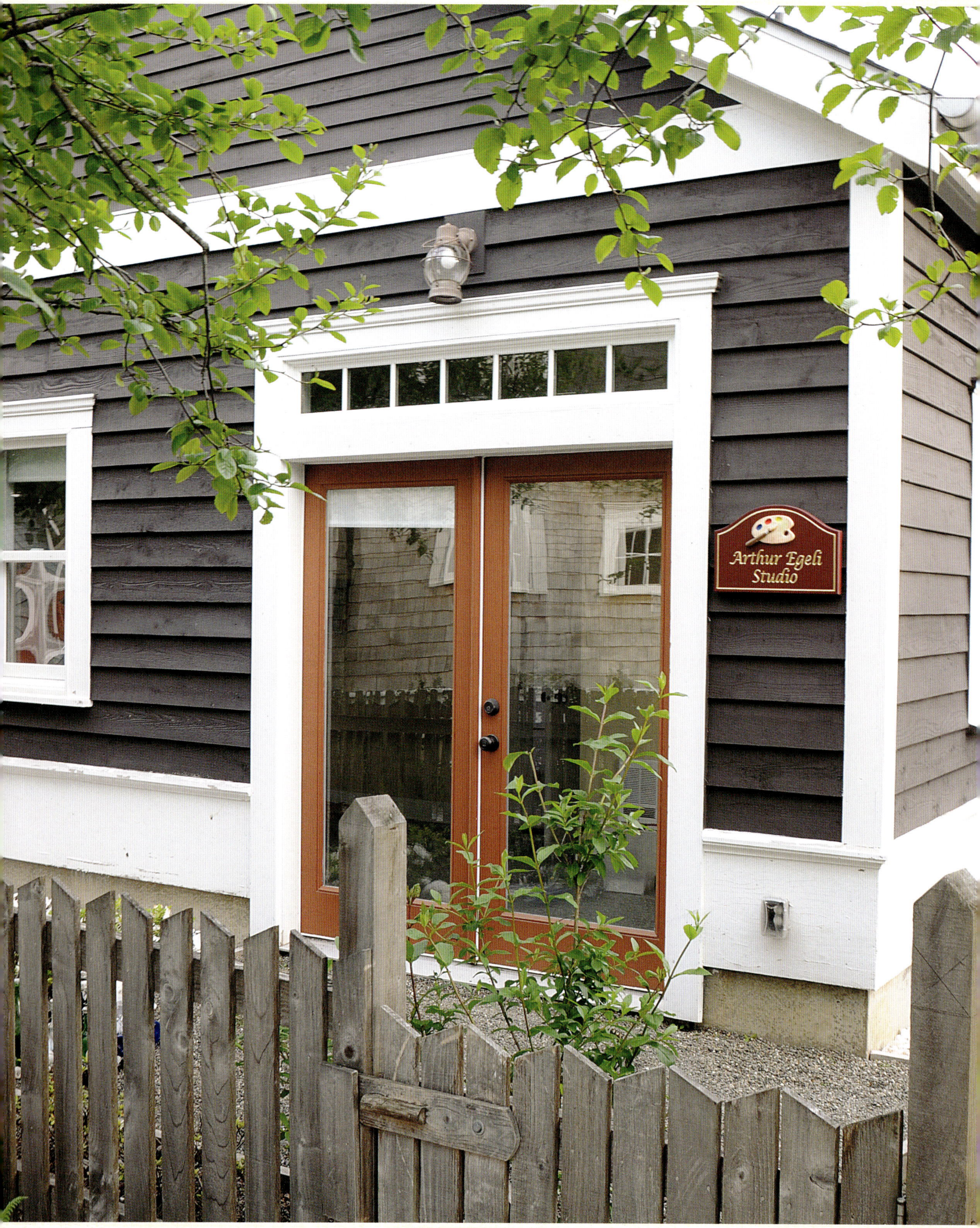
Arthur Egeli
Studio

CHAPTER FOUR

Converting Spaces

"Change is so essential to creativity: a change of tools, size of canvas, location ... all feed the creative soul."

—Cathie Harrison

← French doors lead from a community pathway into Arthur Egeli's studio.

Dennis Doheny
A Simple Garage Makeover

Dennis Doheny converted his two-car garage into a studio almost twenty years ago. The work involved was not great. He finished putting up drywall throughout the space and placed carpet over the concrete floor. The mild California climate, with its absence of frost, made insulation and heating requirements minimal. The only construction involved walling off a domestic water heater and water softener that had been housed in the garage. Doheny installed a space heater and a ceiling fan but chose not to install air conditioning. The other major consideration was the installation of windows. The artist installed a double set of French doors facing north for optimum light, and another doorway was replaced with a single French door. The addition of halogen track lights and studio furniture completed the task.

In general, the artist is pleased with his choice. "The only real challenge has been the lack of storage in the rest of the house," he says. "I have no basement and no real attic. It helps me stay neat, and I tend not to stockpile." Doheny also sometimes wishes that his space were bigger. "If I'm doing a large painting, I can't get far enough away from it," he says. However, the pluses of working in the converted garage are considerable. "I often get up very early in the morning and start painting at 5:30 A.M. or 6 A.M.," he says. "And then, of course, I have no rent to pay." Doheny estimates that over the years he has spent no more than $3,000 on the space. "It was well worth it," he says.

For more on Dennis Doheny, visit his website at www.dennisdoheny.com.

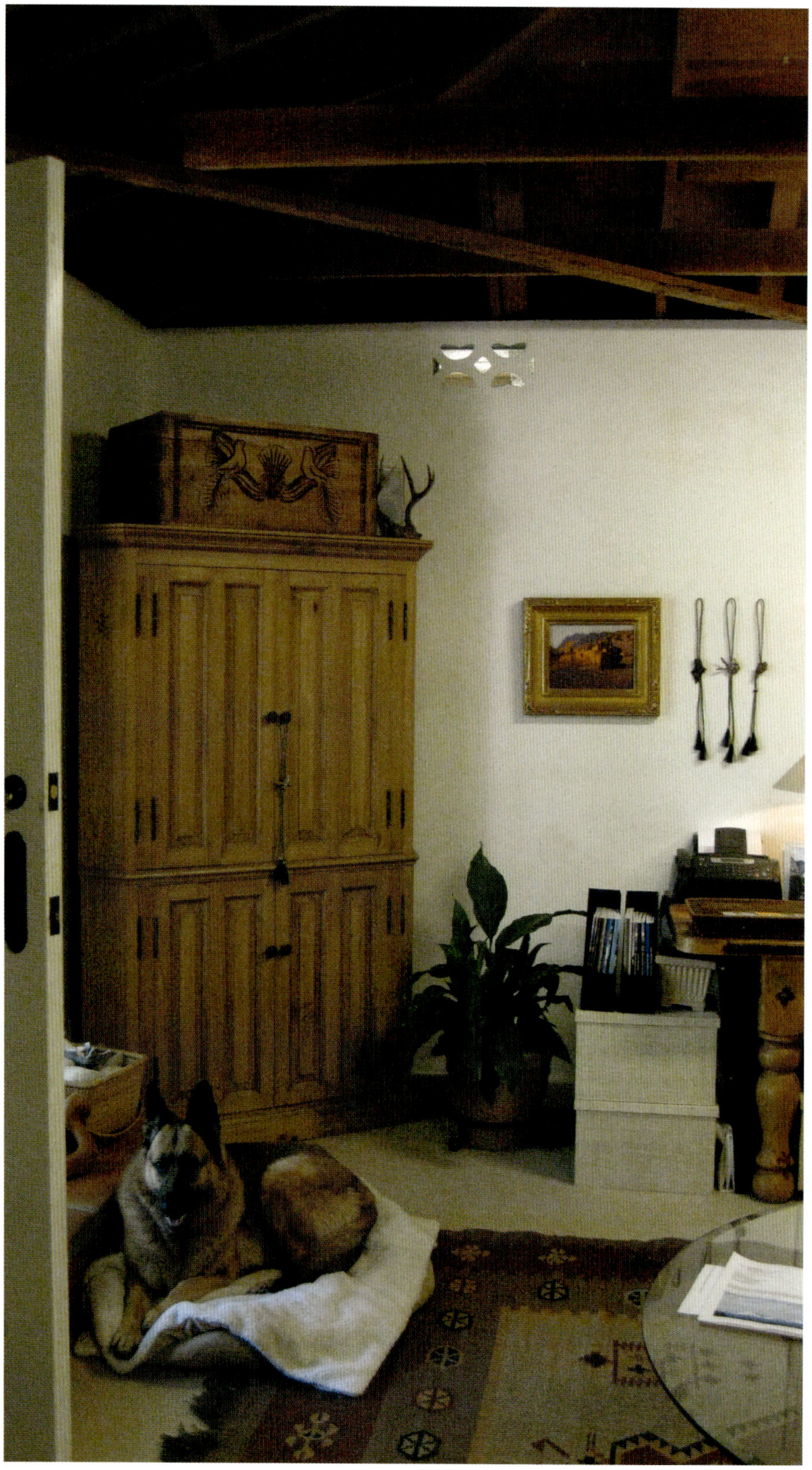

Although he would like to have a larger studio when working on large canvases, Doheny appreciates that his studio is next to his home.

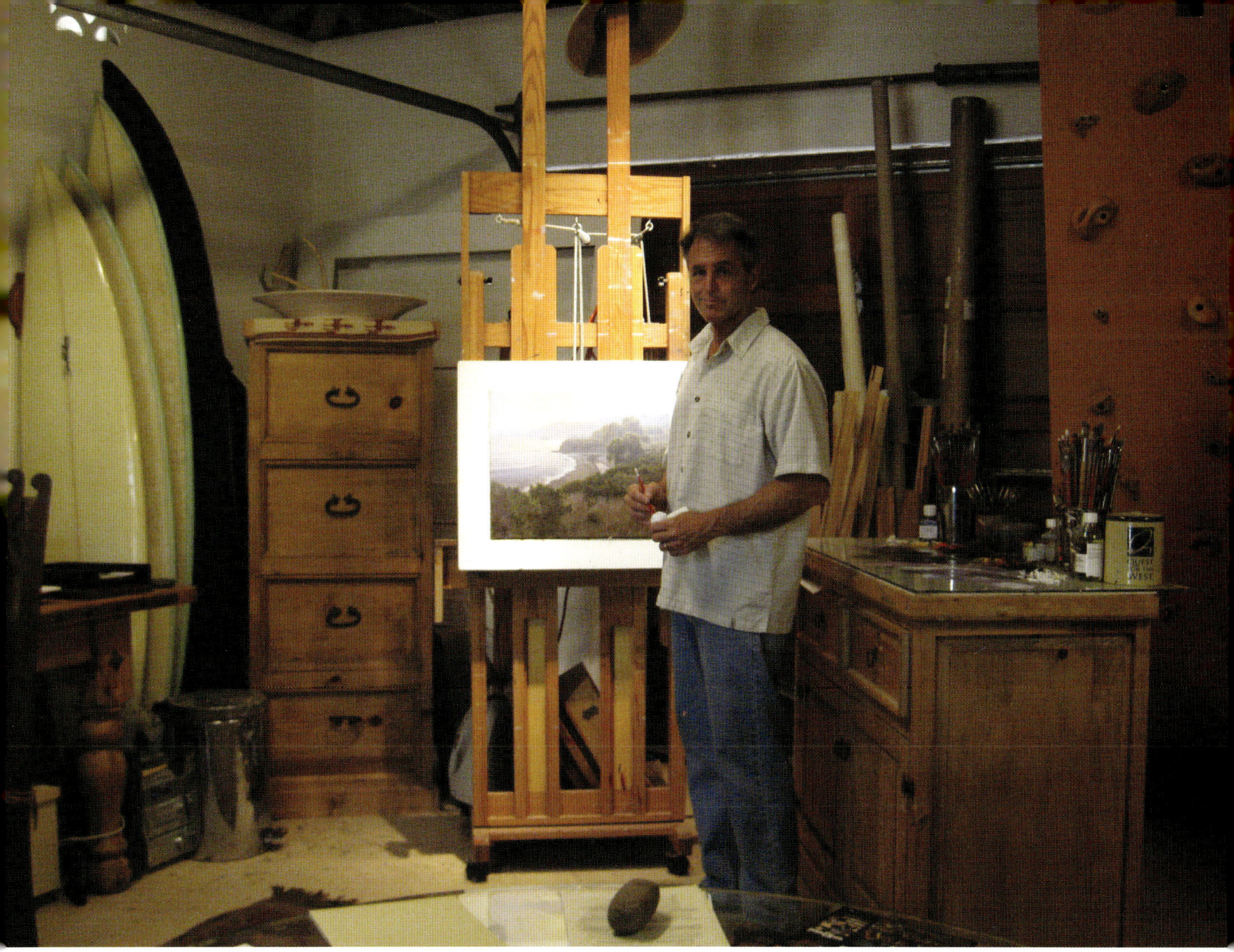

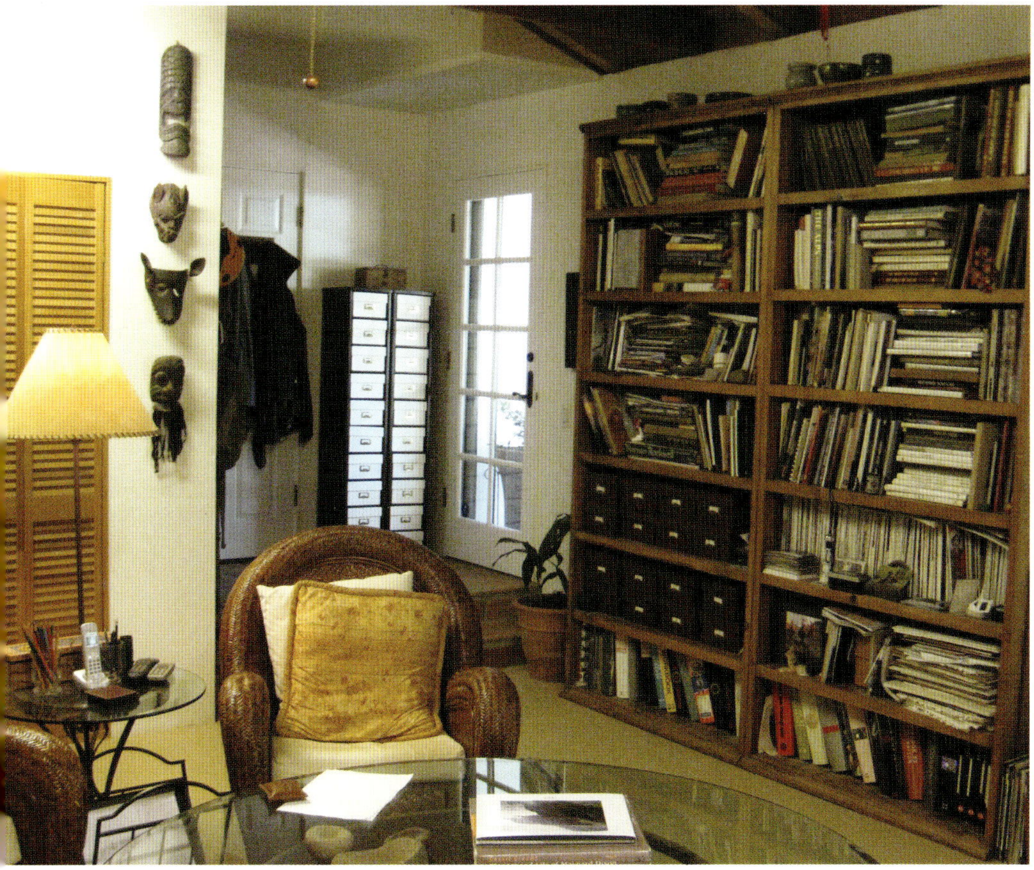

↑ Doheny standing in the Santa Barbara, California, studio he built in what was originally a two-car garage. Because Doheny lives in an area with a mild climate, he only needed to cover a water heater and a water softener in his garage to convert the space to a painting studio.

← After twenty years of using the converted garage, storage is the artist's biggest problem.

Kathy Caudill

Using a 'Bonus' Room

In 2007, Kathy Caudill found that her rented studio space had problems with overhead leaks and was a growing security issue. She decided to move her studio to the "bonus" room above her own garage. Because the new space was going to be much smaller, she had to rent storage space for excess furniture, mat board, flat files, and other miscellaneous items. In renovating her new space, the creation of storage areas was a prime concern. "My husband and I removed one knee wall and installed unfinished oak cabinets into the wall space. It was necessary to shorten the cabinets slightly so that they would fit under the slanted roof," she says. "Shelves were added to the cabinets, and the heights of materials to be stored there were taken into consideration." The artist constructed bookshelves out of medium-density fiberboard to be placed above the cabinets.

The space behind a second knee wall was turned into a storage closet by installing a second access door and adding insulation covered with oriented strand board. Shelves and lighting completed the long narrow space. The existing carpeting was removed, and prefinished hardwood flooring was installed.

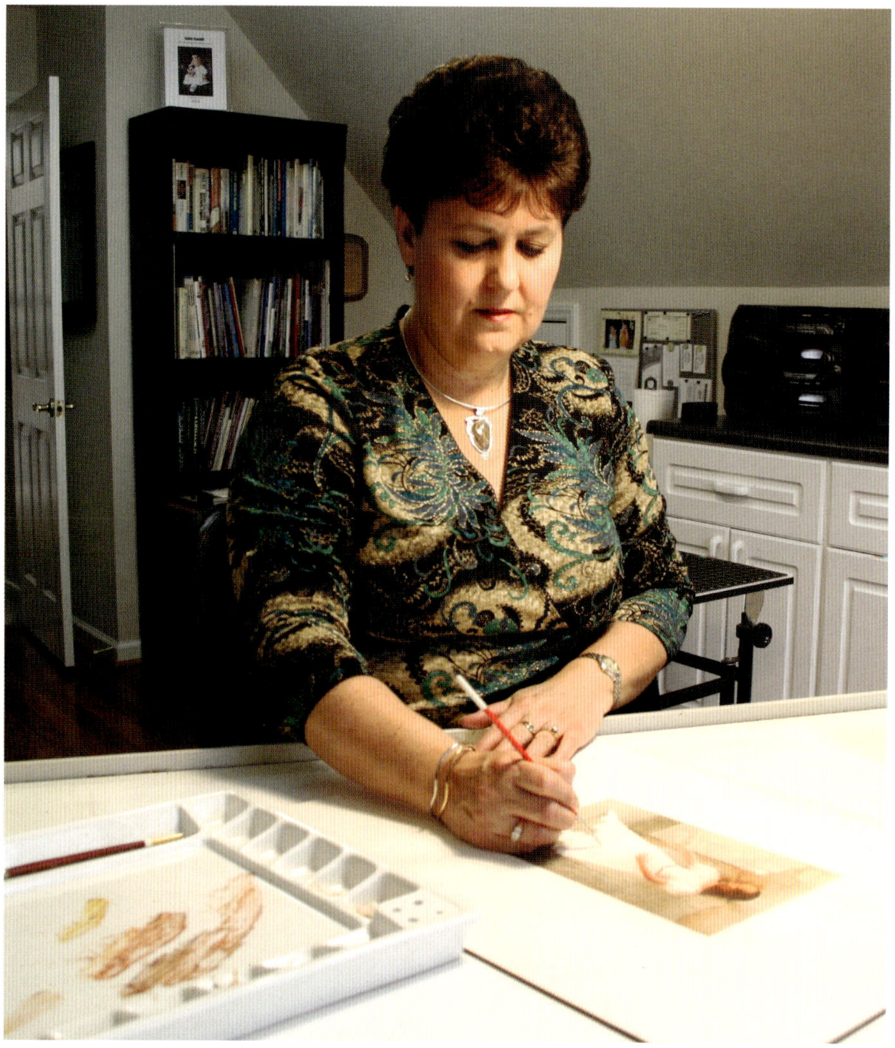

After converting the room above the garage into a studio, North Carolina artist Caudill now has a convenient space in which to create her watercolor paintings.

Given the modest window space in the room, lighting was a real issue. "I have two flexible combo lights in the space," says the artist. "These are a combination of incandescent lights and daylight fluorescents, which do a good job of mimicking natural daylight." The artist uses one on a rolling light stand so that it can be moved at will. The other combo light is attached to the larger of the two drawing tables in the space. Lighting is supplemented by two overhead daylight fluorescents and a four-bulb track light in the ceiling fan. "Plans include adding a large shed dormer across the back of the room," says the artist. "It will raise the sloped walls and flood the room with north light."

Because the walls of her studio are sloped, Caudill uses the entrance corridor for display. "I purchased a Walker Display system so that paintings can be moved around without damaging the walls," she says. "I used a round track light for lighting in the hallway."

Caudill is pleased with her space but has further plans. "Our final project will be to construct a one-and-a-half story building in the backyard," she says. "It will serve as a second studio for my large 8-foot (2m) oak easel, framing equipment, and other items that are too big for the 'bonus'-room studio. I enjoy the intimacy of this smaller studio and look forward to the additional space of a larger one, too."

For more on Kathy Caudill, visit www.providencegallery.net.

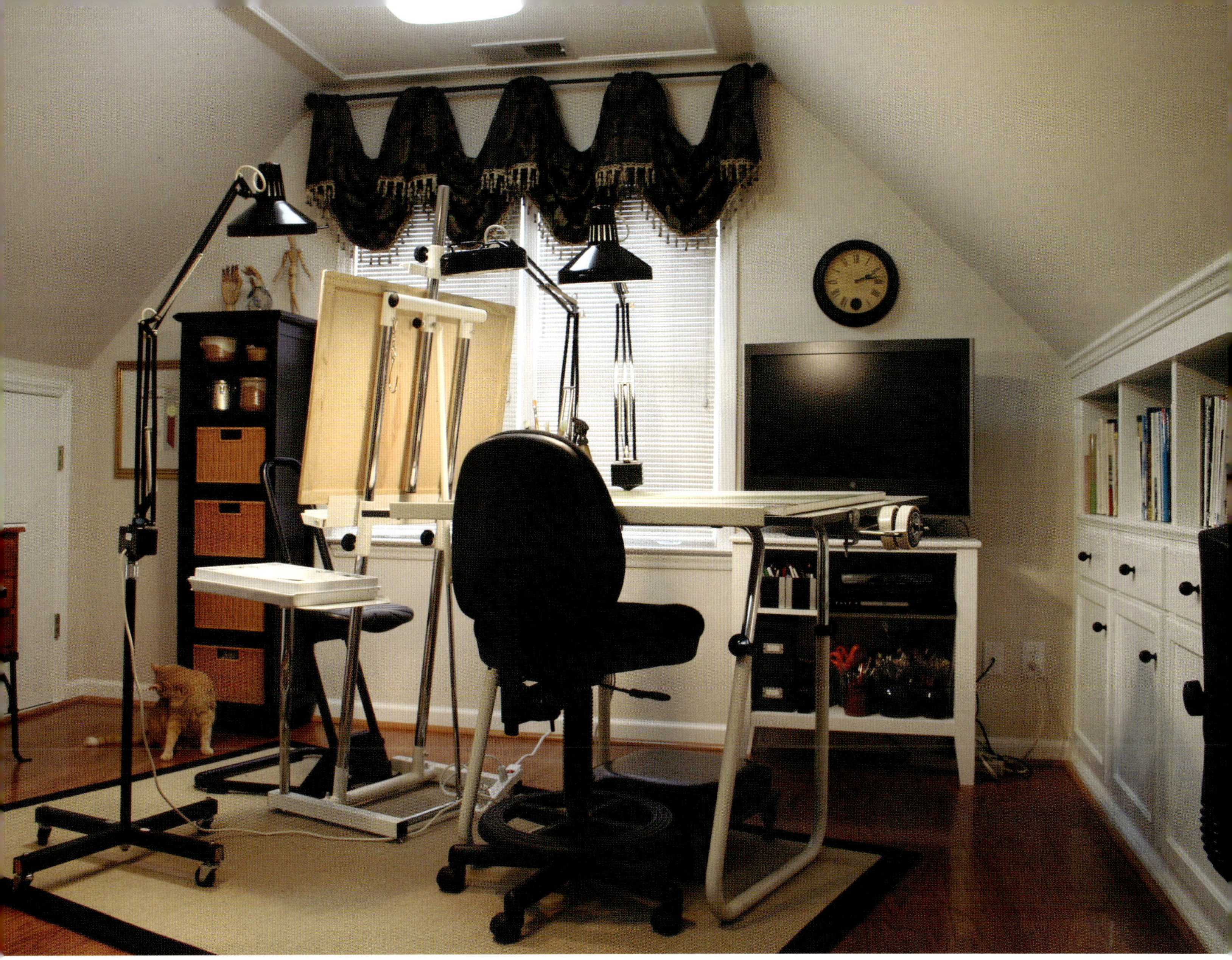

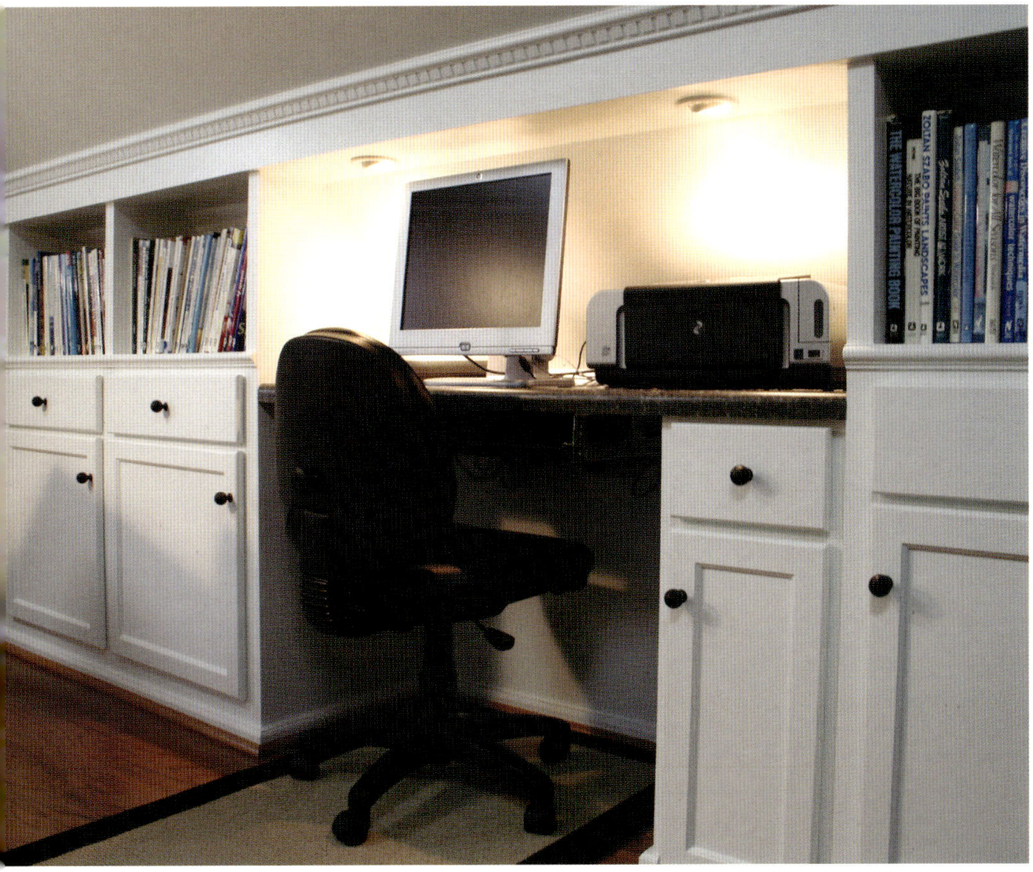

↑ Caudill's easel and flat worktable are located near the window, and two flexible combo lights offer a mix of incandescent and fluorescent illumination.

← A knee wall was removed to make room for storage cabinets and a shallow computer workstation.

William A. Schneider

Building a House to Surround a Studio

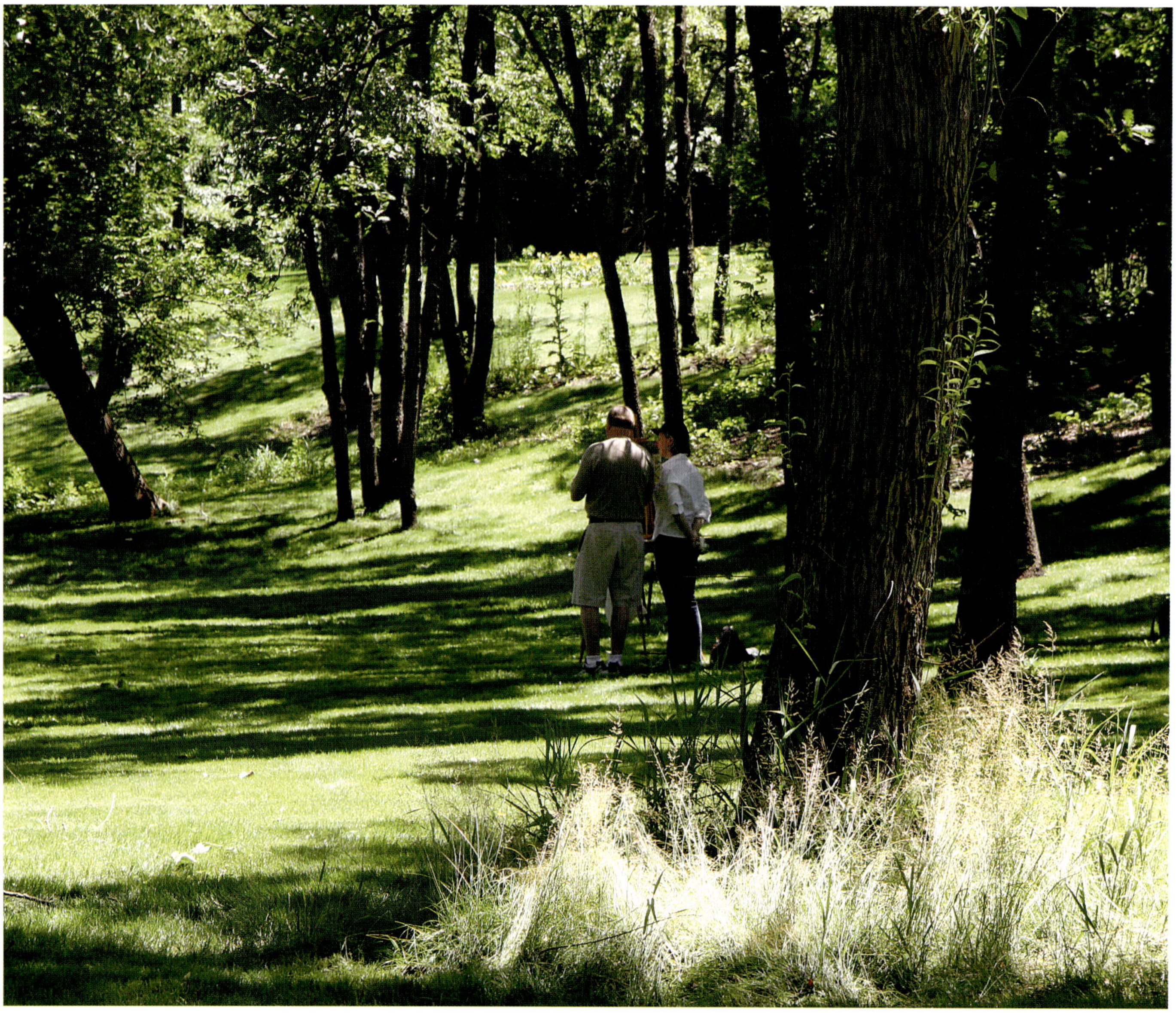

Schneider worked on a plein air painting in the backyard of his home during a recent workshop on composition.

Most artists don't have the opportunity to design a dream studio from start to finish, so instead they turn an existing spare bedroom, basement alcove, or outbuilding into a studio to take advantage of available rent-free space. They make compromises on the lighting, storage, scale, or layout of the work space in order to save money and remain close to their living quarters. That's what William A. Schneider did for years while he was transitioning from a career in managing investments to one in fine art. In the home he shared with his wife, Caren, until August 2008, he worked in the dining room because it was the only large room with a northern exposure. "It worked for a while, but the ceiling was too low for a big easel, and the room was still connected to the main living areas of the home," he explains. "I wanted to construct a stand-alone building on the property, but the town would not give

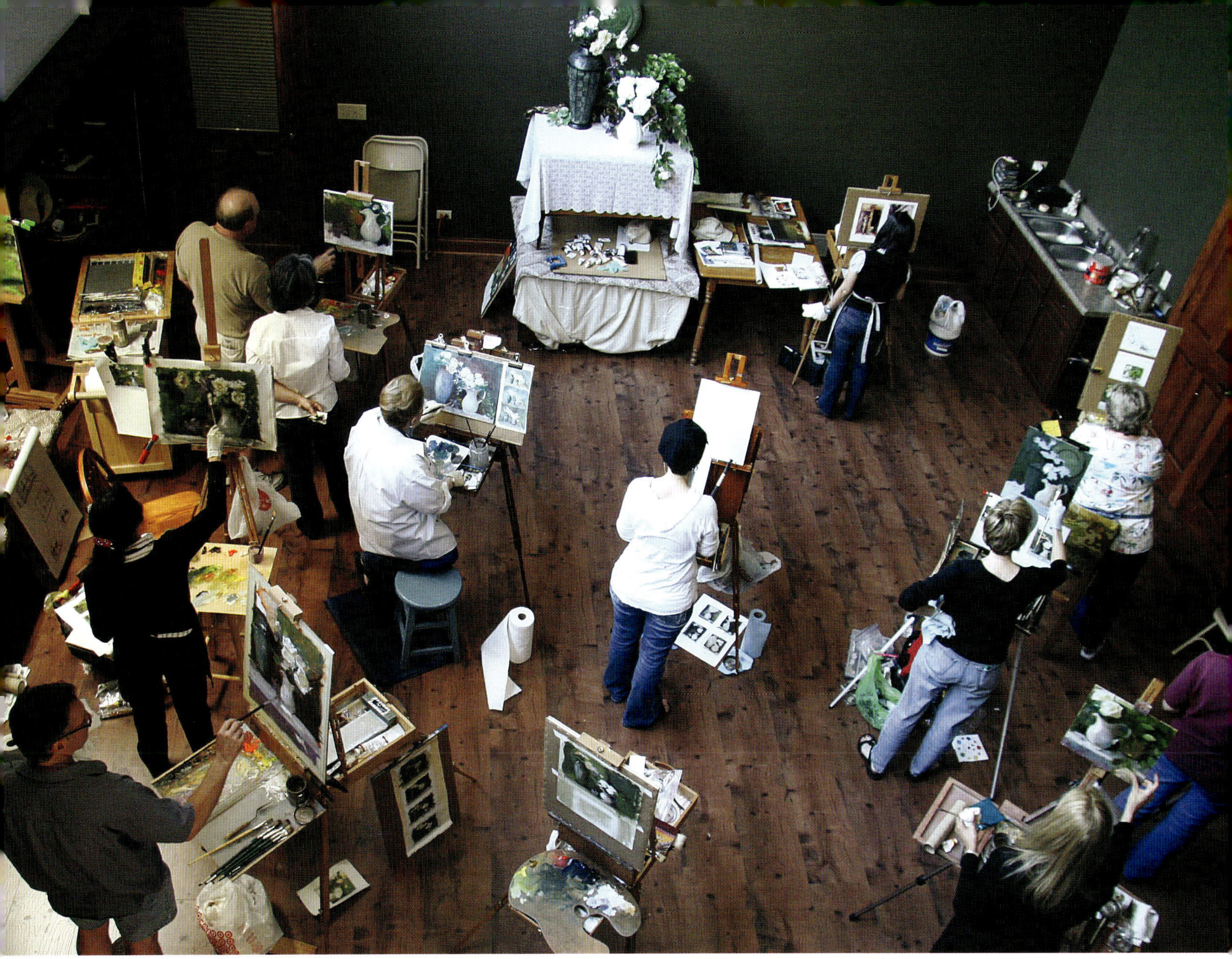

The interior of Schneider's studio in Illinois.

approval for a separate structure. We were forced to buy property in a nearby neighborhood and design a house to fit around a studio."

Knowing he might someday have this opportunity, Schneider spent years making mental notes of what he liked about other artists' work spaces. "Every time I visited another artist's studio, I asked questions," he explains. "I got a lot of advice from my friend Daniel F. Gerhartz who, in turn, received advice from Richard Schmid; and I researched studios of some of the great masters such as Sargent and Sorolla. I also investigated such issues as flooring, air purification, supplemental lighting, wall coloring, and furniture. Finally, we started designing the studio in January 2007 and moved into the new home in August 2008.

"The studio is all about controlling the light," Schneider continues. "The main studio is 26 feet x 30 feet (8m x 9m) with a 20-foot (6m) ceiling. On the north end of the room is an overhang where the ceiling is only 8½ feet (3m) high. The north windows are above that lower section, and that allows me to have a dark area for posing a model or still life while positioning my Hughes easel under the north light. Those windows are 11 feet (3m) above the floor, 60 inches (152cm) high, and 48 inches (122cm) wide. I have shades on each of them that operate by remote control. I can pose a model in the alcove with only a candle for illumination while my canvas is lit by the northern windows."

The artist also noted that he had three canvas-drying shelves built in the northeast corner of the studio as well as a model stand. He also installed a row of five 48-inch (122cm) four-lamp fluorescent fixtures fitted with Vita-Lite color-corrected bulbs below the northern windows so that he can paint at night or on overcast days. There is a sink on the southern wall of the room near the double doors that lead to the living quarters of the house where Schneider's extensive art collection is on display.

At the top of a spiral staircase in the southwest corner of the studio is a 19'-x-13' (6m-x-4m) office that overlooks the work space and can be accessed through a 30'-x-18' (9m-x-5m) storage room that connects to the second-floor hallway in the home. On the ground

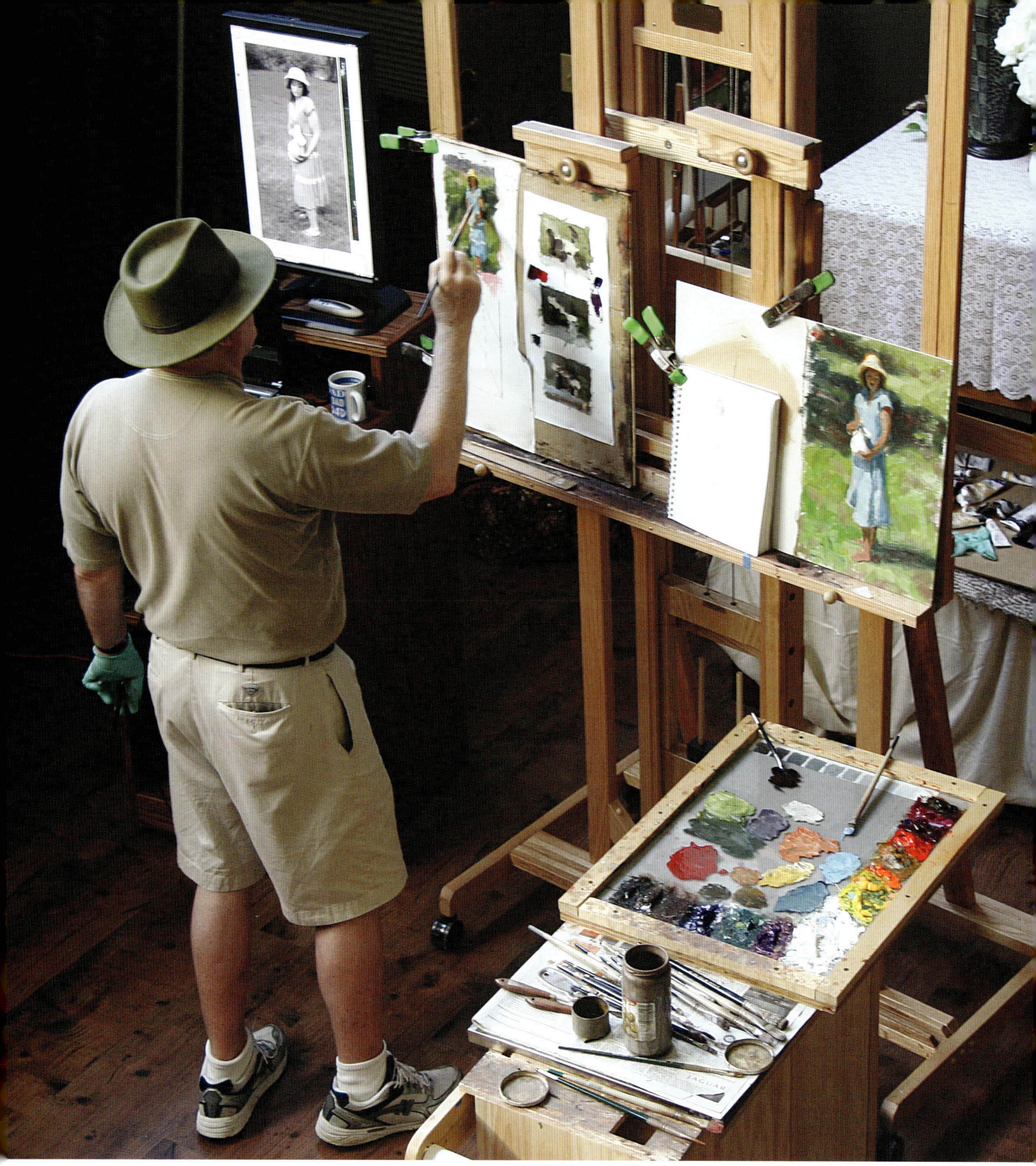

Schneider stands at his Hughes easel to work on compositional sketches.

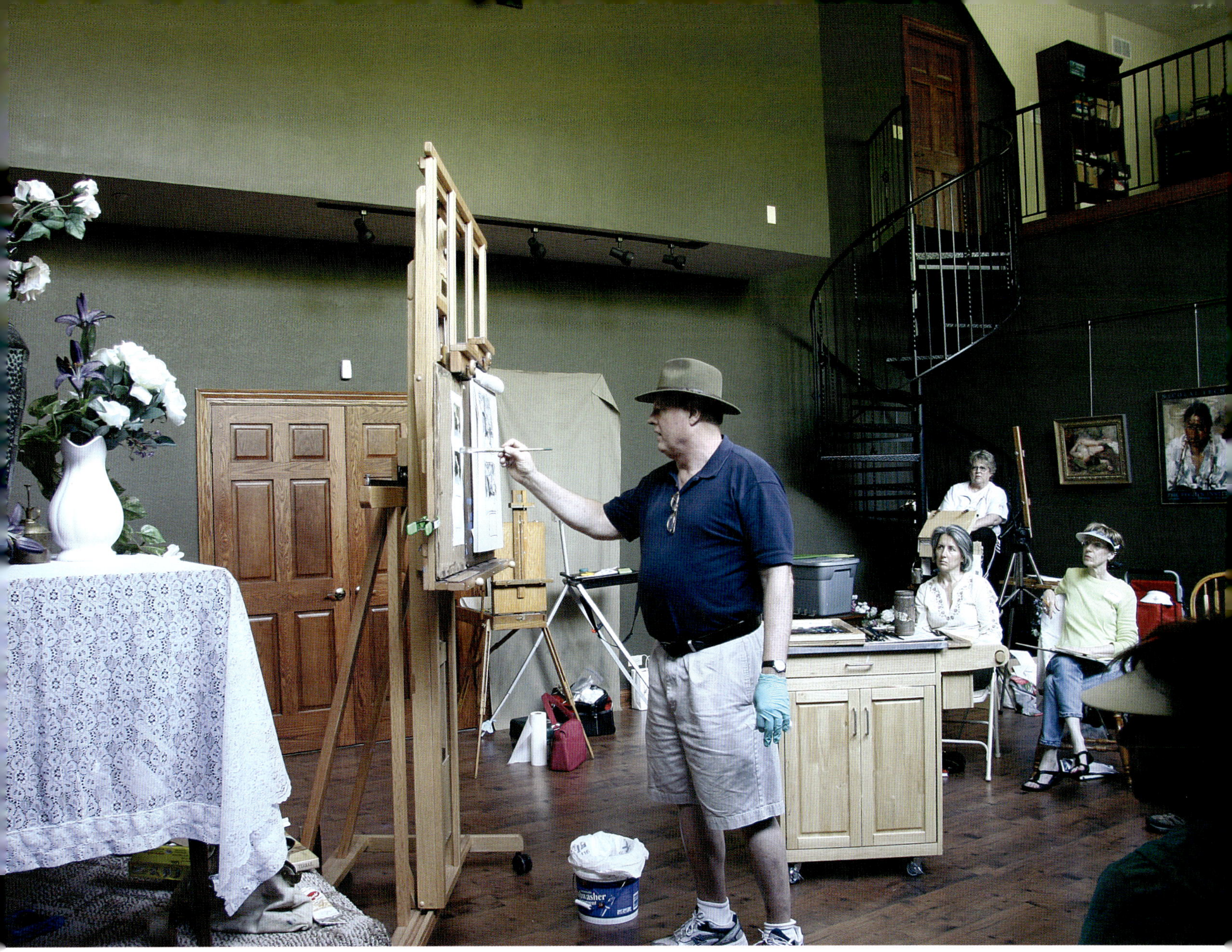

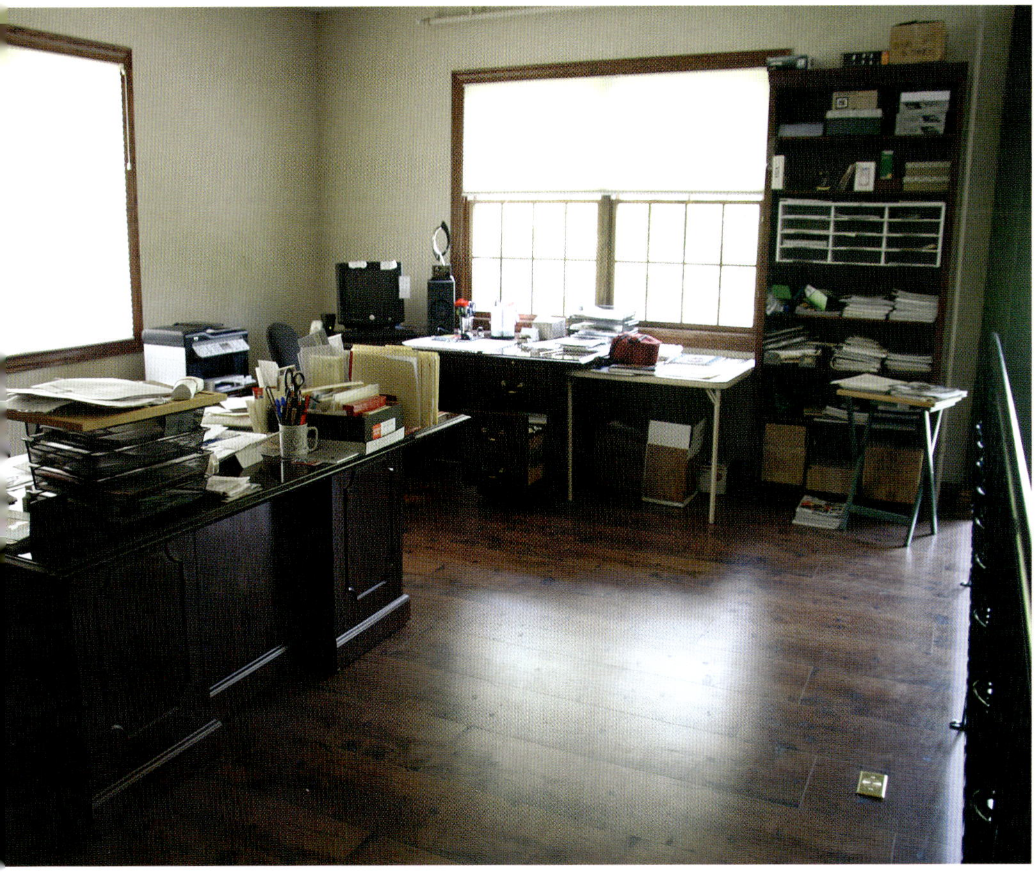

↑ The view from Schneider's easel toward the spiral staircase that leads to the office.

← The artist's office, which overlooks his studio.

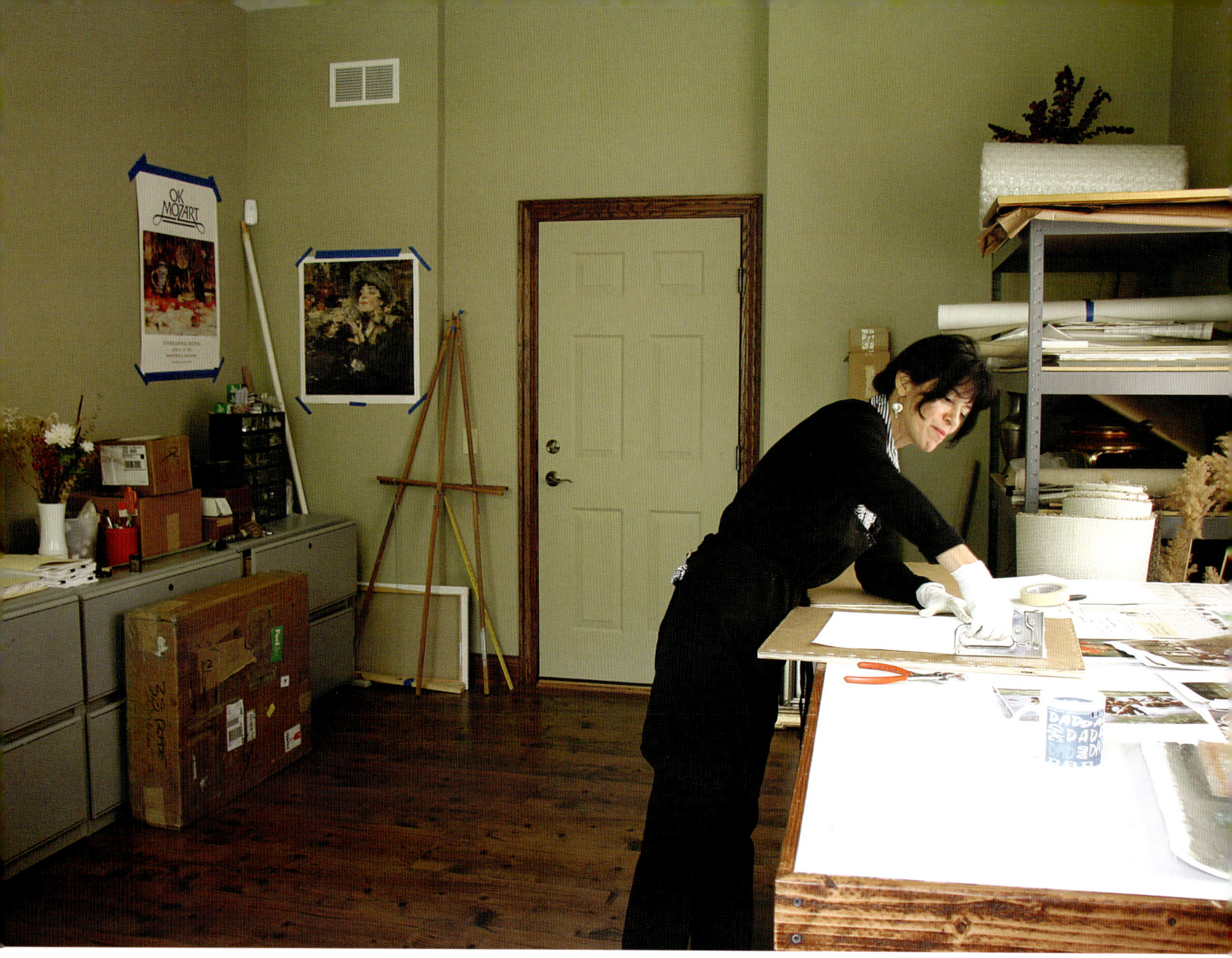

During one of Schneider's recent workshops, a student prepared a canvas in the workroom adjacent to the studio.

floor, there is a workroom with a 6'-x-4' (2m-x-1m) worktable, flat files, filing cabinets, frames, and shipping supplies.

One of the best pieces of advice Schneider received from the builder, Greg Kotlowski, was about the flooring used in the studio, workroom, and office. "The original plans called for hardwood flooring, but Greg recommended a synthetic product called Fausfloor," the artist recalls. "I resisted the idea because I thought it would look cheap, but Greg gave me a sample to test and after spilling paint thinner, denatured alcohol, and other solvents on it and pounding it with a hammer and screwdriver, I was convinced that it would be durable enough. We selected an antique, heart-pine style of flooring, and it has worked extremely well."

Schneider planned to offer workshops in the studio and wanted to make sure the air quality would be safe when he was painting or when a large group of artists was working with oil paints and solvents. First, he made sure there was a completely separate heating and air-conditioning system to handle the studio, workroom, and office that could exhaust the fumes and quickly bring in fresh air. He installed high-volume exhaust fans at a low height on the studio walls and workroom since solvent vapors are heavier than air, and he placed a portable AllerAir air filter near his easel for additional air cleaning. The air filter has a 3-inch (8cm) bed of anthracite charcoal that helps to remove solvents. Finally, Schneider installed fire-safe cabinets for storing paint thinner, mediums, and varnish; and he had a fire-sprinkler system built into the entire home and studio.

"So far the studio design has worked really well for me, and the students who have participated in several workshops have found it a comfortable, spacious place in which to work," says Schneider.

For more on William A. Schneider, visit his website at www.schneiderart.com.

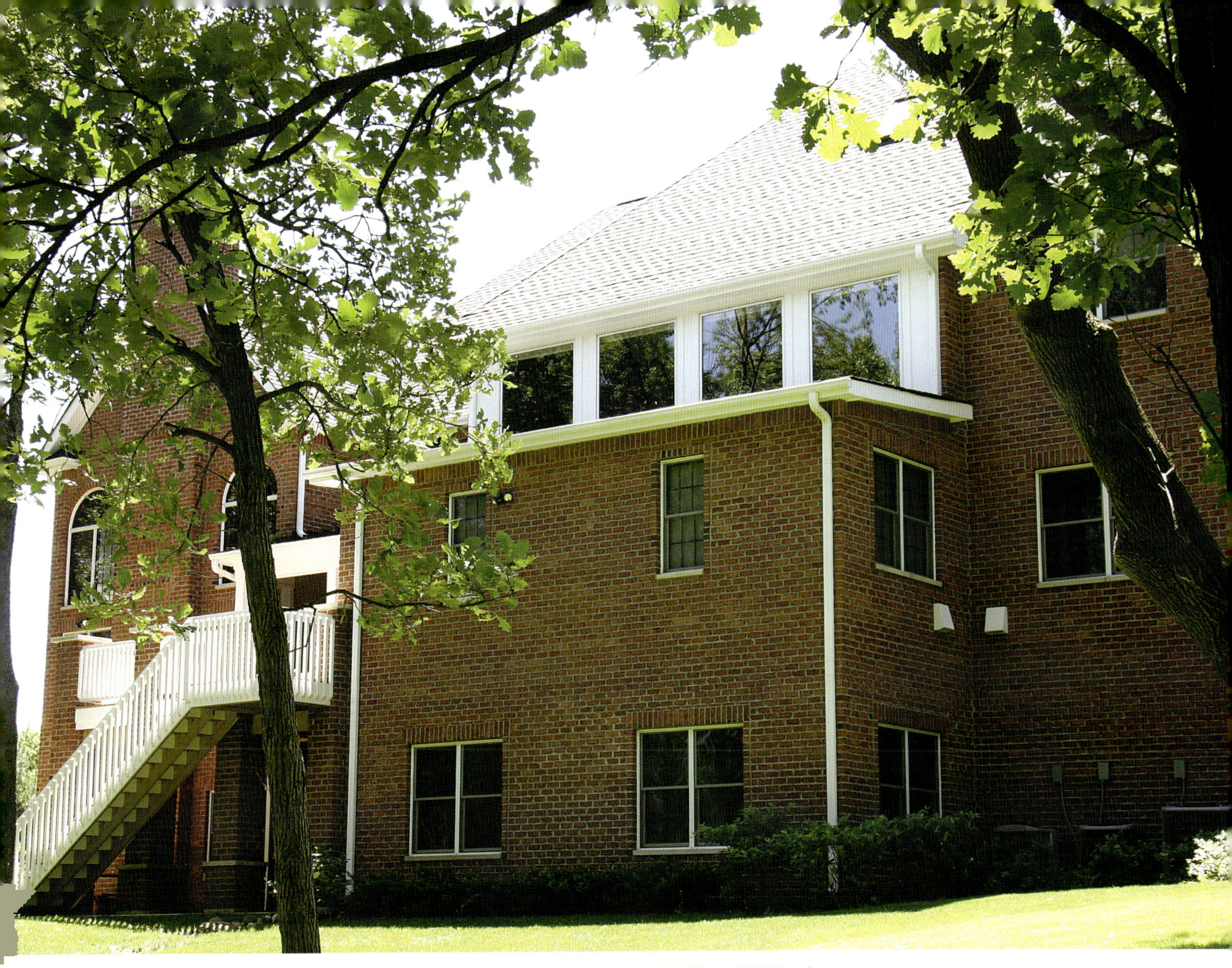

↑ From the exterior of the home, one can see the north-facing windows Schneider installed to ensure proper lighting on his canvas.

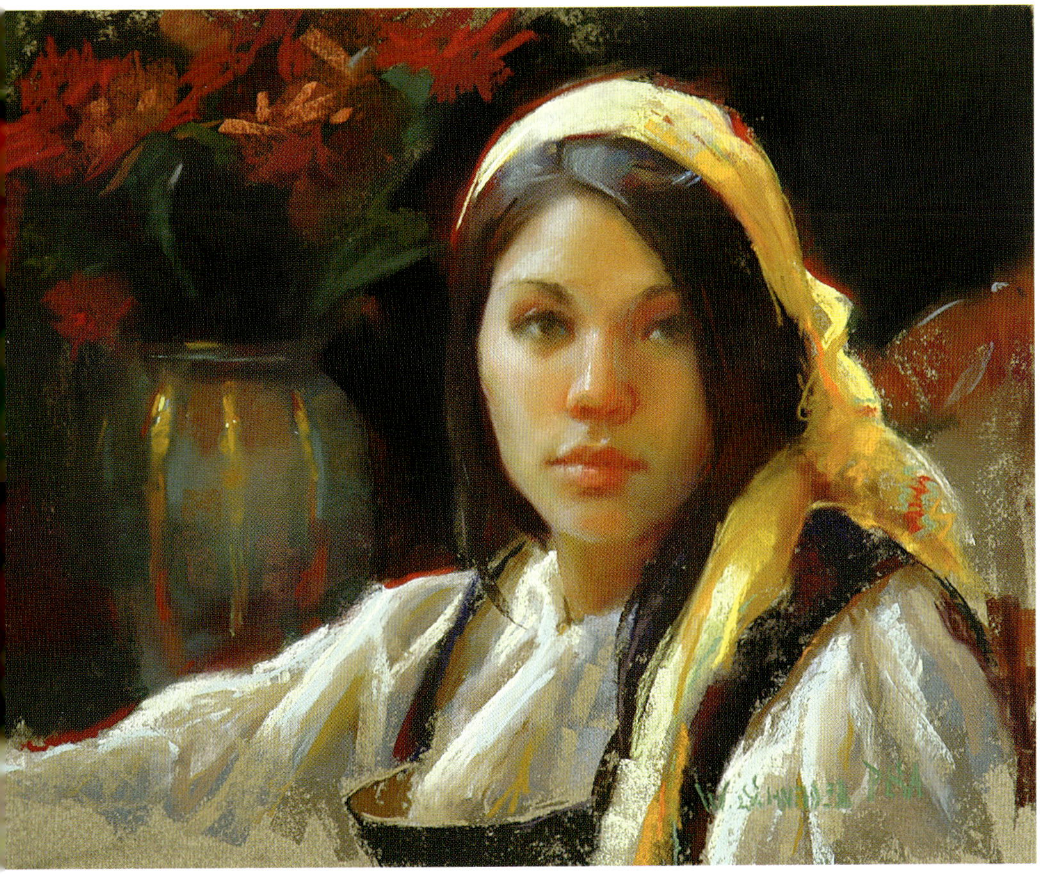

← **Pirate Queen**
by William A. Schneider, 2008, pastel, 16" x 20" (41cm x 51cm). Private collection.

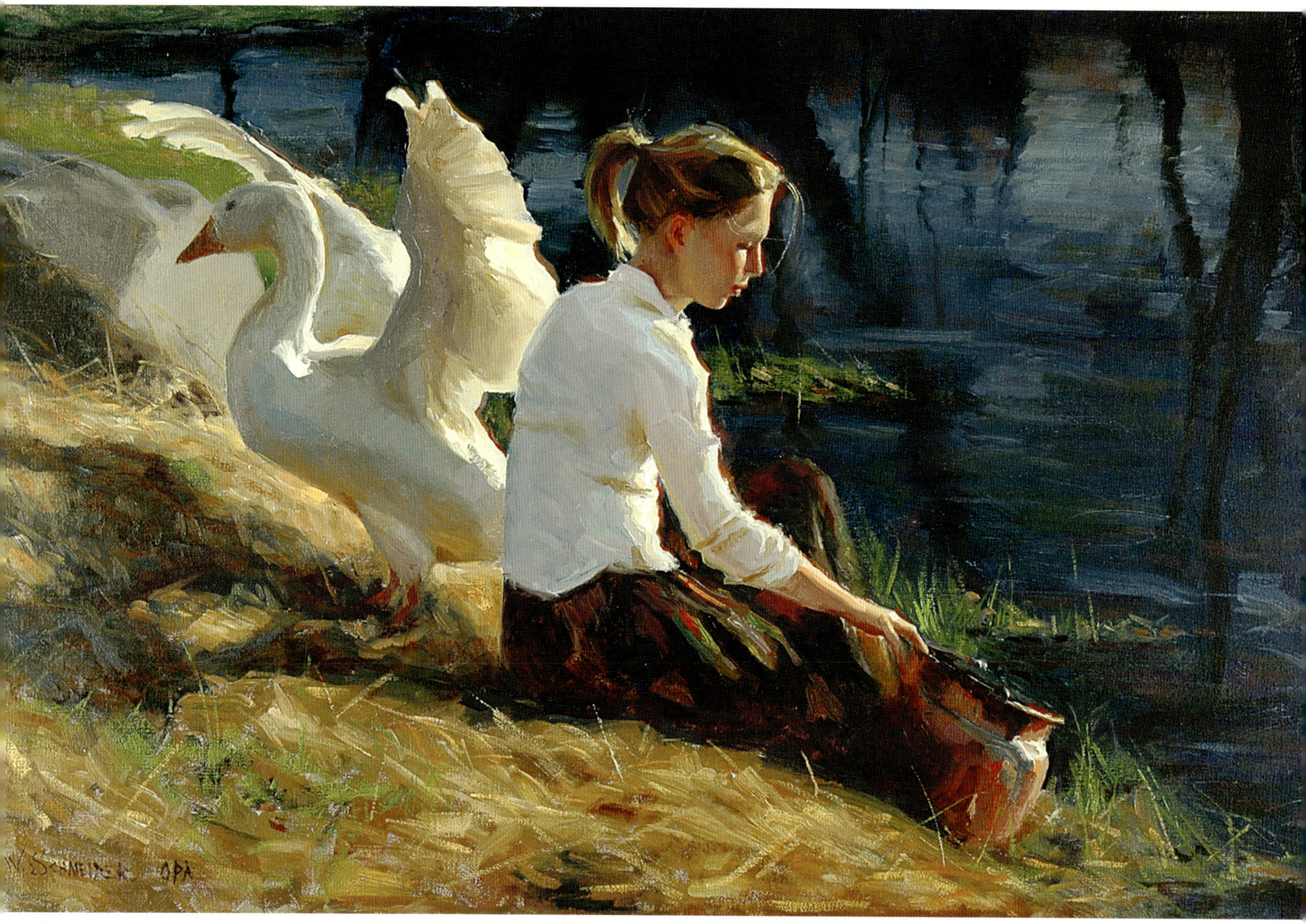

↑ **Evening Chores**
by William A. Schneider, 2007, oil, 26" x 40" (66cm x 102cm). Collection of the artist.

→ **Lady in Waiting**
by William A. Schneider, 2010, oil, 40" x 30" (102cm x 76cm). Collection of the artist.

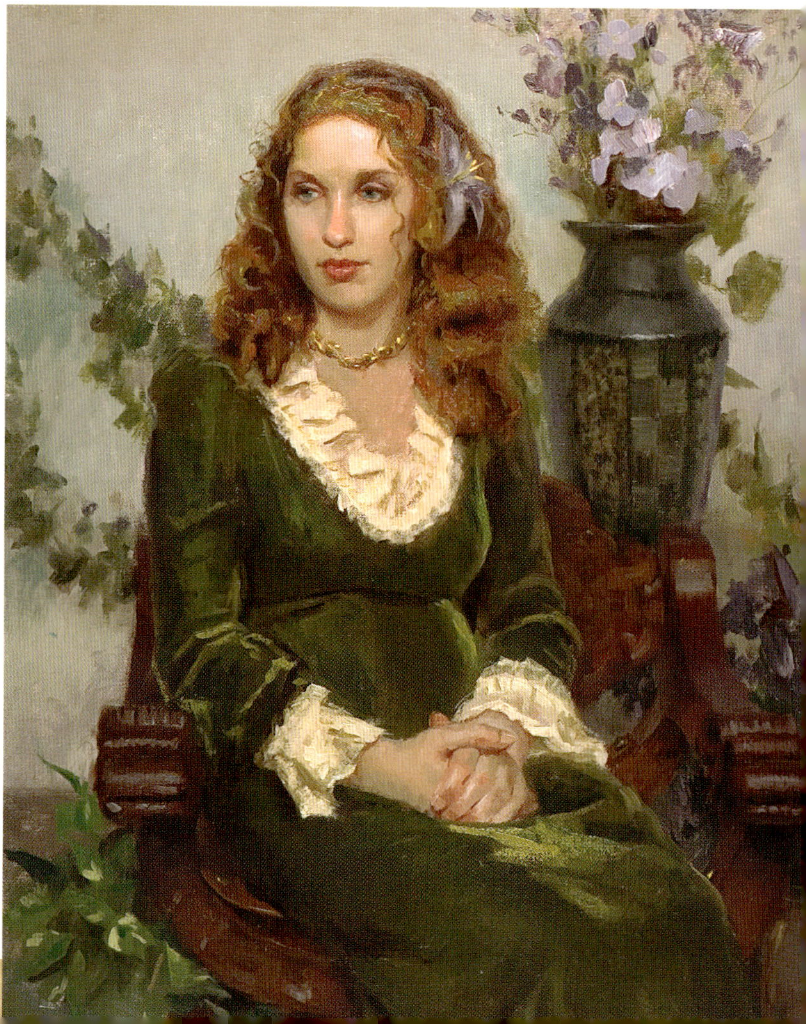

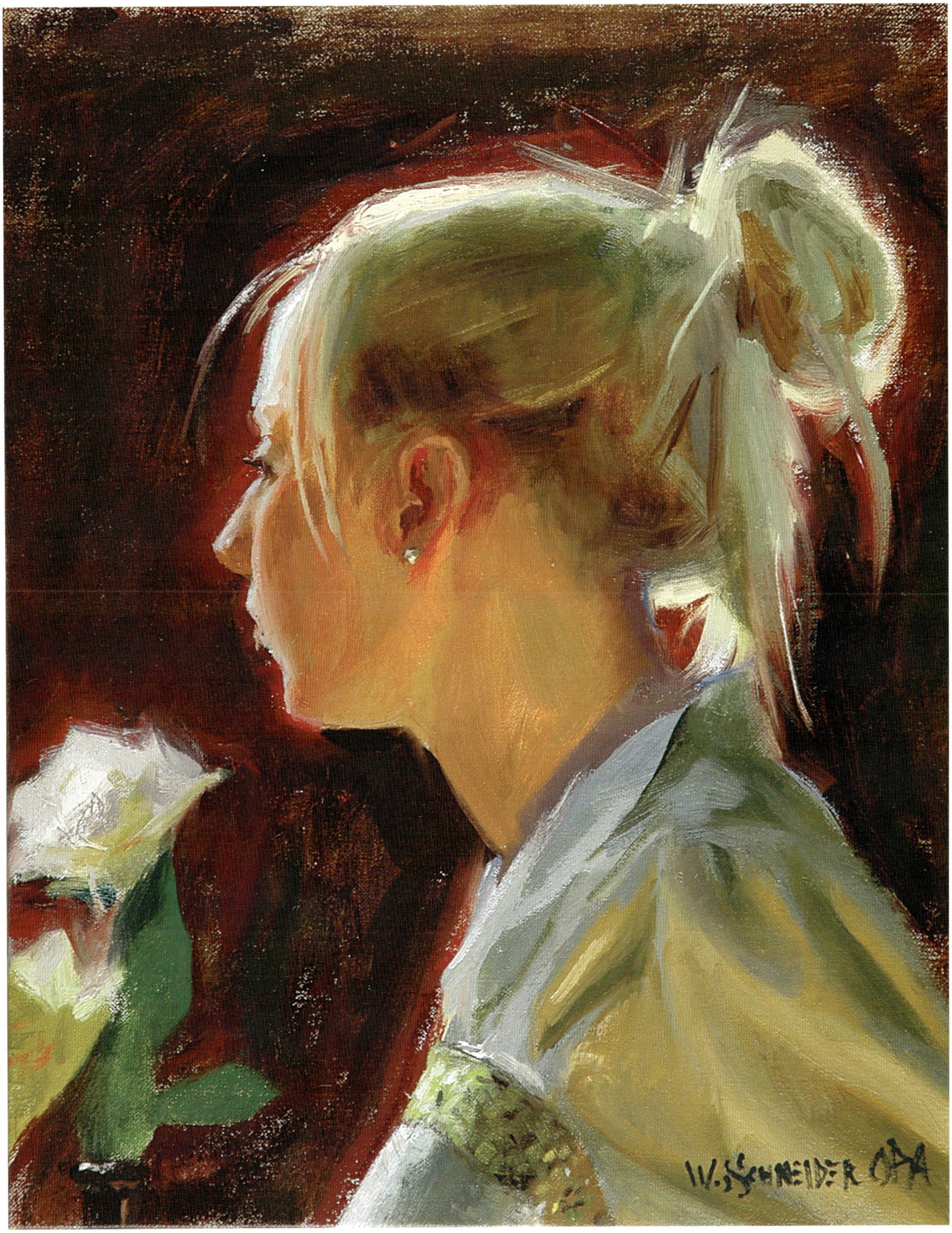

Aglow
by William A. Schneider, 2008, oil, 20" x 16" (51cm x 41cm). Private collection.

Gail Descoeurs
Insulating a Garage

Gail Descoeurs and her husband undertook their garage conversion themselves, transforming a 15'-x-27' (5m-x-8m) space into a generous studio. They insulated the walls and covered them with Sheetrock, which was then painted white. The floor was raised above the cement slab, and a plastic barrier was placed to block humidity coming from below. They painted the new plywood floor in a neutral color with oil-based paint for easy cleanup. "I have a north window, and on the opposite wall I placed a large mirror to bounce the light," says the Quebec artist. "The mirror is also very useful in checking my painting for any errors."

Descoeurs installed a sink on a high counter with a storage area beneath, in which she stows moveable bins laden with supplies and studio accessories. The plumbing for the sink turned out to be one of the most challenging parts of the project, along with drilling holes into the cement for the joists to raise the floor. The artist also added a refrigerator to store snacks for her students and to keep palettes fresh overnight. One of the most important considerations was lighting. "We invested in an excellent track lighting system," says Descoeurs. "The track allows me to add, remove, or reposition my lighting." The artist installed a set of rails, hooks, and chains to hang pictures from but is not entirely satisfied with this system. "The chains work well, but it is not easy to hang large paintings," she says. "It's difficult to get them level." She is currently considering a commercial hanging system.

Heating was another important issue, as winters are harsh in Quebec. "This year we added a propane fireplace, which I love," says Descoeurs. "There is a bathroom off the studio, which is great for my students, and I have a back door that leads to my yard and faces an open field." In the warmer months the screen allows for good air circulation. The artist decided to keep the garage door but added a blanket for insulation. "The door allows easy access for the public to view the studio when I open it for a studio tour in the fall," she says. The door is also useful when it comes to transporting extra-large paintings and canvases. In addition to a drawing table

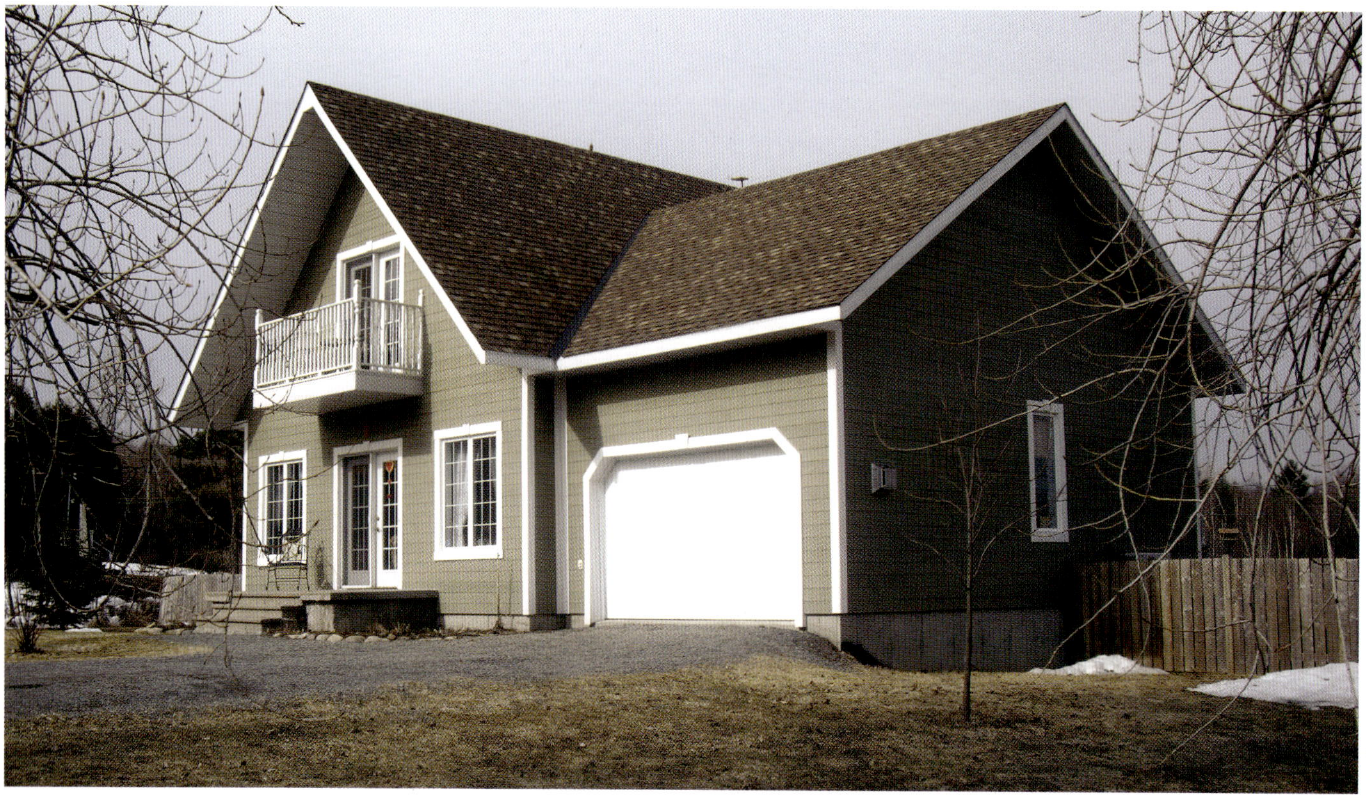

The artist kept the garage door when she converted the space to a studio so that she could open it during warm weather and move large paintings in and out of the space.

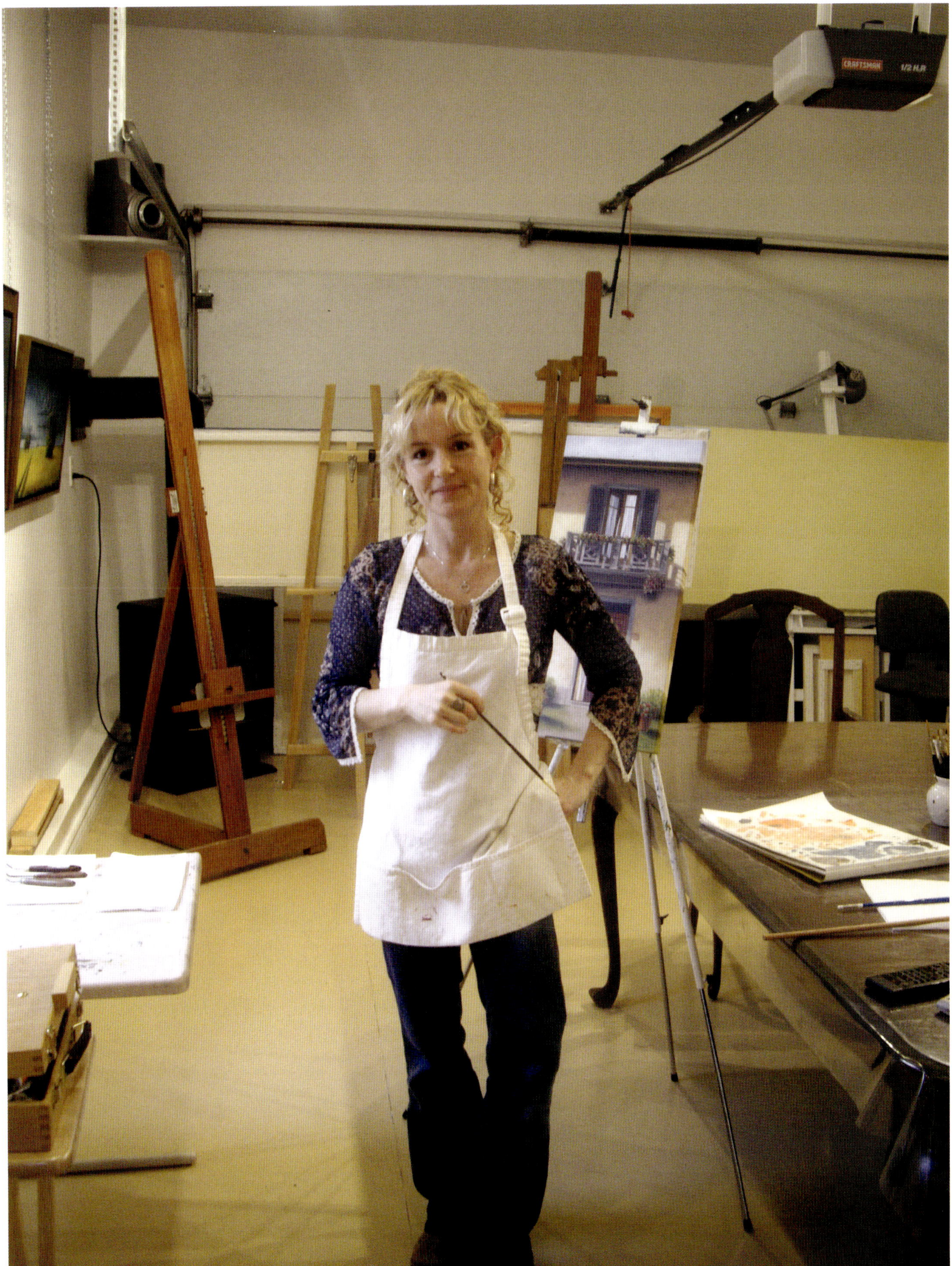

Because of the cold winters in Quebec, Descoeurs insulated the walls, added a raised floor above the concrete flooring, and installed a propane fireplace in her converted garage studio.

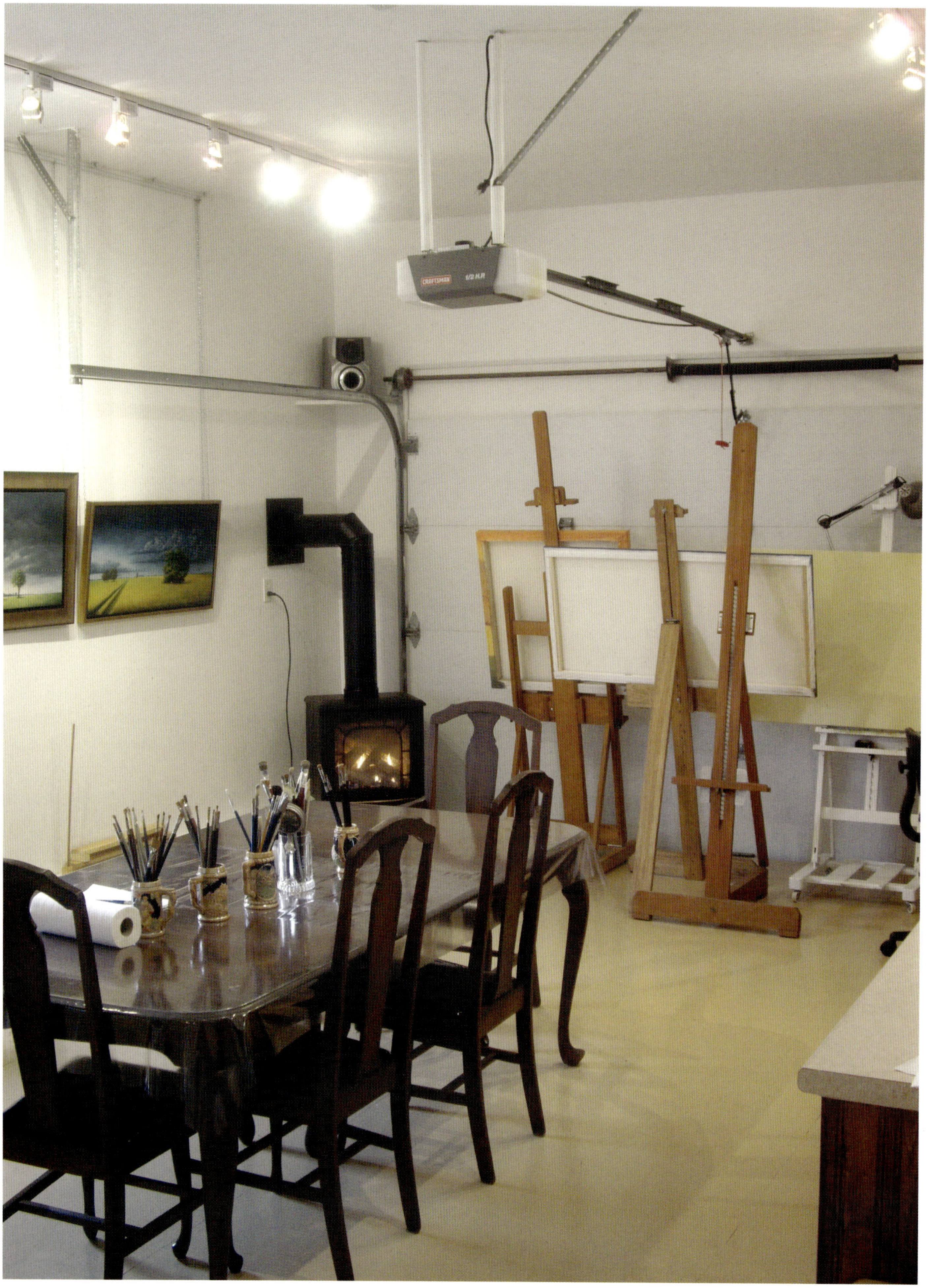

A dining-room table and set of chairs lends a professional look to the converted studio and offers plenty of room for the artist or her students to work.

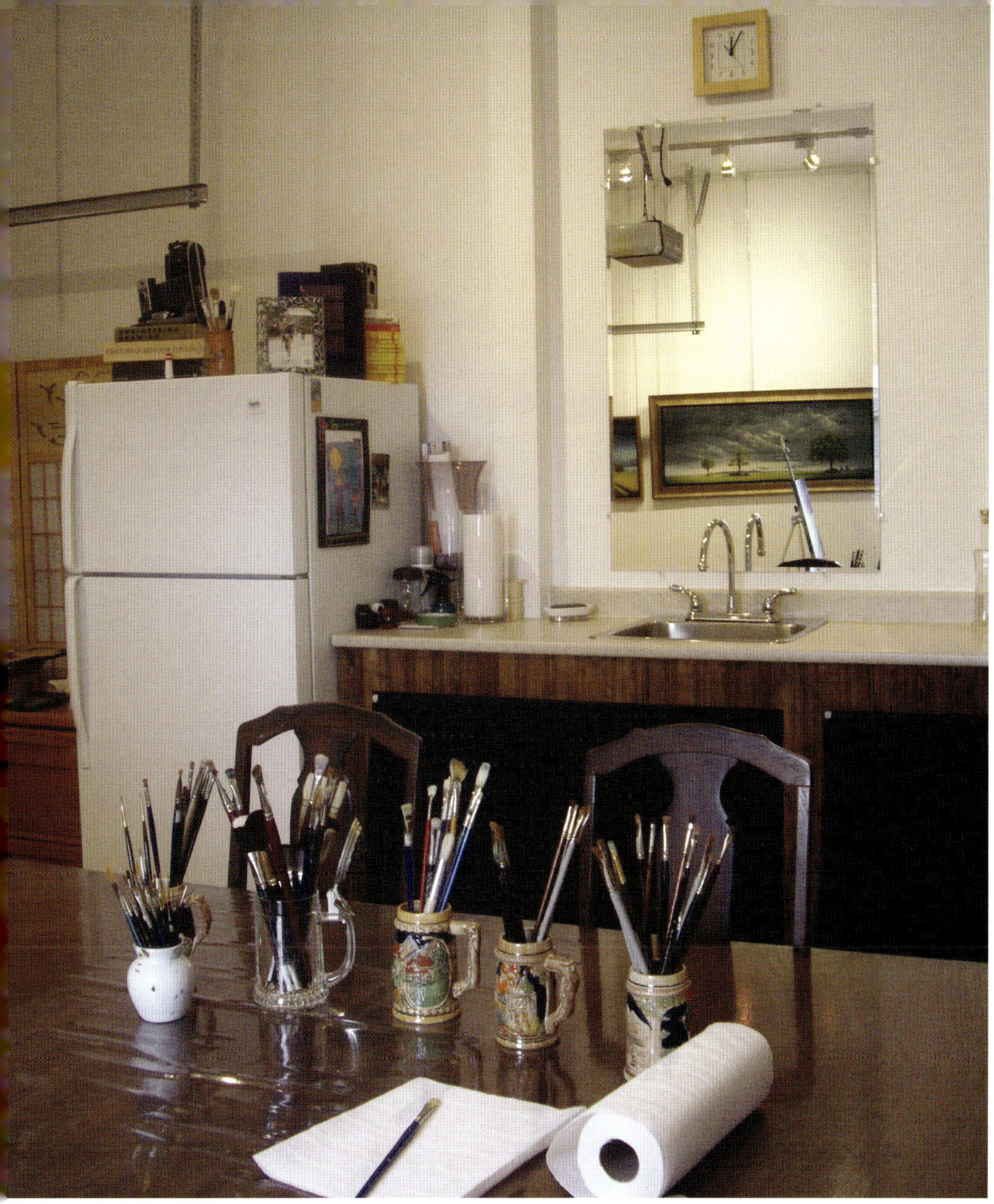

and easels, the artist moved in a large old dining table she covered in clear plastic. "Not only does it add a special feel to my studio, but it also gives me lots of space to spread out my artwork when I am painting," says Descoeurs. "It also allows space for my students to paint using tabletop easels."

The artist is extremely pleased with her new studio and plans to improve it by adding either a drying room for her paintings or an active ventilation system. "I never thought that I would spend so much time in a garage or that a garage would become my favorite room," she says.

For more on Gail Descoeurs, visit her website at www.gaildescoeurs.com.

← During the garage conversion, the artist and her husband installed a sink and refrigerator in the new studio space. A bathroom is just inside the home for easy access.

↓ Windows and track lighting bring in enough light for painting or for displaying framed artwork.

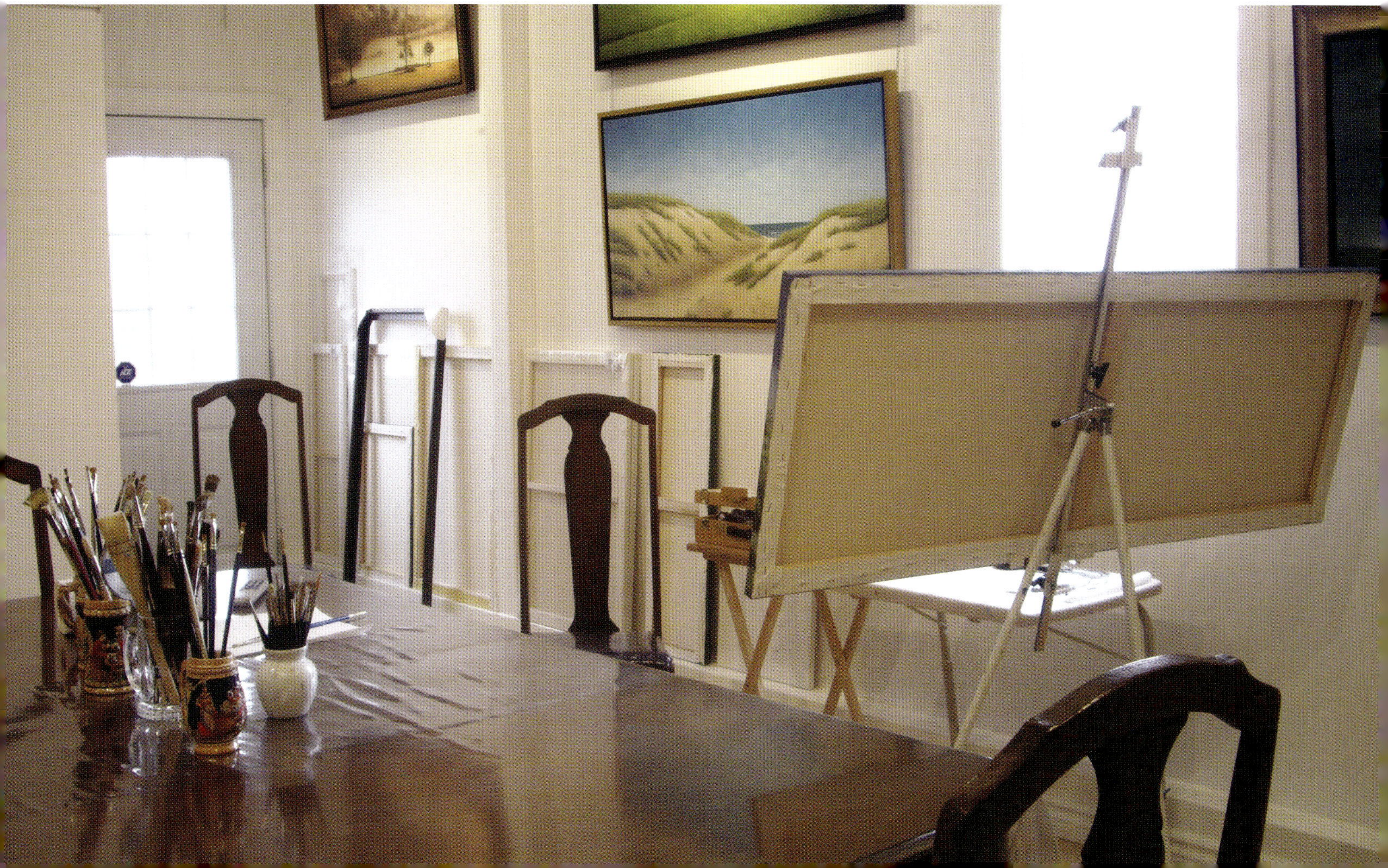

Amy Mann

Using Living Space

After working for some time in studio space in the basement, Amy Mann decided to convert some of her home's living space into a studio. "The first difficulty was getting over the idea that it was somehow wrong to replace our conventional living room with an art studio just inside the front door of the house," she says, "but in retrospect, it was a great decision." Mann and her husband realized that they were spending much of their time in the family room of their home anyway, and the conversion would allow for a far more pleasant working space. The room was 16' x 16' (5m x 5m) and had two large, northwest-facing windows.

The project was "aided" by a recent fire that had burned the fitted carpet in the room. An insurance payment helped with the cost of installing a hardwood floor. The only other structural expense was the installation of two sets of French doors to close the two wide entryways into the room. This assured privacy, quiet, and protection from the artist's three cats who dream of a life of knocking over paint jars and desecrating still-life arrangements. Mann has augmented her space with simple shelving for books and her large collection of still-life materials. She has plenty of room for an easel, a drawing table, a still-life table, and a comfortable chair for reading or for posing a model.

Moving the studio onto the main floor of the house had the added benefit of freeing up the artist's former space in the basement, which she has now converted into a storage area. "I built a painting rack and keep a flat file in there for works on paper," says the artist. "I installed shelves in the closet to increase storage space for canvases. As my studio becomes cluttered with finished paintings, I move them out and down to the storage room." Mann is also planning on making her small, one-car garage into a workshop for matting, framing, and stretching canvases. "Unconventional use of space is the key," she says, "letting go of what the rooms of the house 'should' be used for."

Mann is thrilled with the results of her project. "The studio has been a wonderful aid to my work as a painter," she says. "Having the dedicated space, not having to dig my supplies out or set up my easel every time I want to work makes it much easier to paint. It is quiet in there, and peaceful. It is all mine! It's great to be able to leave a still life up for long periods, or to just sit and look through art books. It has helped me become much more organized."

For more on Amy Mann, visit her website at www.amymann.com.

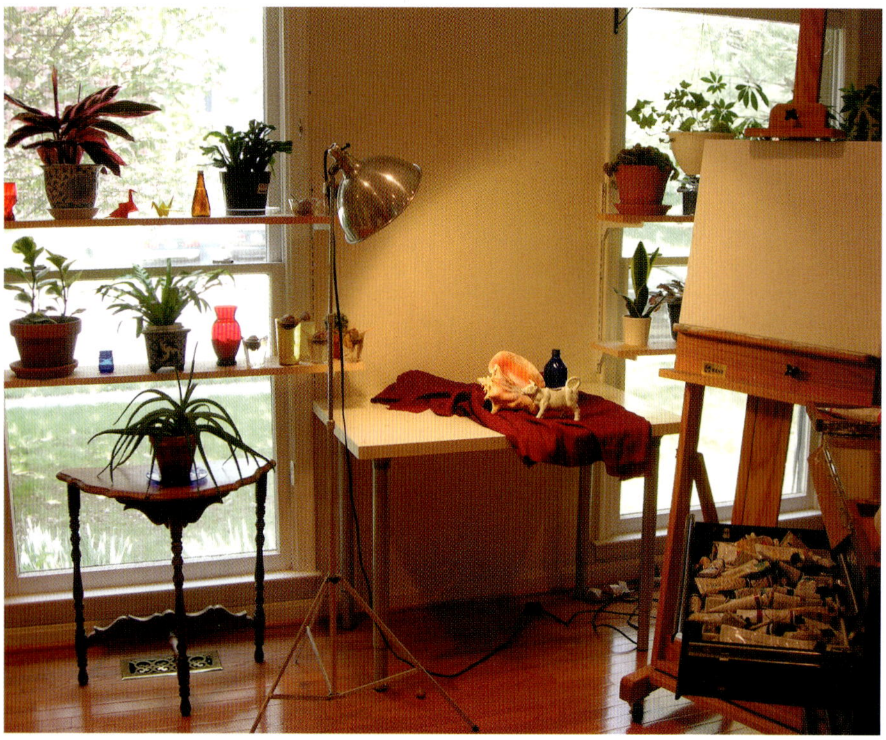

← North-facing windows allow the artist to illuminate her still-life arrangements with either natural or artificial light.

→ Mann has adequate storage for her still-life props, painting supplies, and sound system.

Opposite top: Converting the living room of Mann's Virginia home to a studio involved the addition of new flooring, French doors, and shelving. The French doors lend privacy to the studio in which there are two drafting tables, an upright easel, movable storage units, shelving, an easy chair, and a skeleton.

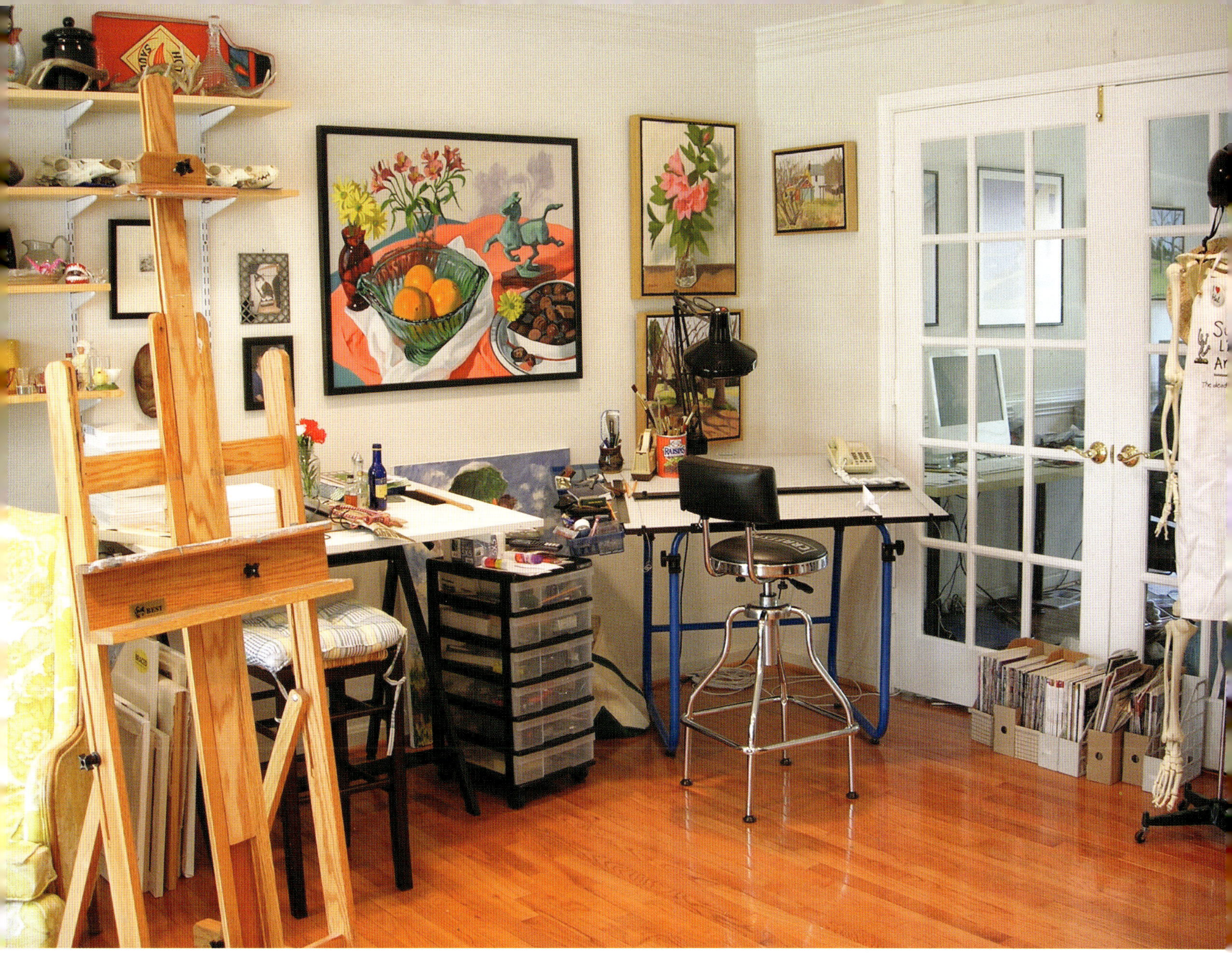

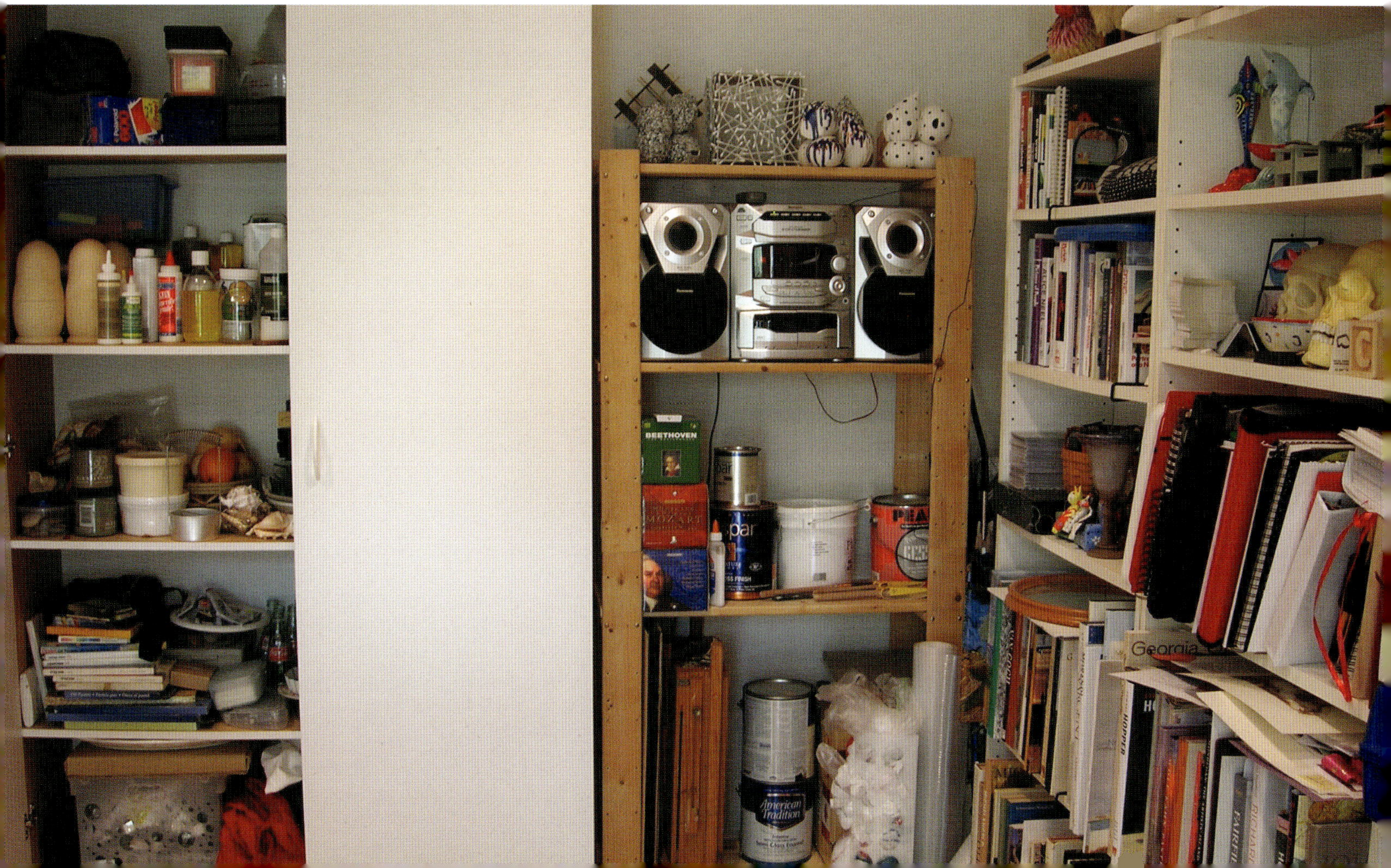

Ruth Ann Greenberg
Adding Upward

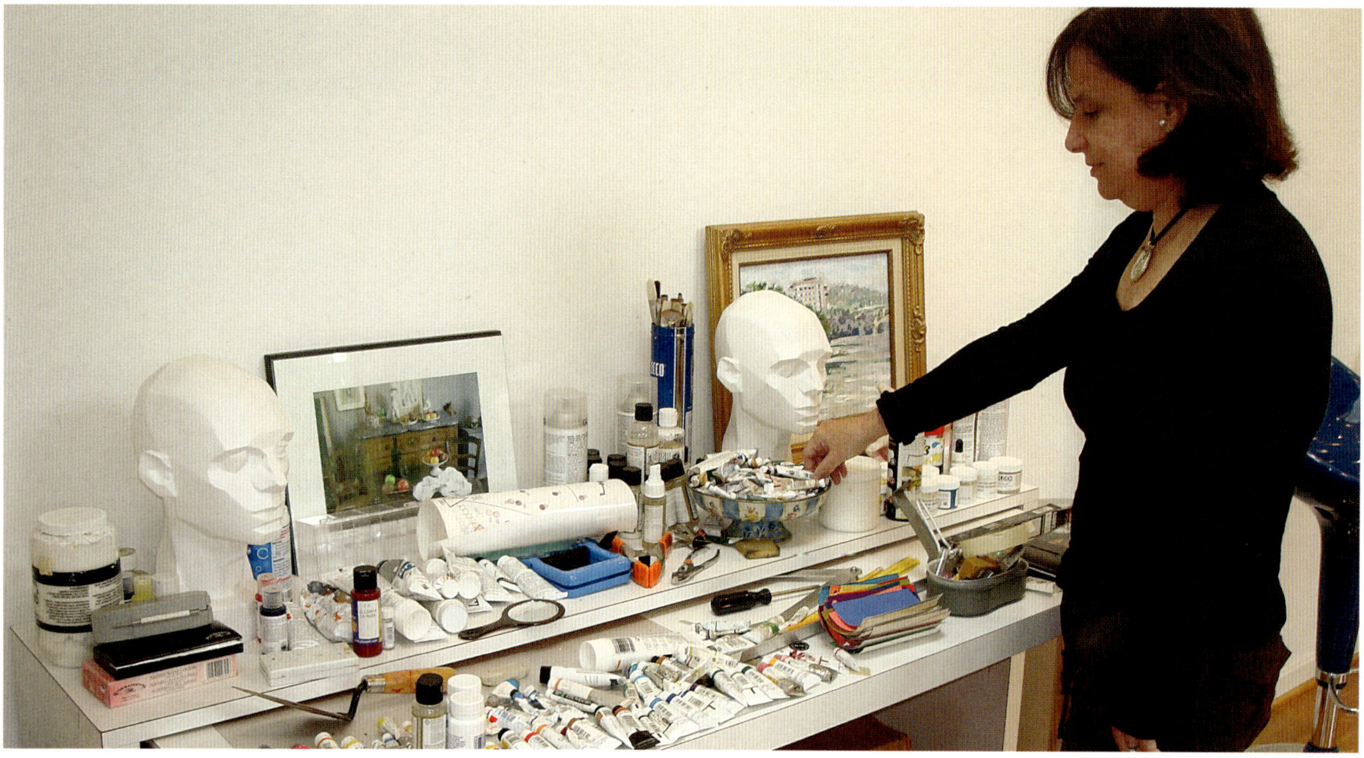

One of the storage areas that holds the artist's brushes, paints, Asaro Planes of the Head, and mahlstick.

After considering a number of alternatives for renting or building a studio space near her home in Bethesda, Maryland, Ruth Ann Greenberg decided to hire an architect to design a spacious work space above the garage she was going to build next to her home. Edwin Lee came up with a plan for a 16'-x-32' (5m-x-10m) room with a 14-foot (4m) ceiling, three skylights cut into the ceiling, windows on three sides of the building, a separate utility room, and an exterior balcony where the artist can paint or spray fixative. "The studio is separated from my home by several walls, and there is an entrance in the back," Greenberg says. "If I want to paint, teach, or meet clients, I can do so only a few steps away from home, but the studio is completely private."

Greenberg's studio has a separate ventilation, cooling, and heating system from the main house, and she can control the light by blocking any of the windows or by turning on one of the recessed halogen or fluorescent lights in the ceiling or the track lights around the room. She can also add task lighting by turning on one of the light stands fitted with Verilux daylight bulbs. "I can quickly change the lighting to focus on displayed paintings, student work stations, or my own easel," she explains. "I work in oil, acrylic, and watercolor, and when the weather permits, I like painting outdoors. For that reason I have easels I can move in and out of the work area, including an Anderson swivel easel for oil painting, a Stanrite for watercolor painting, and both a Douglas Smith handmade pochade box and a Jullian French easel for painting outdoors."

Greenberg has been a full-time artist since she ended her career as a stock broker and part-time painter. "I used to rent a studio on F Street in the district and worked there after spending my days as a broker," she explains. "I studied art in the 1970s and 1980s, and I participated in workshops on watercolor painting and portraiture. I am now a member of Oil Painters of America and several regional plein air groups. I accept commissions and exhibit in area galleries, and I have an entrance area in my studio where I can sit down with clients to discuss their needs. I also teach two students and have plenty of room for them to work."

For more information on Ruth Ann Greenberg, read her blog at ruthanngreenbergart.blogspot.com.

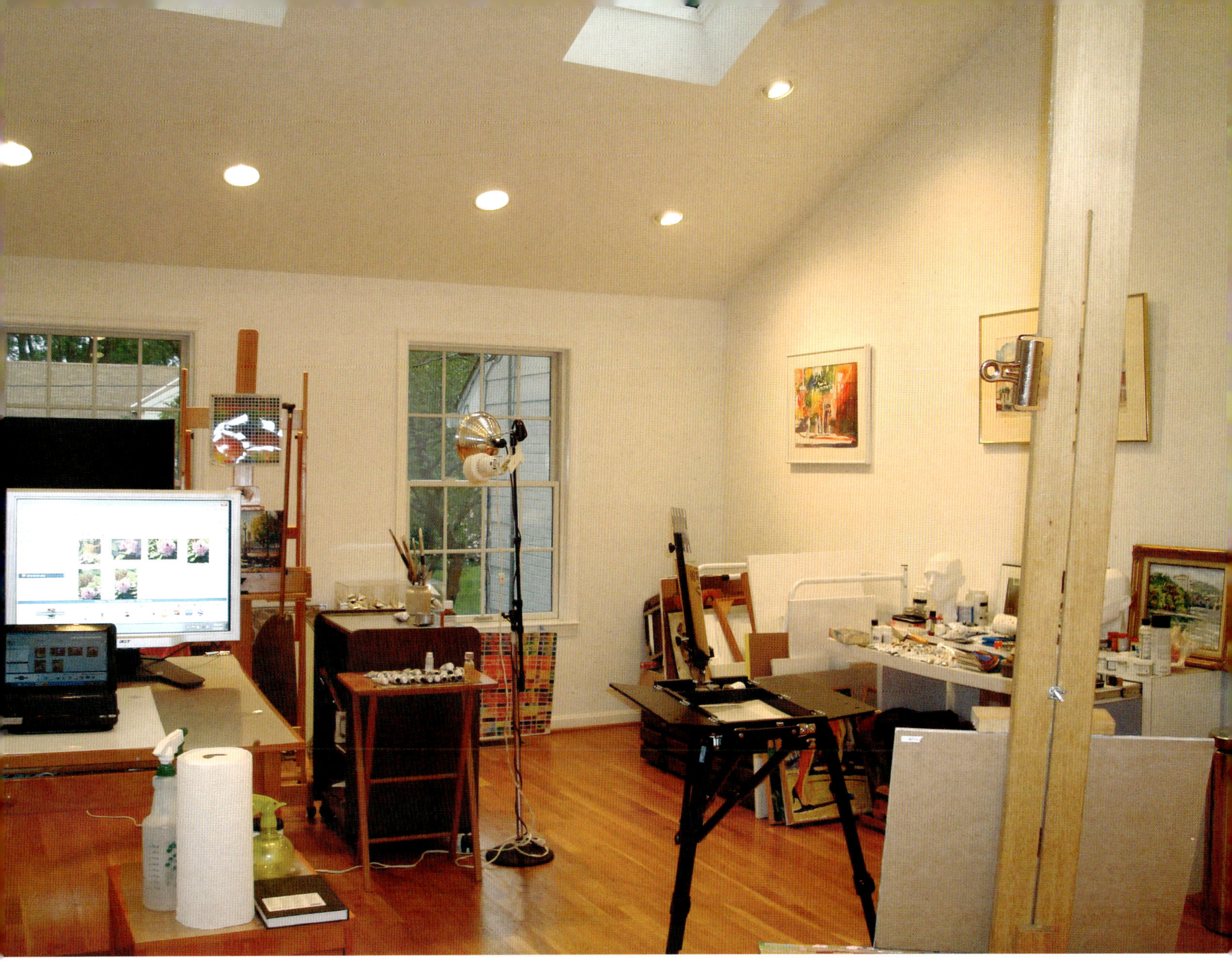

↑ The interior of Greenberg's studio above the garage of her home in Bethesda, Maryland. The skylights above the studio, as well as the windows, bring in light from three sides of the building.

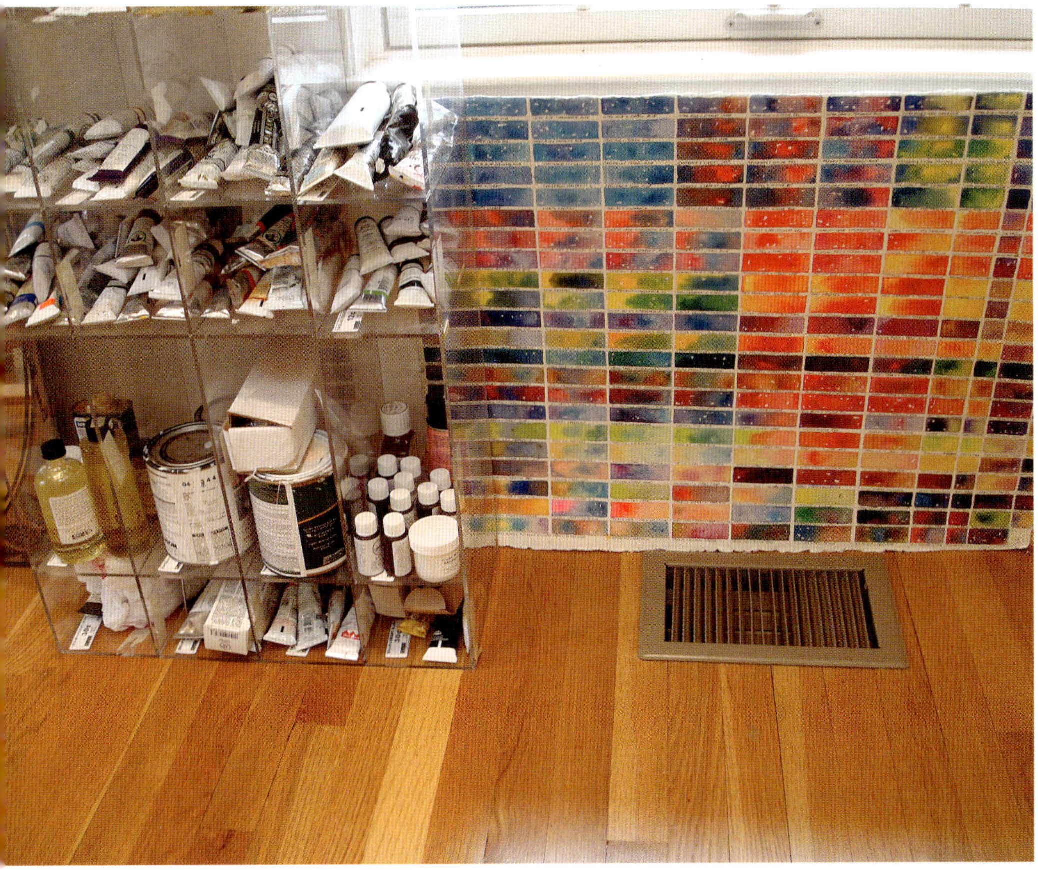

← Greenberg keeps a color chart near her paints and mediums to allow for easy reference.

Christine Ivers

Adapting a Studio to a Changing Economy

For fifteen years starting in 1986, Christine Ivers ran a successful advertising agency in a Connecticut ranch house she converted for commercial use. But when the last recession hit and clients were going bankrupt, starting in-house shops, or sending their production work to Mexico and China, Ivers had to either give up or adjust. "I decided to go from one unstable industry to another," she says with a hint of sarcasm. "I made up my mind to completely change the working space in my office and my home to create two studios in which I could paint, teach, and hold workshops."

Ivers enlisted the help of her husband, three of her four daughters, their boyfriends, and a son-in-law to break down, move, or convert the office space and all the furnishings to serve her new priorities. "In the place of my desk, computers, cabinets, and furniture, I made room for myself and as many as eight students," she explains. "The photo lamps became light sources for evening students, the conference table became a work surface for artists who didn't want to stand at an easel, a trade-show stage became the backdrop for still lifes or models, and storage units were converted to bookcases for art books instead of client files."

Because the basement and recreation room at her residence were larger than the office, she made use of the space for workshops. The area in the basement next to the furnace, hot water heater, and refrigerator became her personal studio. She was then able to host up to fifteen students in one of the workshops she conducts every few months.

Many of the skills that made Ivers a successful businessperson have also served her well as an artist and teacher. Because of her experience with computer equipment, she can teach artists to work with digital photographs, adjust images in Adobe Photoshop, set up websites, and upload photographs into art competitions. She hosts classes for adults during the day and in the evenings, and she teaches young students in after-school programs. She also helps high school students prepare their portfolios for college entrance.

"Most of the artists I know work at their kitchen tables, in spare bedrooms, in the laundry room, or wherever they can find space to spread out and be messy," Ivers says. "I'm not alone in having to make adjustments in order to have space in which to create artwork. I've always believed that necessity is the mother of invention, and this has been one more experience that proves that point."

For more on Christine Ivers, visit her website at www.christineivers.com.

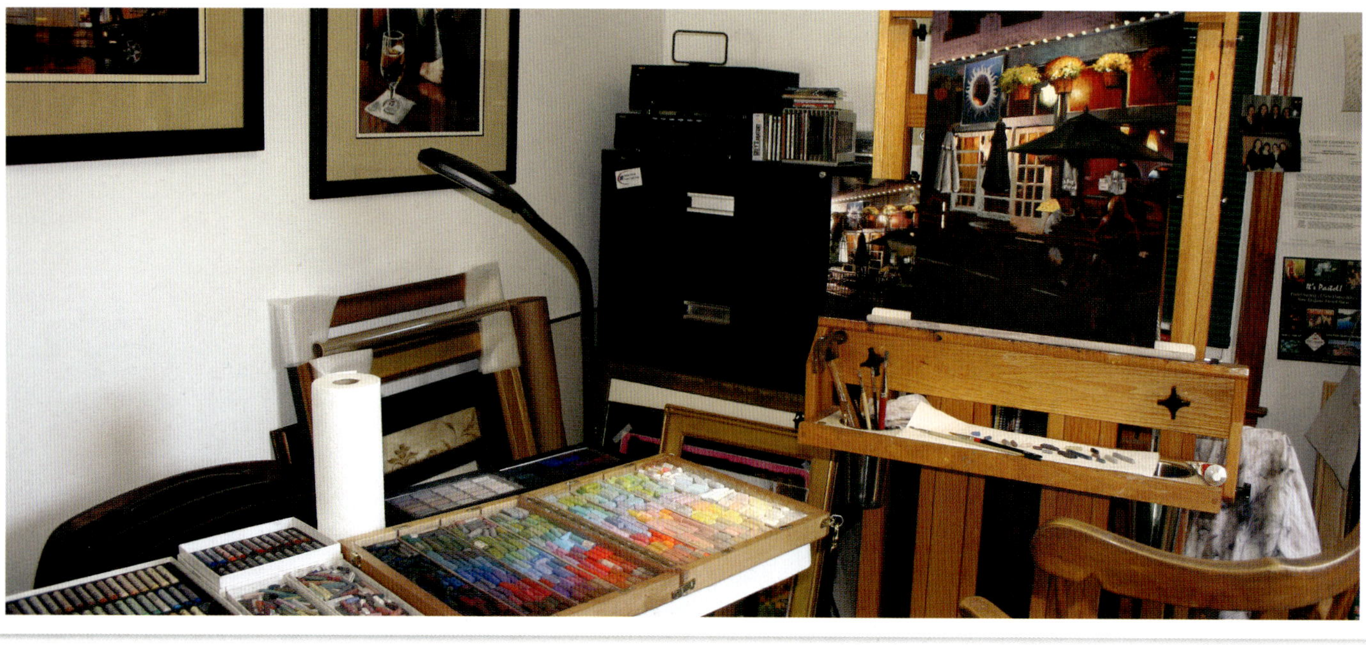

The artist's work space with her supplies. The painting *Mum's the Word* is on the easel.

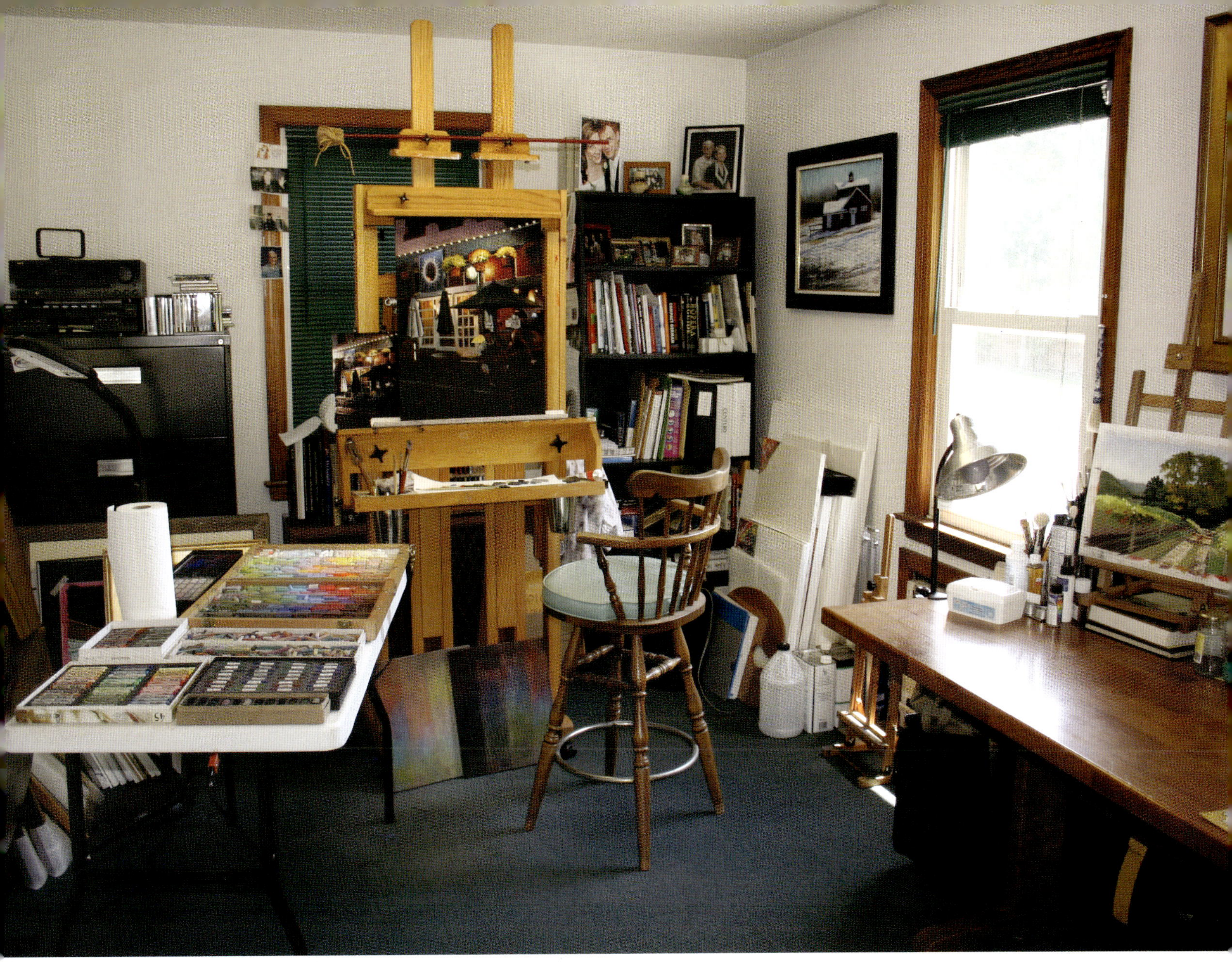

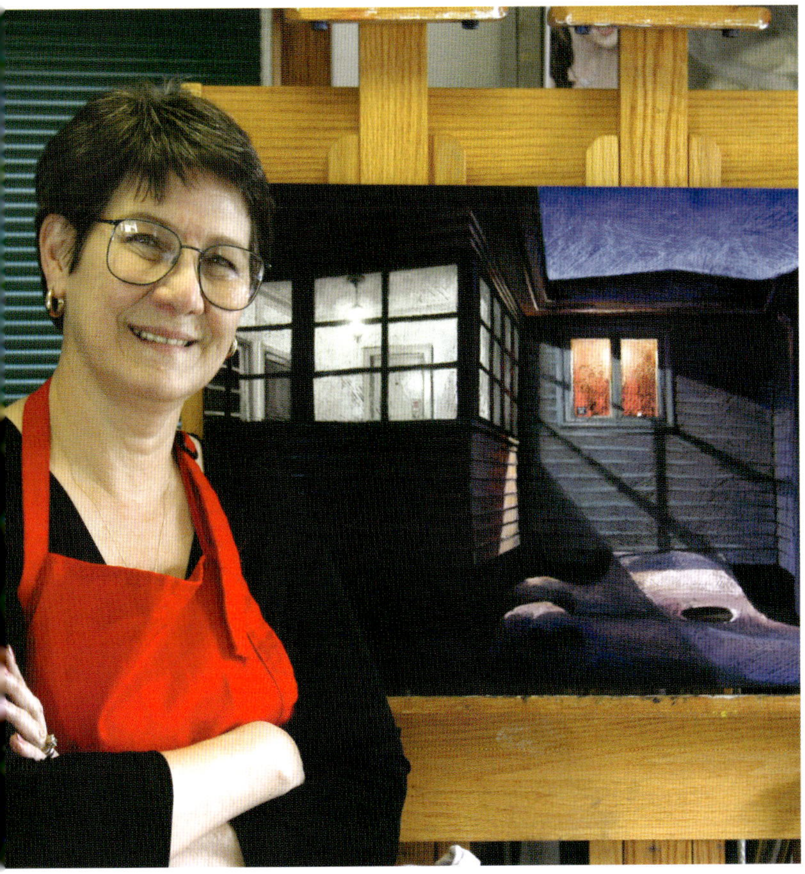

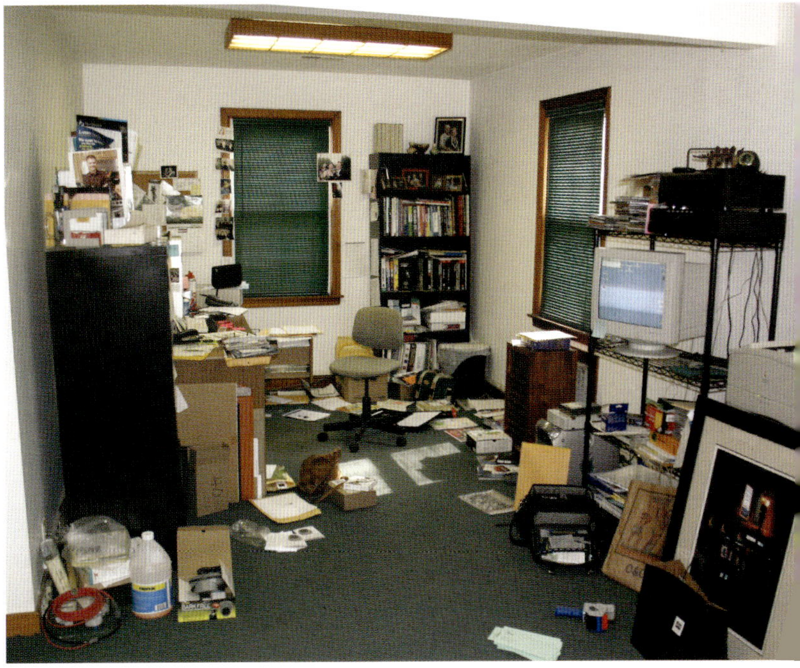

↑ The new studio space.

← Ivers next to a work in progress titled *Insomnia*.

↓ The office before the conversion.

Gerald Simcoe

Putting an Easel Where a Tractor Once Parked

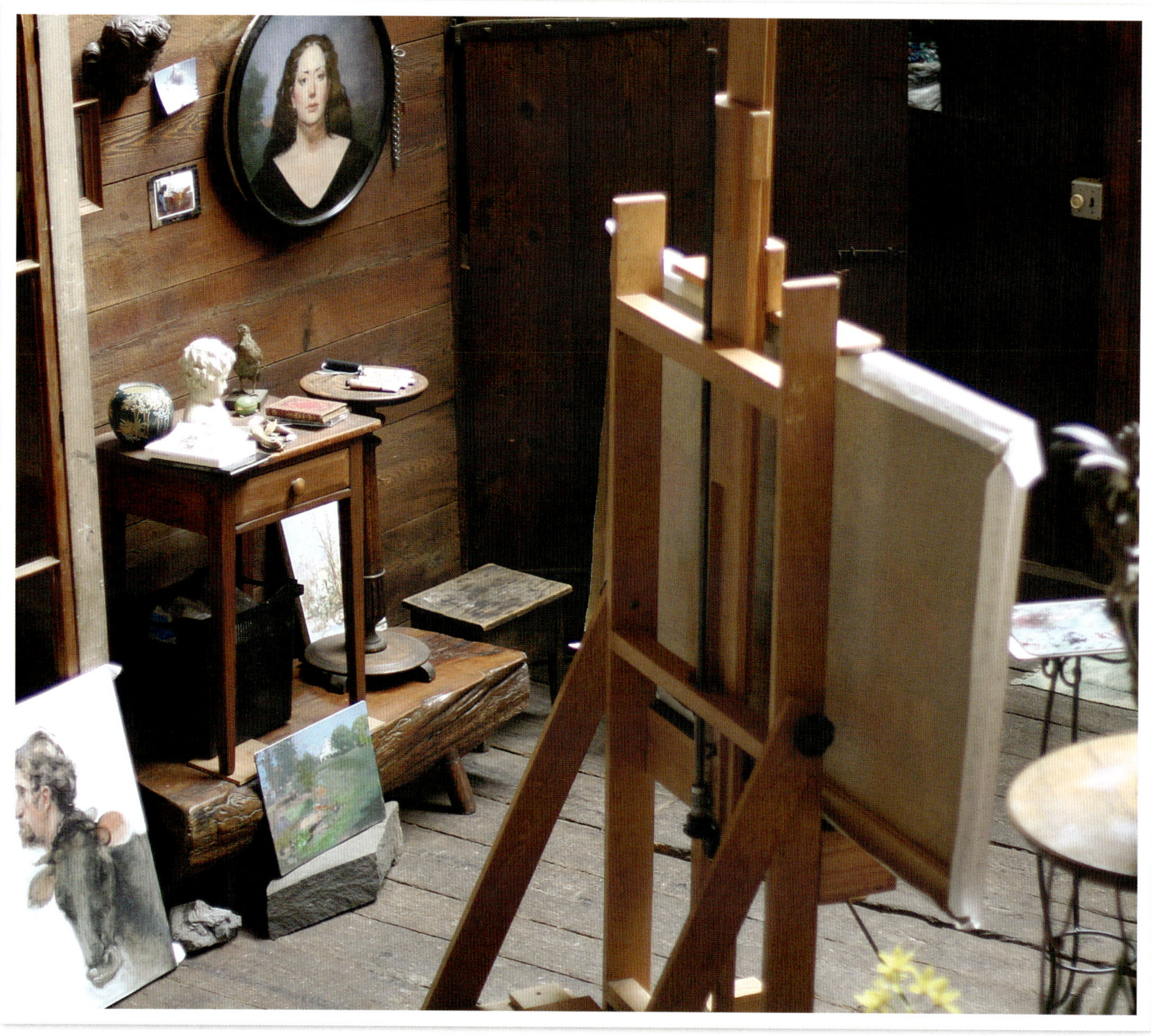

A view down to the studio area of the barn from a storage loft. A skylight is directly above this entrance, which is the thrash floor where the tractor was parked.

In the early 1980s when Gerald Simcoe completed his education at the Art Students League of New York, he decided to move back home to Northampton, Pennsylvania, rather than work in a small, rented New York apartment. "While I was an art student, I lived at the YMCA and then in a tiny apartment," the artist remembers. "It made so much more sense to set up a studio back home and keep the apartment for regular visits to Manhattan."

Simcoe grew up on land that was once a dairy farm, so there was plenty of acreage and scenic views, as well as a large ramp barn built before 1840 that was being used for storage. His parents agreed to renovate the barn in a way that would preserve its historical character while making it possible to use the space as an artist's studio.

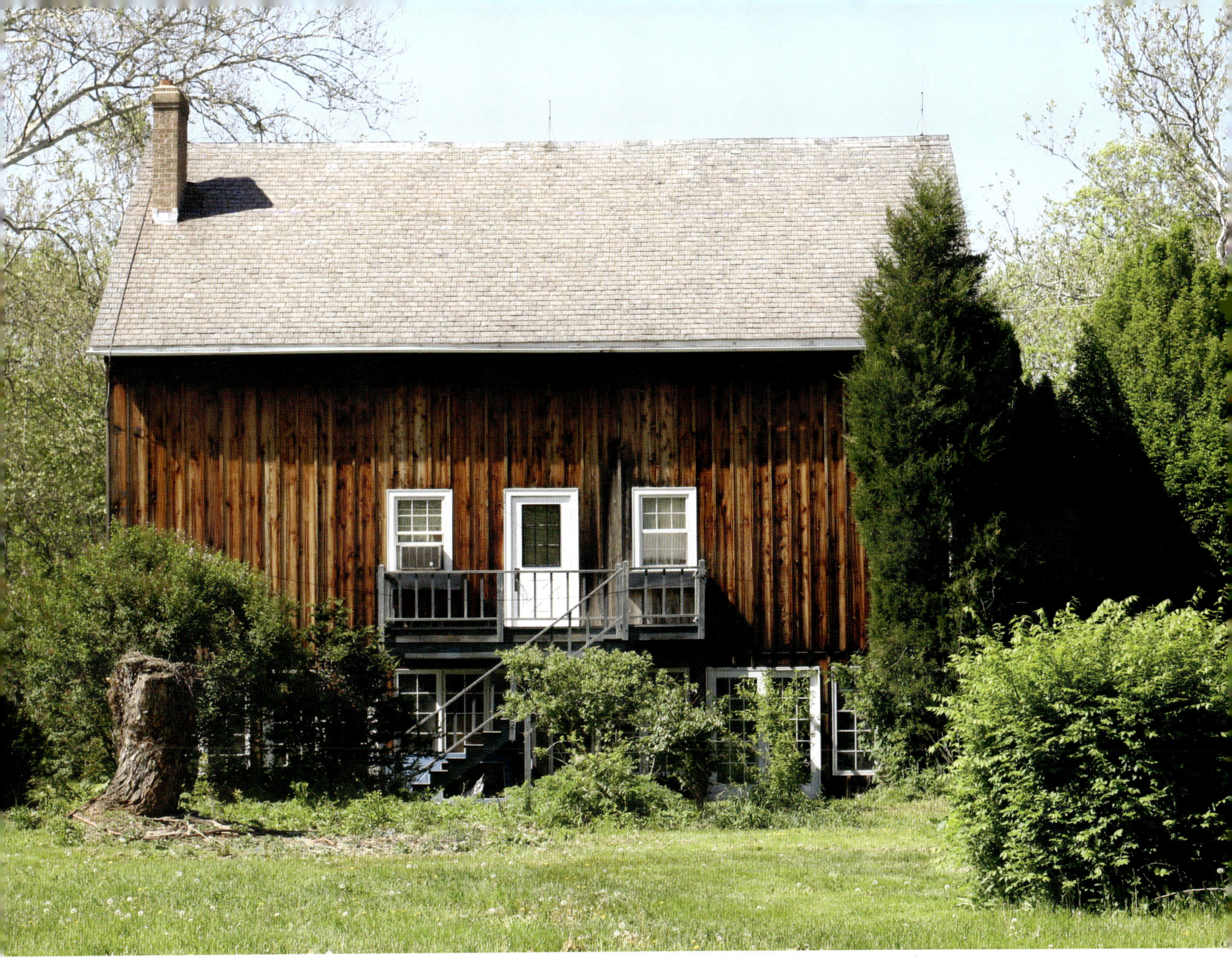

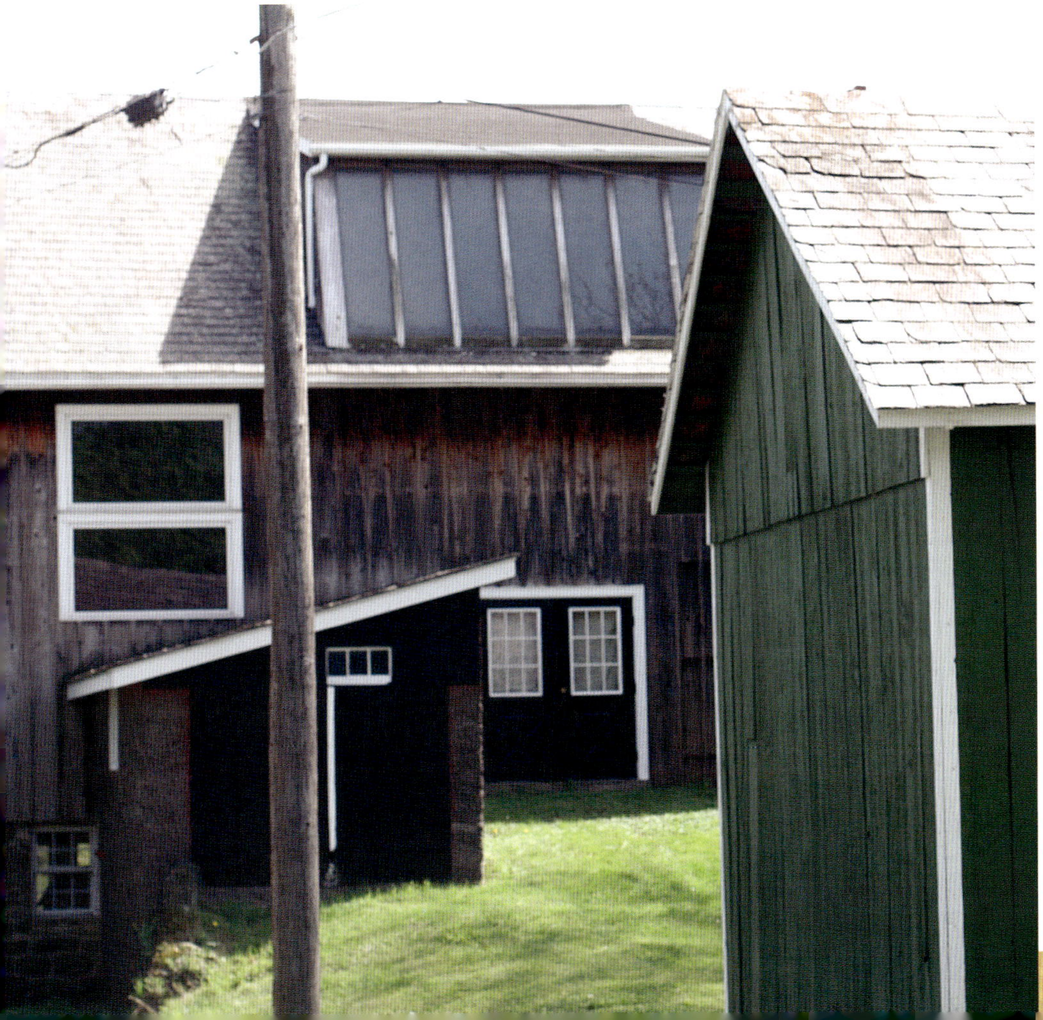

↑ The back of the barn Simcoe uses as a painting studio.

← The exterior of the 1840s barn in Pennsylvania that Simcoe converted to a studio. The large skylight helps illuminate the studio.

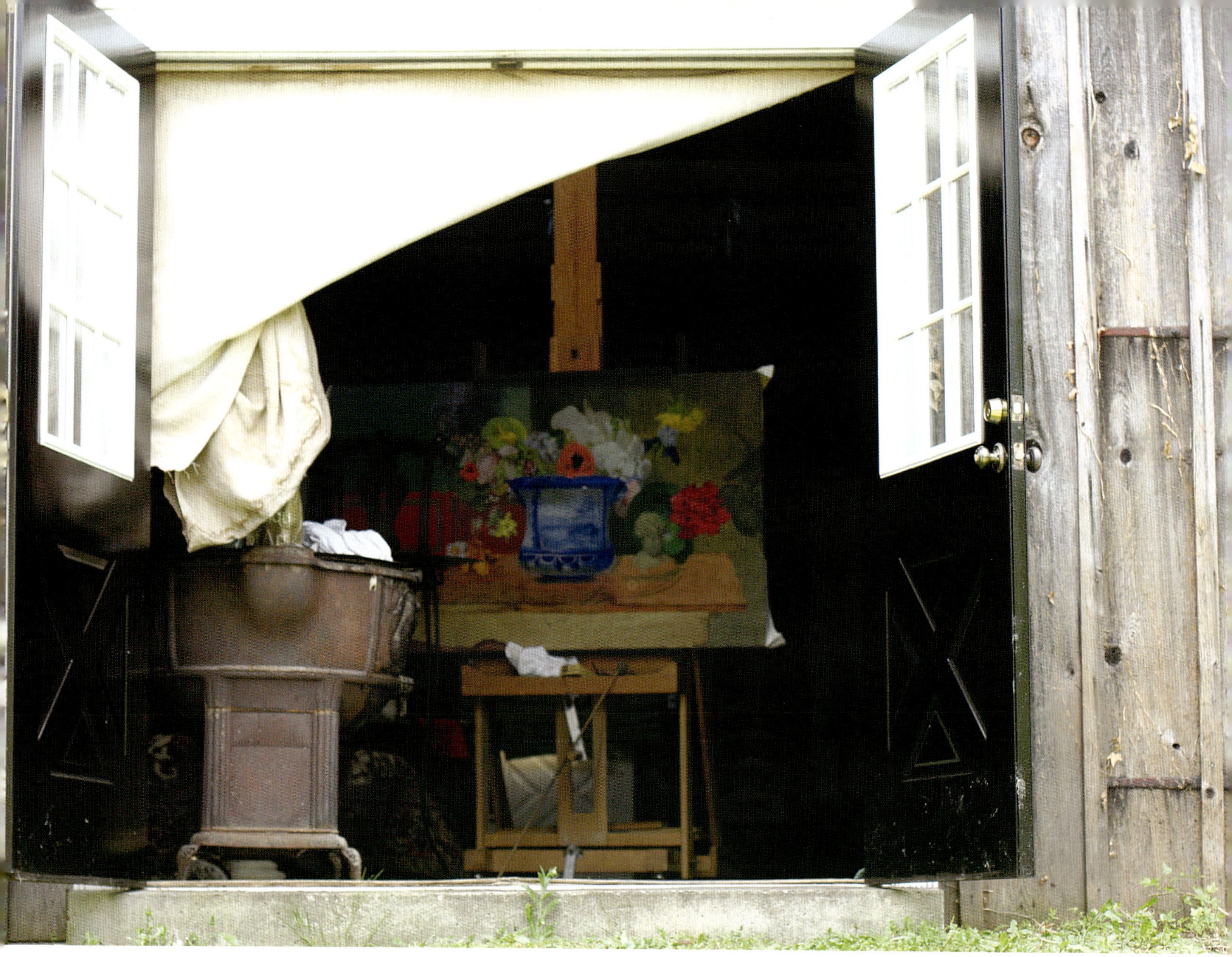

The entrance to Simcoe's Pennsylvania studio.

"The central part of the three-part barn was built with a thicker wooden floor of locally harvested and milled hemlock—the state tree," Simcoe explains. "I wanted to use that section for a studio illuminated with warm daylight, and the eastern third was renovated to have a cool, north-facing window. We also added a skylight over the entrance to the central section to increase the amount of daylight that comes in.

"To keep the space warm in the winter, we insulated the pinewood walls, covered the insulation with the same kind of pine, and brought out the warm tones of the wood by brushing it with linseed oil that helped to preserve the pine," the artist continues.

Simcoe built a model stand to use when his portrait clients posed or when he wanted to raise a still-life arrangement to eye level. He stores a large collection of antiques—which he uses as resources for his paintings—in the barn and his parents' home.

Simcoe is also a talented musician and trained horticulturist who studied at Longwood Gardens, in Delaware. During one period of his career, Simcoe worked on the estate of Ambassador and Mrs. Walter Annenberg; and the artist also plays piano in an annual concert at Swarthmore College, in Pennsylvania.

For more information on Gerald Simcoe, visit his website at www.simcoegallery.com.

→ **View From My Studio**
by Gerald Simcoe, 2010, oil, 35" x 60" (89cm x 152cm). Collection of the artist.

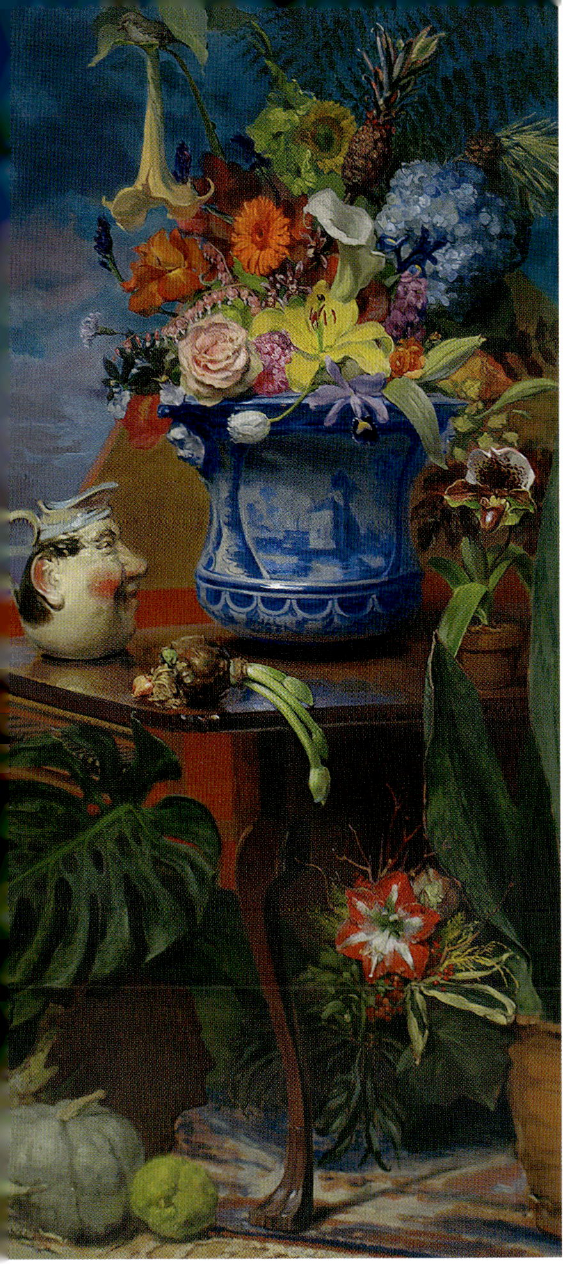

Dutch Influence in Horticulture
by Gerald Simcoe, 2009, oil, 36" x 72" (91cm x 183cm). Collection of the artist.

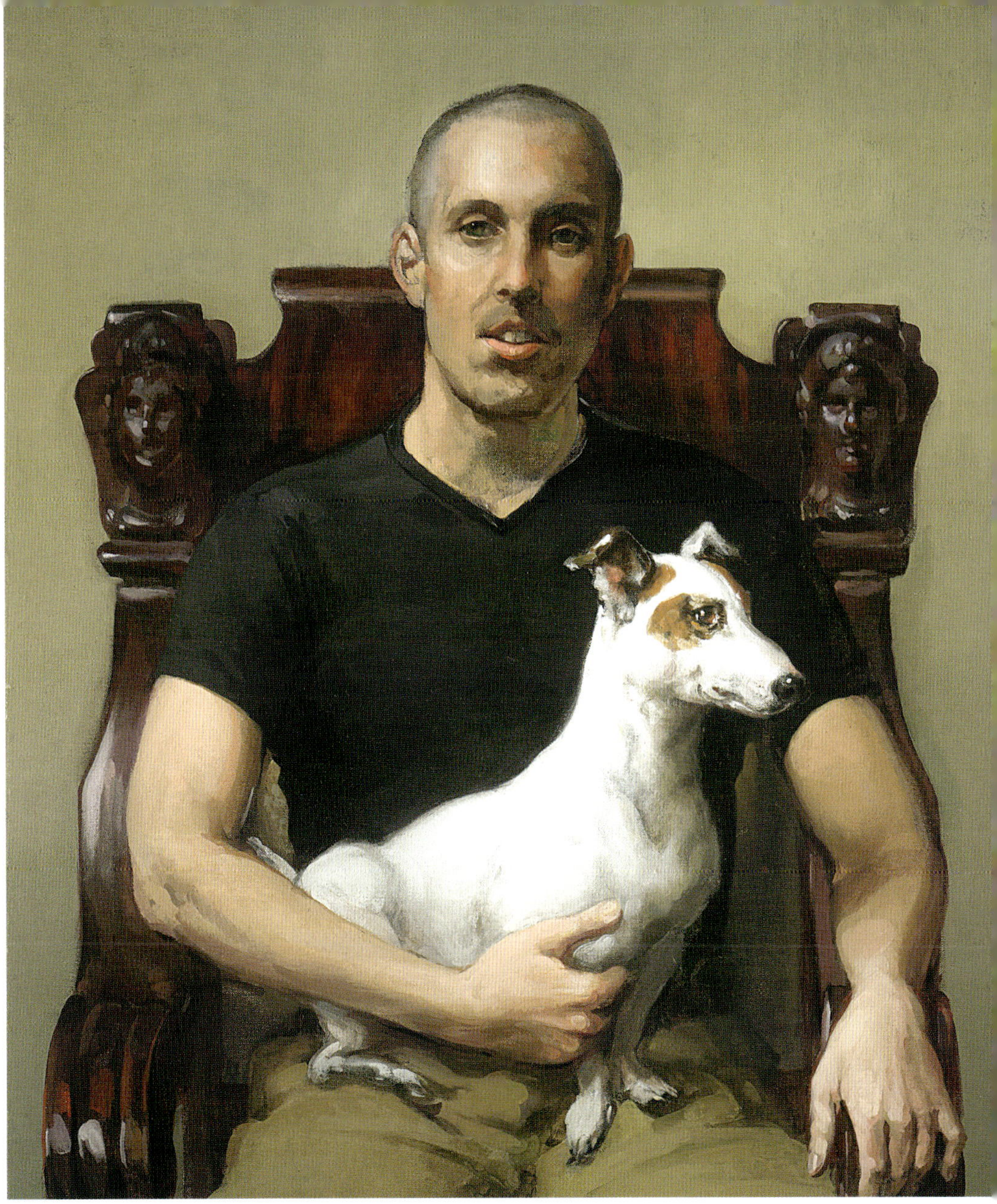

Rob Conti With Peter
by Gerald Simcoe, 2004, oil, 35" x 28" (89cm x 71cm). Collection of the artist.

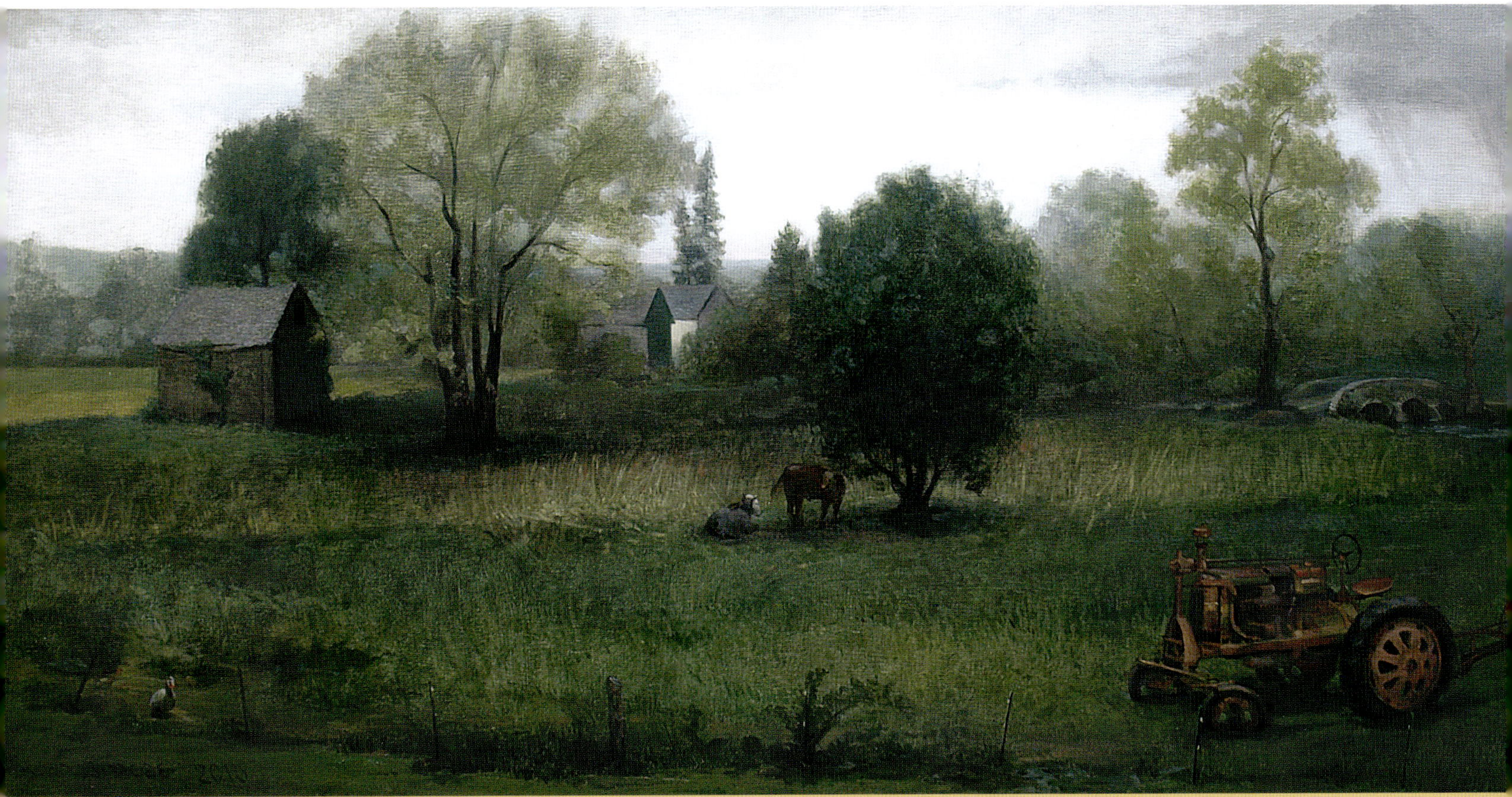

Joan Potter

Building on Art History

In 1912, the year New Mexico became a state, artist Gerald Cassidy (1879–1934) moved to Santa Fe with his wife, Ina Sizer Cassidy, because he suffered from pneumonia and needed to live in a dry region that was connected to the art world by train lines. He created a compound of buildings on Canyon Road, consisting of an adobe house for himself and his family, as well as two temporary structures for his animals. Eventually, in place of these structures he built two more adobe structures—one for a studio and one for guests to stay in. After Cassidy's death in 1934, the property changed hands more than once, and the structures were remodeled. Joan Potter bought the structure on the site of the original "animal house," and she undertook an extensive remodeling and expansion that preserved all of the Cassidy rooms and adopted the same overall style of the Southwestern architecture.

"I was living in New York when I decided to move to Santa Fe, where a number of my artist friends had settled," explains Potter, a graduate of the Massachusetts College of Art and Design, in Boston, and the Art Students League of New York, in Manhattan. "I bought the Cassidy property and added a large studio on the north end of the house along Canyon Road and updated living quarters on the south side. In addition to a north-facing studio, I asked for a long, solid wall on which to display my collection of artwork."

Today, that uninterrupted wall in the dining room is visible as soon as one walks into Potter's home. It holds a large collection of paintings, prints, and drawings by Potter's friends and the historic artists who inspired her. There are two paintings by Cassidy, two etchings by Anders Zorn, a small Edgar Payne oil, an E. Martin Hennings painting, a lithograph by Nicolai Fechin, and oil paintings by Richard Schmid, Scott Burdick, and Matt Smith. Nearby, in a place of honor, is a painting that Potter executed thirty years ago of artist Sherrie McGraw. "I knew Sherrie in New York, and she gave me three modeling sessions as a birthday present," Potter recalls. "I painted her from behind as she looked into a mirror."

Potter's studio measures 20' x 24' (6m x 7m) and is a few steps down from a room in the oldest section of the home. A large, angled window faces true north and can be partially closed by pulling shades up from the bottom. "I started covering the bottoms of the windows when I noticed that tourists in the jitneys were looking in at the nude models posing in the studio," the artist says with a chuckle. "I tend to set up my still-life arrangements on the table on the east side of the room and have the models pose on a bench against the wall on the west side. Having several places for models or still-life arrangements allows me to work on several paintings without having to disturb the setups."

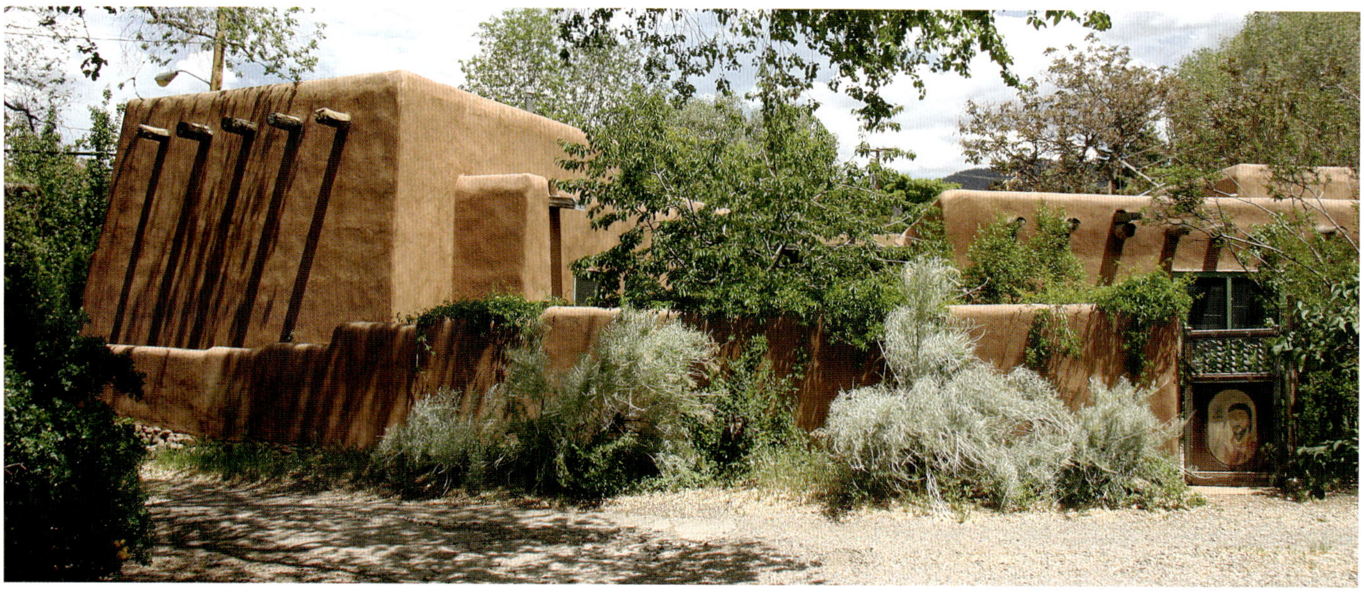

The exterior of Potter's historical home in Santa Fe, with the large studio building on the left.

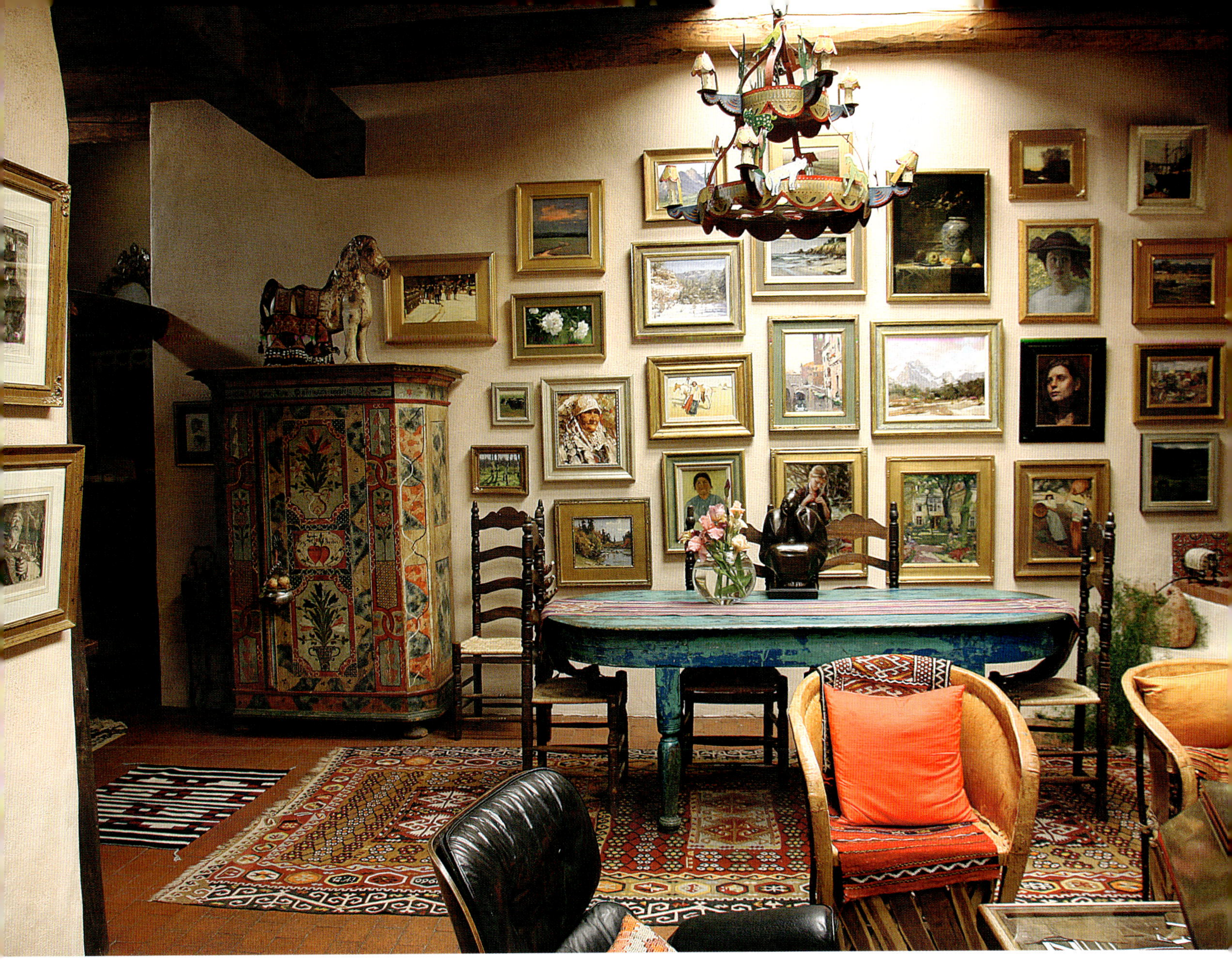

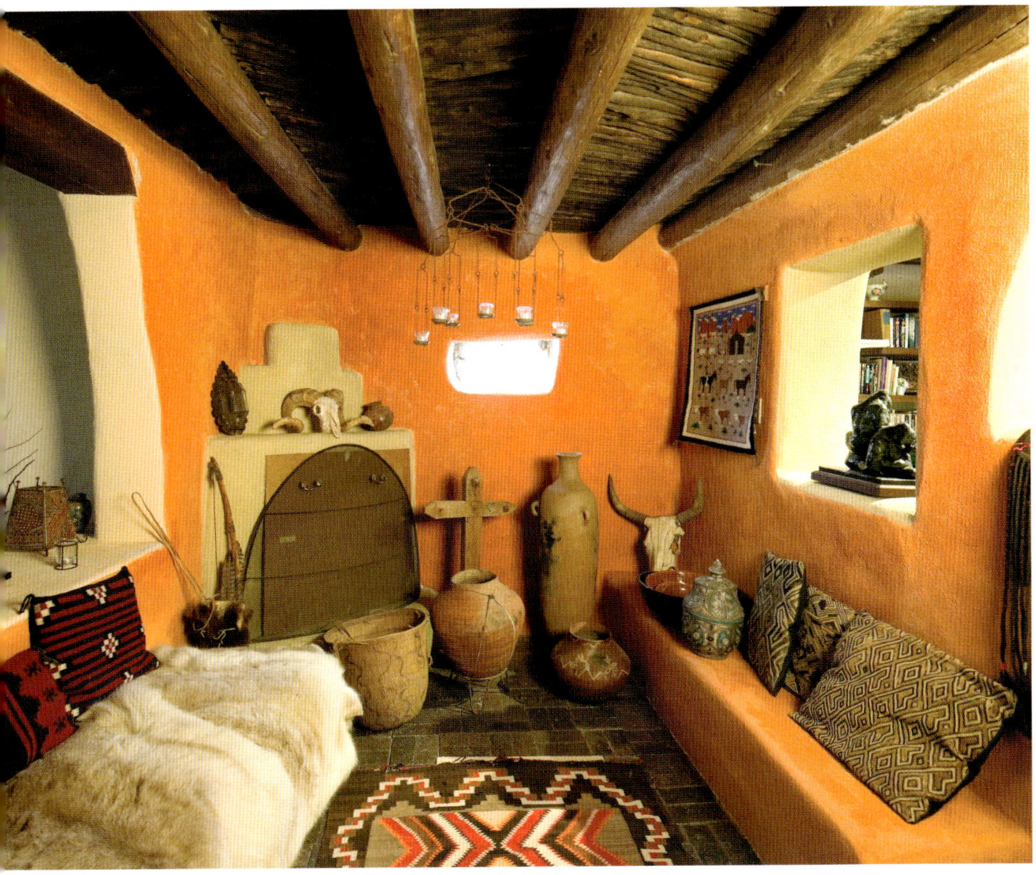

↑ The gallery of paintings in the dining room of Potter's home.

← Part of the original structure built by artist Gerald Cassidy.

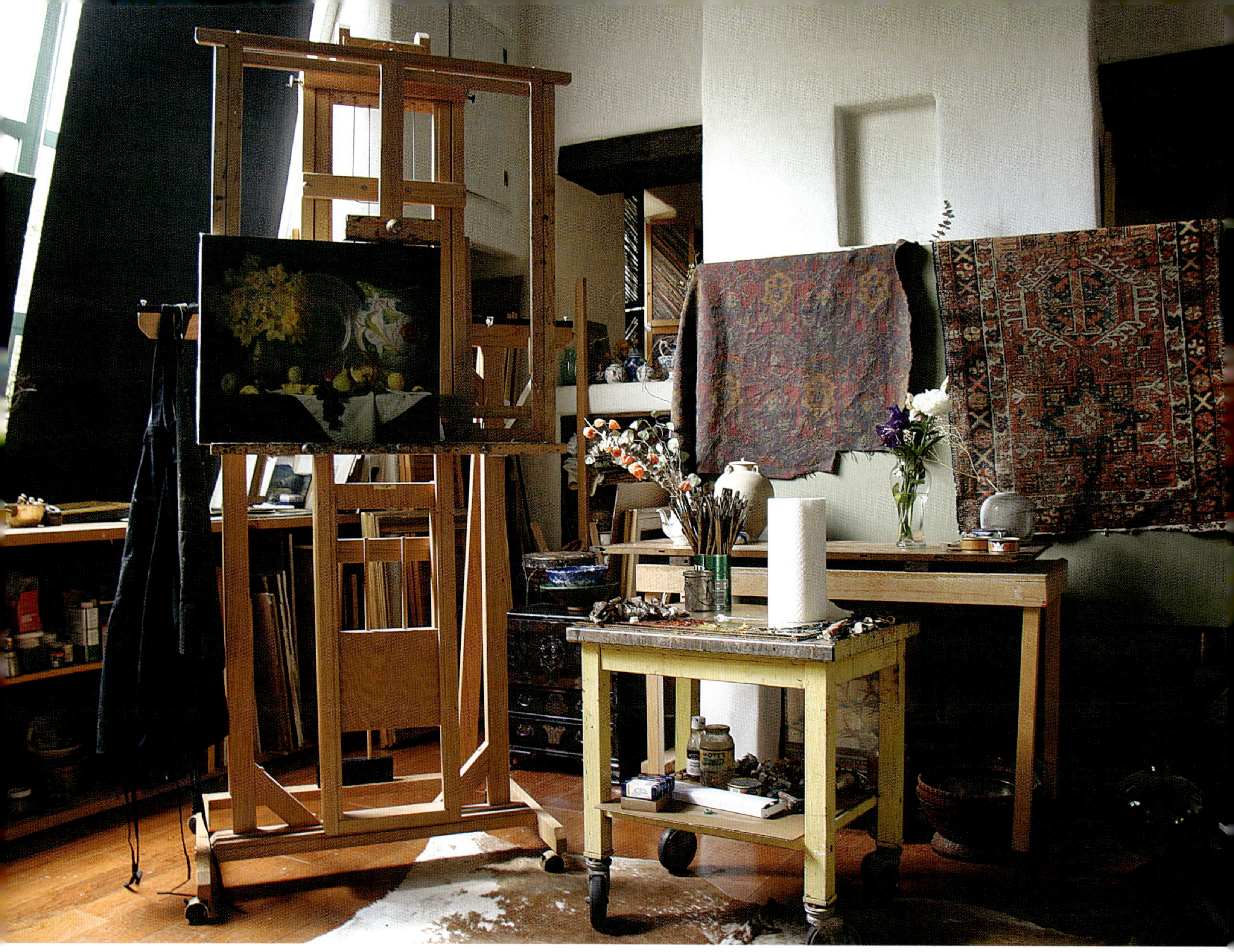

↑ The interior of Potter's studio near the north-facing windows that look onto Canyon Road, a table where she often arranges still-life setups, and some of the many objects she has collected that appear in her paintings.

→ **Gooseberries**
by Joan Potter, 2010, oil, 9" x 12" (23cm x 30cm).

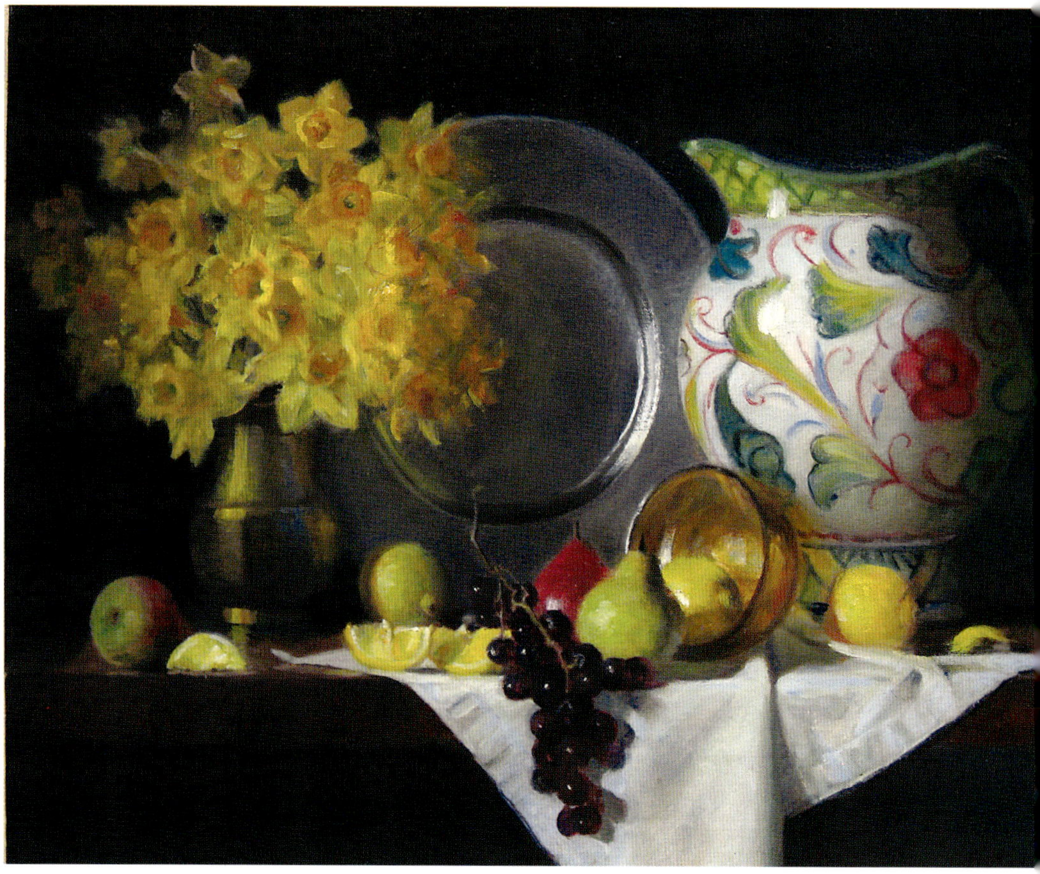

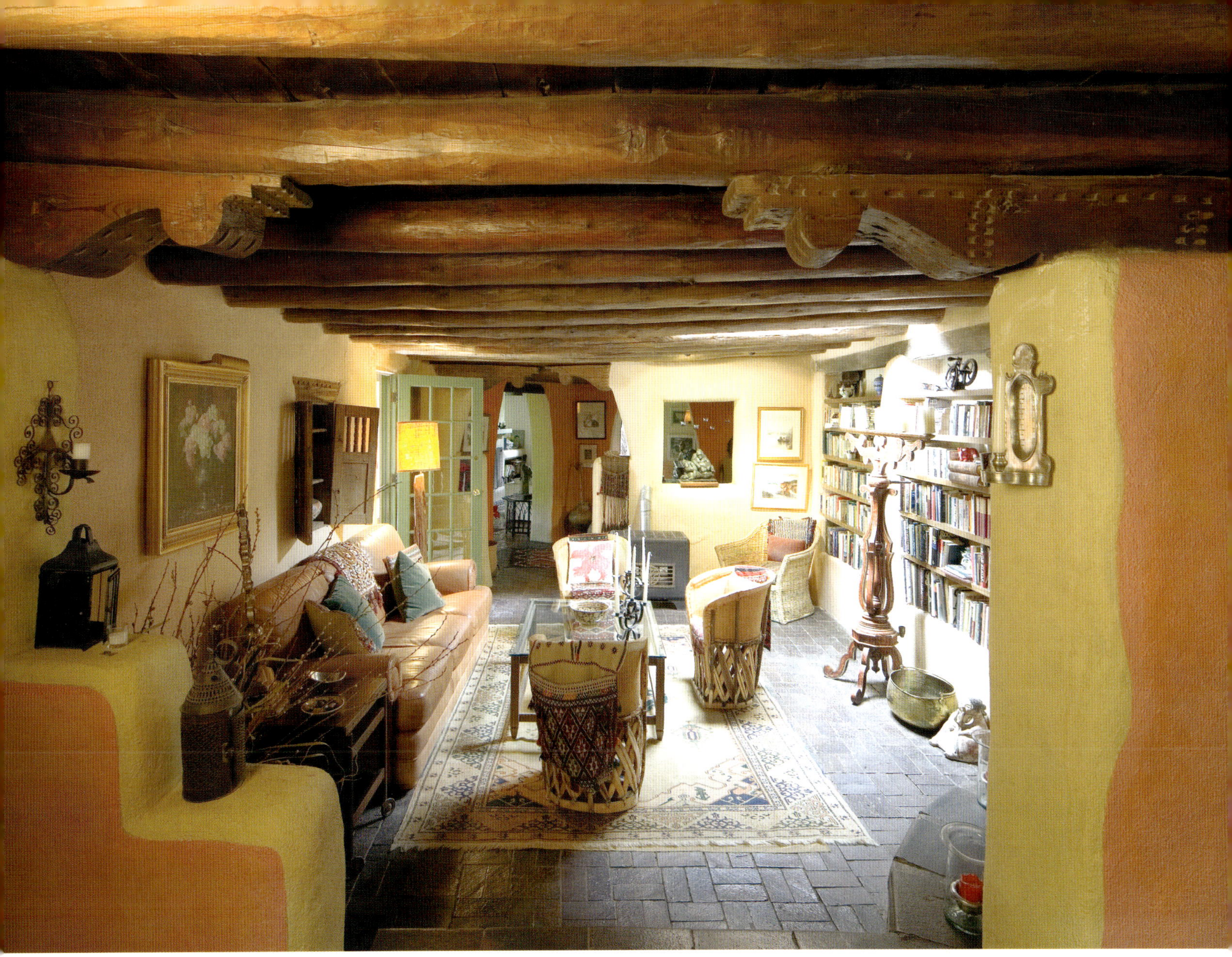

↑ The living room in Potter's home, which is part of the original adobe structure.

→ Potter standing in the studio she added to the adobe structure built by Gerald Cassidy (1879–1934).

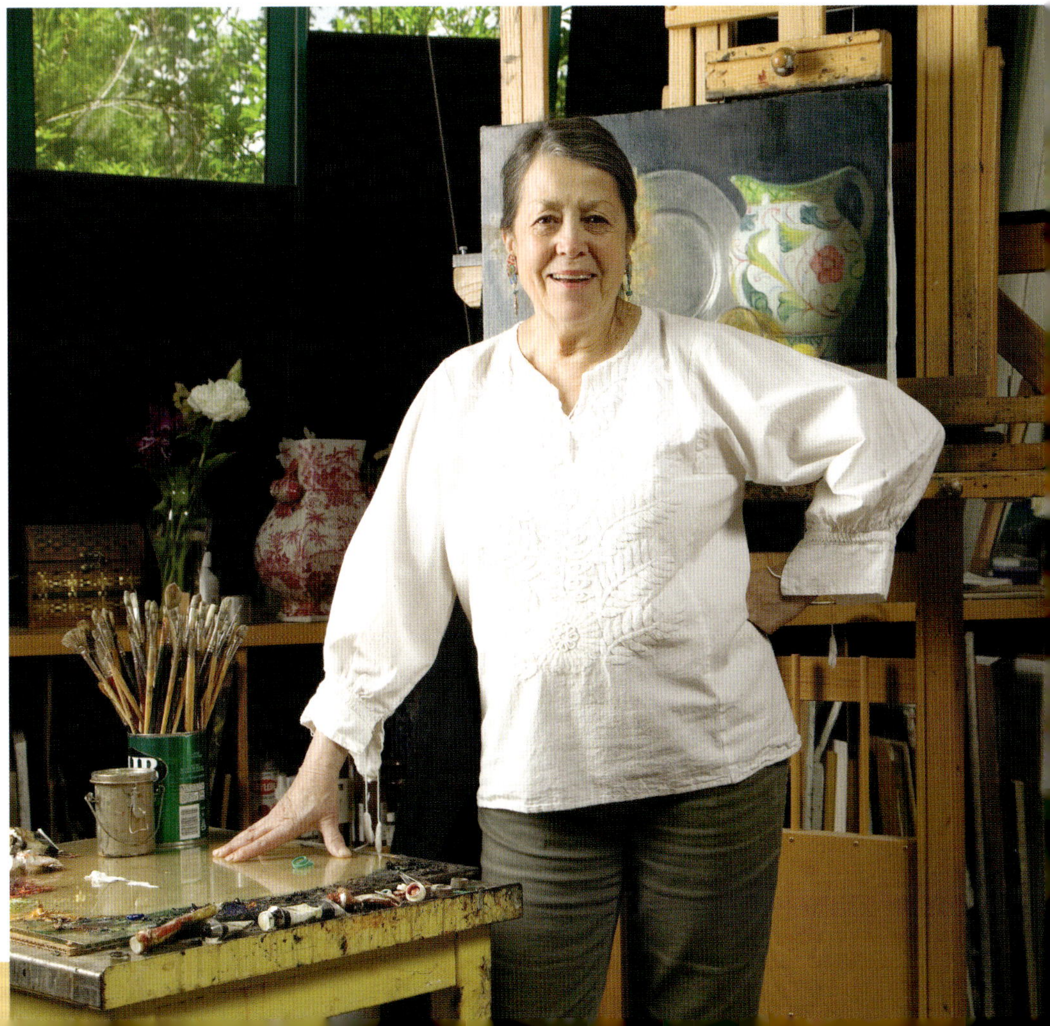

Arthur Egeli

Converting a Garage Into a Professional Studio

The garage behind Arthur Egeli's house in Seabrook, Washington, was a perfect structure to convert to a professional studio. It measures 24' x 24' (7m x 7m), the pathway beside the building connects to the local community, the ceilings are relatively high, and the climate inside remains fairly constant throughout the year. However, the months of work needed to remodel the garage were stressful, especially for an artist who is an active professional and who spends most of his summers in Provincetown, Massachusetts, teaching and operating a gallery.

"I got a lot of good advice from my father, Cedric Egeli, who has built three art studios from the ground up during the course of his career," Arthur explains. "He, in turn, received advice from his father, Bjorn Egeli (1900–1984), on the construction of a professional studio. The most important advice was about the proper way to light a studio, and Cedric urged me to locate a north-facing window at least 5 feet (2m) above the ground and as close to the top of the 12-foot (4m) ceiling as possible." The reason to raise the window so high above the studio floor is to eliminate reflections off the ground outside the studio, such as the green of the grass or the gray of the pavement. And maximizing the height of the window brings in as much consistent, cool light during the day as possible.

Egeli was also advised to add a custom-built window because many standard-size windows have energy-

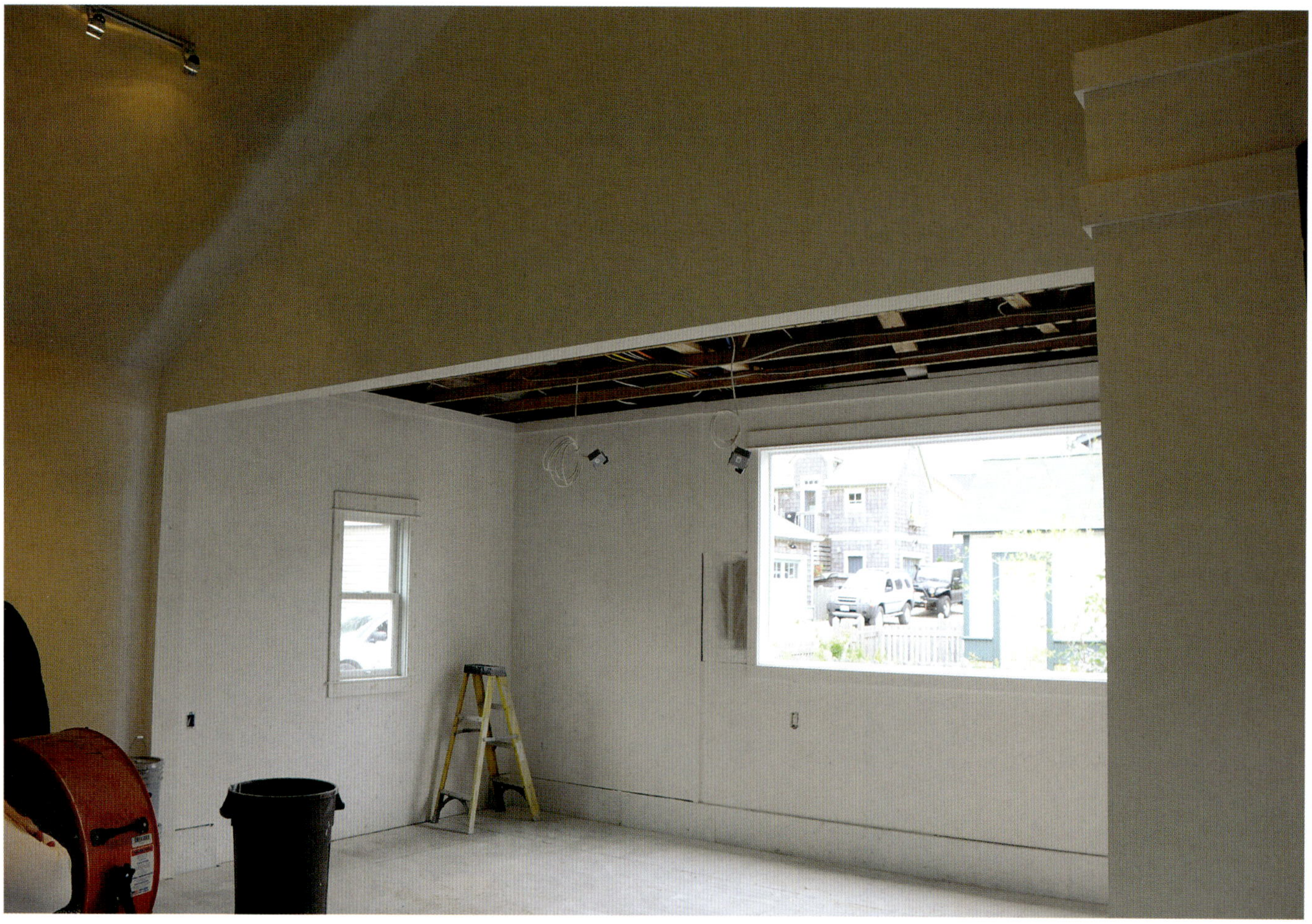

The inside of the former garage before Egeli converted the space into a professional studio.

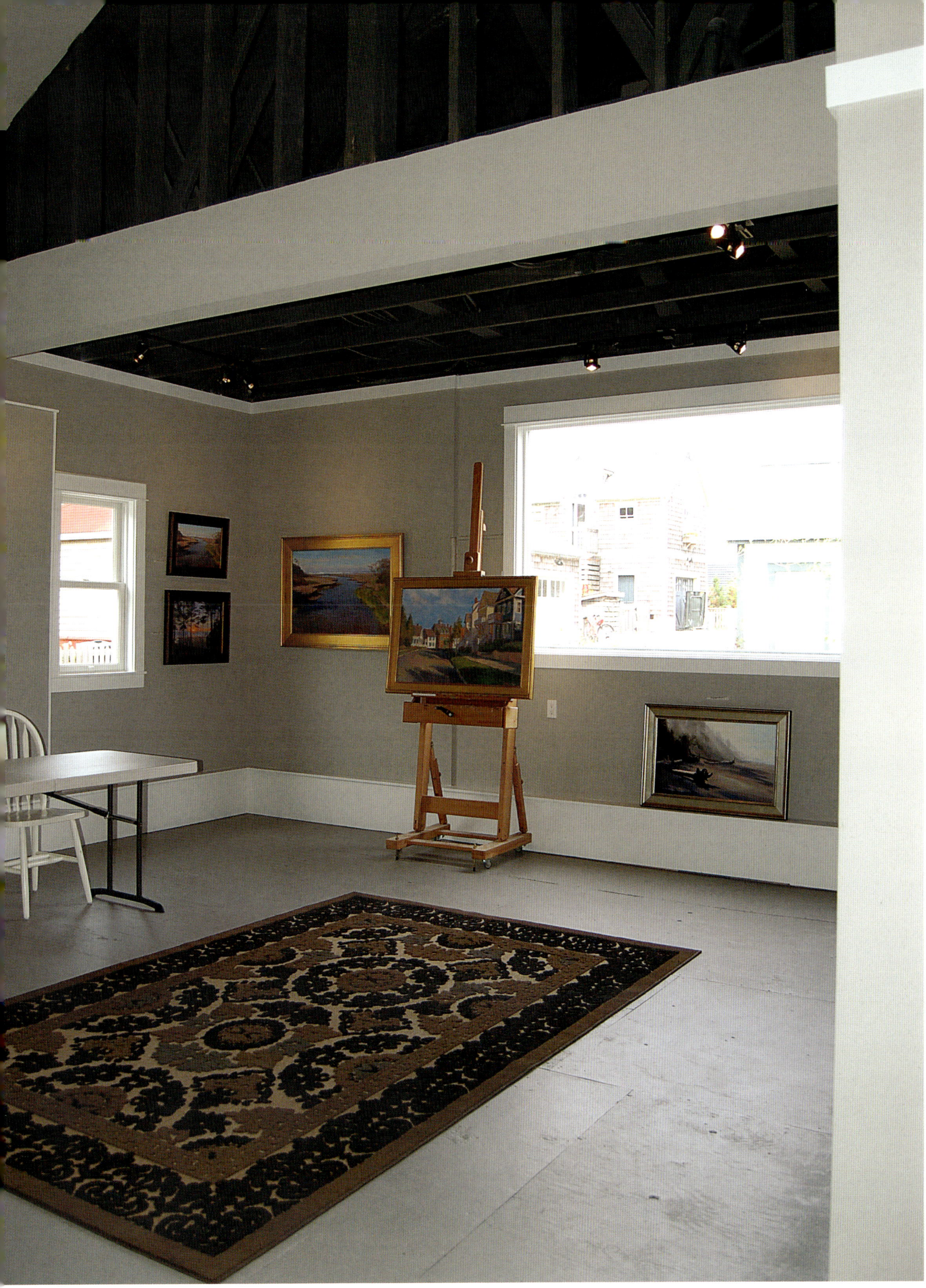

The new studio with its custom window on the north side.

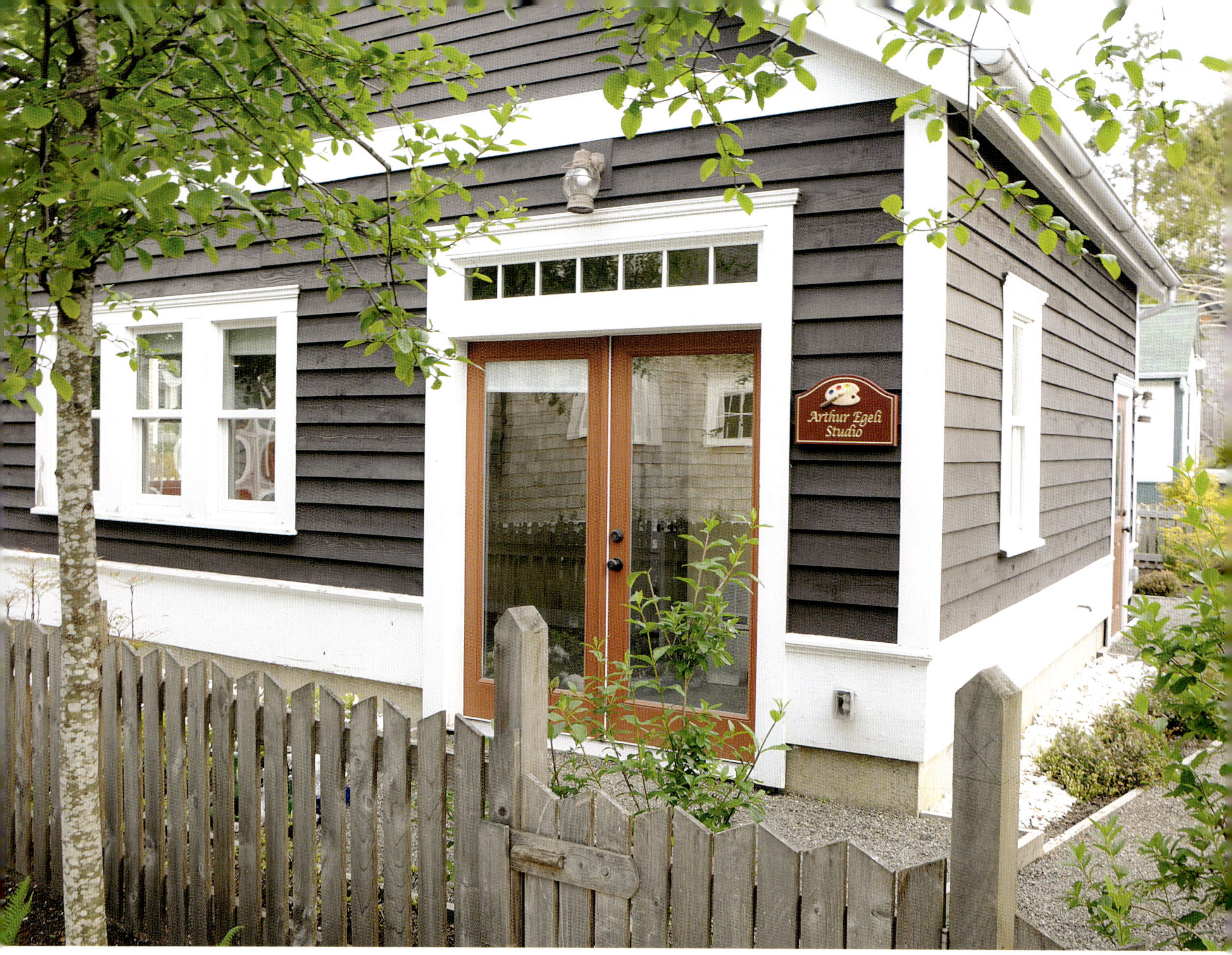

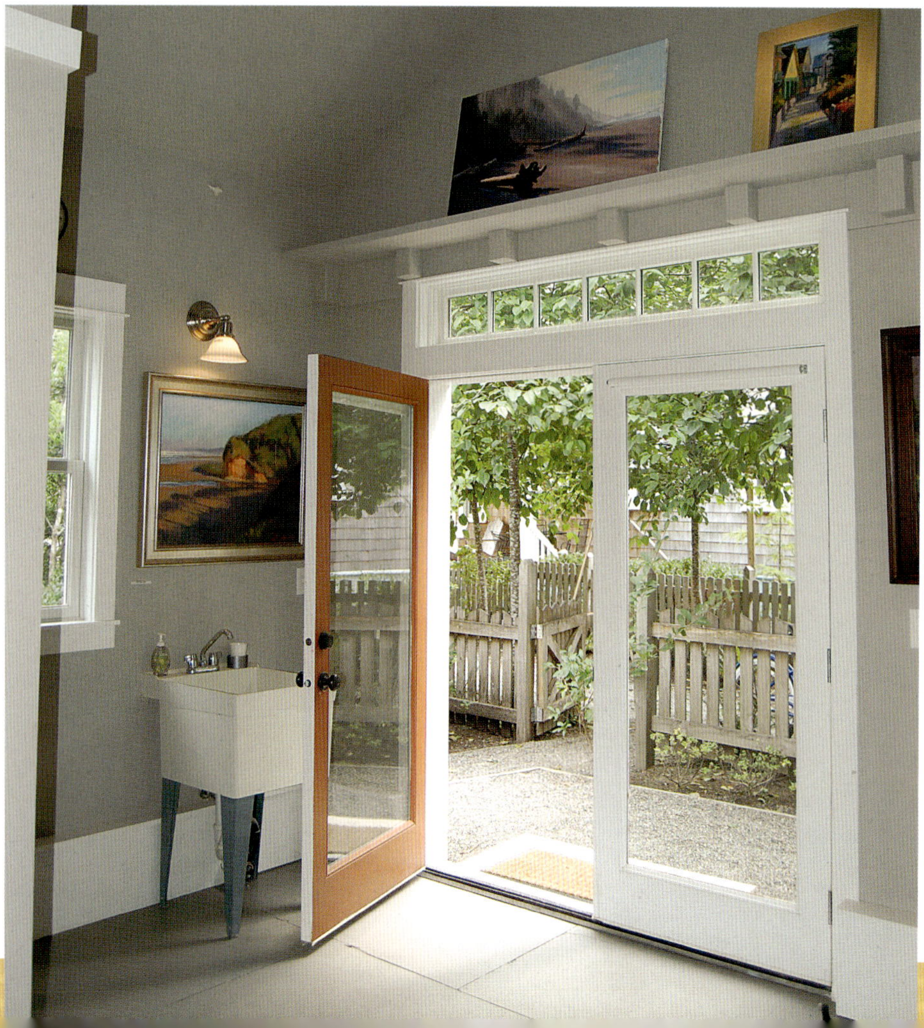

Above and left: The French doors that lead from a community pathway into the new studio.

saving glass that eliminates some of the available light. "The builder, Doug Hughes, prepared the window casing, and then a glass cutter installed ¼-inch (6mm), clear plate glass," Egeli explains. "It is 5 feet x 8 feet (2m x 3m) with the 8-foot (3m) width causing it to occupy about a third of the north wall of the studio. The remaining two-thirds of the wall offer working areas in which there is a soft, indirect light that is ideal for still-life painting and certain desirable effects in a portrait. The space is also perfect for hosting students who can work around a model stand."

Because the large window is relatively close to the ceiling, Egeli had to expose the rafters and trusses and paint

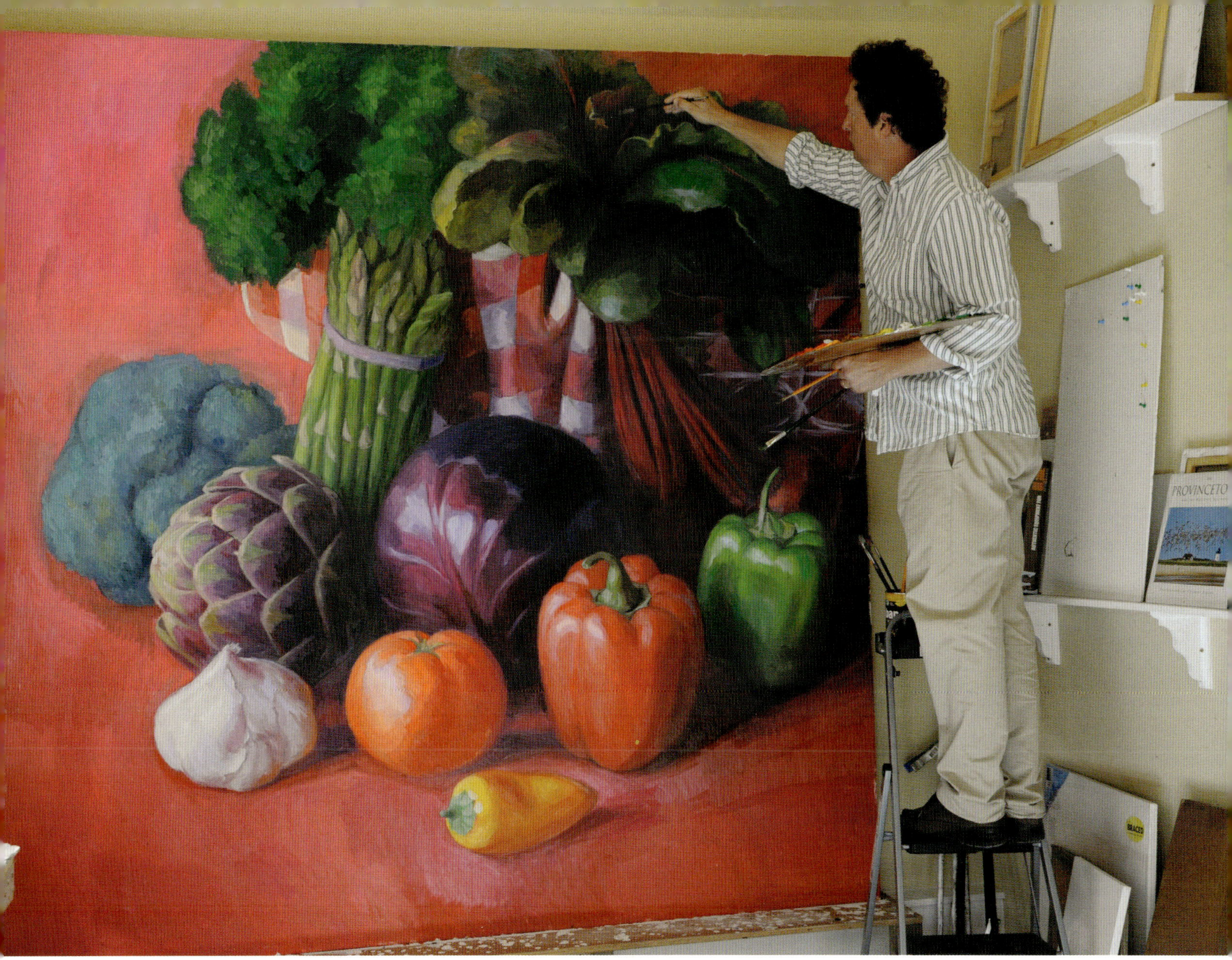

Egeli in his studio working on a commission piece titled *Still Life With Green and Red Peppers.*

them black to minimize the amount of reflected light. He installed a bathroom and a clean-up area, and a pair of French doors was built into the south wall to open the studio onto the community pathway. "We located the French doors opposite the new bathroom area to block the flow of light through the doors into the painting area," Egeli explains.

A canvas storage rack was built above the bathroom, and a large closet for supplies was added next to the bathroom. The concrete floors were covered with slats and insulation, and then plywood was added and painted a dark color. "We designed all these renovations so that the next owner could convert the studio into a guest bedroom or a rental apartment," the artist says.

The remaining walls of the studio were left clean so that the artist could display examples of his work, and halogen track lighting was installed to illuminate the paintings on exhibit. "The path leads to the center of town, and passersby often stop to peek in the windows to see the paintings on display, or they can come in for a visit when the sign on the outside says 'Open,'" the artist explains.

Once a week, Egeli teaches a group of about eight students in his studio, and he encourages others to come in for a visit when he isn't painting. "Having grown up around artists, I'm accustomed to my studio being a small social center," he says. "However, I also know how easy it is to be distracted. That's why I made sure the studio has everything my students and I might need—a bathroom, coffee maker, folding cot, and comfortable chairs. I know myself well enough to know that if I go back into the house for any reason, a few minutes away from the easel will turn into an hour of not painting."

For more information, visit the artist's website at www.arthuregeli.com or Egeli Gallery, in Provincetown, Massachusetts, at www.egeligallery.com.

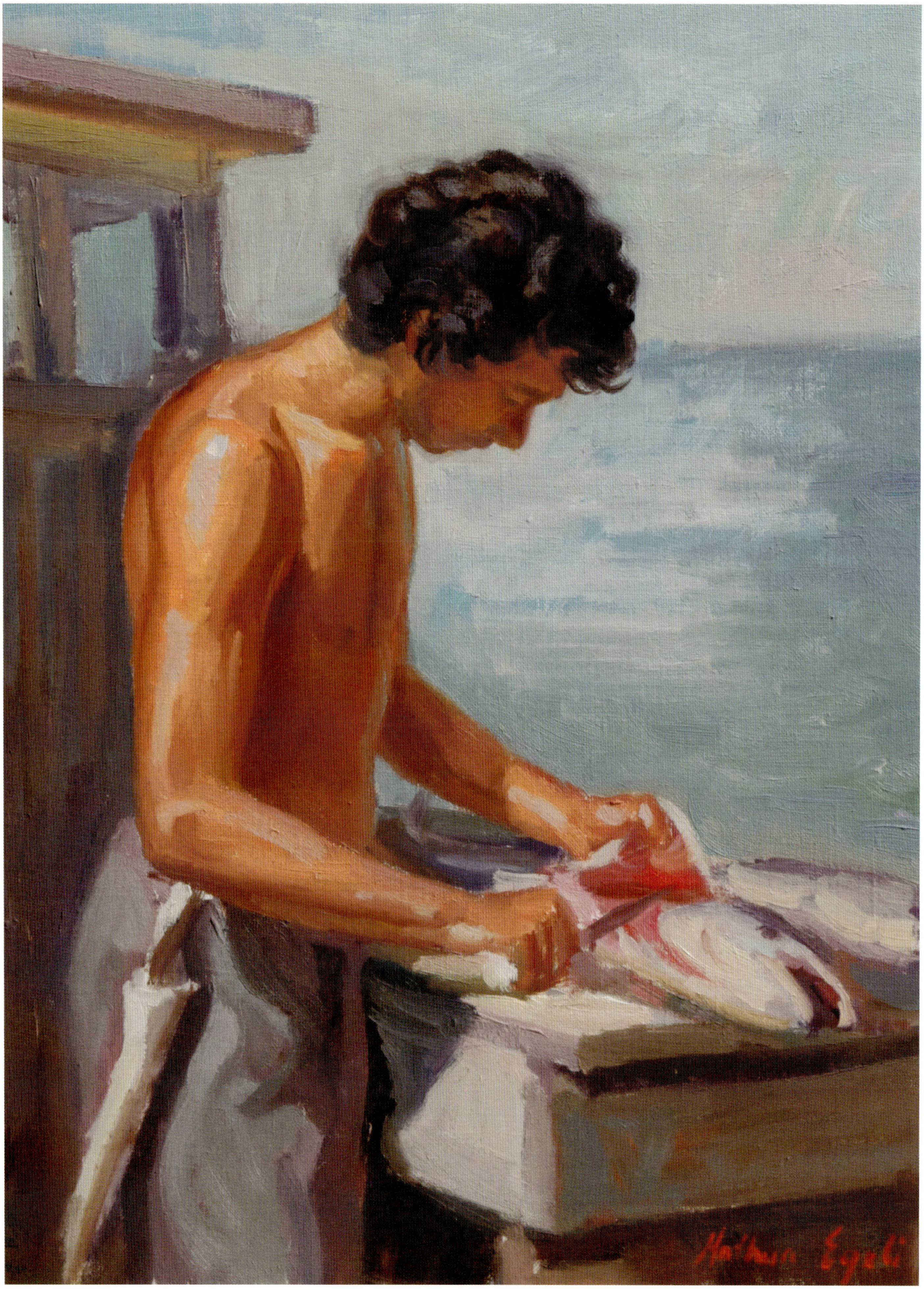

Fish Monger
by Arthur Egeli, 2013, oil on canvas, 14" x 11" (36cm x 28cm). Private collection.

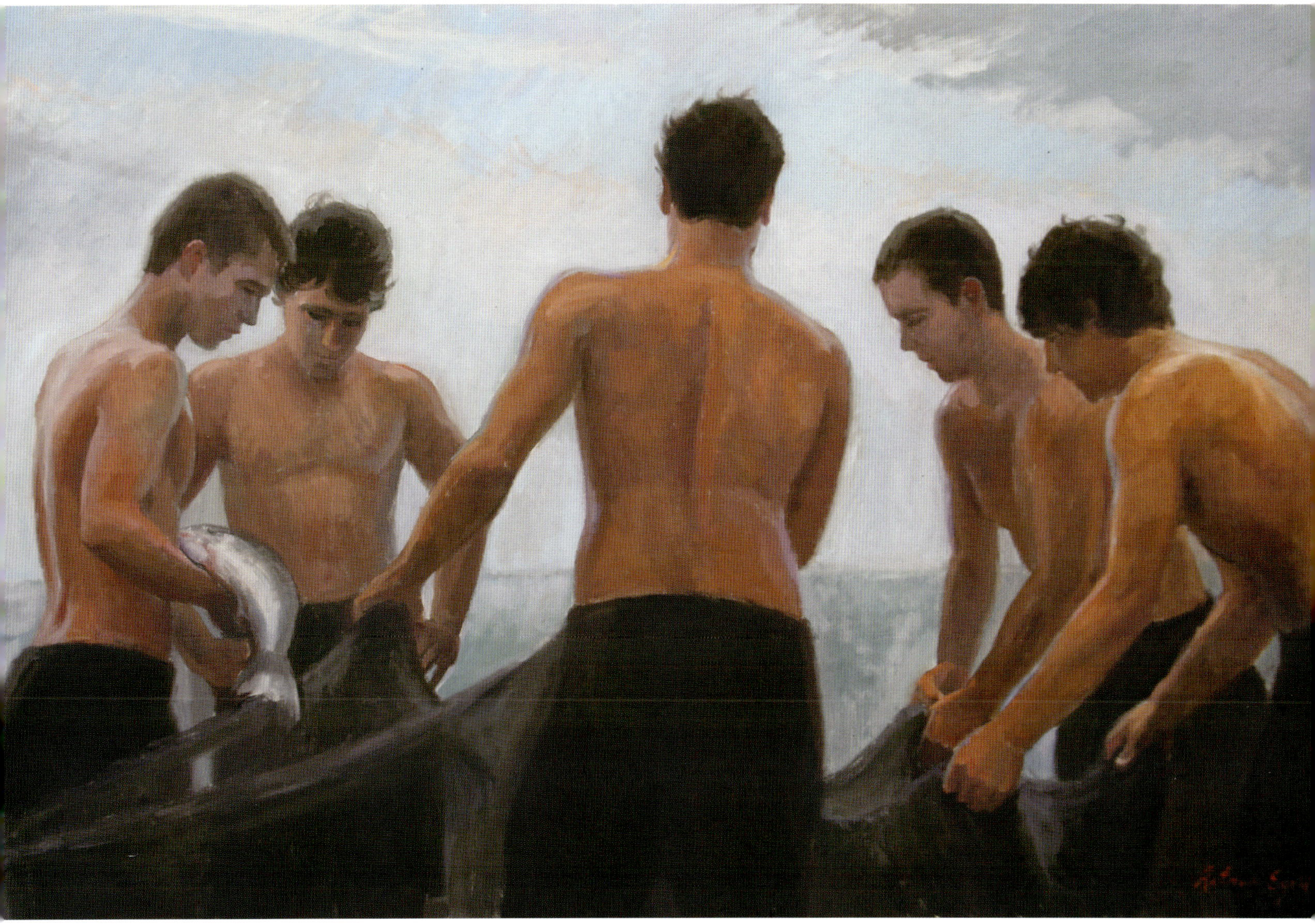

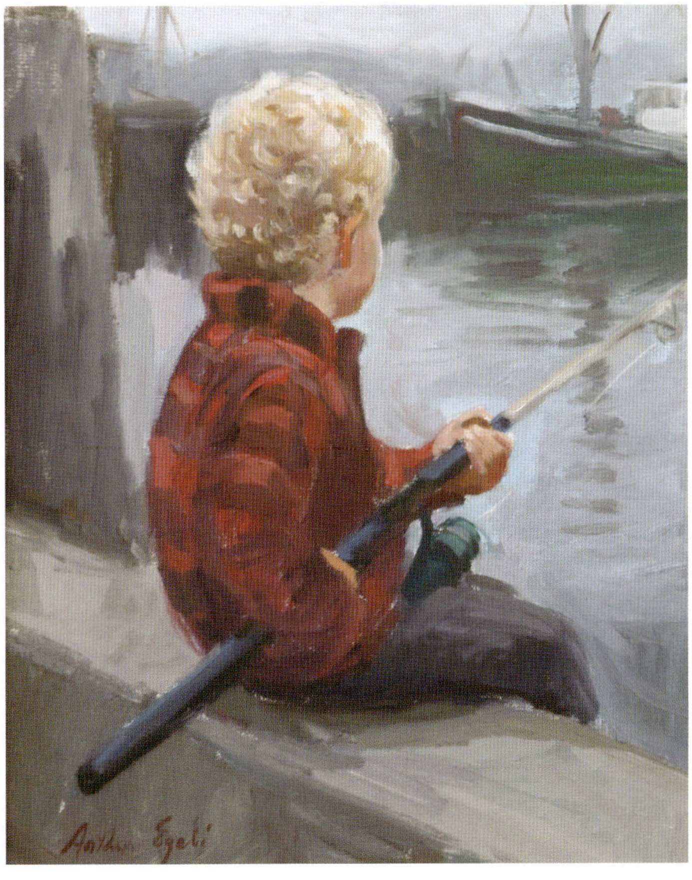

↑ **Checking the Catch**
by Arthur Egeli, 2013, oil on canvas, 36" x 48" (91cm x 122cm). Collection of the artist.

← **The Fisherman (The Artist's Son)**
by Arthur Egeli, 2013, oil, 14" x 11" (36cm x 28cm). Collection of the artist.

John Morra

Turning a Sacred Place Into a Work Space

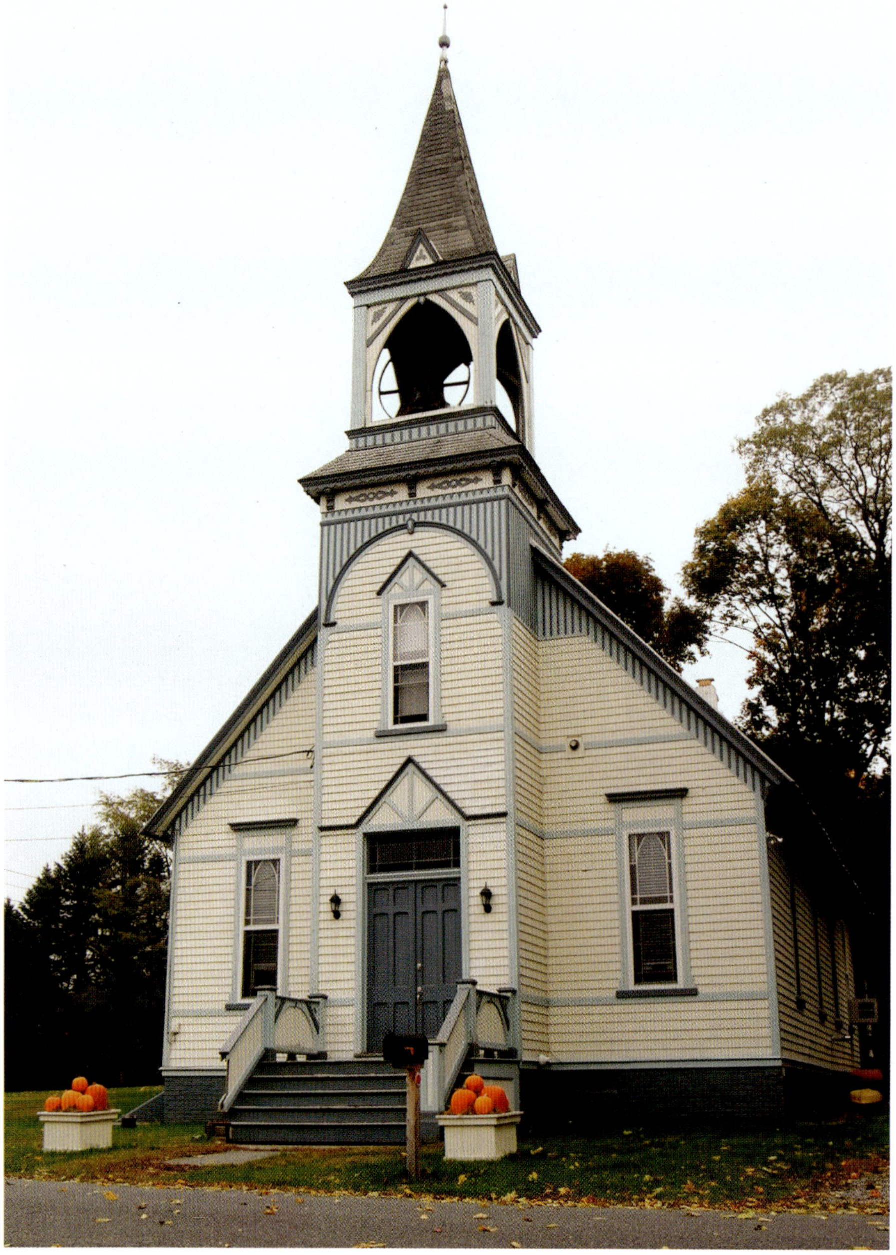

It was during a weekend jaunt in Columbia County, some two-and-a-half hours north of New York City, that John Morra first saw the church that would become his home and studio. As he drove past the "For Sale" sign, a friend in the car said, "You should buy that!" Morra just laughed it off. "I thought every property in the world cost a million dollars, so I forgot about it for a while," he recalls. "Besides, I liked New York City and thought I would be there forever. Then one day I started to think about what it would be like to live in a place that I was not renting, and also what it would be like to live near the Hudson River. I also found out that the price of the church was actually something I could afford." Unfortunately, by this time, someone else had already made an offer on the property. "I was crushed when I heard that someone else had made an offer," says Morra, "but then thrilled when I heard that the deal had fallen through. I took it as a sign to jump in with an offer of my own, and the next thing I knew, I was at a huge table with lots of lawyers and big stacks of paper."

Having taken possession of a full-sized Victorian church, Morra faced the task of converting it into a working studio and a home. Although the building was structurally sound, there was a great deal of renovation and refitting to be done. "I kept thinking that it didn't need much, so I would start a project and then think, 'Hmmm, while we're at it…'" the artist says. "The next thing I knew, all of the walls were ripped out." One project that particularly appealed to Morra was building a finished room in the bell tower. "I was planning for it to be accessible only by ladder," he says. "Then halfway through that, I decided that a choir-loft style balcony was needed as well. So instead of a little nook for taking a nap up in the tower, it turned into a huge guest room/library/study, with yet another folding ladder up to the 'bell room,' a tiny secret chamber for real solitude if you want it. And so it went."

As Morra began work on the space, he had to give careful consideration to the uses he had in mind for it. "I really wanted something beautiful and not just

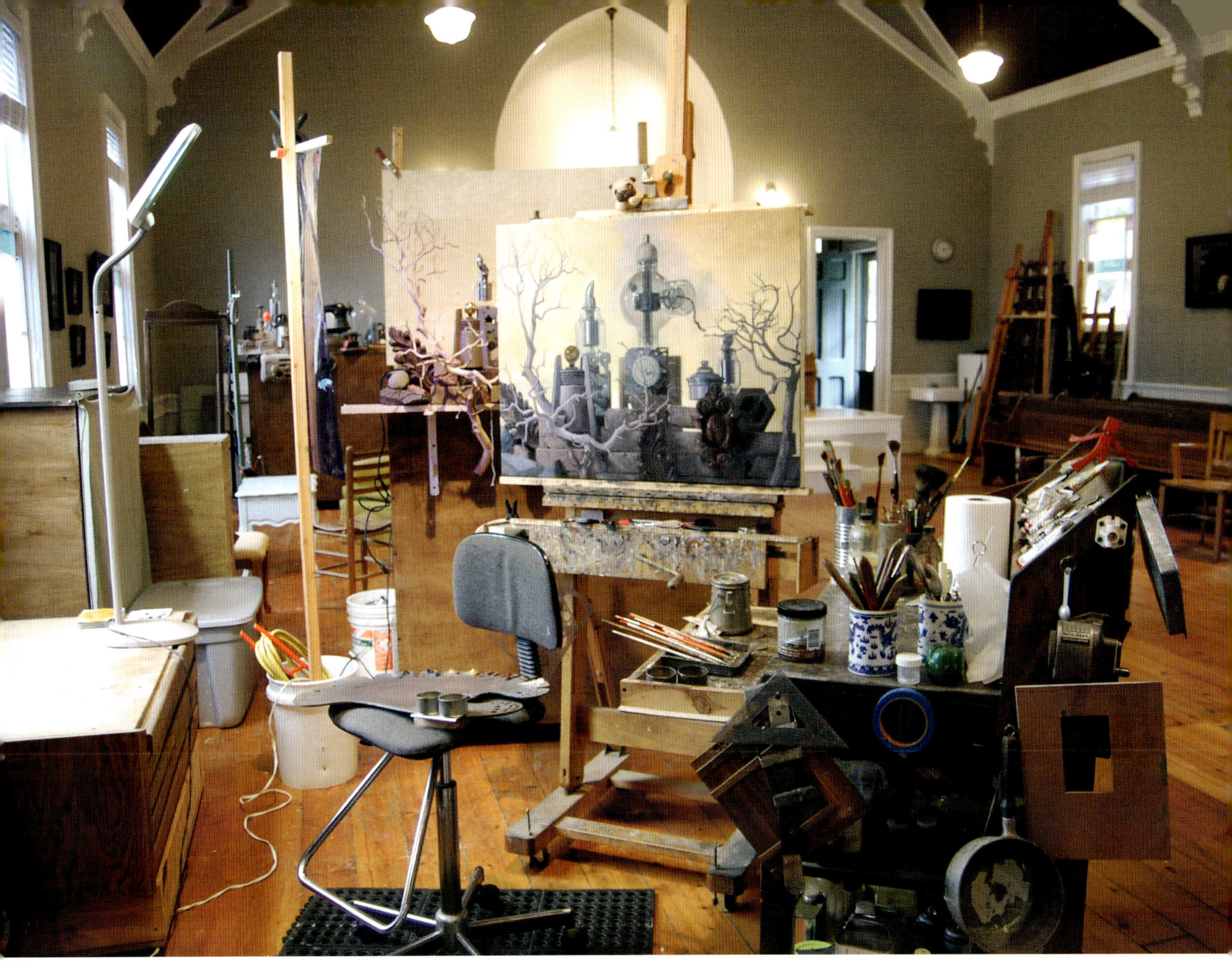

Morra's studio, interior (above) and exterior (opposite).

a warehouse," he says. "The balcony had to fit with the architecture of the rest of the space, and the altar was expanded to allow for concerts—and my wedding." The main consideration was to make the space as functional as possible for painting. "That meant a huge empty main room," says Morra. "I still haven't gotten rid of all the pews, which is starting to annoy me after seven years. In the end, I want it to look as though it has always been the way I've finished it. One of the saddest renovation principles is the concept of 'the obvious addition.' Additions should be invisible and inevitable."

In undertaking the work on the building, Morra says that the major difficulties involved contractors. "Certain workers misrepresented their skills and abilities," he recalls. "I was shocked to find out that I knew as much or more than they did. For instance, on one occasion I decided to inspect the framing of a room up in the attic and was shocked to see that the entire weight of the structure was going to be held aloft by a handful of drywall screws. I asked the builder if he was trying to kill me! Of course, I fired him, but it wasn't easy—I wanted to give the guy a chance. But he didn't know what he was doing at all. It was my fault, really. I should have checked his entire work history instead of just trusting him."

As for the experience of taking over a place formerly reserved for religious practice, Morra says that he is completely comfortable with the idea. "I never get asked about it from people who actually believe in Jesus," he says. "When I was in France a few summers ago, where the people are much more secular, I noticed how the French forcefully raised their eyebrows when they heard that I was painting in a church. It was as if I had just told a very raw joke in front of their grandparents. They would then ask, 'Did you have to have it deconsecrated?' I don't get it. Buildings are not spiritual. If mere flesh and blood cannot inherit the kingdom of heaven, then why should plaster be able to do so? Of course, I will not oppose anyone who finds great meaning in the geometry of the glorious churches of old. I, too, am attracted to old ideas about geometry as evidence of divine intelligence or presence. But I do not think the building itself has some sort of embedded spiritual stuff in it. I am glad that saints

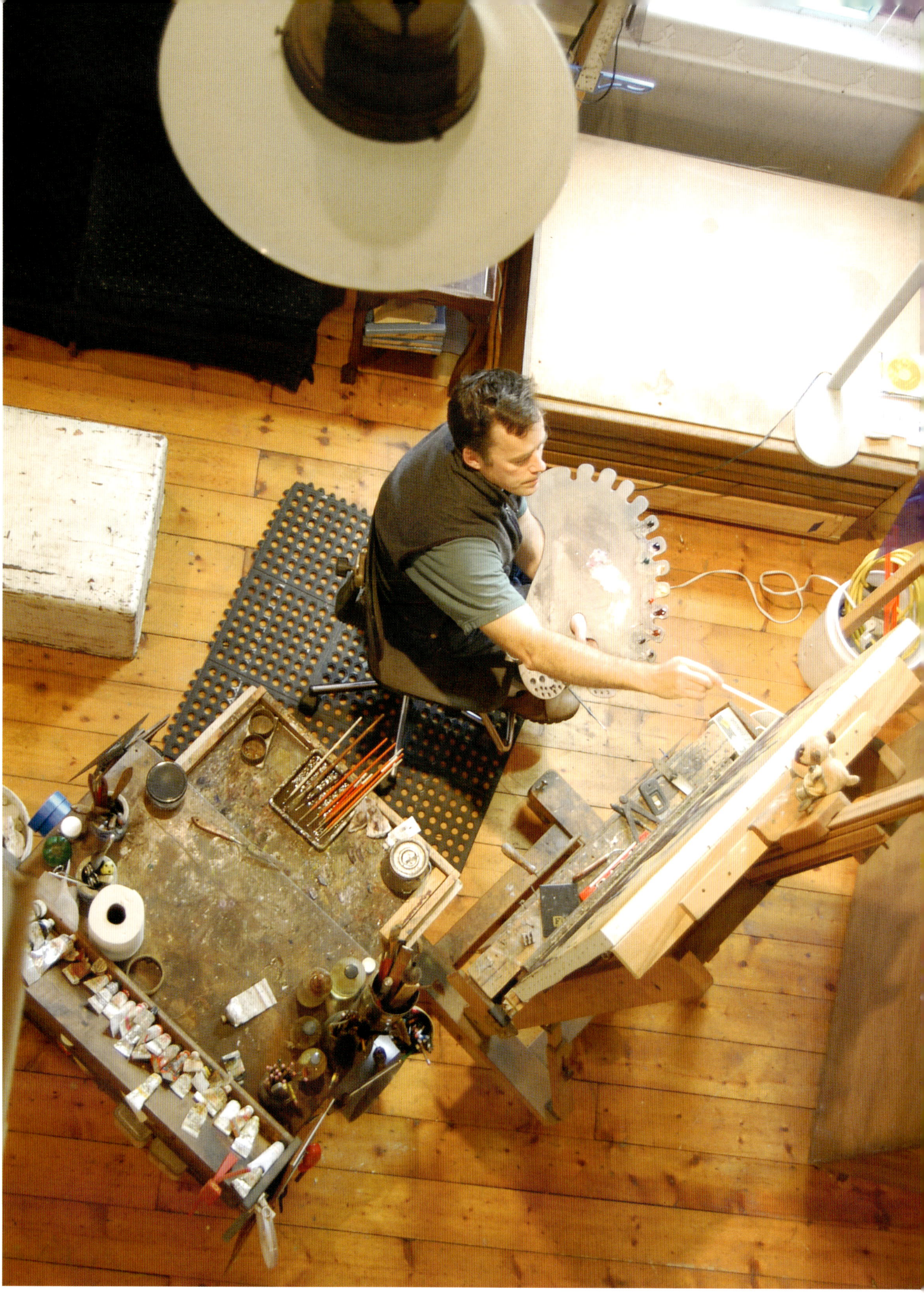

From the balcony, one can look over Morra's entire studio.

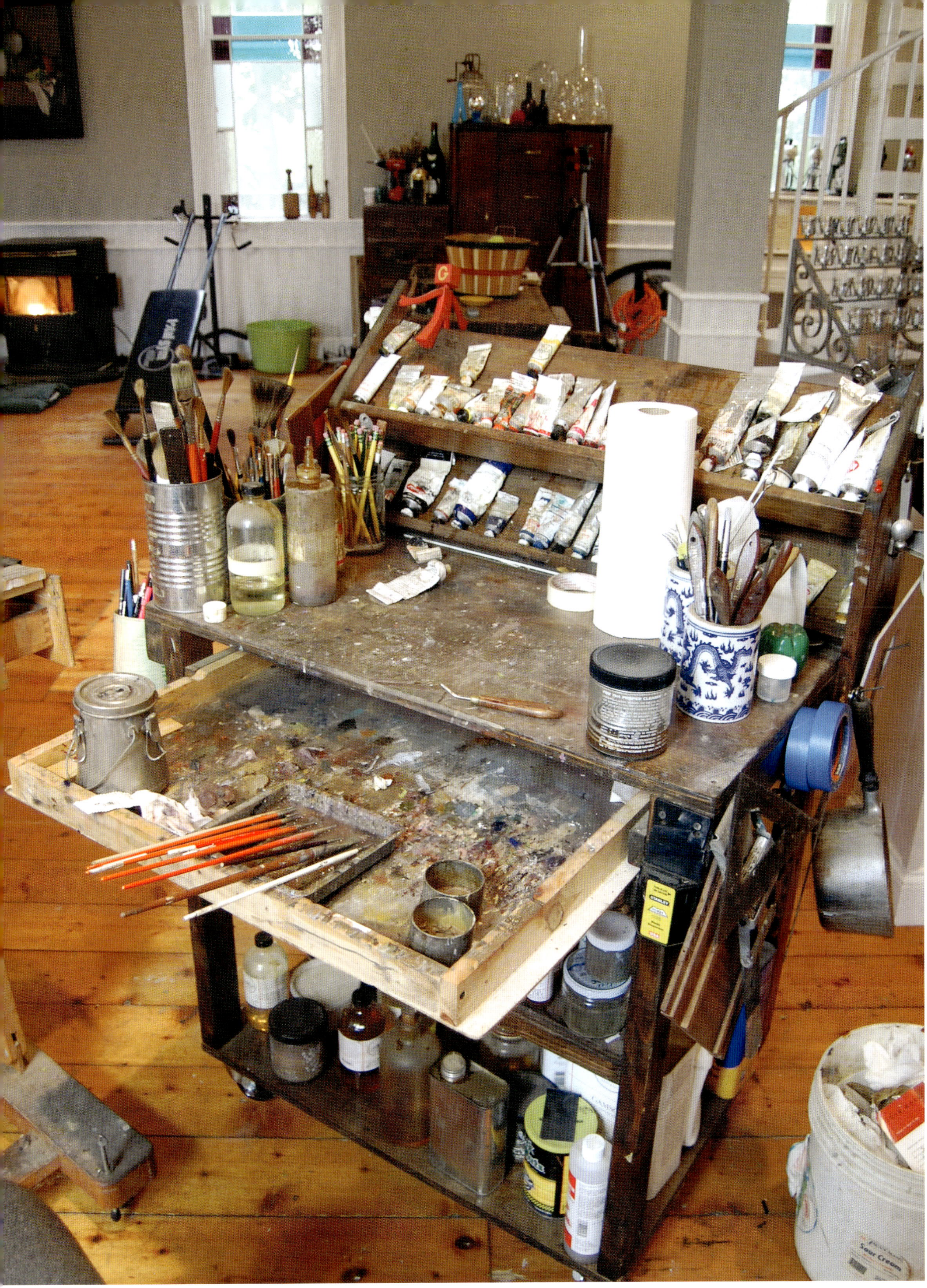

Morra's mobile workstation, which provides ample storage space for materials.

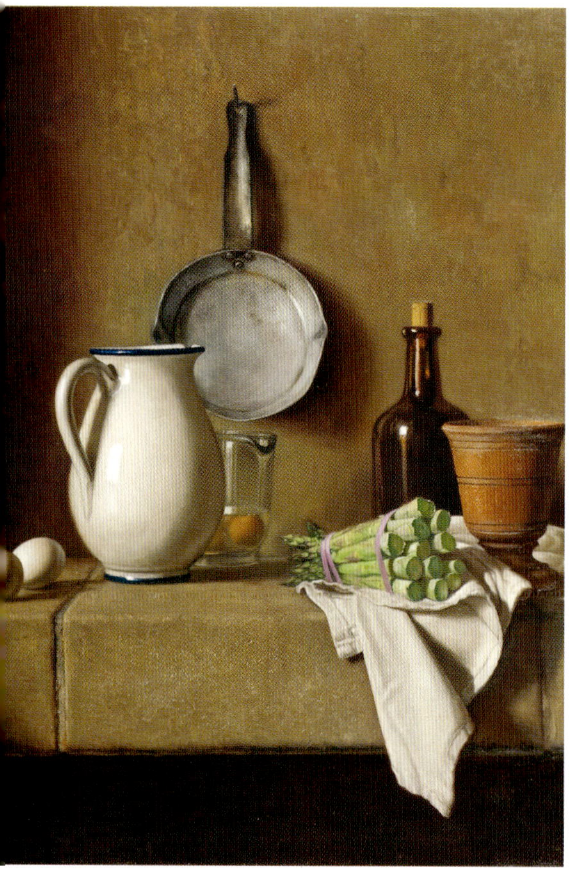

Still Life Asparagus Skillet
by John Morra, 2009, oil, 30¾" x 24" (78cm x 61cm). Artwork courtesy of Eleanor Ettinger Gallery, New York, New York.

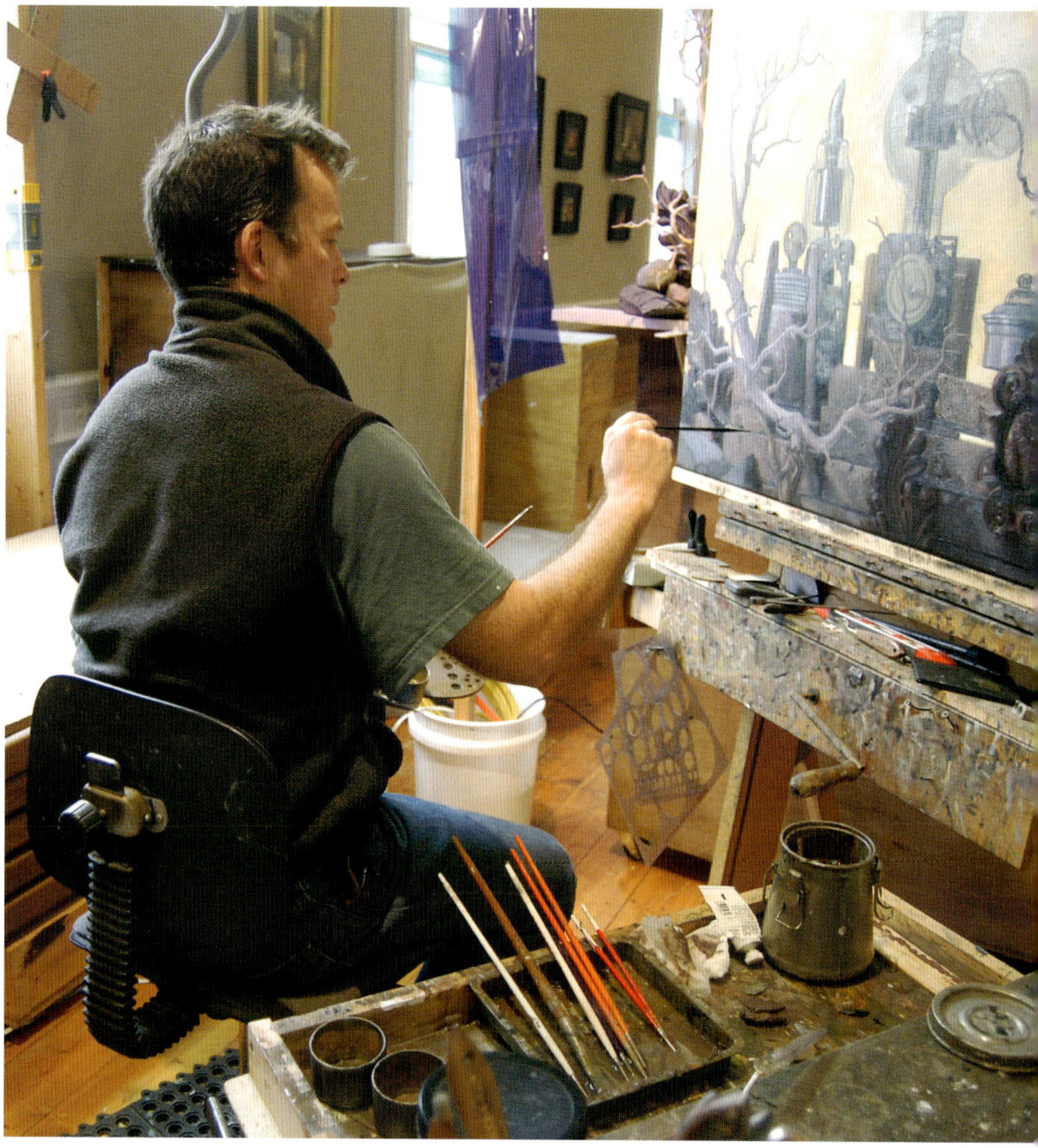

Morra painting at his easel, which he situates near the natural light of the windows.

before me worshiped in Chartres, and when I visit I feel a connection to them in eternity. I feel the same way about those who were worshiping where I am now painting. But the building itself? Ultimately, no. It is certainly lovely, but in the end the people in the building are the treasure in the vessel of clay. No matter how ornate that clay is, it is still clay and will one day be gone."

Looking back on his triumphs and difficulties with the project, Morra feels that his biggest mistake was not putting enough time into planning. "I lost a huge amount of money and time because I didn't plan," he says. "You have to talk to people who really know their stuff when you undertake something like this. My problem was that I didn't know enough people when I first came up to this area. I should have waited and then gone for it." As far as the completed work itself, Morra has only a few regrets. "I wish I had done more sealing of cracks with foam when all of the walls were off," he says. "And I wish I had put in a million more possibilities for outlets, too. I should have been more patient, because once you seal up a wall, that's it—unless you want to make a mess. I also wish I'd taken more photos before, during, and after. With digital cameras, there is really no excuse."

For all the difficulties and challenges of the renovation, the finished studio is everything that an artist could ask for: a light airy space that is both elegant and highly functional, somewhere that feels special yet doesn't feel precious. It's a place where serious work can be done. "I love being able to get back and look at my picture from a distance," Morra says. "You can really see if there is a design that makes sense or not. This is especially true of a painting's value structure. I can see if there is one from afar." Morra also loves having a lot of separate spaces for different activities. "There is one spot where I draw from imagination and from books," he says, "and there is another where I have all the tools for building sets. I have a table set aside for writing, I have a chair for praying, and then, of course, I have at least three stations for setting up paintings. In the past my jigsaw might have been at my feet where I was painting. These days

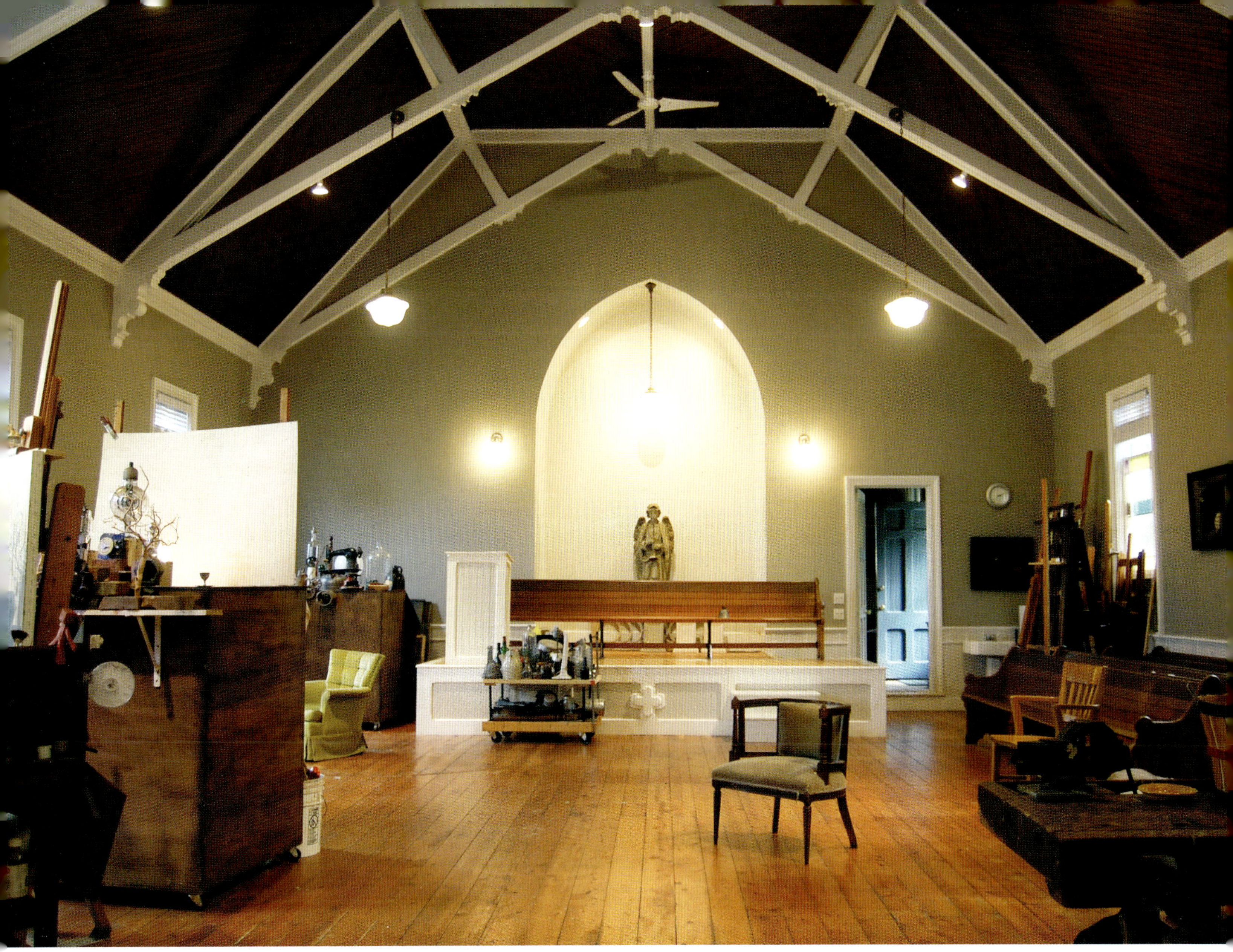

Morra expanded the original altar to make room for performances and his own wedding ceremony.

it's over there with all the tools. I used to have one wall for still life, and now I have huge mobile stages with mobile plaster niches on top of them. Basically, I can do anything I want in here because of the abundance of space." Morra also finds that the scale of his surroundings suggests new avenues for his painting. "I am currently exploring the possibility of depicting vast distance in a still life, like a landscape, which I could have never done in my New York apartment," he says. "I also want to stage sets for figurative paintings."

Of course, a building of such size will continue to present endless projects, and for a mind as active as Morra's, the to-do list never ends. He says that he is still finding new spaces to renovate. "The most recent was the attic, and the final frontier will be the basement," he says jokingly. "I guess if you can't go any higher, you can always go deeper into the earth. I want to put in a woodshop and experimental rocket-propulsion laboratory down there, and of course a wine cellar and gym." Given the curious retro sci-fi elements that sometimes find their way into Morra's still-life paintings, the rocket-propulsion laboratory might not quite be a joke. "There's also the yard," he adds, on a more serious note. "I need a good fence, but not one you buy in sections. I want it to look like something made long ago, so it will be hand-made little by little. I also want to do formal boxwood and gravel in the backyard with a fountain so I can stroll around and contemplate the created order."

These additional projects may only ever exist in the fertile imagination that has given rise to so many extraordinary paintings over the years, but Morra has clearly been energized and inspired by the building he chose to make his studio. In the end, that is, perhaps, the most wonderful thing about the place.

For more on John Morra, visit his website at www.johnmorrapainting.com.

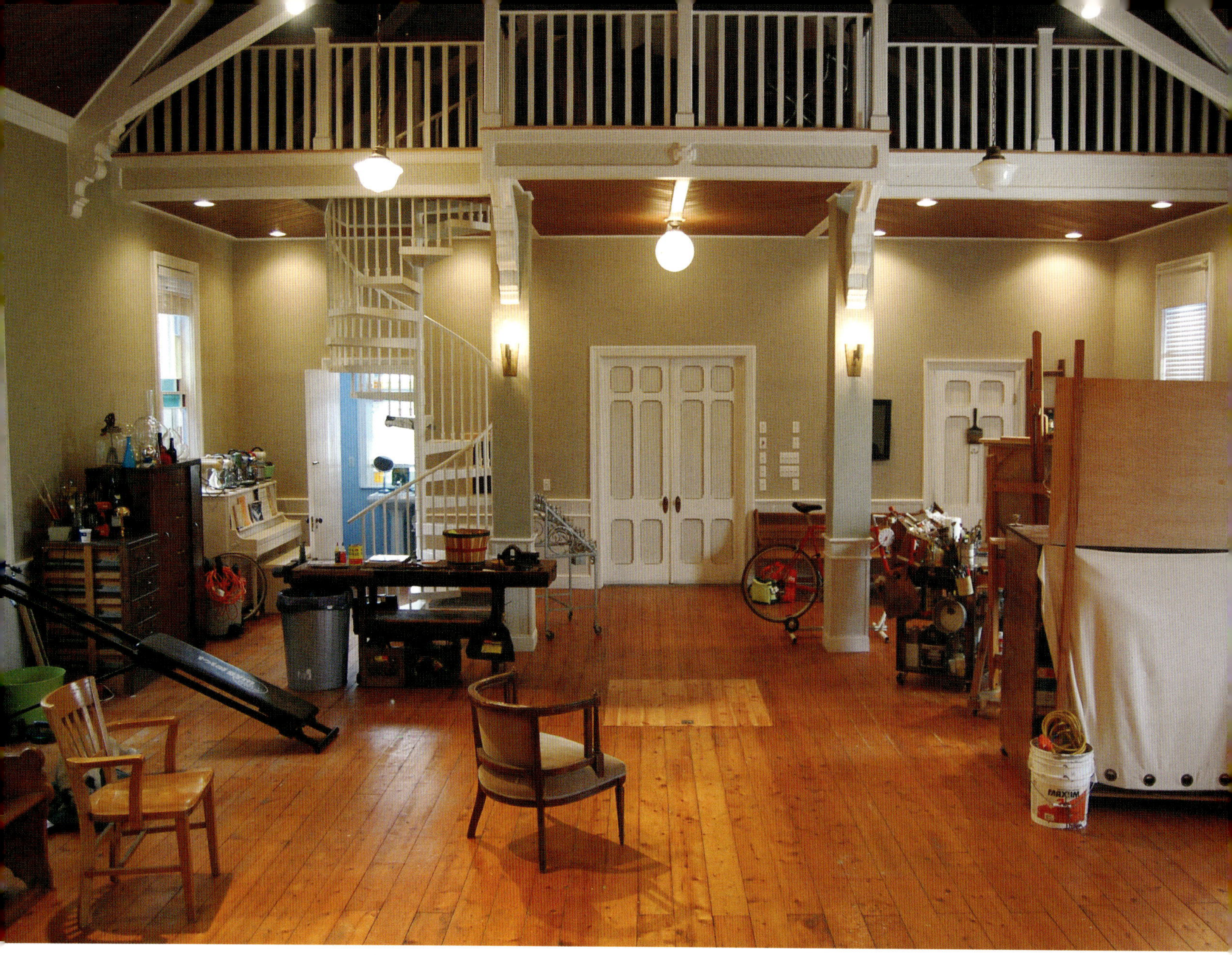

↑ The view of Morra's studio from the altar.

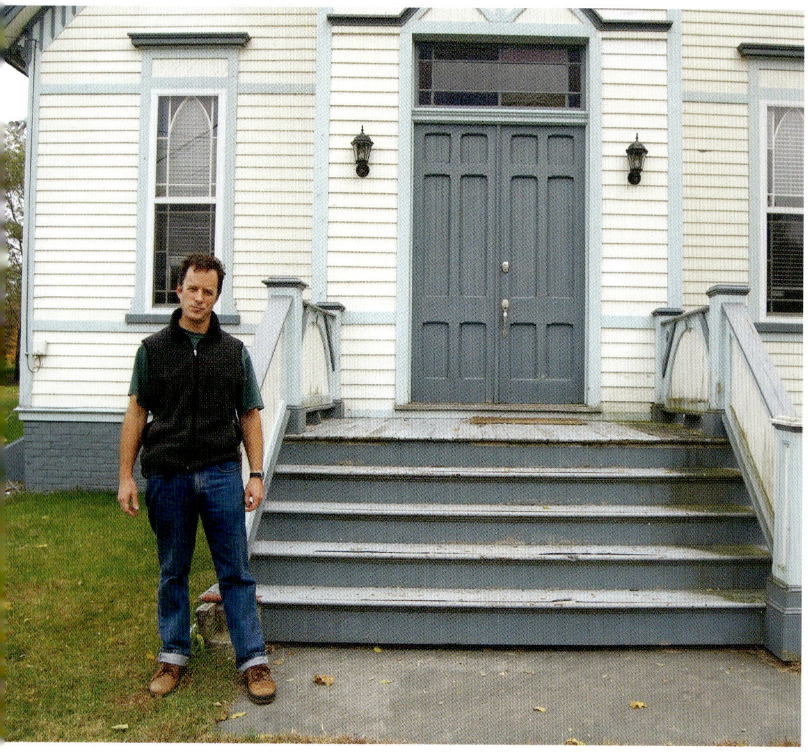

Morra at the entrance of his home and studio.

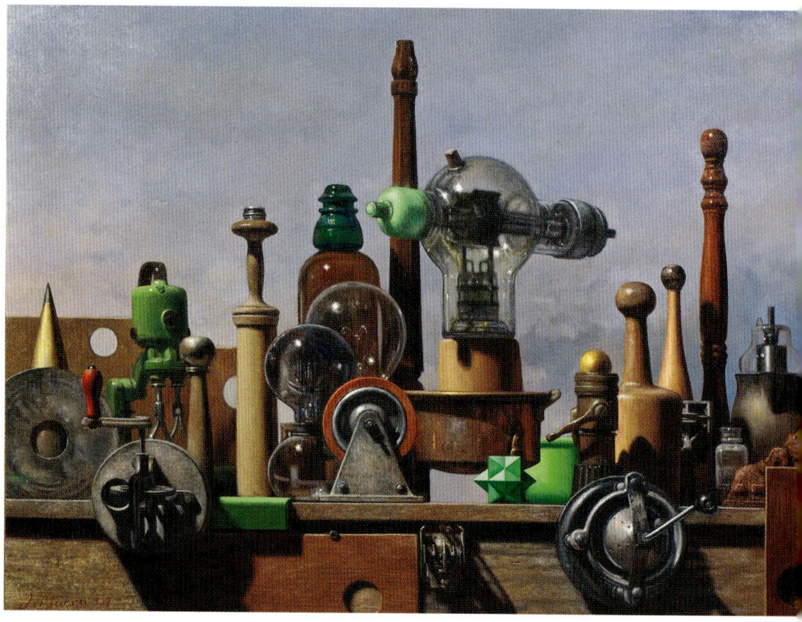

↑ **Mertz No. 12**
by John Morra, 2009, oil, 32" x 44" (81cm x 112cm). Artwork courtesy of Eleanor Ettinger Gallery, New York, New York.

→ The spiral staircase leading to the balcony.

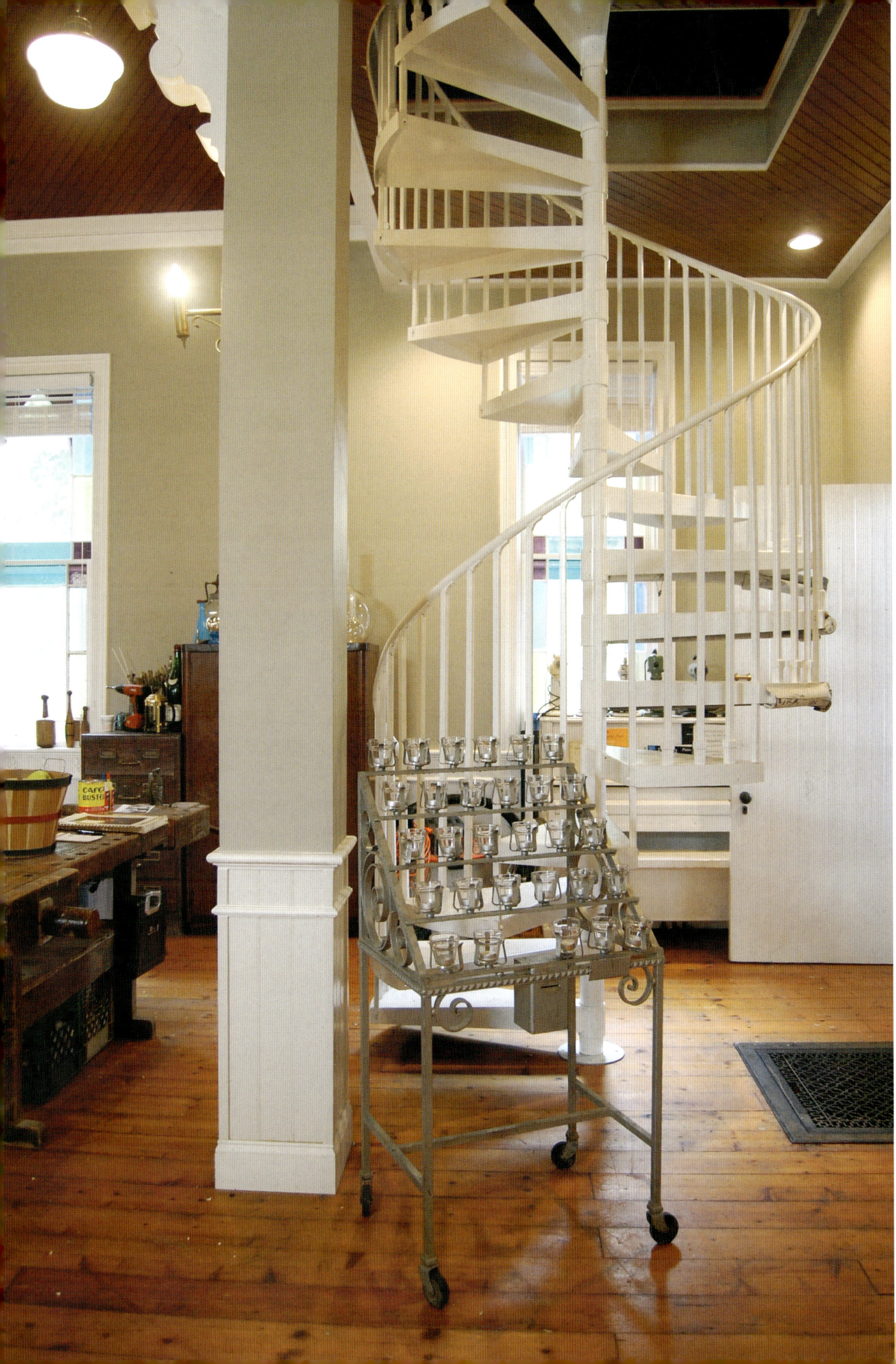

Index

Featured Artists

Kathy Anderson
www.kathyandersonstudio.com

Artpost Austin
www.artpostaustin.com

Betsy Ashton
www.ashtonportraits.com

Babette Bloch
www.babettebloch.com

Ryan S. Brown
www.ryansbrownart.com

Richard Bruce
www.richardgbruce.com

Wende Caporale
www.wendecaporale.com

Kathy Caudill
Represented by The Providence Gallery, Charlotte, NC
www.providencegallery.net

Center for Academic Study & Naturalist Painting
www.cas-utah.com

William T. Chambers
www.williamchambers.com

Gail Descoeurs
www.gaildescoeurs.com

Dennis Doheny
www.dennisdoheny.com

Arthur Egeli
www.arthuregeli.com
www.egeligallery.com

Cedric Egeli
www.egelistudio.com

Ruth Ann Greenberg
ruthanngreenbergart.blogspot.com
artecon@yahoo.com

Daniel Greene
www.danielgreeneartist.com

Christine Ivers
www.christineivers.com

Everett Raymond Kinstler
www.everettraymondkinstler.com

Judith Kudlow
www.judithpondkudlow.com

Amy Mann
www.amymann.com

Paul McCormack
www.mccormackstudios.com

Marc Mellon
www.marcmellon.com

John Morra
www.johnmorrapainting.com

Joan Potter

Rick Price
www.rickprice.net

James Prosek
www.jamesprosek.com

Anthony Ryder
www.tonyryder.com
www.theryderstudio.com

John Howard Sanden
www.johnhowardsanden.com

William A. Schneider
www.schneiderart.com

Charlotte Schulz
www.charlotteschulz.com

Gerald Simcoe
www.simcoegallery.com

Teaching Studios of Art
www.teachingstudios.com

Wendy Walworth-Schrijver
www.wendywalworth.com

About the Editor

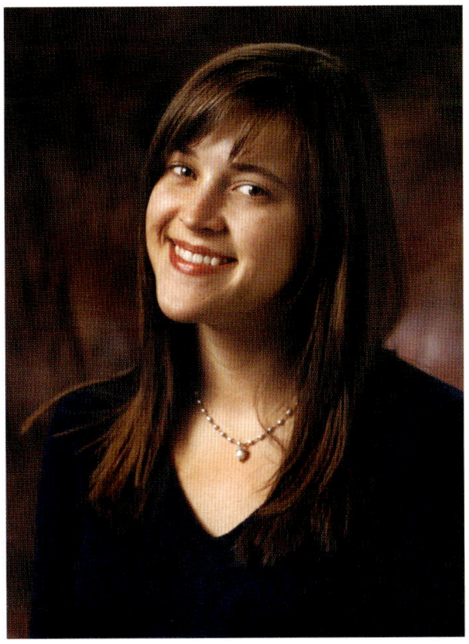

Mary Burzlaff Bostic is the editor of *Photographer's Market*, *Artist's & Graphic Designer's Market* and ArtistsMarketOnline.com. She has eight years of experience editing and acquiring projects for North Light fine art and IMPACT Books and has worked on a variety of titles covering a broad range of art topics. She is a graduate of Georgetown College (bachelor of arts, English) and the University of Cincinnati (master of arts, art history) and resides in Cincinnati, Ohio.

 Published by North Light Books, an imprint of F+W, a Content + eCommerce Company, 10151 Carver Road, Suite 200, Blue Ash, Ohio, 45242. (800) 289-0963. First Edition.

a content + ecommerce company

Other fine North Light Books are available from your favorite bookstore, art supply store or online supplier. Visit our website at fwmedia.com.

18 17 16 15 14 5 4 3 2 1

DISTRIBUTED IN CANADA BY FRASER DIRECT
100 Armstrong Avenue
Georgetown, ON, Canada L7G 5S4
Tel: (905) 877-4411

DISTRIBUTED IN THE U.K. AND EUROPE
BY F&W MEDIA INTERNATIONAL LTD
Brunel House, Forde Close, Newton Abbot, TQ12 4PU, UK
Tel: (+44) 1626 323200, Fax: (+44) 1626 323319
E-mail: enquiries@fwmedia.com

DISTRIBUTED IN AUSTRALIA BY CAPRICORN LINK
P.O. Box 704, S. Windsor NSW, 2756 Australia
Tel: (02) 4560-1600; Fax: (02) 4577 5288
E-mail: books@capricornlink.com.au

ISBN 13: 978-1-4403-3698-0

Edited by Mary Burzlaff Bostic and Christine Doyle
Cover designed by Hannah Bailey
Interior designed by Laura Spencer
Production coordinated by Mark Griffin

METRIC CONVERSION CHART

To convert	to	multiply by
Inches	Centimeters	2.54
Centimeters	Inches	0.4
Feet	Centimeters	30.5
Centimeters	Feet	0.03
Yards	Meters	0.9
Meters	Yards	1.1